Lament

The Azrieli Series of Holocaust Survivor Memoirs: Published Titles

ENGLISH TITLES

Judy Abrams, *Tenuous Threads*/ Eva Felsenburg Marx, *One of the Lucky Ones*
Amek Adler, *Six Lost Years*
Ferenc Andai, *In the Hour of Fate and Danger*
Molly Applebaum, *Buried Words: The Diary of Molly Applebaum*
Claire Baum, *The Hidden Package*
Bronia and Joseph Beker, *Joy Runs Deeper*
Tibor Benyovits, *Unsung Heroes*
Pinchas Eliyahu Blitt, *A Promise of Sweet Tea*
Max Bornstein, *If Home Is Not Here*
Sonia Caplan, *Passport to Reprieve*
Felicia Carmelly, *Across the Rivers of Memory*
Ben Carniol, *Hide and Seek: In Pursuit of Justice*
Stefan A. Carter, *A Symphony of Remembrance*
Judy Cohen, *A Cry in Unison*
Tommy Dick, *Getting Out Alive*
Marie Doduck, *A Childhood Unspoken*
Marian Domanski, *Fleeing from the Hunter*
Anita Ekstein, *Always Remember Who You Are*
Margalith Esterhuizen, *A Light in the Clouds*
Leslie Fazekas, *In Dreams Together: The Diary of Leslie Fazekas*
John Freund, *Spring's End*
Susan Garfield, *Too Many Goodbyes: The Diaries of Susan Garfield*
Myrna Goldenberg (Editor), *Before All Memory Is Lost: Women's Voices from the Holocaust*
René Goldman, *A Childhood Adrift*
Elly Gotz, *Flights of Spirit*
Ibolya Grossman and Andy Réti, *Stronger Together*
Pinchas Gutter, *Memories in Focus*
Anna Molnár Hegedűs, *As the Lilacs Bloomed*
Rabbi Pinchas Hirschprung, *The Vale of Tears*
Bronia Jablon, *A Part of Me*
Helena Jockel, *We Sang in Hushed Voices*
Margit Kassai, *Between the Lines: The Diary of Margit Kassai*
Jack Klajman, *The Smallest Hope*
Eddie Klein, *Inside the Walls*
Michael Kutz, *If, By Miracle*
Ferenc Laczó (Editor), *Confronting Devastation: Memoirs of Holocaust Survivors from Hungary*
Eva Lang, David Korn and Fishel Philip Goldig, *At Great Risk: Memoirs of Rescue during the Holocaust*
Nate Leipciger, *The Weight of Freedom*
Alex Levin, *Under the Yellow & Red Stars*
Rachel Lisogurski and Chana Broder, *Daring to Hope*
Fred Mann, *A Drastic Turn of Destiny*
Michael Mason, *A Name Unbroken*
Leslie Meisels with Eva Meisels, *Suddenly the Shadow Fell*
Leslie Mezei, *A Tapestry of Survival*
Muguette Myers, *Where Courage Lives*
David Newman, *Hope's Reprise*
Arthur Ney, *W Hour*
Felix Opatowski, *Gatehouse to Hell*
Malka Pischanitskaya, *A Mother to My Mother*
Marguerite Élias Quddus, *In Hiding*
Maya Rakitova, *Behind the Red Curtain*
Henia Reinhartz, *Bits and Pieces*
Betty Rich, *Little Girl Lost*
Paul-Henri Rips, *E/96: Fate Undecided*
Margrit Rosenberg Stenge, *Silent Refuge*
Steve Rotschild, *Traces of What Was*

Judith Rubinstein, *Dignity Endures*
Martha Salcudean, *In Search of Light*
Kitty Salsberg and Ellen Foster, *Never Far Apart*
Morris Schnitzer, *Escape from the Edge*
Joseph Schwarzberg, *Dangerous Measures*
Zuzana Sermer, *Survival Kit*
Rachel Shtibel, *The Violin*/ Adam Shtibel, *A Child's Testimony*
Maxwell Smart, *Chaos to Canvas*
Gerta Solan, *My Heart Is At Ease*
Zsuzsanna Fischer Spiro, *In Fragile Moments*/ Eva Shainblum, *The Last Time*
George Stern, *Vanished Boyhood*
Willie Sterner, *The Shadows Behind Me*
Ann Szedlecki, *Album of My Life*
William Tannenzapf, *Memories from the Abyss*/ Renate Krakauer, *But I Had a Happy Childhood*
Elsa Thon, *If Only It Were Fiction*
Agnes Tomasov, *From Generation to Generation*
Joseph Tomasov, *From Loss to Liberation*
Leslie Vertes, *Alone in the Storm*
Anka Voticky, *Knocking on Every Door*
Sam Weisberg, *Carry the Torch*/ Johnny Jablon, *A Lasting Legacy*

TITRES FRANÇAIS

Judy Abrams, *Retenue par un fil*/ Eva Felsenburg Marx, *Une question de chance*
Amek Adler, *Six années volées*
Molly Applebaum, *Les Mots enfouis : Le Journal de Molly Applebaum*
Claire Baum, *Le Colis caché*
Bronia et Joseph Beker, *Plus forts que le malheur*
Max Bornstein, *Citoyen de nulle part*
Tommy Dick, *Objectif : survivre*
Marie Doduck, *L'enfant du silence*
Marian Domanski, *Traqué*
John Freund, *La Fin du printemps*
Myrna Goldenberg (Éditrice), *Un combat singulier : Femmes dans la tourmente de l'Holocauste*
René Goldman, *Une enfance à la dérive*
Pinchas Gutter, *Dans la chambre noire*
Anna Molnár Hegedűs, *Pendant la saison des lilas*
Helena Jockel, *Nous chantions en sourdine*
Michael Kutz, *Si, par miracle*
Eva Lang, Fishel Philip Goldig, David Korn, *Un si grand péril : mémoires de sauvetage durant l'Holocauste*
Nate Leipciger, *Le Poids de la liberté*
Alex Levin, *Étoile jaune, étoile rouge*
Fred Mann, *Un terrible revers de fortune*
Michael Mason, *Au fil d'un nom*
Leslie Meisels, *Soudain, les ténèbres*
Muguette Myers, *Les Lieux du courage*
Arthur Ney, *L'Heure W*
Felix Opatowski, *L'Antichambre de l'enfer*
Marguerite Élias Quddus, *Cachée*
Henia Reinhartz, *Fragments de ma vie*
Betty Rich, *Seule au monde*
Paul-Henri Rips, *Matricule E/96*
Margrit Rosenberg Stenge, *Le Refuge du silence*
Steve Rotschild, *Sur les traces du passé*
Kitty Salsberg et Ellen Foster, *Unies dans l'épreuve*
Morris Schnitzer, *Sur la corde raide*
Joseph Schwarzberg, *Sur les sentiers de la guerre*
Zuzana Sermer, *Trousse de survie*
Rachel Shtibel, *Le Violon*/ Adam Shtibel, *Témoignage d'un enfant*
George Stern, *Une jeunesse perdue*
Willie Sterner, *Les Ombres du passé*
Ann Szedlecki, *L'Album de ma vie*
William Tannenzapf, *Souvenirs de l'abîme*/ Renate Krakauer, *Le Bonheur de l'innocence*
Elsa Thon, *Que renaisse demain*
Agnes Tomasov, *De génération en génération*
Leslie Vertes, *Seul dans la tourmente*
Anka Voticky, *Frapper à toutes les portes*
Sam Weisberg, *Passeur de mémoire*/ Johnny Jablon, *Souvenez-vous*

Lament

Moishe Kantorowitz

Fondation Azrieli Foundation

FIRST EDITION

First published by the author as *My Mother's Bequest: From Shershev to Auschwitz to Newfoundland* in 2004.

The Azrieli Foundation · azrielifoundation.org

The Holocaust Survivor Memoirs Program
Publisher, Naomi Azrieli · Director, Jody Spiegel · Managing Editor, Arielle Berger
Edited by Devora Levin, Arielle Berger and Emily Standfield
Book design by Gareth Lind · Cover design by Endpaper Studio
Endpaper maps by Martin Gilbert · Interior map by Merritt Cartographic

Library and Archives Canada Cataloguing in Publication
Title: Lament / Moishe Kantorowitz.
Other titles: My mother's bequest
Kantorowitz, Moishe, 1923–2008, author | Azrieli Foundation, publisher.
First edition. | Azrieli series of Holocaust survivor memoirs ; XVII
First published as My mother's bequest: from Shershev to Auschwitz to Newfoundland in 2004. | Includes bibliographical references and index.
Canadiana (print) 20250188546 | Canadiana (ebook) 20250188570
ISBN 9781998880249 (softcover) | ISBN 9781998880256 (EPUB)
ISBN 9781998880263 (PDF)

LCSH: Kantorowitz, Moishe, 1923–2008. | LCSH: Jews—Belarus—Shereshevo—Biography. | LCSH: Holocaust, Jewish (1939–1945)—Belarus—Shereshevo—Personal narratives. | LCSH: Holocaust survivors—Canada—Biography. LCSH: Auschwitz (Concentration camp) | LCGFT: Autobiographies.

Classification: LCC DS135.B383 K36 2025 | DDC 940.53/18092—dc23

MIX
Paper from responsible sources
FSC® C004191

PRINTED IN CANADA

Contents

BOOK TWO

World War II (1939–1941)

BOOK THREE

German Occupation (1941–1943)

BOOK FOUR

The Camps (1943–1945)

BOOK FIVE
The Wandering Refugee (1945–1948)

BOOK SIX
A New Life in Canada (1948–2000s)

Series Preface: In Their Own Words

> In telling these stories, the writers have liberated themselves. For so many years we did not speak about it, even when we became free people living in a free society. Now, when at last we are writing about what happened to us in this dark period of history, knowing that our stories will be read and live on, it is possible for us to feel truly free. These unique historical documents put a face on what was lost, and allow readers to grasp the enormity of what happened to six million Jews — one story at a time.
> **David J. Azrieli, C.M., C.Q., M.Arch**
> Holocaust survivor and founder, The Azrieli Foundation

SINCE THE END of World War II, approximately 40,000 Jewish Holocaust survivors have immigrated to Canada. Who they are, where they came from, what they experienced and how they built new lives for themselves and their families are important parts of our Canadian heritage. The Azrieli Foundation's Holocaust Survivor Memoirs Program was established in 2005 to preserve and share the memoirs written by those who survived the twentieth-century Nazi genocide of the Jews of Europe and later made their way to Canada. The memoirs encourage readers to engage thoughtfully and critically with the complexities of the Holocaust and to create meaningful connections with the lives of survivors.

Millions of individual stories are lost to us forever. By preserving the stories written by survivors and making them widely available to a broad audience, the Azrieli Foundation's Holocaust Survivor Memoirs Program seeks to sustain the memory of all those who perished at the hands of hatred, abetted by indifference and apathy. The personal accounts of those who survived against all odds are as different as the people who wrote them, but all demonstrate the courage, strength, wit and luck that it took to prevail and survive in such terrible adversity. The memoirs are also moving tributes to people—strangers and friends—who risked their lives to help others, and who, through acts of kindness and decency in the darkest of moments, frequently helped the persecuted maintain faith in humanity and courage to endure. These accounts offer inspiration to all, as does the survivors' desire to share their experiences so that new generations can learn from them.

The Holocaust Survivor Memoirs Program collects, archives and publishes select survivor memoirs and makes the print editions available free of charge to educational institutions and Holocaust-education programs across Canada. They are also available for sale online to the general public. All revenues to the Azrieli Foundation from the sales of the Azrieli Series of Holocaust Survivor Memoirs go toward the publishing and educational work of the memoirs program.

The Azrieli Foundation would like to express appreciation to the following people for their invaluable efforts in producing this book: Pierke Bosschieter, Vivian Felsen, Dr. Bożena Karwowska, Dr. Piotr Setkiewicz and Alison Strobel.

Editorial Note

THIS MEMOIR WAS written about a time when territories in Eastern Europe were frequently changing hands. As borders shifted, names of cities, towns and villages changed, as did official languages. The territory where Moishe Kantorowitz lived, now Belarus, was ruled by the Russian Empire, Poland, the Soviet Union and Germany. After World War II, it became part of the Soviet Union until Belarus achieved independence in 1991. The various languages and names of places used in this memoir reflect the historical conflicts and territorial shifts in the region as well as the author's memories of a particular community, time and place. Names of shtetls and towns with large Jewish populations have been recorded with their Yiddish, rather than Polish, names. The memoir was originally written in Yiddish and translated into English by the author, a translation that preserved many Yiddish and Hebrew words and phrases, reflecting Moishe's upbringing in a Yiddish-speaking community that emphasized biblical and Hebrew-language education. The Yiddish words and phrases have been transliterated according to the standard of the YIVO Institute for Jewish Research except for where the author used more common Hebrew transliterations, such as for the names of prayers and holidays.

Foreign-language words and historical terms that may be unclear without additional context have been added to the glossary beginning on page 575.

Introduction

OVER THE PAST eighty years since the liberation of Auschwitz, publishing houses have produced an impressive number of memory-based Holocaust works, inviting the question of how important it is to add new memoirs to the existing canon. Though each life story is unique, readers tend to favour the same, well-known texts. Moreover, in recent years, the category of Holocaust memoir has been overshadowed by so-called airport fiction, often with "Auschwitz" in the title. While it is vital that Auschwitz and the Holocaust are kept alive in the collective minds of the public, replacing memories of actual events with fiction essentially suggests that what happened to Jews in Auschwitz was not horrible or interesting enough on its own. At the same time, historians have traditionally built their knowledge from documentation of the Holocaust—most of which was produced by the perpetrators—and the literature of personal experience, or egodocuments, has only recently gained a respected place among other primary sources for historical research. Thus, while many aspects of the Jewish experience during the Holocaust have been relegated to the margins, each new personal recollection published yields unparalleled historical and educational value, showing the depth of the tragedy for individuals, communities and all of European Jewry in a way that cannot be compared to any documents or fictionalized representations.

The story of Moishe Kantorowitz is one of these valuable personal recollections, providing readers with unique insights, even against the backdrop of the many other memoirs available. The author's detailed memories and deep understanding of events are conveyed in a well-written narrative that doesn't force the reader to share his way of thinking but invites us to accompany him as he revisits his past. As in all personal stories related to the Holocaust, this recounting is saturated in tribulations and tragedies, as well as in the beauty of the life he remembers from before the war and the challenges of the one he built afterwards. When recording his life story, Moishe referred to the historical and cultural backdrop that shaped his experiences. This contextual information is important, especially in light of the growing distance from the Holocaust and the rise of nationalistic sentiments in contemporary societies around the world.

Jewish life as it existed before the Holocaust is now only a memory. However, Kantorowitz's story brings to life one such long-gone community in Shershev, a shtetl (a small, primarily Jewish town) in the Brest region in Belarus, which was Poland at the time of his childhood. Moishe was born in 1923 in the part of Europe whose political reality was shaped by war. The end of World War I and the international political processes that followed it, including the Treaty of Versailles, established a political order in Western Europe, significantly leaving Eastern Europe, and especially its eastern borders, open to negotiations, both peaceful and violent. Though Poland was brought back onto the map of Europe as a united, sovereign state in 1918, its borders were undefined and unstable.

It was only a couple of years before Moishe's birth that the eastern borders of Poland were established during the war with the Soviet Union in 1920, and the territory of the Russian Empire called the Pale of Settlement (or "Kresy," meaning "the end" or "borderlands" in Polish), where Jews were allowed to settle, became part of Poland, bringing relative peace and stability to its inhabitants. The changing political landscapes and political instability in Eastern Europe in the first decades of the twentieth century brought a wave of anti-Jewish pogroms in Eastern Europe and stirred up local antisemitic sentiments.

Characteristically, though the territory was populated to a large degree by its native Belarusians, Shershev's political, religious and social life, as Moishe remembers it, was shaped by Poles and Jews. As we learn at the beginning of Moishe's memoir, his father, injured during the war, was taken care of by the Polish government, which granted him the right to sell alcohol. In a typical gesture of colonization, the Polish government gave the land in this newly regained region to former military officers, also rewarding Jews, who were not permitted to own land, by granting them various permits and so rewarding their loyalty to Poland and its legendary marshal, Józef Piłsudski.

From early childhood onward, Moishe and his family were steeped in Jewish community and a Jewish way of life, though even as a child he understood, to a degree, the multicultural nature of his environment. His world consisted of Jews, local Belarusians and Poles. The time and place in which Moishe grew up shaped him not only as a Polish Jew and a member of this religious community, but also as a political being, a person who took an active part in creating his community, consciously building his political and social views and shaping his own future. Often called the "age of nationalisms," the nineteenth century was a time when citizens of European countries began forming national loyalties—moving away from previously prevalent loyalties to religions, families, social groups or rulers. While it is indisputable that nationalism as an ideology has resulted in a number of genocides, including the Holocaust, it framed the thinking of people of that time who were looking to create new ways of life, aligning themselves with one of the many "isms" of the first decades of the twentieth century. For European Jews, this became a period of building their political identities in addition to religious and cultural ones. As a child in Shershev, Moishe formed his connections and loyalties to the idea of a state for the Jewish people, a state that did not yet exist. While he does not engage in large-scale politics in his memoir, he discusses his relationship with Israel insofar as it impacted the plans that ultimately defined his life. Later, as a grown man, he writes about Israel in the context of his long struggle to fulfill the dream of his youth—to contribute to building Israel as a state and country for Jews.

In the mid-1930s, Moishe experienced what he describes as a surprisingly sudden wave of anti-Jewish attitudes and acts after the summer vacation period of 1935. It was after Józef Piłsudski, the Polish leader, died in May of 1935, that the nationalistic political groups that gained power after his death could freely introduce new antisemitic measures. Even in the nationalistic and antisemitic society that existed before 1935, there was a certain consensus on accommodations and tolerance, such as Moishe and the other Jewish children in Polish school being permitted not to write on Saturdays, their Sabbath, a day when doing any work, including writing, was not allowed according to Jewish law. After 1935, the wider circles of Polish society were openly unwilling to accept Jews as Poles, a dynamic spearheaded and supported by their political leaders and the government, which introduced several anti-Jewish policies and practices, including the boycotting of Jewish businesses, limiting the number of spaces for Jews at universities (*numerus clausus*) and forcing Jewish students to sit in separate sections in lecture halls, areas that were called "ghetto benches."

On September 1, 1939, Germany attacked Poland, and Moishe, as a teenager, witnessed from a distance the defeat of the Polish Army and the fall of the state, which lead to chaos and uncertainty. On September 17, Poland was attacked from the east by the Soviet Union, and, a few days later, a group of local peasants took over as representatives of the underground Communist organization that was cooperating with the Soviet Union. Young Jews in Shershev tended to be Zionists rather than Communists. Soviet ideology promoted international rather than national movements, so in the eyes of the Soviet leaders, being Zionist meant being counter-revolutionary. The Jews of Shershev knew they had to be careful.

The two years of living under Soviet control—from September 1939 to June 1941—was also a time of great change in the Jewish community, which was united to a large degree by their traditional religious and cultural lives. Under the Soviets, these aspects of Jewish life were limited to clandestine meetings, and the Communist Party exercised enormous power, repressing what they saw as anti-Soviet activities and punishing those who were even suspected of being involved. People began to be careful about how they spoke for fear of being sent to Siberia for saying the wrong thing. The local peasants, as Moishe calls Communist or Soviet Belarusians, dismantled the old synagogue, and Jews had to adopt a non-religious, Soviet lifestyle. They were required to work on the Sabbath and on Jewish holidays. This is when, amid food shortages and an ideologically motivated lack of kosher products, Moishe tasted his first non-kosher food.

Life under Soviet rule was not easy, but things drastically worsened after the arrival of the Germans in the summer of 1941.[1] Antisemitic Nazi rules and regulations were implemented almost immediately, and Jews were openly and publicly beaten, tormented and killed. In August of 1941, the Jews of Shershev were told they were being relocated to a labour camp. It is difficult to know to what extent the Jewish community members believed in such plans, though labour camps were not uncommon then, Treblinka I (close to the future killing site of Treblinka II) being one of them. But rather than being sent to a labour camp, the Jews of Shershev, as well as those from other towns in the region, were sent on marches from one place to another, marches during which many people were killed by German guards. Moishe and members of his community were led to Antopol, and from there, he and his family went from place to place, learning about the tragedies of local Jewish communities. Mass executions of entire communities, massacres that historians now refer to as "the Holocaust by bullets,"

1 For insight into the ways the occupations of both Soviet and German forces during World War II resulted in millions of civilians being killed, see Timothy Snyder's *Bloodlands: Europe Between Hitler and Stalin* (Basic Books, 2010).

were the main means of killing Jews in 1941 and 1942 in the East European territories, primarily in what is now Ukraine and Belarus.[2]

Eventually, Moishe's family decided to go to Pruzhany and settled in the ghetto there. Jews were forced into ghettos at a time when the Nazis' persecution of Jews was intensifying, leading up to the "Final Solution," the plan to murder all of Europe's Jews. In the ghettos, hunger, overcrowding and sicknesses killed hundreds of thousands of Jews, yet, as Moishe notes, many families moved into the ghetto voluntarily because it seemed like the best chance of finding safety. Soon it became obvious that they were mistaken, and that creating self-governments was a deceptive way the Nazis maintained power over the Jews in the ghetto.

The situation became even more dire beginning in the spring and summer of 1942. Moishe attributes the worsening situation to both the difficulties the German army faced on the Eastern Front and to the acceleration of the Nazis' overt goals. In 1942, during the conference in Wannsee, it was decided that the cooperation of all levels of power would be focused on implementing the "Final Solution," and the mass killing of Jews in killing centres was planned. By the early spring of 1942, the liquidation of ghettos was already taking place, and by the end of 1943, the majority of Jewish ghettos ceased to exist, as their inhabitants had been murdered.

While Moishe does provide some background on Nazi German politics and policies, he focuses on the ways of thinking, behaviours and fates of the Jewish communities of the region, and especially on the people he was acquainted with. But although he writes about other ghettos and towns in the region, it is unlikely that he knew what

2 It is believed that around 1.5 million Jews were killed in these massacres. The exact number is unknown, as in 1942, Heinrich Himmler, the head of the SS, ordered his men to dig up and burn the bodies of the victims. By 1942, the gas chambers in Nazi death camps were the main means of killing Jews en masse. See Father Patrick Desbois's *The Holocaust by Bullets: A Priest's Journey to Uncover the Truth Behind the Murder of 1.5 Million Jews* (Palgrave Macmillan, 2008).

was happening there in detail at that time; there were likely different chains of gossip and partial pieces of information that circulated among Jews in the region. However, the fate of all Jews in the region ultimately became clear.

When writing this part of his memoir, years after the events of 1942, Moishe knew what happened next. He knew that the rest of his family would be killed, and still, while rendering the horror—the mixture of hope with an understanding of what would happen next—he holds on to the last moments of being with his parents and siblings. As winner of the Nobel Prize in Literature Wisława Szymborska writes about remembering the dead:

> The photograph halted them in life,
> and now keeps them
> above the earth toward the earth.
> [...]
> I can do only two things for them—
> describe this flight
> and not add a last line.[3]

In a similar gesture, Moishe keeps his family, or the memory of them, alive through narrative, by writing about them and not adding the last line as long as he can.

Moishe's description of life in the Pruzhany ghetto in the last weeks of its existence is a contribution to the historical knowledge of the Nazi German crimes, but also a way to preserve the memory of many Jewish communities, their desperate attempts to survive, to not give up. His narrative points the reader toward the bigger picture of what life in the ghetto looked like, especially in the so-called open ghetto with its connection to partisan groups, but at the same time, gives voice

3 Wisława Szymborska, "Photograph from September 11," in *Monologue of a Dog*, trans. Clare Kavanagh (Houghton Mifflin Harcourt, 2005).

to the author's individual and personal feelings about his experience. It may seem surprising that Moishe remembers small events like not giving his sister a potato when she asked for it, but he regretted that moment for the rest of his life, and by writing about it and sharing his feeling of guilt with his readers he is able to confront some of the trauma in the memory. It is specifically these memories of moments when he turned away from his family members or chose to focus on himself that accompanied him his entire life.

At the age of twenty, Moishe became the only survivor of his immediate family. His parents and siblings, together with the entire family living in Shershev, were killed even before Moishe was transported to Auschwitz. Moishe was one of few survivors of Shershev's and neighbouring Pruzhany's Jewish communities. His memoir allows us to revisit the past and learn about Jewish life in the shtetls of Belarus, a history now preserved only in the memories of survivors.

At the end of January 1943, Moishe Kantorowitz, together with other survivors of the Pruzhany ghetto, was forced to board the cattle car of a train going to the Auschwitz concentration and death camp. At this time, there was an urgent need in Auschwitz for workers who could fill the quota the SS had promised the neighbouring industrial plants. This is why this group of men was sent to Auschwitz, unlike people in earlier transports, who had been sent to be killed in Treblinka II, one of six killing centres in German-occupied Poland. Functioning since the summer of 1940, the Auschwitz camp was initially established as a prison for Polish men, so-called political prisoners, meaning, those who could potentially create or join underground organizations against Nazi Germany. It also served as a prison for the district. Auschwitz commandant Rudolf Höss had agricultural ambitions for the area, but Heinrich Himmler, one of the most powerful politicians of Nazi Germany and the leader of the SS, wanted to cooperate with various German industries, which soon translated into creating a camp complex consisting of three main camps (Auschwitz, Birkenau and Monowitz) and over forty subcamps. These camps exploited the work of prisoners and de facto used them as slave labour for the economic gain of the SS, strengthening its power.

Plans to expand the camp and the building in 1942 of the second, larger site in Birkenau happened at a time when the Nazi leaders counted on an endless influx of Soviet prisoners of war, whose labour was to be sold to the industry. As the Soviet Union at that time was not a signatory of international treaties, Soviet prisoners of war were not protected by international laws. After an initial territorial gain following the outbreak of the German-Soviet war in the summer of 1941, the German army faced a long struggle and finally a defeat. Instead of bringing workers to the camp, prolonged war meant that German men were drafted into the army en masse, resulting in a shortage of workers. Thus, among all the Nazi killing centres, only in Auschwitz were Jews not automatically sent to the killing facilities, but upon arrival, underwent a selection on the unloading ramp.

The train holding Jews from the Pruzhany ghetto passed the Auschwitz station, pulled over to the side and arrived at a provisional ramp, the Alte Judenrampe, located a few hundred metres from Birkenau. Here the Jews first encountered the realities of Auschwitz. The ones the SS doctors deemed able to work were registered in the camp to become slave labourers for the SS. The rest walked to one of the provisional gas chambers set up inside two village houses with their windows and doors sealed, known as the "little red house" and "the little white house." The crematoria and gas chambers eventually set up in Birkenau had yet to be built but soon would be.

Contrary to popular belief, Auschwitz was built to accomplish more than fulfilling the Nazi antisemitic agenda. A famous Polish writer, Zofia Nałkowska, a member of the Special Committee to Investigate Nazi Crimes Perpetrated on Polish Soil, wrote in 1946:

> Studying the unique phenomenon of Auschwitz through material made available by both eyewitness testimonials and the examination of the camps, we are struck by the fact that the system

> and camps were established in order to carry out a twofold task: political and economic, that is, ideal and practical.[4]

The political included proving the superiority of Germans and the Germanic race, and killing European Jews who, according to the Nazis, were the source of all the political and economic problems of Germany. It also included exploiting the natural and cultural resources of occupied lands and making them available to German settlers, in line with the colonial attitudes of the Third Reich. The economic meant accumulating revenue, which was achieved by looting Jewish possessions and even pilfering their dead bodies, and by selling prisoners' slave labour to the industry.

The economic interests of the SS (and the Third Reich) translated into a shift in several policies in Auschwitz before Moishe's arrival. In March 1942, a camp for women was opened, adding to the workforce needed by the Nazis. In fact, the memory of women in the death block stayed with Moishe his entire life as one of the worst scenes he witnessed in the camp.

Additionally, not long after Moishe arrived in Auschwitz-Birkenau, the SS limited selections in the camp among the non-Jewish prisoners and stopped conducting them by August 1943. Non-Jewish prisoners were allowed to receive food parcels. Jews were also not allowed to visit the newly opened brothel, or "puff," for prisoners in Auschwitz, which was meant to provide an incentive for better work. These policies deepened the differences in the conditions for Jewish and non-Jewish prisoners in the camp, though from the very beginning, camp officials were more relentless in their abuse of Jews, who were not meant to survive longer than three weeks. According to survivors from the first transport to Auschwitz, Karl Fritzsch, the deputy commandant of the camp, addressed the first 758 inmates brought to the camp in June 1940, with the following words:

4 Zofia Nałkowska, *Medallions*, trans. Diana Kuprel (Northwestern University Press, 2000).

> You came here not to a sanatorium, but to a German concentration camp, from which there is no other way out but through the chimney. If someone doesn't like it, they can go straight to the wires. If there are Jews in the transport, they have the right to live no longer than two weeks, priests a month, the rest three months.[5]

By the same token, although Jews were among the functionaries, the prisoners with more power, there were no Jews among the so-called old numbers, or prisoners from the first transports, who were some of the most privileged prisoners of Auschwitz at the time of Moishe's arrival. Those who had survived the first two years of Auschwitz existence, when the inhumane conditions in the camp were the main means of killing prisoners, were able to obtain the best work positions in later years. Mass transports of Jews to be killed only began coming to Birkenau in 1942.

It is impossible for us, people who live in a free world, to understand the internal dynamics of the camp, a place governed by its own laws and customs. The Italian survivor and writer Primo Levi called the camp the "grey zone"—a territory where the prisoners were victims but also perpetrators, as the SS created a system in which there was little to no cooperation between prisoners. No moral codes and laws as we know them applied to this realm, creating a reality that, to many survivors, seemed unreal. It took Primo Levi, who himself was a prisoner of Auschwitz (Monowitz), years to form some level of understanding of the inner workings of the system and to underline the fact that the Nazi system deprived their victims of innocence. In his philosophical book of essays *The Drowned and the Saved*, he called this one of the most gruesome of the Nazi crimes. Describing the work of the Sonderkommando, the groups of prisoners who had to assist the SS in bringing Jews to the gas chambers and then search and burn their bodies in the crematoria, Levi wrote:

5 APMAB, Zespół Materiały Ruchu Oporu, t. VII, k. 464.

> Conceiving and organizing the squads was National Socialism's most demonic crime. Behind the pragmatic aspect (to economize on able men, to impose on others the most atrocious tasks) other more subtle aspects can be perceived. This institution represented an attempt to shift onto others—specifically, the victims—the burden of guilt, so that they were deprived of even the solace of innocence.[6]

On a much smaller scale, this was also Moishe's experience. His tormentors, the people he was the most afraid of in the camp, were not the SS officers and guards, but his fellow prisoners, namely the functionaries. As a Jew coming to Auschwitz without especially valuable skills, unlike Primo Levi, who was a gifted chemist, Moishe was one of many replaceable workers and was never in a position of power over others. His narrative thus gives his readers a thorough description of the ordinary prisoner's life in the camp.

Moishe refers to Auschwitz as "Hell itself." However, like many other authors of Holocaust memoirs, he refrains from extensive emotional language when describing his life in the camp. If he wanted to remember, it was for one reason: to provide a testimony, to be a witness. And so, he invites the reader to engage with his narrative as a description without many reflections on the meaning of the events that he was not supposed to be able to survive. When recollecting Auschwitz, and later his time in the Sosnowitz subcamp, on a death march, and then in Mauthausen and Gusen, there is no concept of surviving in the sense of having a future. There is just one moment and then the next. And in this way, he lives.

One thing that is clear from Moishe's descriptions is that many prisoners formed national alliances among themselves, drawn together by cultural, religious and linguistic similarities but also by the policies set up by the SS. Moishe refers to other prisoners as Poles or Soviets,

6 Primo Levi, *The Drowned and the Saved*, trans. by Raymond Rosenthal (Viking Penguin, 1988).

for instance, seeing them not as fellow prisoners, but as members of national groups with their quite stereotypical characteristics. Interestingly, though he refers frequently to Polish prisoners as antisemitic, when it comes to his descriptions of specific people, their nationality ceases to be the main factor in Moishe's opinion of them. In fact, he is very open with stating that he survived the camp thanks to a Polish "privileged" prisoner, Leon Kulowski.

Moishe being helped by another prisoner does not necessarily testify to any exceptional circumstances. To the contrary, it proves one of the rules of the camp: to protect prisoners who survived what was impossible to survive. Working under an especially brutal foreman, Pilarek, along with constant hunger and suffering from dysentery, after three months in the camp, Moishe was quite sure that his end was near. However, Leon Kulowski, one of the so-called old numbers, a Polish inmate from the first transport, learned that Moishe had survived working under the infamous Pilarek for six weeks and took him under his wing for protection. One can only speculate that this idea—that those who had survived the impossible deserved protection—was a remnant of an old religious way of thinking; there was a common tradition that if a rope broke during an execution, the convict was set free by the will of God. This concept is what gave the prisoners who survived the first years in conditions that made survival impossible relatively more power. It may also be what saved Moishe Kantorowitz, a young Jew who did not succumb to a brutal German foreman. Ultimately, Leon Kulowski and Moishe Kantorowitz saw beyond the national and racial stereotypes that were successfully promoted among Germans by the Nazis.

Years later, in 1965, Moishe met Leon Kulowski, who was working on a Polish trawler as a doctor, on a street in St. John's, Newfoundland. Their surprising meeting was covered in the local news in Newfoundland and in Poland, and it was also the beginning of a lifelong friendship. The letters that Moishe kept reveal that he generously supported Kulowski's family with gifts and parcels containing items that were hard to come by in Communist Poland. The letters also reveal his deep gratitude and a profound emotional connection between the two men. Moishe thought of Leon as a brother, and referred to him as his only brother still alive. Shared experiences of Auschwitz translated into a brotherhood that thrived despite the two men's religious, political and cultural differences, defying all stereotypes. Their letters are often about the weather, but also about their families, and with the passing time, Leon shared some of his memories of the camps and observations about the fading interest in learning about Auschwitz. Life after Auschwitz had a special meaning for Moishe and Leon. Leon reflected how, when he got sick, Moishe commanded him to take care of his health, writing, "After Auschwitz we have to live long and happy lives."

After the war, Moishe moved between camps for displaced persons, and like other survivors, had to find a place for himself. Jewish survivors faced continued displacement, homelessness, ongoing discrimination and the trauma of what they had lived through. Moishe's desire to go to Palestine and build the country that would become Israel could not become a reality for him because of the British-imposed restrictions on immigration. The United States, too, had restrictive immigration policies, so Moishe, with the help of his uncle in New York, found a sponsor, a woman originally from Shershev, who would bring him to Canada. Canadian immigration restrictions also made it difficult for Jews to come to Canada after the war. As Moishe writes, Canada favoured giving visas to men who had experience working on farms, which automatically excluded Jews, as traditionally they had not been allowed to own land in the countries where they lived, and made it easier for Ukrainians or Belarusians with dubious pasts to immigrate to Canada.

When Moishe finally arrived in Canada, he did not have any specific plans for his future; he simply dealt with problems as they came up. Nonetheless, he got married, started a family and worked hard, and his memoir gives the reader a vivid account of what life in Canada looked like for a young Jewish refugee at the time.

In Moishe's narrative, the memory of his family comes up only sporadically as he describes his experiences in the camps. His focus is on surviving, one day at a time. He moves chronologically from the first weeks in Birkenau to his time in the main camp of Auschwitz I, and then to the Sosnowitz subcamp and the death march to Mauthausen. His narrative voice is consistently limited to his current experiences as he moves through this time. But the memory of his family becomes prominent later, in Canada. Moishe names his children after the members of his family he lost in a gesture to immortalize the people he loved, to keep their memory alive and to bring back the continuity of generations that the Nazis attempted to sever. His children in turn continue the tradition, so that all his close family members are remembered in his descendants. Through his life, Moishe preserved the high values attached to notions of family and community that he acquired as a child, supporting his wife and children, and, in his later years, building a Jewish community in St. John's, Newfoundland. It is the community he builds in his new country and the family he raises that connect him, and his readers, to the past and tie the past to the future. Historical narratives are shaped by those with the power to define key terms like "freedom" and "victory." In building his life anew and in writing his memoir, Moishe is among others who are telling and publishing their Holocaust memories, claiming this power, defining their own freedom and victories, and contributing to a deeper understanding of history.

Dr. Bożena Karwowska
Department of Central, Eastern, and Northern European Studies, University of British Columbia
2025

Moishe Kantorowitz Wartime Map

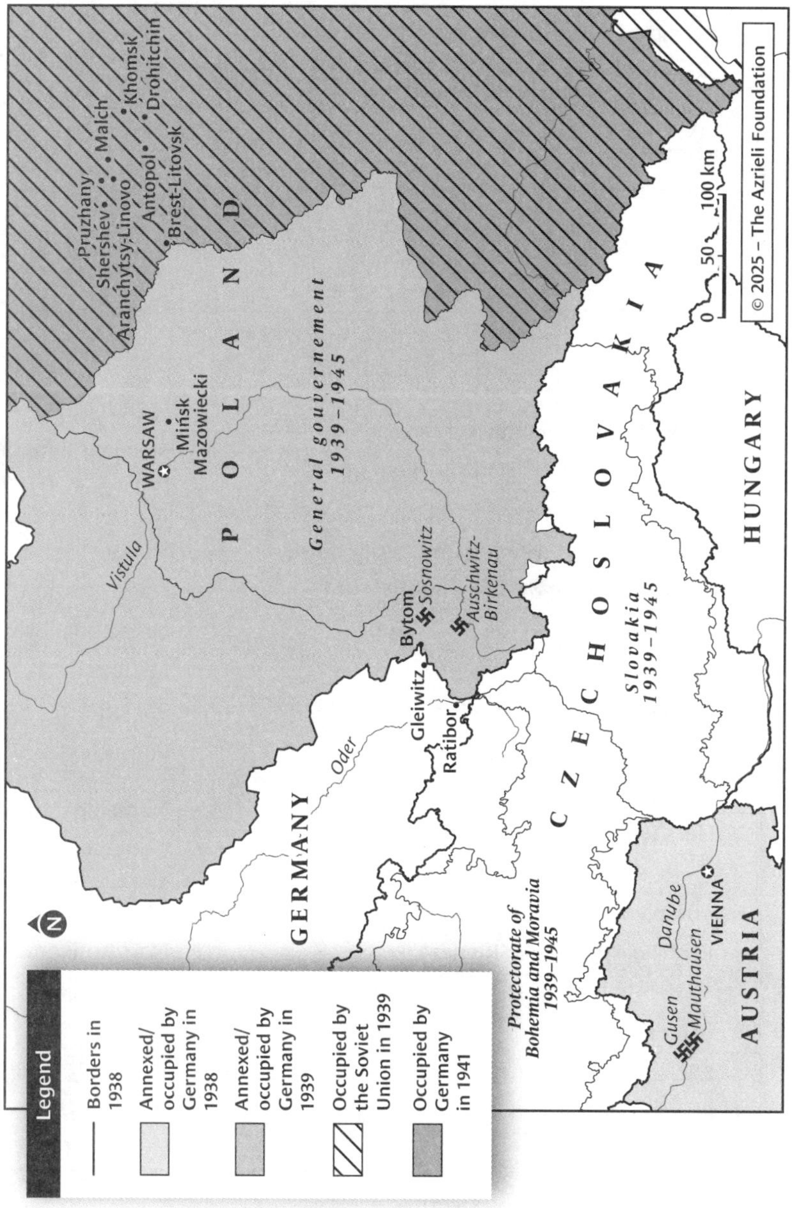

Moishe Kantorowitz Family Tree

PATERNAL GRANDPARENTS
Yaakov Kopel Kantorowitz* m. Chinkah Granitzki*

- **UNCLE**
  Shevach
- **UNCLE**
  Shalom m. Sarah
  - Name unknown
- **AUNT**
  Sheindl* m. Leibel Pinsky*
  - Leah (Lisa)*
  - Shalom (Sioma)*
- **UNCLE**
  Joshua* m. first wife Mushka Leshtchinsky
  - Shalom*

  m. second wife Freda Goldberg*
  - Name unknown*
  - Name unknown*
- **UNCLE**
  Reuven* m. Chashkah Pinsky*
  - Michla*
  - Shalom*
  - Shevach*
- **UNCLE**
  Hershel* m. Sheine*
  - Name unknown*
  - Name unknown*
- **AUNT**
  Pesl (Pola)* m. Zelig Remez*
  - Max*
  - Name unknown*
  - Name unknown*
- **UNCLE**
  Eli*
- **FATHER**
  Yitzchak (Isaac)*

*Murdered in the Holocaust

MATERNAL GRANDPARENTS

Laizer Ber Auerbach m. Freida Leah Goldfarb

UNCLE

Shloime m. Esther Leiba Winograd
- Yankl (Jack)
- David
- Chvolkah (Helen)
- Avreml (Abe)
  m. first wife Chana
  m. second wife Rebecca
- Rose
- Lippa (Leo)
- Elchonon (Harold)
  m. Eva
- Eli m. Shirley

UNCLE

Pesach (Philip) m. Esther
- Names unknown

UNCLE

Lippa (Leo) m. Rebecca
- Irving m. Ruth

MOTHER

Esther Beila*
- Sheva*
- **Moishe** m. Ruth Pleet
  - Ken m. Lisa Nathanson
  - Sharon m. Meir Gazit
    - Orly
      - Emma
      - Gabriella
    - Eitan
      - Noah
    - Erez
      - Nathan
  - Aviva
    - Ariella
    - Genevieve
      - Shayna
      - Elijah
- Leibel (Liova)*
- Sarah (Sonia)*
- Leiba*

For my children—Ken, Sharon and Aviva.

For my grandchildren—Orly, Eitan, Erez, Ariella and Genevieve.

For those who perished.

For the memory of my entire family, their friends, their neighbours—to all their martyred lives, and to all those who have no relatives left to remember them or mention their names.

Prologue

IT WAS MY destiny to be born and live in one of the most brutal and savage centuries in human history, and specifically in the history of my people, the Jewish people. In my time, I have seen my people standing at the edge of an abyss as they were thrown down to its bottomless depths by the tens of thousands daily. I have seen the destruction of more than a third of my people, six million in all—men, women and children—and the destruction of the source and cradle of Hebrew and Yiddish literature, from which countless generations drew their inspiration and boundless hope. I saw the destruction of almost two thousand years of Jewish creative life in Europe—and the immensity of that horror cannot be comprehended.

It was also my destiny and privilege to witness what I consider to be the greatest event of the past twentieth century: the transformation of the remnants of European Jewry from Holocaust victims to a liberated people who returned to their rightful homeland after two thousand years of exile and untold persecution.

The calamity and disaster that befell the Jews of Europe from the mid-1930s to the mid-1940s annihilated the majority of European Jewry, including my father and mother, my only brother, my three sisters, my paternal grandparents, six uncles, five aunts and all their children—a total of fifty-one souls. As I am the sole survivor of my entire family that I had in Europe, it is my wish that they be remembered and that their memory be perpetuated so that their lives, their suffering and their agonizing, untimely deaths should not be forgotten with my passing. It is also my wish to leave on paper my experiences of that era. For deep in my heart, I believe that my life was spared in order to bear witness to the tragedy that befell my people during the darkest era in Jewish history.

I would also like to record memories of my village and the people I still remember, among them childhood friends, neighbours, teachers, rabbis, the so-called pious and the secular, scholars and ignoramuses, rich and poor—all those who made up an ordinary shtetl before the catastrophe, who were slaughtered without leaving behind any remnant, not a single person to remember them, to mention their names, to shed a tear over their mass graves or mounds of ashes. Those mass graves and mounds of ashes are the only witnesses, the only testimony to them ever having walked on this earth.

It is my hope that my children and their children will read this account, will get acquainted through the written word with family they never knew and learn about what their ancestors' world was like. Maybe they will emit a sigh on my behalf and light a candle on the anniversary of their ancestors' martyrdom. Hopefully, there will come a time when people of goodwill in all nations will join together to remember the millions of innocent martyrs and be inspired to dedicate their time and effort to the struggle of equality and acceptance among all races and religions and to the betterment of humanity.

BOOK ONE
Growing Up in Shershev
(1923–1939)

1
Omens for Good Luck

I WAS BORN on February 6, 1923, or the 20th day of Shvat 5683, according to the Jewish calendar, in Shershev, a shtetl in the Brest region in what was then part of Poland (now Šarašova, Belarus), to my parents, Yitzchak (Isaac) Kantorowitz and Esther Beila, née Auerbach. In my younger years, my father lived in a different village than the rest of our family. Because he had been injured while serving in the army in World War I, in 1924, the Polish government gave him a permit to run a restaurant in which alcoholic drinks could be served and bottles of liquor sold. The sale of liquor was under strict government supervision in Poland, and whoever had such a permit was assured a reasonable livelihood. Every district had an allocated number of permits, and one had to accept the permit where it was given. My father received his permit for a place called Verkhy, a large village in the district of Volhynia. The village existed mainly because of two large sawmills, where farmers from the surrounding villages found employment in the off-season months.

My father had to move to Verkhy, but as only a handful of Jewish families lived there, my mother preferred to remain with me and my sister, Sheva, in Shershev, at her parents' house, which was almost across the street from where we lived, on Ostrowiecka Street. My grandparents' house, which had been the house of my mother's grandfather Nathan Shepsl Goldfarb, after whom I am named (one of my middle names is Nathan, the other is Aaron), did not differ much from our house; it was just a bit smaller. I was three years old when our house was sold and we moved in with my grandparents. Behind their house was a shed where firewood was kept for the winter and a stable that served as a storage place for all kinds of odds and ends. Why it was called a stable I never knew. My great-grandfather was a tailor by trade, and I doubt he ever had a horse or a cow.

My grandparents' house stood away from the street, and in the space between the house and the street was a well-kept garden with two big maple trees. Neighbours collected the maple leaves in the fall and placed them under loaves of bread while they baked. A much larger garden containing a pear tree extended behind the house. It was a long, low-lying house built from the standard timber from which the houses in Shershev were built. Because of its age, part of the wooden floor had sunk almost to the ground. The bedroom floors were higher than the rest of the house, so there was a slight elevation at the entrance to the bedrooms. I can see myself as a young child, sitting on that elevation, with my feet resting on the lower part of the floor, singing a children's song about a little room containing a hammer, a metal bowl and other things.

I can still hear the melody of a couple of lullabies and remember some of the words that my mother sang to me when putting me to bed. One lullaby told the story of a maiden who was forced to marry a king and leave her true love behind. The song, especially the melody, always made me sad. Another song was about a maiden in whose garden was a well to which her lover would come every evening to get his fill of the cool, quenching drink. My mother sang to me in Yiddish, but years later I learned that it was a translation from the Hebrew song "Yesh li gan" (I have a garden), written by the great Hebrew poet Hayim Bialik. Still later, I realized that the poet wasn't referring to cool water literally.

I have an early memory of a spring morning before the holiday of Passover, or Pesach, when the snow had recently melted, exposing the unkempt garden beds left from the previous fall. My grandfather, Laizer Ber, placed a large copper boiler in the middle of the garden, elevating it with three stones. Carrying two pails at a time, he made a couple of trips to the well to fill up the boiler. Then he lit a fire under the boiler and shoved the end of a long metal rod into the fire. After a long while, the water in the boiler started bubbling, and the end of the metal rod turned red. My grandfather wrapped his hand in a rug, picked up the cooler end of the rod and stuck the red-hot end into the boiler. The water exploded with a geyser of hissing steam and bubbled furiously. By then, there was a circle of neighbours around, each holding a bundle of cutlery. Each piece of cutlery was tied to the same string, like a long string of jewels. My grandfather took the strings from them, one at a time, dipping them three times each in the boiling water. After the cutlery came all sorts of other dishes. Several years passed before I learned that this ritual made the cutlery kosher for Passover, clean and ready for the holiday according to Jewish law.

A few months after we moved in with my grandparents, I got sick with pneumonia. My grandparents' old house was built at a time when people were more concerned about preserving heat than about overhead space or fresh air. As a result, there wasn't much air for a young boy with a bad case of pneumonia, and I nearly died. In desperation, my mother sent for her only brother who was still in Shershev, my uncle Shloime Auerbach. He immediately noticed the lack of air in the house, and he opened a window, picked me up and took me over to the fresh air. According to my mother, he saved my life, for I began to breathe regularly and freely. Later that day, a doctor named Olia Goldfein was brought in from the neighbouring town of Pruzhany, and she immediately suggested that I be moved to a larger and roomier place. My mother decided to move to my other grandparents', my father's parents, Yaakov Kopel and Chinkah.

My grandfather Kopel was the mayor of the village, an office that was shared between him and a Christian named Szlykiewicz. Kopel was a respected member of the community of Shershev and the vicinity. He was of medium height, broad-shouldered, with a little protruding stomach, a rosy, healthy-looking face and a red beard that showed few grey hairs despite his age. My grandmother Chinkah was a tall slim woman who had absolute authority in the house. Even my grandfather Kopel, accustomed to giving orders, would submit to all my grandmother's decisions. At least that is how it seemed to me as a child.

My grandparents from my father's side were rich by the standards of the community. They lived in a big house on the main street, Mostowa, or "bridge street," so named because of the bridge crossing the street. Behind the house was a building constructed from the same thick timber that the houses were built of. That building served all kinds of purposes. During World War I, my grandfather kept horses, a wagon and some farm machinery there. Those four years of war were very lean years in our part of the world, and my grandfather farmed in order to feed his wife and nine children. My father and his brother Shevach were both of military age. Shevach never returned home after World War I, and he was buried somewhere in the vast expanse of Russia. For over fifty years, my grandfather had a hardware store that gave him a comfortable living, and the building behind the house served as a woodshed and warehouse for the store, which mainly sold metal wagon parts. My mother, sister and I took up three rooms in my grandparents' house. Sure enough, I got better soon.

Close to a year after we moved in, a fire broke out on the other side of the river, no more than a hundred metres from our house. There was a volunteer fire brigade in Shershev, consisting of two dozen men with little training and even less equipment. This volunteer group was unable to bring the fire under control, and it spread, engulfing the neighbouring houses along the riverbank. There was a danger that the fire could cross the river, putting the entire main street in danger, including my grandparents' house. My mother hired a wagon driver, loaded the wagon as high as possible, and we set out to our other grandparents'. My maternal grandfather, who was in his seventies, came for me in person, not letting me climb on the wagon. He carried me in his arms, a distance of over a kilometre. While he carried me, I looked up and saw that the sky was covered with flying sparks and small cinders that floated slowly to the ground and showered the houses we were leaving behind.

The fire was eventually put out with the help of Pruzhany's fire brigade, which arrived with a fire truck and motorized pumps. The next morning, we returned to the house and found out that half a dozen houses had gone up in flames during the night, but the fire hadn't crossed the river. My mother took Sheva and me to look at the devastation and the still-glowing cinders. It wasn't until 1937 that Shershev got its own motorized pump with enough hose to reach from the river to any point in the shtetl. A year after that, Shershev got its own fire engine, a brand-new shining vehicle, even more modern than the one in Pruzhany.

My father would come to Shershev for the holidays, and in the summer of 1927, we made our first trip to Verkhy. To get to Verkhy from Shershev, one first had to get to Pruzhany, a three-hour ride by horse and buggy. Then one had to get to the railway station at Aranchytsy-Linovo by a narrow-gauge train, and from there, we took two different trains and an omnibus, which looked like a little bus with no motor and was pulled by a team of four horses. The wheels were made of wood framed in metal railings, just like the farmers' wagon wheels. On one of our trips to Verkhy, one of the wheels broke and thanks to a sturdy wire in one of our suitcases, the driver managed to continue the trip.

In Verkhy, we stayed with our father in his cramped quarters. My father took me to one of the sawmills to show me the huge steam engine. In the noisy engine room, one of the attendants climbed a ladder and pressed the steam whistle. It frightened me immensely, and I would have run out had my father not been holding my hand.

I still remember the Jewish *porets*, or landowner, in Verkhy, a rarity in Poland, as Jews were not permitted to own land. Only a handful of Jews who had owned land before World War I, under the czar, were permitted. The Jewish *porets*'s estate was close to the village, and he would ride into the village on horseback, a tall man in riding boots and breeches with a rifle over his shoulder. Once he rode into my father's restaurant sitting on his horse. He always had a pocketful of candy, which he never failed to give me when he visited my father, which was often. He even tried to have a conversation with me in Polish and Russian, but at that age I spoke neither.

The handful of Jewish storekeepers and tradesmen in Verkhy made a living from the non-Jewish population that was employed in the local sawmills, many of whom would drink away a good part of their month's earnings come payday. I still remember the Jewish blacksmith and his assistant, a young man with extraordinary strength. A circle of gentiles would gather around to admire the young Jewish strongman. He would pick out the biggest and heaviest man around, lift him over his head and throw him several metres away.

In between our trips to Verkhy, we would go on a summer vacation to a shtetl called Domatcheva, where my father would meet us for a few days. The shtetl was near the river Bug, about forty kilometres south of Brest-Litovsk, or Brisk to Jews, and it operated as a summer resort. There were a couple of rows of wooden houses built on a sandy terrain and cobblestone streets where vacationers walked in the late summer afternoons. I remember peeking inquisitively into the open doors and windows of the Jewish homes and seeing the local Jews in their *arbe kanfes* (a ritual undershirt with fringes), working in the sweltering midday heat, making paper bags for grocery stores to supplement their income. The main attraction in Domatcheva was the surrounding pine forest, where vacationers spent most of their time. The local baker would walk among the groups of vacationers, yelling, "Cheesecake, butter cake, preserve cake!" a large baking pan resting against his midsection suspended from a cord around his neck and loaded with baked goods.

Getting to Domatcheva was no easy matter, and once there, my mother had to do her own baking and cooking. There were no dishes available to buy or rent there, so half a household of dishes, utensils and clothing had to travel with us. I never understood how my mother managed to bring all the above and two small children along on such a long and tiresome trip.

While we lived with our paternal grandparents, my father's sister Pesl and his two youngest brothers lived with them as well. The older one was Hershel, and the younger one was Eliyahu, or Eli. Eli was a student at the Hebrew gymnasium, or high school, in Pruzhany, but he came home for Shabbos, Jewish holidays and vacation times. I remember my uncles with pliers in hands, splitting old automobile tires. There were no motorized vehicles in Shershev at that time, so I don't know where my grandfather bought tires. The tires were split in half and then given to specialized artisans who made them into a sort of shoe that was held together with rivets and tied onto cloth-wrapped feet with long leather straps. That was sturdy footwear that could last for years and was affordable to the local farmers. My grandfather sold these shoes to them in his store.

In 1928, I turned five, the age when Jewish boys attended traditional Jewish religious school, or cheder. There were a few *melamdim*, or cheder teachers, in Shershev. Taking her father's advice, my mother sent me to a *melamed* by the name of Kepele Potshinker. He lived with his wife in one of the alleys that ran off the main street, Mostowa, toward the swamps that surrounded a good part of the shtetl. The little street on which he lived was a swamp, too, and as far as I can remember it was never dry, even on the hot summer days. Kepele was a tall man with a long beard, and his attitude toward his little charges was grandfatherly.

The night before my first day in cheder, my mother sent me to sleep over at her parents' house. The next morning, my mother was there bright and early. After breakfast, she and her father took me by the hands, and the three of us walked out the kitchen, into the hallway and to the outside door. They both stopped at the door and told me to step over the threshold with my right foot first, a remedy and omen for good luck and success according to Jewish custom. And so, we stepped across the threshold as they blessed me with every blessing they could think of. I felt safe holding the hands of the two people I loved and trusted most in the world, who were now walking on either side of me like two guardian angels. This is how I started the first day of my Jewish education.

My grandfather Laizer Ber had made me a little wooden lantern with glass panes on all sides. One side served as a door through which the rabbi would light a candle for me before I went home, so that I could find my way in the dark and muddy alley.

In cheder, I first learned to recognize the Hebrew letters, and from there I graduated to reading slowly from a prayer book, or *sider*. The six months went by quickly, and on the last day of cheder, my mother and grandfather came to take me home, just as they had accompanied me to cheder on the first day. I guess the *melamed* wanted to show them that he had earned his pay, so he put me at the head of the table, opened the *sider* at random, and told me to read. I read to the bottom of the page, not understanding a word. As soon as I finished, a handful of change began to fall onto the table, rolling in all directions. My grandfather said that angels from heaven threw the money, a reward for my being such a good student. I trusted my grandfather and loved him so much, and it took me years to realize that he was the one throwing the money. Going home after that final day of cheder, my mother and grandfather walked on either side of me, a little to the back, and like six months earlier, my mother was on my left side and my grandfather on my right.

Around this time, the first autobus was introduced in the shtetl. It was bought by a partnership of several local merchants for service between Shershev and Pruzhany, and it was parked overnight in my uncle Shloime's shed, which had high and wide enough doors for the bus to pass through. I can still see the name of the bus, "Warszawianka," meaning "woman from Warsaw," written in large letters on both sides. The bus would cut down the travel time between Shershev and Pruzhany from three hours by horse and buggy to half an hour. The fare was one złoty by bus against half a złoty by horse and buggy. A złoty was a day's pay for an unskilled labourer.

My uncle Shloime was married to Esther Leiba (née Winograd). Their two oldest sons, Yankl (Jack) and David, had left Shershev in the early 1920s and lived in the United States. My mother's other two brothers also lived in America. By then, one of them, Lippa (Leo), had passed away, leaving a wife, Rebecca, and a young son, Irving. The other brother, Pesach (Philip) was living in New York with his wife, Esther. But my mother hardly knew these brothers, as they had left Shershev while she, the youngest, was just a child. Although Shloime was twelve years older than my mother, the bond between them was very strong. I was a frequent visitor in my uncle Shloime's house. How lively that house was, always full of young people, family members and their numerous friends. We all knew that my uncle was expecting an entry visa to the United States, but it only struck home when he got his papers and began getting ready to leave. At the time of my uncle's departure, he had young children still at school. Like other married men who left for the United States, my uncle planned to send for the rest of the family after two years of residence.

I wonder what it was like for my grandparents, who were then already in their early seventies. What chance did they have to see their son again? Their other two sons had left more than three decades earlier, and they never saw them again. To see their last and only son leave Shershev for America must have been traumatic. My mother really knew only this one brother all her life, and she was tied to him with a thousand knots. Now she had to part with him, and it turned out to be forever. She was the only one remaining of all the Auerbach children, taking on the burden and responsibility of looking after her aging parents. After my uncle's departure, not one day passed that my mother didn't mention his name at least once. She would wait for his letters as eagerly as a devout Jew waits for the Messiah, hoping that they would bring the "good news," meaning that his older daughter Chvolkah (Helen) had become betrothed.

It was the wish of almost every Jew and non-Jew in Eastern and

Central Europe to immigrate to the United States. In addition to economic reasons, Jews wanted to get away from centuries of persecution and pogroms. I don't think that the United States ever had greater patriots than the Jews of Eastern Europe in the early twentieth century. And to think that it let them down so heartlessly in the years to come.

My father came to spend the autumn holidays of 1928 with us—Rosh Hashanah, Yom Kippur and Sukkos. He took me with him to the Rabbi's Synagogue, where my grandfather Laizer Ber was the *gabe*, the synagogue warden. It was quite a walk, and we passed by three other synagogues on the way.

On the eve of Yom Kippur, my father and I went to the synagogue for Mincha, the afternoon prayer, and distributed alms at the entrance of the synagogue. The floor of the synagogue was covered with hay, as many of the older worshippers wore no shoes inside, as was the tradition on Yom Kippur. Hundreds of large candles were lit, giving the synagogue a solemn and mystical air. How mysterious and awe-inspiring, yet how heart-rending those prayers were. At the age of five, I could not understand the meaning of the words, but the dignity of the moment was enough to instill in me and in all the children a feeling of respect and solemnity. In the morning, the seats of the synagogue were filled, and there wasn't enough room for all the children to sit down, but how long could one expect a child to sit during daylong prayers anyway? So we used to run around.

My grandfather prayed all day in his stockinged feet. I wanted to make sure that he would have plenty of hay under his feet, but I did not want to be conspicuous in hoarding hay, so I walked around the synagogue, dragging my feet, pretending not to notice the growing pile of hay under them as I got closer to my grandfather. However, he was so engrossed in prayers that he wouldn't move his feet for me to put the hay under them. I suspect that I was more attached to my grandfather than to my father, who had been away for much of my life.

From my playmates of that age, I can recall my cousin Eli, who was my uncle Shloime's youngest son, and two cousins from his mother's side, Avreml Winograd and Sarah Leiman. The four of us became classmates in the Hebrew school a year later. At times I would play with my cousin Michla, who was the daughter of my father's brother Reuven and his wife, Chashkah (née Pinsky).

My mother, Sheva and I lived in my paternal grandparents' house until the end of 1928, after which we rented rooms in a house owned by Yudel and Reizl Zubatzky. I stayed home from school with my mother and my sister Sheva during the winter of 1928–1929. Right after Passover, in the early spring of 1929, I started attending Yankl Berl Eisenstein's cheder, in which about twenty boys of different ages and levels were studying. His method of teaching was considered modern in local terms. Not only did he teach Chumash (the Five Books of Moses) and the rabbinic discussions of the Mishnah, but he even taught Gemara, the commentary on the Mishnah. He taught Hebrew as a living language, which was something new in the shtetl. Besides his qualities as a teacher, Yankl Berl was also a good violinist. Passersby would stop to listen to the sweet melodies pouring out of the open windows of his living room on warm summer evenings. For good measure, he was also a carpenter who made all the furniture in his house by himself, a shoemaker who made shoes for his entire family and a violinmaker whose violins were the most highly priced in Shershev.

Yankl Berl ruled the cheder with an iron fist. He sat at the head of a long narrow table, around which the boys sat tightly together. He held a long thin rod in his hand and kept the attention of his charges with well-aimed lashes over ears, no matter how far away a boy sat. A boy sitting next to Yankl Berl could expect to receive a stab from his thick finger that would leave a mark for several days.

After the holiday of Shavuos in the spring of 1929, I was enrolled in the Hebrew kindergarten for the summer to prepare me for starting at the Hebrew school, Yavneh. I attended the kindergarten for half the day and spent the rest of the time at my mother's parents' house and my uncle Shloime's, though he had emigrated a year earlier.

In the early years of my life, I spent a lot of my time at my maternal grandparents' home and often slept over. They had a modest and peaceful way of life. My grandfather divided his time between his children and grandchildren and his synagogue. Only a few years later, when I got a bit older and they were already gone, I realized how much they loved us and how much I missed them. Their love and devotion to family was boundless, and so natural, so innate in the Auerbach side of our family. There wasn't much to do in the evenings with my grandparents. My grandfather got exercise books that were lined and written on with silvery ink in beautiful calligraphy. The writing was in Latin letters but I don't know in what language. My grandfather gave me a pencil and told me to trace the silvery writing. Being left-handed, I initially picked up the pencil with my left hand, but that was unacceptable in those days, and I had to learn to hold a pencil in my right hand. How fondly I remember those long-gone evenings with my grandparents—the little house, the room that was poorly lit by a kerosene lamp, the attention they gave me and, above all, their love.

When I slept at their house, I would watch my grandfather tending to his vegetable gardens. He opened a new world to me, vistas I can still remember. I could hardly wait for vacation time, when I could go to sleep at my Auerbach grandparents.' Their little house seemed to me like a fairy tale. In the summer, it was sheltered from the street by a garden and trees. An embankment made of pine needles hugged a wall of the house and kept it warmer in the winter. Women from the neighbourhood would sit on the embankment, telling each other stories and local news with not a small degree of exaggeration.

My grandparents rented a room to an elderly lady by the name of Rachel Krenitzer. Her livelihood, if that is the right word, was selling milk. In summer or winter, she was at her milk suppliers by six in the morning at the latest. Those were poor Jews, owners of a cow, who would sell the cow's milk to supplement their meagre livelihood. Some owned two cows, and the milk was their only source of income. Rachel Krenitzer would buy the milk from those poor cow owners and carry it in two containers to her customers. We were among her customers, and she was at our door before seven every morning, rain or shine. I can still see my mother commiserating about that woman's lot as she watched her approaching our house on the cold winter mornings, knee-deep in snow, with a heavy container in each hand.

My grandparents' house was not big. What was immense in my grandparents' home was the warmth and love that my sister and I received from them.

In the summer of 1929, my mother gave birth to my only brother, Leibel, or in Russian, Liova. I can still recall my feelings of panic as well as marvel, looking at the new life my mother had just brought into the world. My grandparents called my father, who came to Shershev the next day. The local mohel, Shmuel Tzemachowitch, performed circumcisions on at least a generation of Jewish males in Shershev. He made a living from the slaughter of fowl and animals, buying up the hides of the animals he slaughtered and selling them to the tanneries. On the day of the bris, the circumcision, many children from the neighbourhood came around, uninvited guests, asking me to bring out to them what we called *nasheray*, or snacks. That consisted of *beblekh* (fava beans), *nahit* (chickpeas) and *yodern* (pumpkin seeds). It made me feel good to be in the role of a generous giver, particularly in front of the older boys.

Around this time, my father moved back to Shershev for good. He concluded a deal with a Pole who had a licence for the retail sale of liquor in Shershev in exchange for my father's licence in Verkhy. The new business, a store on the main street, not far from where we lived, was much easier for my father. No more long hours and catering to drunks. Now it was a regular store open from eight in the morning till six in the evening and dealing with a much nicer clientele. Sheva and

I were delighted to have our father home every evening. It must have been a treat for him too, for he spent a fair amount of time with us.

One evening, my father gave my sister and me a stack of receipt booklets that he brought from Verkhy. The pages were sticky on one side, and my sister and I made designs on the wall with them. One of us noted that the unused sheets had a date of the year 192__. The conversation turned to the following decades of 193__, 194__, until we reached the year 2000. One of us wondered aloud what it would look like to see a two followed by three zeroes. Our parents responded that there was no reason why we children should not live to see it. How wrong they were.

In the late 1920s, violent upheavals were taking place in the Land of Israel, then called Palestine. The large Arab population turned against its small and defenceless Jewish minority. They killed individuals and slaughtered and drove out entire communities. In the ancient community of Hebron, Arab rioters killed almost seventy Jews, including women and children, wounding many more. When my mother put me to bed at night, I would ask her why the Arabs were doing that, and she had no answer. To calm me down, she would begin to say with me the bedtime Shema, ending the prayer by wishing a good night to every member of the family individually, including the most remote cousins. She said that this prayer would protect me from all evil. I memorized the prayer and said it nightly after that, even on the darkest and most despairing nights of my life. I always ended by wishing every member of my family a good night, even when I knew only too well that they were not alive anymore.

2
Foundations

IN THE FALL of 1929, I was enrolled into the first grade of Hebrew school and right away had three friends there: my uncle Shloime's youngest son, Eli, and his cousins, Avreml and Sarah. I became friends with two other boys, Hershel Schneider and Tevye Krugman. Our class had more than twenty pupils, mostly boys. In those days, parents put more emphasis on educating boys, particularly when it came to Jewish education. The more affluent parents sent their daughters to Hebrew school too. The poorer parents sent their daughters to the Polish school, where the education was free. Only a few girls attended cheder and just for a few months or a year, while some boys continued for years at a time.

The school was modern for that time. The teachers spoke only Hebrew among themselves as well as to the pupils, in school and in the street. Except for one hour a day that was dedicated to the Polish language, all the subjects, like Chumash, mathematics, geography and history, were taught in Hebrew. Given that the Jewish children spoke Yiddish at home and among themselves and a Belarusian dialect with the Christians, it is no wonder that Polish was a foreign language to us, even though we lived in Poland.

My parents began to look for a house closer to the centre of the shtetl, which was a cobblestoned square surrounded by the biggest houses in the shtetl. Some of those houses had been converted into stores, inns and restaurants. In the middle of the square was an ancient building whose origin nobody knew. It was built from large bricks that had not been used for over two hundred years. The building was referred to as the *rond kromn* (row of stores). During the winter of 1929–1930, my father bought one of the larger stores in this building, and in the late fall of 1929, we moved to a new home, owned by Judke, the shoemaker. He had two separate houses under one roof, and he lived in one of them and rented out the other. Now we lived no more than a hundred metres from the town square and marketplace. The distance to school got shorter too, which helped on the cold wintry mornings.

When our store was ready to be opened, the district government in Pruzhany decided to send a commission to check the distance from the store to the nearest church. In prewar Poland, the law determined that a liquor store had to be a certain distance away from a church, though not a synagogue. The nearest church, a Russian Orthodox one, was on Kamieniec Street. In the end, the distance from the store to the church was found to be sufficient, and the store was opened on time.

In the summer of 1930, my uncle Shloime had been living in the United States for two years and received his first papers, so he applied for the rest of his family to come over. Two of his sons were already in the United States, and his son Avreml had married a girl from Shershev by the name of Chana Meister, an extraordinarily beautiful girl, the daughter of Daniel, the blacksmith, and Malka. Shortly after the marriage, Avreml left for Argentina, temporarily leaving his wife in Shershev with her parents until he was able to bring her over four years later.

The day of my aunt and cousins' departure came. There was a kind of tradition in the way people left Shershev. A couple of crates and sacks were filled with what was considered indispensable in the New World, like samovars, copper pots and pans, candlesticks, feather pillows and comforters, some personal clothing. The crates were loaded onto a hired wagon, which proceeded slowly, the departing people following the wagon and entering every house they passed to say goodbye to its residents. After all, we knew each other from birth. The residents would join the family behind the wagon, and the crowd grew, family by family, as the wagon went down Mostowa and turned right on Pruzhany Street to the very end of the shtetl. The Jewish population of Shershev would cry along with the departing people. In this way, we accompanied my aunt Esther Leiba and her children. I remember crying as we got back home, though I don't know how much I understood about what was happening. It is quite possible that I cried in sympathy with my mother, who was crying bitterly.

Whenever I think of those events, I can't help but wonder what it was like for the people who were departing. They left behind all their loved ones, their place of birth, where they grew up, all their friends and acquaintances. For most of those immigrating to America, they left behind their entire world, for their world did not extend much beyond the perimeter of the shtetl. They were born there and could trace their ancestry back generations, even centuries. It must have been frightening for a small-town person to set out across oceans to a distant land, a stranger among strangers, without a penny in their pocket and without the language of the new place. And what about the family members left behind—parents, brothers and sisters, even wives and children? In retrospect, despite the pain and hurt of parting and the years of longing and yearning, it was really a lucky thing that they left Europe when they did.

The only one of my Kantorowitz grandparents' nine children to leave his birthplace and look for new horizons was my uncle Shalom, who immigrated to Argentina with his young bride Sarah sometime in the 1920s. In 1930, Shalom, who had been influenced by socialist idealism, left Buenos Aires for the Soviet Union with Sarah. They travelled via

Warsaw, and my father secretly went to Warsaw to meet them. At that time, Communists were being arrested and persecuted in Poland, and meeting someone who was travelling to the Soviet Union would make my father a suspect in the eyes of the Polish authorities. That could put the entire Kantorowitz clan in danger. But my father did go to see him, and their meeting remained a secret for a long time. As soon as my grandparents received the first letter from Shalom announcing that they had arrived safely in the Soviet Union, my uncle's whereabouts were not kept a secret anymore. But my father never talked about meeting Shalom in Warsaw.

In the spring of 1931, we moved again, this time to the very centre of the shtetl, to the north side of the town square. At about the same time, my father bought the only empty building lot in the square, intending to build a house. The lot was situated on the east side of the square next to the Large Synagogue, which was indeed the largest in the shtetl. The Large Synagogue had been built to replace the beautiful synagogue that had burned down around World War I. That synagogue had been built about the same time as the *rond kromn,* judging by the size of the bricks and the thickness of the massive walls. It stood at the northeastern corner of the town square, but set back from the houses, thus leaving a large space in front of it that reached to the town square. It was assumed that this space had been used for the town Jews to assemble in times of festivities, with the ability to accommodate the Jewish population of Shershev when it was much larger.

The old, burned-down synagogue still had four massive walls and four impressive columns on which a huge pediment was resting, giving the entire edifice an imposing and magnificent Roman-style distinction. The inside of the structure was cavernous, and two immense pillars supported the ceiling. Because it was impossible to keep this building warm in winter, the community decided to build another synagogue for year-round use. So there was a newer synagogue in front of the old one—the Large Synagogue. It was one of three of the Shershev synagogues to be built of bricks. The other four were built of wood.

In front of the burned synagogue was a building lot that belonged to an elderly man by the name of Pellet Aprik. Pellet had left for America as a young man, before World War I, and after several years he came back with enough money to buy a house in the town square with a garden backing onto the burned shul, a store in the *rond kromn* and another house in an alley off Mostowa. It seems that his luck turned around shortly after he returned to Shershev. His big house in the town square burned down, and he could not afford to rebuild it. The building lot remained empty, and with time, grown over with grass and weeds. All that remained visible were the large stones that were part of the foundation. My father bought this lot from Pellet Aprik for the equivalent of 450 US dollars, a fortune in those times.

In August of that summer, my mother gave birth to a girl. She was named Sarah, but we called her Sonia. We were now four children in the family.

Around that time, the members of our synagogue decided to get an additional *seyfer toyre* (Torah scroll). There was in Shershev a *soyfer stam* (ritual scribe), and he undertook the job of writing it. Just about every Jew in the shtetl went to visit the scribe as he was writing the Torah, and my mother took me too. The scribe sat at a large table on which lay the open Torah scroll, partly covered with writing. He was writing carefully on the parchment in amazingly uniform letters and in a straight line with a feather quill. There were a few people ahead of me, and when my turn came, the scribe, as with the others, handed me the pen for a second and then took it back and wrote a word on the scroll, I assume on my behalf. Everyone left some change with the scribe, a contribution toward the Torah scroll. The scribe was a respected man, and there were all kinds of stories circulating about his piety and devotion to God and to the Torah.

Eventually, the Torah scroll was ready. The scribe brought it to the rabbi shortly before Rosh Hashanah. From there, it was carried under a chuppah to our synagogue with great fanfare. The Torah scroll under the wedding canopy was surrounded by almost the entire community. As it grew dark, everybody held a lit candle and the men sang passages from the Psalms and other prayers. For us youngsters, it was an experience that came up in our conversations years later.

From early spring, my grandfather Laizer Ber would come to my school, bringing me different dishes or treats that my grandmother Freida Leah or my mother had made for me. At 11:00 a.m., during our long break, my grandfather was always there waiting for me with a special treat. While eating, I would try to talk to him and share with him my experiences from the morning, but he never failed to remind me: "It is written that one does not talk while one eats." He wanted me to finish everything before the bell.

That summer, during my many visits to my Auerbach grandparents', I noticed my grandmother changing dressings on my grandfather's neck, at the base of his head. It looked like he had a fair-sized ulcer. Over the summer, it got bigger. It seemed to me that they intended to cure it without a doctor's help, as it did not interfere with his daily movements or activities. By the fall of 1931, the sore on my grandfather Laizer Ber's neck had gotten worse. Finally, the doctor suggested taking my grandfather to the Pruzhany hospital. As soon as the doctors there took a look at it, they told my mother to rush him to Brest-Litovsk, where there was a much bigger hospital and better-qualified doctors. My mother took him to the hospital in Brest-Litovsk, where he was operated on immediately. A couple of days after the operation, the surgeon told my mother to go home, as it was going to be a long process and she would not help anybody by being there. At the time, my mother was pregnant with her fifth child.

My mother returned home, leaving her father under the attention of the surgeon and some relatives there. Two days later, she received an urgent telegram from the hospital to come immediately. In those days, a trip from Shershev to Brest-Litovsk took twenty-four hours. When she got to the hospital, the surgeon informed her that it had become necessary to operate on my grandfather again, and he could not wait for my mother's consent. He also told her that the operation had taken place without anaesthesia because of his age and state of health. When my mother was permitted to see her father, he asked her if she had heard his screams during the operation. She answered, "You know that I was in Shershev then," to which he replied, "You could have heard them there too."

My grandfather's condition deteriorated rapidly. The doctor told my mother to take him home, as they could do nothing for him in the hospital. My mother said, "Only God in heaven can help him now."

When I saw my grandfather the next evening, he seemed to be unconscious. The only word he continuously said was, "water," and he was oblivious to everything else. My mother and grandmother, who were constantly at his side, kept wetting his lips, as the doctor had ordered not to give him anything to drink. Right after school, Sheva and I ran to our grandparents' house. There were always people there, neighbours and members of the synagogue. Maybe because of the many people there, or maybe because I had never been confronted with a death in the family, I did not understand the severity of the situation.

Two or three days later, a classmate of mine who lived near my grandparents told me unceremoniously that my grandfather had died early that morning. The teacher sent me home right away. I ran to my grandparents', where I found the house full of people. My grandfather was lying on the floor covered with a white sheet, and two candles in candlesticks were burning on either side of his head. Bent over him stood my mother and my grandmother, crying bitterly. The other women in the house cried with them. A few minutes later, my mother, grandmother and a few other women began whispering. They sat me down on the floor with my back to my grandfather. My grandmother took his already rigid hand by the wrist and rubbed it over my back, chanting something quietly. The whole process took a minute or two.

I still don't know what it meant or what sort of a remedy or ritual it was. Nor do I know why they didn't do the same to my sister Sheva or to my almost three-year-old brother Liova.

The *khevre kedishe*, the voluntary burial society, started the process of purifying the body, called *tare*. They washed the corpse and dressed it in traditional *takhrikhim*, or shrouds. This was done by men if the departed was a male and by women if it was a female. I stood by and watched as they pulled out from the hole at the base of my grandfather's head a wad of dressings that left a space in which a man's fist could easily fit. I looked at it in horror, and a shudder went through me. In my nine-year-old mind, I could not comprehend what had been done to my grandfather and how cruel and merciless the doctors must have been. I was glad when they put the shrouds on him and wrapped him in his *tales*, his prayer shawl, so I didn't have to see the gaping hole in his head. When they finally put him on the *mite*, the stretcher on which the corpse is carried, and carried him out of the house, I saw that my entire school, students and teachers, had lined up in front of the house, waiting for the funeral. As far as I know, this was the only time that the Hebrew school participated in a funeral.

My grandfather was buried on October 29, the 18th day of the month of Cheshvan according to the Jewish calendar. There was a large crowd in the street. The schoolchildren stood two in a row, the teachers keeping an eye on them. In Shershev, as in all small shtetls in Eastern Europe, the *mite* was carried all the way to the cemetery on the shoulders of volunteers, and it was considered a mitzvah, a good deed, to be a stretcher-bearer. The procession took a detour to the Rabbi's Synagogue, where my grandfather had been the *gabe* for many years, to his very last day. There, from the porch, he was eulogized and then carried to the cemetery, where his grave was waiting for him.

I looked on with curiosity and grief as they lowered my grandfather into the cold and damp ground, where four boards had been placed around the sides of the pit at the bottom. A small white sack filled with earth was placed above my grandfather's head. Two pieces of broken black pottery were placed over his closed eyes, and his face was sprinkled with earth from the Land of Israel. Between the fingers of each hand, a small twig was placed. After being gently wrapped in his *tales* again, boards were placed over him, resting on the edges of the other boards, forming a kind of box around him. As soon as this was done, men began to fill in the grave, and I looked on with a grieving heart as the earth covered my grandfather. He was the human being I loved most, second only to my mother.

My grandmother Freida Leah did not remain in the house long. She sold it and rented a room with an elderly widow by the name of Temma Kwelman. It must have been difficult for my grandmother to get used to her new lifestyle, losing a husband after fifty-five years of marriage and leaving the house in which she had been born and lived her whole life. All she had left in Shershev was my mother and us children. My grandmother corresponded regularly with her son, our uncle Shloime, since he had left Shershev, but very little with her other son, Philip, who wrote rarely. Shloime was a prolific and eloquent letter writer. Freida Leah was a loving and devoted grandmother, and despite our tender age, my siblings and I understood it and felt her love and devotion to us. Now, we felt that the time had come to reciprocate for all that she had done for us, though in a small way, and there was not a day that my sister and I did not visit her. If, God forbid, it was getting dark and we had not seen her that day, our mother would remind us.

That autumn, my father hired a tree expert named Benjamin Goldberg, and together with a government agent from the Forestry Department, they went to pick out the right trees to be cut for the construction of our house. Shortly thereafter, local peasants began hauling in the huge pine trunks, unloading them on our new lot and the adjoining yard of the synagogue. A couple of crews worked continuously through the winter to saw the logs into planks.

In early spring of 1932, hired men started building the foundation for the house. The large stones of the previous foundation were used, and more were brought in from outlying farms. The stones were cemented together, forming a quadrangle, giving the appearance of a metre-high fortress. On this foundation, the builders lay the first row of heavy beams, which were fitted together in the corners by interlocking niches. For good luck, a little hole was drilled in a bottom beam, and an old coin was deposited, plus a piece of bread and some salt as a blessing for long and plentiful life for the residents.

The building of the house took most of the summer, and I spent a lot of time watching the progress with my friends. An extension was added to the back of the house under which a large cellar was built. In the cement walls of the cellar were niches in which shelves were inserted that could hold all kinds of jars and pots. In the roof of the extension, a movable part, called a *fligl*, was added, and it could be opened so that a *suke* could be erected under it during the holiday of Sukkos. Two carpenter brothers were hired to do the woodwork. Our house was the only one in Shershev that had a double floor with space between that was filled with charcoal to absorb dampness and keep warmth inside the house.

During that same summer of 1932, electricity was introduced in the shtetl. All summer long, we watched as tall wooden posts were dug in and copper wires were strung along their porcelain insulators. In most houses, a direct wire led to a single bulb and the proprietor paid a flat rate per bulb. We must have been one of no more than a dozen households that had a meter, for we had electric bulbs in every room. With electricity and lit streets, Shershev came into the modern era, and one could walk at night on the wooden sidewalk without the danger of tripping over a protruding board. The street lights came on at sunset and went off at midnight.

Right after the start of the school year, we moved into our new home. Something strange and inexplicable happened to me then. A day or two after we moved in, I began to get headaches in the mornings as soon as I got out of bed. The pain would ease up during the day, but it never left me completely. A day before Rosh Hashanah the *mezuzes* arrived, and as soon as my father affixed the rolled-up pieces of parchment in their cases to the doorposts per Jewish law, my headaches disappeared for good.

3
Village Life

THE FIRST VEGETABLE to appear in the spring was the shallot. Local farmers would pinch off the long green stems and sell them by the bunch. We would open the stems to make sure there were no little worms in them, then wash and cut them into little pieces. Mixed with some water, vinegar and sugar, they were served as the first salad of the season. The first fruits of the season were the early cherries, a yellow cherry with no taste. A few weeks later, the real cherries appeared, dark red and sweet. Next came the vegetables: lettuce, and a week or two later, small round radishes, and then one after another, cucumbers, cauliflower, carrots, tomatoes, beets and other fruits and vegetables. There were no coolers or freezers in Shershev in those days, yet people had to keep those perishables for as long as possible. So as soon as the fruits appeared on the market, brought in by farmers from the surrounding villages, my mother would begin to preserve and store for the winter.

We had a little wooden barrel that Freida Leah had given us when she sold her house after the death of my grandfather. It was always filled with cherries fermenting in sugar and vodka. It had a faucet on one side to let some of the delicious cherry brandy out. Through the large opening on the side that was plugged up with a cork, my grandmother would fish out with a spoon a few cherries for Sheva and me. As soon as the new cherries appeared, my father bought a whole pail, and my mother, with the help of the maid, washed and pitted them and poured them through the opening of the barrel, which was partly filled with last year's cherries. Then my mother added sugar and a bottle of vodka. This brew would ferment for a couple of weeks and turn into cherry brandy. Privileged guests relished this drink more than the well-known Polish Baczewski liquor that my father sold in our store.

After the cherries came the strawberries, which farmers brought by the wagonful. We ate the strawberries in different ways—plain with sour cream and buttered bread, as a snack or as a dessert. Having a sweet tooth, I usually added sugar. My father would buy ten or fifteen kilos of strawberries at once. My mother and the maid would pick them over, wash them, put them in a large copper pot, cover them with a thick layer of sugar and let them sit for forty-eight hours. The copper pot was then placed on the stove, covering all burners, and cooked for a few hours to make jam. The most delicious thing I have ever tasted was the foam that formed at the top while the jam was cooking.

And so, the season of preparing preserves and jams for the entire year started. Raspberries came next, and they were prepared either the same as the strawberries or they were cooked and strained through a piece of linen, and only the liquid was saved. After staying in the cool cellar for a day or two, it would congeal and turn into a raspberry jelly of the purest quality. The same was done with cherries and plums. Blueberry preserving had an additional purpose, reflected in the saying about it that "it should not be needed." It was believed that blueberries constitute a great medicine for stomach ailments, particularly dysentery.

Last to be preserved in the fall were the cranberries. To make them palatable, they had to be cooked with an equal measure of sugar. For the winter, my mother filled up a shelf with large jars of cranberry jam, and it was used on bread as a snack or eaten with meat.

We would also dry apples and pears. Pears were washed, cut in half and strung with a large needle on a fine cord and put in the oven for twenty-four hours. Apples were more work as they had to be peeled and thinly sliced, and they were not in much demand for us youngsters, as they were not as sweet as the pears.

Although there was no shortage of cucumbers in Shershev proper, grown by the local farmers, most of our cucumbers came from the nearby village of Waszki. This village sat in the middle of a swamp. It had one connection to the world through Shershev, which it reached through a row of wooden planks set atop poles that were stuck into the swampy ground. The villagers would carry their produce on their backs to the market in Shershev. Cucumbers were washed, placed in a large wooden barrel, and spiced with dill, garlic and bay leaves. The barrel was topped up with water and the cucumbers were left in the cellar to sour. Sauerkraut was made with a similar process, except that the whole family took part in chopping up the cabbage at the dining table. Cranberries were added to the cabbage to give the sauerkraut a nice appearance. The sour pickles and sauerkraut would last all winter in the cellar, together with the sacks of potatoes, beets, carrots and the various preserves.

With the winter snow, farmers from nearby villages brought in wagons or sleds filled with firewood cut from the surrounding forest to sell to the Jewish population. The wood was stacked in the yards, where it remained until the next fall. By then, it was good and dry and taken into woodsheds to be used the following winter for heating houses and cooking. This system had been going on for generations and was the only way to get fuel in our part of the world.

We enjoyed the first winter in our own house despite the cold and snow. Our home, in which our father had invested so much of his life and soul, not to mention his money, was big and comfortable, especially compared to other houses in Shershev. It included a large kitchen and seven spacious rooms. There were three bedrooms, a room with a separate front entrance that my father was planning to use as another store someday, a dining room, living room and parlour. As far as I knew, our house was the only one in the shtetl that had permanent double windows and heavy outside doors.

We settled into our new home. No longer did we have to think of moving, and it seemed that we had found permanency where not only I, my sister and brother were born, but also where my parents had been born. Half of my friends lived within a hundred metres of us, and I could see their homes from our windows.

Despite the size and spaciousness of the house, I loathed laundry days, which took place every two months or so. This task was a three-day process, during which the kitchen and nearby rooms were stacked with piles of dirty laundry. First the laundry had to be washed by hand with the help of a washboard and strong soap. Next, the washed laundry was put in a huge copper boiler that stood on the stove and took up all four burners. After the laundry was boiled, it was washed again in a wash tub, in which a tiny tube of a dark blue substance was added with each load to make the white laundry whiter. After the second washing and wringing, everything was hung out to dry in the sun. On rainy or cloudy days, or in winter, the laundry had to be hung in the attic. In the winter the wet clothes would freeze before they had a chance to dry, and they had to be brought into the house still frozen and in the shape of the person it belonged to. This was especially true for men's underwear, which was always subject to a remark or a joke. Before the laundry was put away, it was pressed with a heavy rolling pin and ironed. Then everything was put in its place by my mother and the maid. To help with the laundry, my mother hired a woman by the name of Izbyta. She had spent many years in Jewish homes doing laundry and learned to speak Yiddish as well as any Jew.

My mother was busy from the moment she awoke early in the morning until she went to bed. I cannot remember my mother sitting idle for one moment. After cooking and baking, washing and cleaning, she would do other things in the evenings, like sewing and darning socks. My mother made sure that we were always dressed clean and proper. On hot summer days, my mother and other housewives spent their time in a sweltering kitchen, where the cast-iron plate on the cooking stove made the heat unbearable.

In contrast to my mother, who never stopped working all day long, my father opened the store at eight in the morning, then sat and waited for customers to come in. On hot days, people would come into the store just to relax and talk because the store was cool. Serving them required little effort. All he had to do was hand them a bottle and collect the money. My father truly worked hard most of the year, however, he also had time to read the newspaper every day and discuss the news with friends and acquaintances, who were all trying to solve world problems.

The main attraction for my friends and me in the summers of our preteen years were the seemingly endless swamps around Shershev. After taking off our shoes and socks and rolling up our pant legs as high as they would go, we would start moving slowly into the murky water that was full of all kinds of creatures—beetles of all sizes and shapes and slimy wormlike creatures that frightened us. Most of those swamps and marsh denizens were green and blended in with the lush surroundings. As we got deeper in, we'd take off our pants so that we wouldn't get a tongue-lashing from our parents.

The challenge was to see how far one could get into the swamp before falling into it. The trick was to find with your foot a root or vine under the water that was strong enough to support you, lower your weight onto it and then look for the next one. Of course, some vines or roots would give just when you thought you were safe, and you would get an unpleasant dunking. The most unpleasant company in the swamps were the many leeches, who did not wait for an invitation to attach themselves to your exposed body. But neither the leeches nor the inevitable dunking stopped us boys from spending days of our vacation time in that natural amusement park.

On Saturday afternoons in the summer, after the Shabbos lunch of cholent, we boys would go wandering or exploring in the nearby woods. We called our favourite place "the alder woods." It wasn't much of a forest, just a small bit of woods that was constantly struggling for its territory between a thick pine forest and the nearby swamps. The forest was always mucky if not outright wet and was overgrown with all kinds of weeds and vegetation. All this was covered by a canopy of alder bushes and trees. There we had the opportunity to acquaint ourselves with the diversity of the bird kingdom in our part of the world, and we observed as birds lay their eggs and then the hatchlings left the nest. Another place where we spent time observing birds was in the Jewish cemetery on Beis HaChaim (Cemetery) Street, or Nowa Street in Polish. There, in the old part of the cemetery, which was thickly overgrown with ancient trees, we climbed among the dense branches and came across birds' nests. Some were empty, but some held birds' eggs or chicks. We would come back often to watch their progress, until one day we would return and the nest would be empty.

In the winters, there were long, clear moonlit evenings when one could read a book without the help of additional light. On those beautiful evenings, we children went sledding. The only hill in Shershev led from Ostrowiecka Street into the market square, with an elevation of no more than one metre. We piled on a sled, one on top of the other, as high as we could. Then one of us ran in front, pulling the rope attached to the sled. When the sled reached its highest speed, the runner would jerk the rope to the side, causing the sled to tip over and spilling the pile of us into the snow. We would jump up filled with exuberant energy and enthusiasm to run up the hill and do it all over again.

One of my favourite activities was reading books, which I borrowed from the Hebrew school library. The library consisted of about 250 books. Most had been written in Hebrew, but there were a few dozen that were translated into Hebrew from other languages. I read a good part of the library before I left Hebrew school after finishing Grade 4. There was also a Yiddish library in Shershev, which had been founded by a group of young people ten years earlier. One of the founders and initiators of the idea was my cousin Avreml Auerbach. He and some of his friends lay the foundation for the Yiddish library, which grew to several hundred books by the time Avreml left Shershev a couple of years later. Those young and idealistic individuals saw it as their duty to provide worldly reading material for the Jewish youth of Shershev, who slowly began to drift away from the cheder tradition to a more modern educational system that exposed them to new horizons.

The father of my two friends Laizer and Litek Rotenberg hailed from near the town of Chelm and brought from there an inexhaustible supply of stories that he shared with us boys during the long winter evenings. Some of the stories were from his childhood, which had been quite different than ours. Some were true stories and some were fictitious, and many had to do with witches, ghosts and demons. Being a good storyteller, he could keep us boys hypnotized for hours. We lived in a society where many adults believed in ghosts, and we kids were inclined to believe in them too. After listening to these stories for a few hours, I would walk home with my friends at night. To get to my house, I had to cross the empty town square. Then I would see the large synagogue, enveloped in darkness, and behind our house, the ancient synagogue, destroyed except for its immense walls and imposing facade. Birds and small animals made their homes in the ruins, and at night, one could hear strange voices, rumoured to be ghosts and demons. The closer I got to my house, the louder the sounds became, and the more scared I was. Relief came the moment I got hold of the handle on my front door.

My days started early, as school began at 8:00 a.m. When I was eleven, prayers were introduced in school before the classes, and all boys had to attend, so I would get up before daybreak. In our home, as in the few other well-off households in Shershev, winter breakfast often consisted of buckwheat pancakes. An elderly woman carried them around to her regular customers in the early winter mornings in two baskets covered with heavy shawls to keep the heat in. My mother would look at her with compassion and give her a couple more pennies, or groszy, than she was owed. Breakfast could also consist of black bread and butter with milk or tea. Usually we had it with what we called Swiss cheese, though it was produced locally, or with honey, halvah or sausage. I took the same food I had for breakfast to school for lunch, which was eaten during the twenty-minute break at eleven o'clock. For the lower grades, school ended at one, and there was always something to eat when we got home to tide us over until dinner, which was usually eaten at four. There was nothing tastier than my mother's potato kugel on a cold winter afternoon.

On the coldest winter days, the tile ovens that warmed the house had to be lit twice a day. As soon as the wood in them was burned almost completely and all that was left were the embers, the cast-iron doors of the stoves were closed to retain the heat. The most preferred place in the house during a long winter evening was next to the stove with one's back pressing against it, the warmth radiating from it and through one's body. Our family would sit around the stove conversing or trying to solve problems, just as it is done nowadays sitting around a table.

In such an oven, my mother baked her potato kugel in a fair amount of animal fat. When ready, it was moved to the upper part of the stove where it was kept hot until we came home from school. Then my mother would take it out of the oven in its round earthenware pan, narrow on the bottom and wide on top. She would flip the pan over a flat wide plate, leaving a pyramid pudding with a flat top, a hot glistening delight that filled the house with the most appetizing aroma.

Dinner in winter always consisted of meat and soup, a nourishing and filling meal, and supper always included bread. With every meal came cheese or halvah or smoked whole fish with golden skin.

In mid-summer of 1933, my mother gave birth to her fifth child, a girl, my third and youngest sister. My parents named her Leiba after my grandfather Laizer Ber.

Around this time, the correspondence between my Kantorowitz grandparents and their son Shalom, who was in the Soviet Union, suddenly stopped. The entire family became uneasy, for we knew a bit about the situation in the Soviet Union, though many of the rumours were attributed to Polish anti-Bolshevik propaganda. Late in fall 1933, a letter arrived for my parents from Shalom's wife from Argentina. She wrote that she had given birth to a baby girl in Birobijan, and shortly thereafter her husband had passed away and she returned to Buenos Aires with her three-month-old baby.

My father and his brothers were not in a hurry to pass on such news to their parents, but my grandmother had an intuition that something had happened to her son, and she wrote a letter to her daughter-in-law's parents in Argentina and asked them for the date of her son's death. They took it for granted that she knew of his death and sent her the date. My grandmother observed a full year's mourning from the time she found out, thus being stricter in observance than required by tradition. At that time, my father's two younger brothers, Hershel and Eli, were single and still lived at home with their parents. My grandmother removed the arm of their record player so that no music should be heard in the house for a year, as is the tradition while mourning for a close relative. She gave the removed arm to my father for safekeeping, after extracting from him a promise that he wouldn't return it to his brothers before the year was up.

Shalom was the only one of the nine children of my Kantorowitz grandparents who got out of Europe before the war. With his demise, the fate of the entire Kantorowitz clan was sealed together with that of most of European Jewry.

4
Holidays

ONE DAY CLOSE to Rosh Hashanah of 1933, I went to visit my grandmother Freida Leah and noticed in her just-arrived mail an open *shone toyve* card with good wishes for the Jewish New Year. On it were pictures of the Western Wall, Rachel's Tomb and the Tomb of the Patriarchs, holy sites in the Land of Israel. It was good material for pasting in the notebook I used for my class on the geography of the Land of Israel, and without thinking, I asked my grandmother, "Bobeh, kenst mir gebn der shone-toyve?"—*Can you give me this New Year's card?*

She answered, "Yo, mayn kind. Du kenst hobn der shone-toyve un mayn gut yor oykh."—*Yes, my child. You can have this card and the good things intended for me too.*

To a ten-year-old, sickness is far from mind and death is unthinkable, and to a ten-year-old, a person in her seventies is a very old person. Why would my grandmother want to give me, in her old age, the good things destined for her? I felt as if I was depriving her of something, or that she was giving me the most precious thing she had—her health. I wished she had not said it, but knowing her love and devotion, I understood she meant every word, and I wanted her to be able to give me that gift.

From the beginning of the Hebrew month of Elul, a month before Rosh Hashanah, there was a sense of solemnity in the air, which grew in intensity by the day. The Jews of Shershev felt indeed that the Day of Judgment or reckoning was approaching. It was not just imaginary or a presumption but a very real feeling that on Rosh Hashanah "we will stand in judgment," as the liturgy states. People were calmer and spoke in a more polite manner, and attendance at the synagogue increased daily. People even exchanged less gossip at that time of the year. Gossip was quite popular in Shershev; after all, we had to have something or somebody to talk about.

Avrom Ber was an elderly Jew who went around the Jewish streets on Fridays and on the eve of the holidays before sunset and yelled in a loud voice, "In shul arayn!"—*Go to the synagogue!* This was the signal for the Jewish stores to close, for the workers and artisans to stop working and for the women to light the Shabbos candles. During the month of Elul, he would walk through the Jewish streets between two and three in the morning, knocking on doors and shutters and shouting, "Get up for Selichot!" And the Jews, mostly the older men, would get up and go to the synagogues to say the penitential prayers. Avrom Ber also went to all the Jewish homes every Thursday to collect donations for performing his sacred work. Aside from his work waking up the Jewish inhabitants of Shershev, Avrom Ber was the only chimney sweep in the village. This old man would climb onto every roof in the shtetl with a small broom stuck onto a long thin stick, positioning himself so that he could jam the broom down the chimney. Having repeated the process several times, he would climb down and empty the stove below of the soot that had come down from the chimney. Despite his efforts, he was as poor as they come, having to support a wife and two children, both of whom were past the marriageable age for Shershev. The only benefit of his profession was that his beard was always black, and nobody had ever seen his face. Even Avrom Ber lowered his voice before the Days of Awe. This must have been difficult for him, for I believe that he really had forgotten how to speak in a normal voice. As far as I remember, his voice always thundered from one end of the shtetl to the other.

For the Days of Awe, the synagogue members would arrange for a better *bal tfile*, prayer leader, and not settle on one of our own volunteers. They preferred Yankl Kleinerman or Tzalkah fun di zamden (Tzalkah from the sand dunes) or Bendet Lifshitz, who had better voices. Understandably, such voices did not come for free, and the entire treasury of the synagogue had to be emptied for such a pleasure.

After the short Rosh Hashanah evening prayer, the men would wish each other a *shone toyve* (a good year) and go home without the customary short chat. The welcoming greeting at home was always "Leshone toyve tikoseyvu"—*May you be inscribed for a good year*. After the Kiddush, the blessing over the wine, we sat down for the meal, which always started with golden chicken soup with noodles. My mother used to say that the noodles were a reminder of our long-lasting *goles*, our exile. This dish was followed by fish, meat, *kreplakh*, which is a type of dumpling stuffed with meat, and other dishes, but never anything sour or bitter, to symbolize that we would have a sweet year. Rosh Hashanah was spent between the house and the synagogue. We boys would go to the river to watch the crowd of worshippers gathered for the Tashlich ceremony, when we cast our sins away into the water.

The Ten Days of Repentance between Rosh Hashanah and Yom Kippur passed in a subdued mood. On the day before Yom Kippur, early in the morning, all members of the family would participate in *shlogn kapores*, the traditional ceremony of atonement done with a chicken—during which a rooster (for the men) and a hen (for the women) was waved over our heads and a short prayer recited. After the ceremony, it was my task to take the chickens to the *shoykhet* to be slaughtered according to Jewish law.

The *shoykhet*, a respected elderly man, stood on the porch in his backyard, wrapped in a bloodstained apron, a long thin knife in one hand. With his other hand, he took the receipt for the twenty-groszy slaughtering fee for each fowl, which I got from his wife or daughter. After putting the receipt in a little box, he passed the nail of his thumb over the length of the sharp edge of the knife to make sure that there was no nick on it, a requirement to make the slaughter as painless as possible. After this inspection, he cut the chicken's neck with a quick slash and threw it down to the ground. Not losing a second, he turned to the next customer. The slaughtered chickens would flap around for several seconds after they were dead. I would then pick them up and take them home to be prepared for the meals before and after the Yom Kippur fast.

Mid-afternoon before Yom Kippur, the men went to the synagogue for the afternoon prayers. On a table right inside the synagogue were a dozen or more large plates with signs indicating the names of the charitable organizations or purposes for which donations were being collected—for the synagogue, visiting the sick, burial associations, poor locals and others, including international organizations like the Jewish National Fund (JNF). One had to come with some change in one's pocket. The saddest part was that most of the attending worshippers could have used the money themselves.

After prayers, we lit the traditional candles in memory of the departed, and they would burn until after Yom Kippur. Almost all worshippers brought candles with them, one for each departed person, and the synagogue was filled with lit candles that contributed to the already suffocating conditions in the crowded room. Many candles would start melting and bending because of the heat.

All the Jewish population of the shtetl was in the synagogues for Kol Nidre, the opening prayer of the eve of Yom Kippur, and the following prayers, except for those who were bedridden.

The worshippers were all familiar with the prayers and melodies and would sing along with the *khazn*, the cantor. Many of the Yom Kippur prayers are in the ancient language of Aramaic, and even though I could already converse in Hebrew, I could not fully understand those prayers, so my father would translate them for me, keeping me engaged and encouraging me to understand what I was reading. I believe that my father had a gift for languages, for there were no Hebrew schools in Shershev in his youth, and in cheder they spoke Yiddish, yet my father was fluent in Hebrew. The same was true for the Polish language, even though my father grew up in the Russian Empire, and Polish was not taught.

The Neila prayer, the closing prayer of Yom Kippur, was a difficult time for the fasting crowd because of the solemnity of the hour and because everyone was exhausted at the end of the long fast. After the prayer, the *gabe* would go outside with some older members to see if three stars were visible in the evening sky, marking the end of the holiday. When they reappeared, they finished with the evening Maariv prayer and then blew the shofar, after which the worshippers would chant loudly, "L'shanah habah b'Yerushalayim!"—*Next year in Jerusalem!* Worshippers then wished each other "Gmar khsime toyve"—*A good final sealing*, and hurried home for the meal breaking the fast.

A few days after Yom Kippur was the holiday of Sukkos, a long and pleasant holiday that indicated the beginning of the winter. It seemed like the first frost always came on Chol Hamoed, during the intermediary days of Sukkos, and terminated the season of the gąska zielonka mushroom that appeared in late summer. Non-Jews would marinate these mushrooms, whereas Jews would fry or cook them. With the frost, the time came to wear *kaloshi*, short rubber boots worn over shoes or boots. They had to be taken off before walking into the school because the wooden floors of the school were sprayed with kerosene to protect them from rotting, and the moment one stepped on the kerosene-covered floor with *kaloshi*, the bottoms of the *kaloshi* began to blister and fall apart.

Preparations for Chanukah started in school a month before the holiday. The teachers wanted to please the spectators and get praised, so instead of regular lessons, a lot of time was taken up with rehearsals, which could be quite entertaining, and the students did not object at all. The performance took place on the Saturday night of Chanukah in the school. It usually remained a topic of conversation in the shtetl for weeks, especially among the parents. Some could not stop raving about their children's artistic qualities, and others felt offended by the insignificant parts their children were assigned in the play or by their children being overlooked altogether.

On Chanukah, we received from our parents Chanukah *gelt*, gifts of money. In fact, we received gifts not only from our parents, but also from our grandparents and even aunts and uncles if one "happened" to be in the right place at the right time. It was not a lot of money, but more than we got for our allowance. We could spend it on anything our hearts desired.

With spring came the nicest holiday of the year, Pesach, or Passover. Right after the holiday of Purim, when we exchanged gifts of food with our neighbours and friends, one room in the house, the parlour, was cleaned and scrubbed and became out of bounds. In that room, my mother made mead from sugar, honey and hops, which was left to ferment. That was the first step in getting ready for Pesach.

The next step was getting the matzos. Usually, a dozen women would get together and bake matzos for themselves in the home of whoever had the largest oven. This entailed making not only the oven and kitchen kosher for Passover first, but most of the house as well, so that the matzos would not come into contact with anything leavened. Some women would bake matzos for others to earn some money, and the more affluent housewives, like my mother, would buy it off them.

Not far from us, on Mostowa, was a bakery owned by a widow named Sarah Neibrief. The women who baked matzos rented her kitchen and a few other rooms to set up their enterprise. A long table was put in the living room, around which a dozen or so women stood, their hair wrapped in clean white kerchiefs to ensure that not a single hair fell into the matzos. Each of them had a wooden roller in hand. A woman nearby bent over a small trough, kneading a piece of dough, making a large piece, called *meyre*. Then, the woman who was kneading pinched off a piece of dough, or *challah nemen*, and gave it to a man called the *shiber* who stood in front of the open oven door in which a hot fire was burning. His job was to put the raw matzos into the oven and take out the baked ones. It was a constant job in front of a furnace-like opening. The man took the *challah nemen* and threw it in the fire. It was only after this that the *meyre* was cut up and divided among the women, who rolled the dough out into flat circles about a foot across. The *redler*'s function was to puncture holes in the raw matzos. This was done by rolling a pizza-like cutter with points on the edge back and forth over the dough, keeping a straight line with the help of a rolling pin held against it. Then the matzo would be passed to the *shiber* to be put in the oven.

For us children it was a stimulating and interesting time of year. Those evenings—the bustle, being permitted to carry the raw matzos on a rolling pin to the *redler*, seeing the matzos handled so nimbly as they were put into the oven and the baked ones were removed—all of it was very exciting. Matzos for one household were baked in one evening and were carried home by family members late at night in specially washed white bedsheets.

Traditionally, one is not permitted to taste matzos before Pesach, but grown-ups pretended not to see as we children sneaked a piece of matzo while we carried it home. It tasted much better then than it did during Pesach. We would bring the matzos into the same room as the fermenting mead, covering them tightly. They were not to be touched or even looked at until Pesach eve.

Having provided these main elements needed for Pesach, my mother turned to getting the house clean and ready, a formidable task. The maid, a strong young village girl, helped out. The closer to Pesach it was, the more frantic the preparations became. As there was no refrigeration, the food had to be prepared no more than a couple of days before the holiday. An important part of the Passover diet consisted of matzo meal and matzo *farfel*. My father was responsible for making it, and when I turned twelve or so, I pitched in. Half a dozen matzos were thrown into a large mortar made from a tree stump and ground with the help of a heavy wooden pestle. After a steady ten or fifteen minutes of hard grinding, most of the matzos in the mortar turned powdery. The crushed matzos were then sifted, and the powder was used as matzo meal and the larger pieces as *farfel*. When we boys went for walks on the evenings before Passover, we could hear the dull grinding and reverberation from the menfolk of the shtetl grinding matzo, pitifully working at this backbreaking task as if God wanted them to taste the slavery of their ancestors in Egypt. However, despite all the hard work, everybody looked forward to Pesach with anticipation, hope and joy.

All the symbolic items of food on the seder plate were made by my mother, except for the *kharoyses*, a mixture of fruits, nuts, spices and wine that symbolizes the mortar the Hebrew slaves made in Egypt. It was a tradition in Shershev to go to the rabbi's house for *kharoyses* and at the same time to sell our *khomets* (bread or leavened products). Each member of the community would leave the rabbi some groszy, supposedly for selling the *khomets* to a non-Jew. This contribution was of great financial assistance to our rabbi, Rabbi Noah Liwerant.

It was a tradition, almost a must, to get a new suit of clothes and shoes for Pesach. Some parents who could not afford new suits for their sons took their sons' Shabbos suits to the tailor and had them turned inside out, which made them appear new, that is, if the boy had not grown too much over the past year. The trick was to have the new clothes ready for Shabbos Hagadol (the Shabbos before Pesach) and to show off the new clothes in the synagogue. Who was equal to us boys as we paraded through the streets in our new outfits?!

The day before Pesach eve, the house was all clean and kosher for the holiday. In the evening, the bathhouse was reserved for the women of the community, who would visit it while the men went through the ceremony of searching for any last remnants of bread in their homes with the *bedikes khomets* ritual. The next morning, the men would go to the bathhouse. The bathhouse was an integral part of any Jewish community in Eastern Europe and was used only by the Jewish population. I used to wonder where the non-Jewish population of Shershev bathed, for there was no public bathhouse in our village and there were no bathing facilities in the homes. As far as I knew, we were the only ones in Shershev with a tin bathtub. There might have been a few wooden ones. Not that a bath at home was such a simple thing. It entailed bringing a dozen pails of water from the well and heating them over the wood-burning stove. It was much easier to go to the bathhouse, which was open every Thursday night for women and every Friday morning for men. Our tin bathtub, as well as the Passover mortar and pestle, had been passed on to us by my maternal grandparents. The story of the bathtub is that my mother, being the youngest child and the only girl, was treated better than her brothers. When she turned ten or so, her overprotective mother decided that the local bathhouse was not clean enough for her only daughter and bought her a bathtub.

Once inside the shtetl's bathhouse, one was confronted by a large furnace with a gaping mouth that was always ready to take in chunks of wood, which Yankl der beder (Yankl the bathhouse attendant) fed between his constant pumping of water and collecting of entrance fees. Yankl was a tall, well-built man. My father used to say that Yankl would have been a strongman had he had a decent meal once in a while. The bathhouse was divided into two parts. One part formed the bathhouse itself, and the other part was the shvitz. In the bathhouse was the pool for ritual immersion, called a *mikve* as well as half a dozen tubs and a row of showers. It could happen that one had to wait for a tub, but never for too long. The Jews of Shershev did not know how to relax in a tub, especially when others were waiting their turns. In the shvitz, the older Jews would lie on the wooden benches in thick steam and rub or massage each other's backs with the help of short brooms made from young birch twigs. My father was not a steam bath enthusiast, and maybe that's why I'm not either.

On the day before Pesach, we returned from the bathhouse and ate the last bites of *khomets* until after Pesach. Whatever was not consumed had to be burned. We ate in a hurry, standing at the kitchen door or in one of the woodsheds. After that meal, we children took the bread crumbs that we had found when searching for *khomets* the night before and the wooden spoon we had used to scoop them up, and we brought them to the bathhouse, where we threw them into the flaming furnace, thereby fulfilling the biblical command to burn our *khomets*.

The rest of the day was difficult for all, especially for the women who had to prepare the seder. To ease the long wait for the seder, my mother served a snack of peeled potatoes and hard-boiled eggs. It was not the fanciest snack one could wish for, but it wasn't matzo, which we were not allowed to eat until the seder.

Finally, the sun began to set, and one could feel the festive atmosphere in the shtetl. The Jewish homes were spic and span and so were their inhabitants. The women began to light the holiday candles, and the men made their way to the synagogues in their best attire.

There were six synagogues in Shershev. The ancient shul, which stood partly behind our house, was beyond repair. Next door, to the right of our house stood *der groyser beys medresh* (the large synagogue), which indeed was the largest in shtetl. It was a two-storey brick building with part of the second floor serving as the *ezres-noshim*, the women's section. The rabbi's synagogue was where my grandfather Laizer Ber Auerbach had been the *gabe* and where my father had his *shtot* (membership seat) at the eastern wall. The third was Reb Isaac's synagogue, where my grandfather Yaakov Kopel was a member. The fourth, the *gemoyerter* synagogue, was an ancient building made of oversized bricks. For us children, the main attraction of that synagogue was its system of interconnecting cellars whose layout we had never figured out. The fifth, the new synagogue, on the *hoyf gesl* (courtyard street), was indeed the newest, built right after World War I. Finally, the last synagogue was called the Chassidic synagogue, although in my time there were no Chassidim in Shershev except for one family that moved there shortly before World War II. Still, one could find Chassidic prayer books in Shershev. We even had some in our house from my paternal grandparents, who had given them to us without any explanation.

After the short prayer on the eve of Pesach, my father and I walked swiftly home, where everything shone with holiday brightness and splendour from the floor to the ceiling, including the members of the household. The big table stood in the middle of the dining room, covered, according to tradition, with seven tablecloths one on top of the other, the best one at the very top. The flames atop the candles in the shining holiday candlesticks flickered happily, and joy and warmth filled every corner of the house. In the middle of the table was the *keare*, the seder plate.

We would be hungry when we arrived home from the synagogue and did not waste any time in proceeding with the seder, which was conducted in an Orthodox tradition. The food in our house was always good, but never as good as on the first night of Pesach, when we ate more than our fill. The next morning, all the men and boys went to the synagogue. The Hebrew school was closed on Saturdays and holidays, so we spent the eight days of Pesach playing games, using walnuts, the most expensive nuts around, as prizes; the loss of a couple was a big loss for a little boy.

The days of the most beautiful Jewish holiday of the year passed quickly, and on the last day, after the evening prayers, we put away the Pesach dishes, a task in which the whole family participated. We wrapped the dishes, pots and pans in old newspapers and packed them tightly in wooden barrels. It was my father's job to carry them up to the attic, where they remained untouched until the next year. As soon as the Pesach dishes were put away, my mother would send me or my sister to the baker, who was just then taking freshly baked rolls out of the oven, and the *khomets*-hungry crowd bought them as if they had not eaten in a week. The next morning, everybody returned to the ordinary and mundane life of the shtetl.

5
Idealism

IN THE SPRING of 1933, before the end of the school year, a rumour spread around the school and in the shtetl that the principal of our Hebrew school, Yaakov Peker, was going to set up a Betar cell in Shershev. The Betar movement was hardly known in the shtetl, and it was doubtful if he would find any followers. However, it turned out that there were some young men who sympathized with this approach to Zionism, which focused on immigration to Palestine and preparation for a Jewish state. Until then we'd had only left-leaning Zionist organizations such as Hashomer Hatzair and HeChalutz in Shershev. But many Jews of Shershev were wary of socialist ideologies. Children nine and older could join the Betar organization, and almost every child in our school did.

Around this time, we children started hearing the grown-ups speaking of a man by the name of Hitler who had gained power in Germany. The faces of my parents and their friends were full of concern when speaking about him. At our meetings in the local Betar, this name came up quite often, and we knew him to be a Jew-hater.

Peker left Shershev before the start of the school year and gave over the command of Betar to Chaim Shemesh, my father's first cousin, who was a bookkeeper in the local Jewish community-owned bank.

Chaim was an exceptionally gifted person, and there was no limit to his quest for knowledge. Chaim was the ideal person to take over Betar, but his leadership didn't last long. A few months later, he succeeded in obtaining a much-coveted permit to go to the Land of Israel. His position was taken over by another local young man who had just graduated from teachers seminary, Yaakov Judelewsky.

The summer of 1933 went by quickly thanks to the activities at Betar, where we came together to be indoctrinated with the ideals and spirit of Revisionist Zionism. Aside from Betar, our favourite place to spend time was Courtyard Street, a short street that branched off Shershev's main street. At the beginning of the lane to the left was a large space used for sporting activities, and behind it was the New Synagogue and two or three farm homesteads. To the right, there was a shoemaker, the home of a government bureaucrat and a stately home in which the Greek Orthodox priest lived with his nine beautiful daughters. Next to that was the Polish public school with its sprawling grounds and the parsonage of the Catholic Church. The main attraction of Courtyard Street was the rows of ancient linden trees growing along each side of it. The trunks were large and hollow, and three or four boys could squeeze inside them.

The legend went that several hundred years earlier Queen Bona, who ruled over Poland and Lithuania, built a palace in Shershev at the end of that lane, and it was then that the linden trees were planted. One day, as the queen's two daughters were walking into town, they were attacked by a swarm of bees. Fortunately, the Jews from the nearby houses noticed and saved the two young princesses from much suffering and maybe death. In gratitude, the queen built a magnificent synagogue for the Jewish community, and it remained one of the most impressive synagogues in Poland until World War I, when it burned down.

Courtyard Street served as a sort of amusement park for the Jews of Shershev, especially on Saturdays, when the Jewish crowd walked there under the wide shade of the linden trees or lay on the lush green grass under them. As youngsters, my friends and I spent many hours there listening to the preaching and lectures of our young idealistic leaders, playing games and dreaming of the future.

At the end of August 1933, I began Grade 4, and we began to learn Chumash and Tanach, the twenty-four books of the Bible, in more depth. We were also introduced to the geography of the Land of Israel. I was indifferent to most subjects, but I became obsessed with the Land of Israel. My mother would say, "Wake him up in the middle of the night, and he will tell you how many cows they have in each kibbutz." I became absorbed in its geography but also with the ideal of Zionism. Our teacher of that subject was Yoel Waldshan. Shortly after he started teaching us about the Land of Israel, Waldshan acquainted us with every town, settlement and kibbutz there. Considering the number of Jewish towns, settlements and kibbutzim in Palestine in 1933, it wasn't too difficult for a young and inquisitive mind to absorb it all. The exercise book that we used for the subject was the heaviest I ever used. In it, we pasted pictures that we cut out from newspapers, booklets or pamphlets. The more pictures we had, the better. My uncle Eli, my father's youngest brother, was very active in Hashomer Hatzair and had access to a lot of printed material about the Land of Israel. Through him I had an inexhaustible supply of pictures. It is no wonder that my exercise book was one of the two outstanding ones in class. The second belonged to Yaakov Waldshan, the teacher's son. We did a project called "fifty years of building," referring to the years 1882 to 1932, during which Jews had been rebuilding their homeland. Waldshan took us through those years as if we were living side by side with those early pioneers. We shared their hardships, hunger and thirst, their defeats and victories, their disappointments and enthusiasm, and above all their dreams and their boundless hope.

As of this writing, it is well over sixty years since those lessons, but I can still see Yoel Waldshan standing in front of our class of ten-year-olds, telling us with so much fervour about the accomplishments, daring and heroism of those *chalutzim*, pioneers, as they stood neck deep in malaria-infested swamps to plant eucalyptus trees and dig ditches, draining the swamps to make them livable and guarding the newly established kibbutzim from murderous Arab attacks. Jewish young people from Eastern Europe left behind warm homes and families and set out to a far and hostile land, exposing themselves to all kinds of dangers and difficulties in order to build a Jewish homeland. My exuberant imagination would get hold of me, and I could barely wait for the day when I'd be old enough to join the ranks of the *chalutzim* to participate in building the Land of Israel.

6
New Environments

IN THE SPRING of 1934, the last few weeks of the school year went by quickly but with a touch of apprehension, for my father had decided to transfer me to the Polish school, as he had done with Sheva. He said that we lived in Poland and we had to know the language of the land, which the students of the Hebrew School hardly knew and only a dozen families in Shershev used at all. Because of my poor knowledge of Polish, I had to lose an entire school year and redo Grade 4 in the public Polish school. The summer vacation was as pleasant as always, yet one could feel a sense of uneasiness among the Jews of Shershev. People began reading the newspapers more thoroughly, but nobody shared their thoughts with us youngsters. I recall the day when the newspapers arrived, carrying the headline announcing the death of the most popular Hebrew poet. It read "Hayim Nahman Bialik is dead." I believe that his death made a greater impact on us youngsters than on the grown-ups, for we had just begun to study and memorize his beautiful and moving poetry.

The two main Jewish papers read in Shershev were the rightist *Der moment* (The moment) and the leftist *Haynt* (Today). Both were printed in Warsaw at midnight and arrived in Pruzhany in the morning and in Shershev by noon. Subscribing to a newspaper was too expensive for one person, so people paired up in twosomes or foursomes. My father and grandfather were partners to one paper. When one was finished with it, the other got it. If there were four partners to a paper, the paper was in use all day, or even on the following morning.

As our family had expanded, my mother gave up our annual summer vacations in Domatcheva, and we settled for a much closer vacation in Shubichi, where my mother could rent a large room and a kitchen. My father stayed at home to keep the store open and came out on Friday afternoons by bus. The inhabitants of Shubichi were farmers. Next to their fields was a large estate belonging to a Jewish man by the name of Brezynski, a respectable, humane and committed Jew. The main attraction of this estate was the part of its forest that sat on high sandy ground and was overgrown with pine trees.

It was stylish in those days to put on weight, and this was the purpose of going to the country. So, my mother spent entire days making delicacies for us. The requisite additional food was two eggs and a glass of milk three times a day. To get me to drink the milk, my mother would bribe me with a piece of chocolate. After this we were supposed to eat a regular meal. It is not surprising that we did not want to eat, and my mother's efforts on those hot days remained untouched on the table. Those tables, laden with all sorts of good food that I refused to eat, later haunted me.

For my mother, one month of such "rest" in the country was enough, and she and the children returned home. I stayed on for a week or two with my aunt Chashkah and the children and returned with Uncle Reuven on a Saturday night by bus, for I did not enjoy the return trip home by horse and buggy, as the buggy was full of bags, bedding, dishes and other items. For my uncle and me to catch the ten o'clock bus going from Pruzhany to Shershev, we had to leave Shubichi and walk along a field for a kilometre to the main road. We gave ourselves enough time and got to the road early. Having nothing to do, I stretched myself out on the grass and looked up to the dark blue sky, strewn with countless stars. It was a dark night, and it seemed that one could count them all. I think that it was the first time, and perhaps the only time, I ever saw such a starry sky.

It was good to come back home to my parents and Sheva, who was always a caring big sister and guardian to me. She followed my mother's actions, pampering me and giving in to my every whim. She behaved the same way toward my little brother Liova, almost seven years younger than me, and to my little two sisters, Sonia, then three years old, and the little one, Leiba, just a year. Our family, like many other families in Shershev in those days, was tightly knit, dependent on and devoted to each other. When my parents went out to visit family or friends for the evening, they would leave my sister and me to look after the little ones. Sheva was not yet thirteen years old, and I was only eleven. If one of the little ones woke up, my sister and I would take turns holding them in our arms and walking with them back and forth until they fell asleep, never running to our parents for help.

With the end of the summer vacation in 1934, I went back to school, but to an entirely new and strange environment. Gone were the familiar friendly faces of my playmates and peers. Instead, I found myself among schoolchildren who spoke a barely familiar language. They knew each other but ignored me. They were rougher in conduct and language than I was used to. Their dress was somewhat different and even their smell. The school was on Courtyard Street, over half a kilometre farther from our house than the Hebrew school. It had many more classes, though as the grades progressed, the classes shrank as students failed or left school. It also had a large yard that was planted with osier, which was used for arts and crafts lessons. A sturdy fence separated the schoolyard from the street. Along the fence in the yard was a long ditch that was full of stagnant water all year long. During an exceptionally hot summer, the water would dry out for a few weeks and the aroma of dead tadpoles and frogs could be smelled from quite a distance. The ditch was overgrown with trees on either side, including a couple of huge oak trees, whose branches reached over the fence and to the other side of the road. At the end of August, a huge number of acorns would fall off those oak trees and cover the road almost ankle-deep.

There were around 450 students in that school, compared to 125 in the Hebrew school. Among those 450, about 100 were Jewish children, mostly girls. The school building itself was the largest wooden structure in the village, and it included the living quarters of the principal. He was a tall man by the name of Falshewsky, about forty years old, a former Piłsudski legionnaire, a fanatical nationalist, patriot and antisemite, and he alienated the local population with his air of superiority.

The school had a special large room for arts and crafts and an adjoining room for tools. There was also a kitchen where meals were prepared for needy children, who would get a bowl of soup during the long break, though Jewish kids did not eat there because there was no ritual kosher supervision. The school executive would refer the Jewish kids to Jewish welfare organizations to look after them.

The language of instruction in school was of course Polish, but the Jewish children spoke Yiddish among themselves, and the Christians spoke a Belarusian dialect among themselves. Conversation among Jews and non-Jews was conducted in the local Belarusian dialect. In the entire school, there were perhaps a dozen students who actually spoke Polish. They were the children of the government employees who came from Poland proper to run things.

My first year in the Polish school was a difficult one. I had trouble communicating with my teachers as well as with the non-Jewish students, but my father made sure that I came to the store after school to review everything I had learned and make sure that my homework was in order. My father's spoken and written Polish was perfect, so when anyone in the shtetl had a problem or was in trouble with the government and had to explain themselves in writing to the authorities, they would come to my father and not to the local barrister. My father didn't do it for pay, just for the sake of the good deed itself.

For some inexplicable reason, I developed a taste for Polish history. My father made sure that I memorized each lesson, and in every term, I got the highest mark in Polish history despite the language problem.

My other highest mark in class was in mathematics, which I continued to receive up to graduation.

The order of school days changed for me. In the Hebrew school, we had attended six days a week, excluding Saturday, which was Shabbos, while Sunday was an ordinary school day. In the Polish school, we had to attend on Saturday under the threat of expulsion. However, Jewish children were not obliged to write on Saturday, as writing is not permitted on the Sabbath. So we Jewish children would sit in school without touching a pen, pencil or chalk.

It was in the Polish school that I came face to face with outright antisemitism for the first time. Of course, I had heard about it, but I hadn't experienced it personally before. There were two teachers, a married couple by the name of Gulawsky. She was a tall aristocratic woman who was aloof, even among the other teachers, and she taught us drawing. Her husband, a shorter man, was always seen with his walking cane. It was in fact a climbing stick with a sharp metal point at the bottom and a metal elongated head on top, which had an axe-like shape on one end and a pickaxe point on the other. A story was going around in the shtetl that when he was asked by an acquaintance what the use of such a cane was when there were no mountains around for five hundred kilometres, he replied that it would come in handy to split Jewish heads.

The following year, he became my gym teacher. Once, he took the class for a walk in a nearby forest. The terrain was covered with conifer cones, and our classmates started throwing them at me and the other Jewish boy. At first, we ignored it, but the throwing intensified. The teacher pretended not to see. Finally, we protested to him. He then turned to the students and said, "One should not deal with Jews in such an obvious way. One should approach this in a more civilized way, like not giving work to Jewish craftsmen or artisans, and more important, not buying from Jewish stores."

Shortly after Sukkos of 1934, my grandmother Freida Leah began to feel weaker and spent more and more time in bed. My mother brought her to live with us, and friends and acquaintances often came to visit my grandmother. I cannot recall one evening when we were left alone. The members of the Linat Hatzedek, the benevolent association, whose volunteers stayed up all night with the sick to give a night's rest to members of the family, were often in our home.

As Christmas approached, my class began to learn and rehearse carols. This was a new and completely alien phenomenon. Jewish kids were exempt from singing but had to attend the rehearsals, just as we had to attend the morning prayer but were exempt from saying it. Jewish students were also exempt from religious classes conducted for Catholic students by the priest and for the Greek Orthodox students by the Greek Orthodox priest, or "pope" as the students called him. The other Jewish student and I did not attend, but we would feel the consequences as soon as the class was over. Insults, name-calling, pushing and kicking happened with renewed rage and fury after every religious class.

My new world was not easy to adjust to. Although we were exempt from attending classes on Jewish holidays, I still missed the pre-holiday atmosphere in the Hebrew school. The relationships with our non-Jewish classmates were quite cool and limited to the subject matter we were learning, particularly math, in which we Jewish boys excelled. When a Christian pupil spoke to a Jewish one more than necessary, his friends would immediately reproach him.

With such a sense of disconnection from my environment, I welcomed the year 1935. Fortunately, after school and homework and after private Hebrew lessons, I still found time to spend with my friends. We still liked to go sledding down the hill or spend time in the local Betar. My original group of six friends had grown to eleven. Because of the large number, frictions were inevitable, which eventually led to the group splitting up.

That winter, our Betar branch received an honoured guest in the person of our former Hebrew school principal and founder of the Betar organization in Shershev, Yaakov Peker. One evening he came to visit us, and we all dressed up in our uniforms: brown hats and brown shirts, navy pants and polished shoes. Lined up in a straight line, like soldiers, not daring to blink an eye, we followed our commander as he strode along our lines in his uniform. Deep in our hearts, we hoped that he still remembered and recognized us. When we were freed from our rigid postures and the atmosphere warmed up, we learned that he remembered most of us by name. Some forty years later, I met Peker at a remembrance gathering for survivors of the Pruzhany ghetto that took place in New York. To the best of my knowledge, he was my only Jewish teacher who survived the Holocaust.

On a warm day in March 1935, we were playing near my friend Moishe Gelman's house when Chashkah Krenitzer passed by. I knew her well, for her mother-in-law had lived in my grandparents' house. She was the elderly lady who brought us milk every morning, rain or shine, summer or winter, as long as I could remember. Chashkah turned to me and almost casually asked me, "How is your grandmother?"

As I had been at home no more than two hours previously, I answered, "About the same."

Without changing her tone, she said, "You'd better go home."

Out of a habit of listening to older people, I went straight home. I found my grandmother lying on the floor, covered with a sheet, with two candles burning near her head. My mother was standing bent over her, crying. There were quite a few people in the house—neighbours, friends and acquaintances, and anybody who had just heard the news. The women cried along with my mother. The men stood in silence with sorrowful faces and downcast eyes or whispered to one another. All that late afternoon and evening, people were coming and going. Finally, they all left except for a couple of old men, who continued to sit with the dead body, reading Psalms uninterruptedly throughout the night.

We kids fell asleep. I was awakened early in the morning by my mother's quiet sobbing. Getting out of bed, I found my mother crying quietly over my grandmother's body. It did not take long before we were all up, and my father tried to quiet my mother down a bit, but with little success. The two old men who had been sitting near the body all night got up and left. Soon the townspeople began to gather. First came the women from the *khevre kedishe*, the burial society, who started with the process of purifying the body. Others began making the shrouds. When I saw my grandmother again, she was already dressed in the shrouds and was being put on the *mite*. She was covered with a black cover, and four men lifted the handles of the stretcher on their shoulders, and in a slow procession began to carry my grandmother in the direction of the Jewish cemetery. Behind them followed my mother, my father and us children, surrounded by various relatives and friends of the family.

It was not customary to reserve a burial place in advance, and people were buried next to each other as they died. As we got to the cemetery, my grandmother's grave was already dug. Somebody noticed that her grave was in front of my grandfather Laizer Ber's stone and said that they must have a lot of ancestral merit to be lying next to each other. It wasn't in the Jewish tradition to take pictures at funerals, but because my grandmother had two sons in the United States, my uncles Shloime and Pesach, Rabbi Liwerant gave permission to take pictures and send them to the sons. My mother was so religious that she didn't have any pictures of herself or of us.

The loss of my grandmother, whom we had loved and who had loved us in return tenfold, and who had become an inseparable part of our daily life in the last few years, was very painful. My mother's heart-rending lament and cries of grief as the earth was shovelled into the grave should have woken my grandmother up from her eternal sleep. Now, after many years, I can console myself and take comfort in the fact that both my mother's parents were favoured with being buried in a Jewish cemetery according to Jewish law. It was only after I matured that I understood my mother's loss. For not only was my grandmother devoted to my mother body and soul, but she was also the last member of my mother's family in Shershev, or in all of Poland.

My grandmother died not quite three weeks before Passover. On the first seder night, the atmosphere was so tense that even the small children felt it. It did not take long before my mother broke out crying.

Sheva and I soon joined her. My little brothers and sisters looked at us with large, uncomprehending, fearful eyes, begging us not to cry. There was no crying on the second seder night, and everyone tried to act normally. The living must go on with their lives.

Right after the holidays, the weather improved and we Jewish students could spend the recesses outdoors and keep a distance from our more aggressive non-Jewish classmates. The warmer weather also carried the promise of summer and the approaching vacation.

One morning in May 1935, we were lining up outdoors for gym class, and our teacher Gulawsky was giving us instructions for an exercise. We saw the chief of police walking along the other side of the fence, not with his usual erect, military gait, but slowly, with his head lowered. Coming to the fence opposite Gulawsky, he stopped and called out to him. Gulawsky went over to him, and they greeted each other warmly, being of the same elite Polish class. After a short conversation, the teacher came back to us and walked toward me. He said quietly, "Kantorowitz, wasz dziadek umarl"—*Kantorowitz, your grandfather died.*

I was taken aback. I had passed my Kantorowitz grandparents' house less than a half an hour earlier, and everything seemed in order. How could the teacher know? Did the chief of police bring him the news? True, my grandfather was the mayor, but to those Poles he was no more than a despised Jew.

So I said to the teacher, "How can it be? Only half an hour ago I passed by their house, and everything was fine."

He answered, putting emphasis on each word, "I did not say *twoj*, 'your' singular. I said *wasz*, 'your' plural—your Jewish grandfather, Marshal Piłsudski." At that moment, as a twelve-year-old boy, I did not understand the weight those few words carried.

I don't remember if that school day was discontinued or not, but I remember how distressed my parents and everybody in the street were. All kinds of rumours began to circulate about rising antisemitism and about the chances of war with Germany. Jews considered the First Marshal of Poland, Piłsudski, to be friendly to the Jews, not only because of his early socialistic sympathies, but because of a story that was told about him.

In his youth Piłsudski was not only a fervent Polish nationalist and patriot, but also an ardent socialist, and the czarist secret police, Okhrana, were constantly on his heels. Once, Piłsudski was found by the Okhrana in a shtetl, and they gave chase. Like most Eastern European shtetls, this one was a maze of interlocking streets and lanes huddled together closely like the Jewish inhabitants in them, as if in proximity there was security. Piłsudski ran into a Jewish home and asked the owner to hide him. The Jew, having little sympathy for the antisemitic czarist police and guessing that the young Pole must be a revolutionary of sorts, and maybe also out of compassion or pity, pushed him into the next room and threw a *tales* over him, covering his head and most of his body. Then the Jew stuck a prayer book in his hands and told him to rock back and forth in the way Jews do while praying. When the police burst into the house, it never dawned on them to look at the Jew engrossed in prayer. So they left to look for him in the neighbouring houses. Piłsudski, it was said, did not forget the favour that the Jewish stranger did for him, and while he was in power, the deep-rooted Polish antisemitism was kept in check. One thing is for sure—after his death, persecution of Jews in Poland started in earnest, intensifying as time went by.

Piłsudski's funeral took about a week, during which schools and offices were closed. The population spent a lot of time listening to the few radios available in Shershev, which were playing funeral marches, or attending memorial services in synagogues. When Piłsudski's remains were laid to rest in Wawel Castle in Krakow at the end of the week, the mourning period continued to the end of the month, after which the country returned to its normal rhythm.

My father's parents, Yaakov Kopel and Chinkah, still had their three youngest children living with them, Hershel, Pesl and Eli, who was turning twenty-one, which was conscription age. According to Polish law, every male turning twenty-one had to appear before a military medical commission that determined if he was physically and mentally fit to serve in the Polish army for two years. Candidates could be exempted if they were the sole supporters of parents over sixty or if there was a younger, underage child in the family. This was how my uncle Hershel had managed to avoid military service. He appeared in front of a commission in 1925, when Eli was only eleven years old.

Jewish young men had little desire to serve in the Polish army. First, there was the problem of the non-kosher food. Second, the Polish army was saturated with antisemitism. A sickly young man was the envy of all his friends, for he stood a good chance of being rejected from the army. One way to be rejected was to weigh under the required minimum of just over a hundred pounds, so many Jewish young men tried to lose weight, forming groups to watch each other so they wouldn't eat or sleep. They spent their days and nights on bicycles, travelling from village to village or from shtetl to shtetl. Not sleeping at night and out of sheer boredom, they sometimes wandered the streets of the shtetl causing minor damage, like removing doors from sheds or pushing over fences. The victims of such pranks understood and had sympathy for these young men.

The parents of those young men didn't sleep restfully either. No Jewish mother wished to part with her son for two years. Especially when her son would be spending his time among *goyem* (non-Jews), eating *treyf* (non-kosher food) and not observing the Sabbath. He would sleep under the open sky on the ground in the summer and in snow in winter. And how could a mother bear to watch her son not eating or drinking, or pushing himself on a bicycle day and night to the point of total exhaustion?

Among these young men was my uncle Eli. I can still see him pedalling his bicycle, stopping to exchange a few words with my father. My father, who was twenty-two years older than Eli, was a father figure to him. Besides, my father had been a soldier, serving under the czar in the city of Kazan, the Tartar capital, and he had faced the Austrian and German armies at the outbreak of World War I, when he lost two fingers of his right hand.

One day, in the summer of 1935, my father and I were standing in front of our store when Eli pedalled by on his bicycle. He pulled over when he saw us. To my father's question as to how he felt, he answered, "Miserable." He could barely keep his eyes open and could hardly stay on his feet from fatigue and hunger. He appeared to me all skin and bones, a shadow of his former self. Two months had passed since he had undertaken the torment of losing weight, and he had two more weeks to go before he was scheduled to appear in front of the commission. He was very much in doubt if he could keep it up. My father asked how much he weighed, and he answered, "A hundred and forty pounds."

"And how much did you weigh before?" asked my father.

"A hundred and seventy-five pounds," came the answer.

"That means that it took you two months to lose thirty-five pounds, and now you have two more weeks to lose forty more," said my father. "You'll never make it. Go home, dear Brother, have a good meal and go to sleep."

My uncle took his advice. A couple of weeks later, Eli and his peers faced the military commission, and they were all accepted into the army.

The summer vacation of 1935 ended, and I found myself in Grade 5. Despite having spent a year in the Polish public school already, through the summer I had forgotten what it was like to spend so much time in a non-Jewish environment. Jewish students in public schools were always subjected to a certain amount of antisemitism. One day, Sheva came home and told my parents that someone had sneaked up on her and smeared her lips with a piece of pork. Somehow the story reached my grandfather Yaakov Kopel. A few days later, a delegation from the Department of Education came from Brest-Litovsk to Shershev to see what could be done to improve the school with respect to education, hygiene, discipline and the curriculum. The representatives from the provincial capital met with the local representatives, among them my grandfather Yaakov Kopel as the mayor. During that meeting, the subject of hygiene came up, and my grandfather announced that he would like to contribute personally toward buying towels. Everybody looked up in astonishment. Why towels? My grandfather said, "So that Jewish students will have towels to wipe their lips with after their classmates have smeared them with pork."

The principal blushed a bit and said that the guilty student had been punished. However, my grandfather insisted that this was not the first time this had happened. The principal promised to put an end to it. However, as far as my sister and I knew, nobody was reprimanded, nor did this behaviour stop.

With the approaching winter, we boys took advantage of the immense expanses around Shershev, where the ground was as flat as a table. The little tributary of the Leśna River that surrounded Shershev from every side flooded its low banks into the surrounding meadows, marshes and fields, turning the tiny river into a wide lake along its banks. This flooded area often froze, creating a skating rink that could take us to the end of the horizon where we discovered lands inaccessible to us in the summertime. The ice was undisturbed and, when clear of snow, transparent. Skating over it, we could see below every blade of grass and plant, even the variety of bugs that went on with their lives below the ice. From time to time, we could see a fish that had ventured away from the river to forage for a snack among the grasses and weeds under the ice. Some boys tried to catch fish by stunning them with a club through the ice. It was not easy to do because the fish were fast, however, there were a few boys who earned a few złoty now and then from the fish they caught. Others made traps from branches and placed them under the ice. They would make the rounds every morning, breaking the ice and pulling the traps out, and if lucky, finding in them a few fish.

On a windy day, we would skate on the ice against the wind for a couple of kilometres, then we would turn around, unbutton our coats and open them as far as we could, letting the wind propel us back to town, our coats serving as sails. The enjoyment of that free ride was worth the effort of the struggle against the wind. After a couple of hours of such exercise, it was a pleasure to come home for dinner.

That year, my father started leaving me alone in the store while he went home for dinner. I spent a fair amount of time there in general, doing my homework with my father. One did not have to be an expert to serve the customers, and the fear of robbery did not exist. Sometimes a friend or two would come in, and the time would pass quickly.

Christmas was approaching, and in school the students rehearsed carols again. The conversations in and out of class revolved around the upcoming holidays. On Christmas night, my parents did not sleep, as it was one of the two best business nights of the year. The Christian population, on their way to Mass or on their way back, wanted to drink. At first, they would come to the house and knock on the door, so my father decided to stay in the store. But it was against the law to stay open at night, so my parents worked as a team. When one of them was in the store with a customer, the other stayed outside. If a policeman approached, a knock on the door was a signal for them to remain inside until the policeman went away. The Russian Orthodox celebrated their Christmas two weeks later, and the same process was repeated. And again, the same thing happened on Easter. Many Jews did not sleep well on those nights because in many places pogroms occurred, especially on Easter. Fortunately, as far as I know, those nights passed without disturbances in Shershev. The five policemen in the shtetl were more lenient to the Jewish storekeepers on those nights. It is quite possible that they preferred to spend that night with their families rather than chasing down Jewish storekeepers.

In general, however, the Jewish storekeepers played cat and mouse with the police every Sunday, when stores were not allowed to be open. A member of the family would keep watch, standing in front of the store, while the storekeeper would take a customer inside. Should a policeman appear, a knock on the door or the windowpane would warn the storekeeper and his customer to remain inside. The policemen were not easily fooled and sometimes stayed outside the store for a long time. The lookouts would put a padlock on the outside door, trying to convince the policeman that there couldn't possibly be anyone inside. However, if a policeman discovered that someone so much as opened or closed the door of a store, that storekeeper was fined five złoty. That could represent a week's earnings to a storekeeper.

I was looking forward to the approaching winter holidays when I didn't have to get up while it was still dark outside. On school days, I had to get out of the house at a quarter past seven in the frosty morning, and by the time I got to school, I could not feel my ears, nose or cheeks. Even my hands within my gloves were numb. During the holidays, I could stay in a warm bed as long as my heart desired, for my mother with her boundless love seldom said no to me, and I took advantage by staying in bed until late morning. If the weather was very cold, I stayed in the house, entertaining Leibel with stories that I remembered from when I was his age or had read in children's books. Sometimes, I even made up stories of my own. Our cousin Shalom would join us. Those two could sit for hours and listen to my stories, never tiring of them. I always found time for my two younger sisters, Sonia and Leiba, although my sister Sheva spent more time with them than I did. My little brother and sisters were being brought up to be well-behaved and obedient children, not only toward our parents, but toward others as well.

That winter, I became bar mitzvah. Not much was made about bar mitzvahs in Shershev then. A few days before his thirteenth birthday, a boy was shown by his rebbe or by his father how to put on *tfilen* (phylacteries). On the Shabbos of his bar mitzvah, the boy was called up to the Torah, usually getting the honour of reading the Haftorah, the weekly section from the Prophets. None of my friends had ever mentioned when they became bar mitzvah, although they were all older than me. Still, my mother invited my friends on Friday night after the Shabbos meal for cake and tea. This constituted the celebration of my bar mitzvah, and it was more than any of my friends had.

I was never enthusiastic about getting up early in the morning, especially in February. But as a bar mitzvah boy, I was expected to attend the daily morning prayers, which meant getting up an hour earlier than usual. Fortunately, there was a synagogue next door to our house. After one month of attending the services, I gave it up. My friends had also stopped attending services a month or two after their bar mitzvahs, a fact that enhanced my argument with my parents about giving it up.

For me, the best time and day was Friday morning. My mother would get up at two o'clock in the morning to start baking challah. I shared a room with Liova, and my bed stood against the back wall of the oven. As soon as my mother lit the fire in the oven, the wall would get warm, and then the bed and room. The unusual warmth of the bed and the sounds in the kitchen would wake me up, and I'd feel a sense of comfort and well-being, knowing that the person dearest to me in the world, my mother, who would do anything for me, was up and watching over me and baking challah and cake for us. While it was bitterly cold outside, I lay in my warm bed, and when I got up, my mother would have a hot potato pancake ready for me.

I spent many of the long winter evenings reading, sometimes until the early hours of the morning. My mother would get out of bed and try to persuade me to put the book aside and get a few hours of sleep before going to school. She was concerned for my health and worried that I was ruining my eyes. She had a difficult job getting me up in the morning after only a few hours of sleep, and I would leave for school with my eyes half shut. I knew how much I was hurting her when she saw me in such a state. Yet my father would never interrupt my reading even if I stayed up all night, which happened a few times.

I loved the long winter evenings with my family and enjoyed my mother's boundless love and endless affection. My mother's unconditional love, selflessness and self-sacrifice were unusual. I only began to understand that a couple of years later, with the onset of the six-year-long period of darkness—first, when I still had her, and later, after I had lost her. All the positive things that have been said and written about mothers were embodied in my mother. If there was such a thing as having a favourite child, it was I, and I suspect I felt it and took advantage of it, to the detriment of my other siblings.

On those evenings at home, we children would sing popular songs we had picked up in school or on the street. Sometimes our parents would get carried away singing a solo or duet, Yiddish or Russian songs from their younger years. To us, they sounded ancient. Sheva loved to sing and could pick up a song after hearing it once, as could my two little sisters, Sonia and Leiba. Singing was often heard in our home.

The holiday of Pesach arrived almost as suddenly as the warm spring weather. The snow on the flatlands began to melt faster than ever, flowing in the direction of the little river which had flooded and frozen over the previous fall. Now, the flooded river was melting, and combined with the melting snow from all around, turning half the shtetl into a sea. My grandparents' yard was covered in water, and many of the houses were flooded.

The spring created a lot of activities in and around the shtetl. The farmers started plowing the fields. The Jews who had gardens got busy working in them. Houses were being built, and carpenters, masons and roofers, all Jews, were working. The blacksmiths, who, except for one, were Jewish, also got busy servicing the farmers' wagons and shoeing their horses.

Shortly after Pesach, my uncle Eli was called up for military service, which he had been expecting for almost a year. His friends, the entire group with whom he had spent sleepless nights and who starved themselves, were called up too. My grandmother cried continuously for a week after Eli, her youngest son, left. My father, as the oldest son, tried to comfort her.

7
Clouds on the Horizon

THE YEAR 1936 WAS one of growing antisemitism in Poland. The Poles did not need encouragement to follow in the footsteps of the Germans, who were implementing anti-Jewish laws. The Nuremberg Laws had been passed in Germany a year earlier, and in Poland, the Jewish political and economic horizon began to cloud over too. Not having anyone like Piłsudski to restrain them, the Polish people started their own antisemitic campaigns. The unrest started with propaganda urging people not to buy from Jewish-owned stores. Next, people were throwing rocks into Jewish homes and businesses and attacking individual Jews. Then there was the first Polish pogrom of the 1930s, which took place in the shtetl of Przytyk, on March 9, 1936, when a mob of Polish antisemites attacked the local Jewish population.

Jews, especially young people, began looking for a way out. The majority wanted to go to the Land of Israel, but in the last few years, the British government had been drastically reducing the number of Jews allowed to enter Palestine. At the same time, the persecution of Jews in Germany increased the demand for permits to Palestine. There were some who got permits. They were young people who belonged to the leftist Zionist organizations, which were authorized by the British to hand them out. Those privileged to get such a permit had to be active and committed members of that organization and had to pass a Hachshara, a special training course to prepare Jews for agricultural work in the Land of Israel. People who had members of their immediate family in Palestine also received permits, as did those who could produce 1,000 British pounds (5,000 US dollars), a huge sum for the poverty-stricken majority of Polish Jewry. Students with gymnasium matriculation could also go to Palestine to continue their studies at the Hebrew University.

Life in Shershev began to change slowly but noticeably for the worst. We sensed that our Polish neighbours envied the fact that in Germany antisemitism was not only out in the open but encouraged and supported by the government. Our non-Jewish neighbours would often say, "Wait till Hitler comes." When I heard antisemitic remarks in school, I could tell myself that they came from the mouths of children. But hearing such comments from grown-ups was depressing and frightening.

The Jewish press was full of saddening and dispiriting news, but one of the Jewish papers also contained stories about faraway places and exotic lands. The stories awoke in me a desire to travel, and certainly a desire to leave Shershev. They also triggered the imaginations of my friends, who, like me, had dreams for their futures. We spent many summer evenings together, walking back and forth on Mostowa Street, the only street with a sidewalk. On warm Saturday evenings, the entire Jewish population could be found there, the sidewalk too narrow to hold us all. We boys used to walk, plan and dream of a future along that sidewalk. Who knows how many more boys like us had walked on that sidewalk and dreamt similar dreams? We also used to walk in the meadow along the riverbank. We would let the wind blow through our hair, which grew during the vacation time, as we were not permitted to grow it during the school year. With the wind in our faces or at our backs, we walked and talked about faraway places, exciting events, and the distant and wide world. Above all, however, we dreamt about our own Jewish homeland in the Land of Israel. We were ready to do anything to realize the dream of our own independent state—even giving our lives would have been a small price to pay.

The news from the Land of Israel was becoming more depressing by the day. There was a difference of opinion among Jews about how to respond to the Arab terror attacks. The main Jewish military organization in British Mandate Palestine had a policy of restraint, but when the revisionist organization started to retaliate against Arab terror attacks with their own attacks, the mood in the shtetl improved, and many were even elated that Jews were willing to strike back, even if they had to hang for it.

Even with all these problems, the summer of 1936 was a pleasant one. We would go to the nearby forest to pick mushrooms. The little river that cut through the main street widened in a couple of places, and the local population would swim in these spots. As the male bathers were stark naked, the women found another spot to swim in, some distance away. Before and after swimming, we would bask in the sun. For me it was no pleasure, knowing that my skin would soon turn red and be covered with blisters by morning. A day later, the blisters would break and the skin peel painfully. A few days later, I would bask in the sun again and go through the same process. I never got used to the sun, and I finally learned to avoid it.

On rainy summer days, I spent hours with my friend Moishe Gelman in the parlour of his house. His father, Meir, loved gardening, especially tending to flowers. From the parlour, two windows looked out onto the beautiful flower beds. A grapevine climbed along lightweight scaffolds near the house, up to the top of the roof. There was just enough room to open the windows and inhale the fragrant smell of the flowers. Moishe and I would sit in front of the open windows, which were protected from the rain by the large grape leaves. We would watch the warm raindrops falling and being soaked up by the sea of flowers. I felt a sense of comfort and security on those days. It must have been there that I developed a liking, even affection, for a summer rain.

With vacation over, the school year of 1936–1937 began. The atmosphere at home was a bit subdued because Sheva left to study in the Pruzhany

Hebrew gymnasium. My sister's departure was difficult on all of us, though she came home every Friday to Saturday night. I am sure there were disagreements between my sister and me at times, but she always smoothed them over. She was very much like my mother, tolerant and forgiving, and she didn't carry a grudge or hold on to anger. My sister would bring home new songs from the bigger town, which we would all pick up immediately, the house filling with song. When she went back to Pruzhany every week, she left us all in a rather gloomy mood.

I was now in Grade 6. To my surprise, we had a Jewish teacher, Glier, from Grodno, who taught geography. The non-Jewish students did not show him the respect a teacher deserved and were much noisier than usual when he was teaching. We, the Jewish kids, tried to make up for it by behaving exceptionally well, knowing that the others were behaving badly out of spite.

With the start of the new school year, we were told that new textbooks on the Polish language were being issued. When I opened the book and looked at the first pages, I realized that it contained a lot of material of a different and ugly nature, like stories about Jews who swindled and cheated the poor Christians. On one page was a picture of a statue of Christ, standing with his hand stretched out. Underneath, in large print, was written: "This statue stands in the village of ______, on the spot where the last Jew of the village lived." This was a book from which we students were supposed to learn the Polish language to prepare us for life in the Polish society. Is it surprising that antisemitism was so rampant in Poland?

Antisemitic persecution was the worst for me during that school year. In my class of forty students, ten of us were Jews, with two boys, me and Laizer Eisenstein, my private Hebrew teacher's oldest son. Scholastically, there was the eternal race between us for first place in mathematics and physics.

My brother Liova was in Grade 2 at the Hebrew school, and on winter mornings, we would leave the house together at daybreak. I turned right down Mostowa to the Polish school, and Liova turned left down Kamieniecka Street to the Hebrew school. After school and a snack, I did my homework, which took two to three hours. I minded the store as my father had dinner, and as soon as he returned, I would try to sneak out, but I was not always successful. He would ask me about school, my lessons and homework. By the time we finished with my schoolwork, I knew it well, but he never let me feel this way and always advised me to go home to read it again. Facing our store was the house of my uncle Reuven. Not daring to leave the store and go straight to my friends, I would tell my father that I was going to my uncle's house, which my father tolerated.

During that winter, my group of friends became even closer knit. At the same time, a group of girls of about the same age formed an equally tight-knit circle. It is unclear to me now how we boys started meeting the girls. I do not doubt that it was deliberate. We always met as a group. A boy meeting with a girl on his own was unheard of in Shershev. One could see eighteen-year-old couples in the streets, but not younger. It was another year before we boys and girls dared to go out on a Saturday night walk together, not, God forbid, as couples but as a group. That took care of Saturday evenings. On the remaining evenings of the week, if we were not at Betar, we boys sat and talked and talked without end—about Zionism, about the unrest in Palestine, about the growing antisemitism in Poland and about the persecution of Jews in Germany. There was no shortage of topics to talk about.

With the arrival of spring in 1937, a series of decrees were issued that affected Jewish homeowners. Suddenly the authorities decided to modernize the streets inhabited by Jews—Mostowa and half of Ostrowiecka, as well as the market square, the town's Jewish centre—by issuing orders to replace the wooden sidewalks that had served Shershev for a hundred years with cement ones. This order was accompanied by an even more oppressive demand: all houses on those streets were to be painted in either dark green or shades of blue and grey, and if any of them were more than a metre away from the sidewalk, which most were, the owners were required to put up a fence and plant flowers. The fences were to be all the same size and the same colour as the house. The paint used in our part of the country had a linseed-oil base, and the thick wooden walls of our houses soaked up dozens of litres of paint, putting a heavy financial burden on the poor Jewish inhabitants of the shtetl. But if they did not comply, they faced exorbitant fines.

No sooner did the Jewish community comply with one decree than others followed. Soon it was a requirement that all chimneys were to be whitewashed and stay white. The same applied to the street gutters. I challenge anybody to keep a chimney white while constantly cooking and heating the house with wood. Better yet, whitewash a street gutter and see what it looks like after the rain. Sure enough, as soon as the rain would stop, the five local policemen would be out in the street writing fines.

The streets of Shershev were paved with cobblestones. An order came to get rid of the grass that was growing up between the stones. One could see men, women and children standing bent over, kneeling or sitting on the ground with knives, trying to get the stubborn grass roots out from between the closely set stones along the Jewish streets and in the marketplace. It was a futile attempt. By the time one piece of road was cleared, new grass was already sprouting in the space that had been cleared the week earlier, and the entire effort was wasted.

Hordes of inspectors and commissioners descended on Shershev and on the shtetls around us to extract from the Jews as much money as possible. It had been a yearly event for every scale and weight in the village businesses to be inspected and punched with an inspector's emblem. This year, an entire group of inspectors came and disqualified every scale and weight. Their own workers supposedly repaired the scales and adjusted the weights, charging exorbitant prices. The poor Jewish shopkeepers had no choice but to pay. There was no one to complain to about this outrageous and blatant robbery, as it was sanctioned by the government. Other commissions found other ways of squeezing out every złoty from Jews.

Another imaginative invention of the government to deprive Jewish shopkeepers of their livelihood was our first co-op store in Shershev. Two non-Jewish homes stood in the town square, and a co-op was opened in one of them. With a wink from the local officials, some local Christians bought shares in this endeavour. Big signs were hung in the windows of the co-op store, calling on the population not to buy from Jews. Soon, another co-op opened down the main street. This event had no effect on our business, but it affected other Jewish storekeepers, maybe more morally than materially.

Jewish families in the villages around us that had majority Christian populations had always wanted to move into a shtetl. It was difficult to keep a kosher home, give their children a Jewish education and, of course, find a match for a child while living among non-Jews. As antisemitism in Poland escalated, the lives of Jews in those villages were put in danger. In a village near Shershev, the villagers locked an elderly Jewish couple into their home, then set it on fire. The couple managed to escape through a window.

Around that time, the government decided to open a health centre in town. They were looking for a suitable place that consisted of four spacious, bright rooms in an easily accessible location in the centre of town. They liked our house. It was centrally located and had four rooms all facing the front, with two front entrances, one that could serve as the clinic entrance and the second as a private entrance for the nurses. A delegation came from the district, looked over our house and, after a short discussion among themselves, made my father an offer. It must have been a tempting one, for my father, after talking it over with my mother, accepted.

A carpenter closed up the three doors that connected the four front rooms to the others and we moved all the furniture into the remaining rooms. Now we had only four rooms and the kitchen. There was no room left for a maid, and it was the first time my mother had to do without one. Surprisingly, she managed, and she was no busier without a maid than with one.

Two countrywide boycotts were now in place in Poland. Jews led one against German-made products, and there were signs in the Jewish store windows in Polish and Yiddish proclaiming "We don't buy German merchandise." The anti-Jewish, Nazi-sympathizing Endek political party of Poland led the second boycott, which was against Jewish businesses and was much more serious and more effective. They were trying hard to deprive Jews of their livelihood.

On the road between Shershev and Brest-Litovsk was the town of Kobrin. It had a large population of Jews, and they owned most of the stores. In late spring of 1937, the government-built booths in a meadow outside of Kobrin and renting them out to Christians only. The farmers from the surrounding villages ignored the newly erected stores in the meadow and continued doing business in the town. One morning, on a market day, the police closed all the streets leading into town, ordering the farmers to unhitch their horses on that meadow—all an effort to deprive the Jewish storekeepers of their livelihood. They didn't realize that the farmers depended on the Jews as much as the Jews depended on the farmers. Almost all the tradesmen, artisans and craftsmen were Jews, and the farmers needed blacksmiths to repair their wagons and shoe their horses. They needed shoemakers, tailors, seamstresses, carpenters, masons and wagon-wheel makers. Above all, the Jews were needed to buy up the farmer's surplus produce. I believe that there could have been a quiet and even a harmonious coexistence between the Jewish and non-Jewish populations were it not for the interference of the government and the church. In Kobrin, the farmers left their horses outside the town and carried their produce on their backs into the shtetl. They were as unhappy with the new decree as the Jews were.

Another antisemitic decree was the one that prohibited the kosher ritual slaughter of animals. The instigator, Janina Prystor, tried to get the decree passed. Jews appealed, protested, wrote petitions, and tried to explain and justify the practice on religious grounds. Unfortunately, the ingrained antisemitism in the parliament was stronger than economic common sense or a sense of tolerance, justice and respect for other faiths. Eventually, the parliament compromised to a degree, allowing a certain number of cattle to be slaughtered according to Jewish law, but the total was minimal and included the entire animal, though Jews are not permitted to eat the hind part of the animal. Polish inspectors frequently visited the Jewish butcher shops to make sure that they were not selling unlicensed meat. The inspectors were not immune to bribes. Knowing the severity of the fine for selling unlicensed meat, they used to extract every groszy from the already impoverished butchers.

Despite the difficulties, life went on. A couple of young Shershev men from the Hashomer Hatzair Zionist movement succeeded in leaving for the Land of Israel. Only a trickle managed to get through the underground route with Aliyah Bet. It was a difficult and dangerous journey. Members of Betar had no chance of getting a permit to go to Palestine, and there was a shortage of inspiring leadership, so the local Betar closed. My friend Kalman Kalbkauf and I assumed the official leadership, but we didn't have a following. All we did was keep contact with the head command in Warsaw, sending them a couple of złoty monthly. But for all intents and purposes, the Betar ceased to exist. In our correspondence with Warsaw, I signed as *mefaked* (commander) and Kalman as secretary. I kept all Betar correspondence, records and stationery in our attic.

Kalman was my closest friend and confidant. What he and I shared was our dream of travelling to faraway places and our hope of a Jewish homeland. To realize our dream, we even started to build a small boat with another friend, Laizer Rotenberg. We worked at it during the entire two-month summer vacation, cutting timber and making the moulding to fit the frame. It was difficult, yet nobody was happier and more enthusiastic than us boys, doing what we thought we needed to do to materialize our dream. Ah! Those youthful years.

That summer, everyone either conversed about world politics or found something to complain about in the local Kehilla, the Jewish community organization. The central leadership of the Kehilla was in Pruzhany, which took in all the neighbouring shtetls, each of which had two representatives, but most of the members were Pruzhany residents. The members were democratically elected every couple of years in the shtetls, but there was always dissatisfaction with the results. How else can it be in a democracy? In Shershev, the same two men were elected time after time. They were my grandfather Yaakov Kopel and my friend's father Meir Gelman, the flower lover. From time to time, Gelman was replaced by Chatzkel Krugman.

In Shershev there was a shoemaker named Meir Chaim. He was a tall man with unusual strength and a loud voice. All week long, he worked long hours to provide for his wife and many children. On Shabbos, he would be up at six in the morning, sitting on the doctor's porch in the market square, his voice thundering halfway across the shtetl as he preached about the state of the world, shtetl politics and Kehilla politics. The doctor did not want to be awakened that early and told Meir Chaim to move on, but the next Shabbos morning, he was back in his favourite place, sharing his thoughts with the shtetl. Nobody wanted to start a discussion with him for fear of getting a punch in the nose, and they preferred to be on his good side.

There were a few tough Jews in Shershev with whom the average community member would not like to have a disagreement. Jews and non-Jews avoided crossing paths with these people. In a sense, they gave the downtrodden Jew a feeling of security, knowing that there were Jews unafraid to hit back. It also gave the roughnecks among the non-Jewish population reason to think twice before starting a brawl with the Jews.

That summer, I spent a lot of time in the store, sitting behind the shelves, reading books. I could sit there undisturbed for as long as I wanted. My father never interrupted me while I was doing my homework or reading. I read a lot, sometimes a book a day. The only bit of work I did was to help my father unpack the wooden cases of vodka and put the bottles on the shelves.

In Shershev, there were a few young men who didn't do much but sit and wait for a girl with a large dowry to marry them. Having nothing to do, they would come into the store and spend time with their peers. One could hear true news and half-truths, assumptions and wishful thinking, anything one wanted or did not want to hear in these conversations. After every lengthy discussion, someone would turn to my father and ask, "*Nu*, what do you say, Yitzchak?" One would think that my father had a direct line to every government leader. Coming home, my father would share with my mother some of the conversations he'd heard during the day. Some were sensible, some naive and some unbelievable.

It was no secret that Germany was arming itself and that Hitler was building a huge and powerful army. Any conversation inevitably turned to talk of war. The topic was familiar to my parents, as they had experienced it first-hand twenty years earlier with World War I, when my father was a soldier in the czar's army and my mother experienced hunger and deprivation under German rule between 1915 and 1918. Their stories triggered my imagination and awoke in me all kinds of fantasies in which I was the hero. My mother was a gifted storyteller, a family Auerbach trait, and her stories were spellbinding.

By late summer, my friends and I made only a half-hearted attempt to finish building our boat; our earlier enthusiasm was gone. The hours we spent working became more mechanical than creative. Deep in our hearts, each of us felt that we were labouring in vain, but nobody wanted to be the first to say it aloud. Our project came to an end at the start of the school year.

I did not look forward to the new school year of 1937–1938 given my experiences the previous year. To my surprise, things had changed. On the first morning of the school year, a few Christian boys started picking on us two Jewish kids, but a couple of other boys told them to leave us alone. Later, the boys were whispering to each other. Apparently, they came to an agreement to leave us alone. The atmosphere in the classroom changed completely. The non-Jewish boys began shaking our hands without making comments. Other persecutions ceased. Moreover, it seemed that the entire class was paying more attention to the teachers. Perhaps because it was the last year of the school, and the students wanted to take advantage of the opportunity to learn. My unwillingness to attend school disappeared.

The growth of antisemitism in Poland went hand in hand with the growth of Polish nationalism. This, in turn, provoked the many minorities living in Poland, including the Belarusian people, among whom we Shershev Jews lived. They considered themselves Russians, or at least closely related to the Russians, and they sympathized with the Soviet Union. I believe that any turnaround of the local population's attitude to Jews did not stem from their love for Jews but from their hatred of the Poles.

That winter was the last unmarred winter our family had together. It passed in dread and apprehension as we didn't know what to expect and what decrees the government would come up with next. Meanwhile, the antisemitic Endek party became less active. Throughout the winter, I sat with my family, doing homework, reading books and keeping an eye on my younger siblings. I felt smug about being able to help them. I also had a hobby collecting stamps, which was fashionable among youngsters in those days.

8
Premonitions

AS SOON AS the snow melted and the roads dried out in the spring of 1938, all kinds of government commissions descended on Shershev: the health commission, sanitary commission, beautifying commission, planning commission. The inspectors' only task was to find any excuse to penalize the Jewish storekeepers, to strangle them economically. Soon, Jews were being beaten up if they walked down a non-Jewish street. An atmosphere of hatred was felt across the land, and there was a series of anti-Jewish attacks. I heard an eyewitness account about a pogrom in Brest-Litovsk from my close friend Laizer Rotenberg, who was studying there. The perpetrators broke into Jewish-owned stores and warehouses and helped themselves to whatever they wanted. The mob dragged sacks of flour, sugar and grains out of the stores, poured the contents out into a heap and drenched it all with oil and kerosene. Going through the Jewish streets several days later, one could see the broken doors and windows of Jewish homes and stores, as well as furniture, pillows and mattresses lying in the streets, feathers flying all over.

With the successful reintegration of the contested Saar region, or Saarland, into Germany's borders, Germany's reoccupation of the Rhineland, and with the recent Anschluss of Austria, the appetite of the Polish government and Polish people for more territory grew. Pamphlets appeared everywhere, portraying beautiful, palm-covered sandy beaches and blue shores, with big letters proclaiming, "We want colonies!!!" Poland soon realized that the powers possessing colonies would not give them anything, so they decided to bully weaker neighbours like Lithuania, demanding that they restore diplomatic ties. Lithuania decided not to rock the boat, and their acceptance of the ultimatum was seen as a victory in Poland. Little did the Poles know what the Germans had in store for them.

And so my school year ended in June 1938, and I got better marks than I expected, but the mood was not conducive for celebrations. During that same summer, my uncle Eli came home after completing his two years of army service. Then my uncle Hershel left Shershev with his wife, Sheine, for Kamenets Litovsk, where he became a partner in his father-in-law's business. Eli's return from military service was not only a happy occasion for him, but for me too. He was only nine years older than me, and I considered him an older brother and looked up to him. I guess he found me to be a good listener, for he liked to share his experiences with me. How glad I was to walk with him as he told me about life in the army, even teaching me some of the songs they sang there.

Sheva spent that summer vacation at home, bringing a new repertoire of songs with her. Some of her out-of-town classmates came to visit her during the summer. I can still hear my mother talking about one of them: "How does such a young girl from a small town come to have such an eloquent Yiddish?"

At some point, young men began to appear in our house. They never remained alone with my sister or any of her friends. The only thing I had in common with those older boys was the game of chess. They were usually better chess players than I was, but from time to time I would beat one of them. I never analyzed why they came to play chess with me. Sheva was a good-looking girl, well educated and she was Yitzchak Kantorowitz's daughter.

My close friend Laizer Rotenberg also came home from Brest-Litovsk for the vacation. With his arrival, our group of friends came back to life. He had the best qualifications of a good friend: trustworthiness, solidarity, dependability, and he was neither an exaggerator nor a braggart. His courage and physical strength were also impressive.

The information from the Land of Israel was not encouraging. Arab terrorism did not let up, and there were new Jewish victims every day. My father took comfort in the fact that some Jews reacted and hit back. My mother mourned the new victims. Once, I mentioned to my mother that I would like to go to the Land of Israel. She would not hear of it. On another occasion I asked both my parents why we stayed in Poland; why didn't we go somewhere else? I received a Jewish answer, that is, my question was answered with a question: "And what will we live on somewhere else? Here at least, we are making a living."

The summer vacation ended in growing tension. There were no facilities for further schooling in Shershev for me. One possibility was the Hebrew gymnasium in Pruzhany, as the chances of a Jew to be accepted into the Polish gymnasium were minimal. Seeing no other viable option, I enrolled in the Hebrew one. But a couple of weeks later, my parents realized that it served no purpose. I would waste years getting a matriculation that was worthless in Poland. In previous years, children of merchants would not become tradesmen or artisans; it was considered beneath their dignity. But the new trade schools, where one could learn a trade and at the same time advance one's education, had become fashionable. My parents decided to take me out of the gymnasium and enroll me in the Jewish trade school in Brest-Litovsk.

The school had its own dormitory for out-of-town students, to which I was accepted. Students came from near and far. There was even a small group of boys from an orphanage in Warsaw. They had grown up in a non-Jewish environment and knew little of Jewish tradition, spoke no Yiddish and conversed only in Polish. That was strange for the rest of us, Jews from eastern Poland.

My school year in Brest-Litovsk started late because of my first few weeks in the gymnasium and the entry formalities. So I was in Shershev for an extra few days and spent it with my friends on the windblown streets in a depressed mood. What added to my foul disposition was the unusual number of ravens, which flew from one naked tree to the other, continuously cawing. They were like ominous messengers of terrible events to come.

In the fall of 1938, Hitler expelled "Polish" Jews from Germany. These were Jews who had settled in Germany before and during World War I, become German citizens, and lived there for decades. The German authorities picked them up in their homes, ordered them to leave behind their possessions and drove them to the Polish border. The Poles, in return, refused to accept these Jews, claiming that they had left their territories before Poland was recreated, that they were German citizens and thus had no right to Polish citizenship.

The homeless Jews were now stranded at the German-Polish border. The Germans even refused to allow anyone to bring them food from the German side. The Jewish communities in Poland campaigned to provide them with food. In Shershev, the entire community gathered in the large synagogue, and rich and poor contributed according to their means.

A refugee camp was set up for the thousands of Jews on the border, where they remained for many months until they were allowed into Poland.

Poland's appetite for more territory was still unquenched. With the dismemberment of Czechoslovakia earlier that fall, Poland had thrown itself over the devoured country like a bird over fallen prey, demanding her crumbs. The crumbs consisted of a piece of territory south of the Polish-Czech border, beyond the Olza River. The dying Czechoslovakia, torn apart by Nazi Germany and sold out by European democracies, was not in the position to challenge Poland and surrendered the territory.

It should have been clear where Hitler's politics and plans were leading. Yet Poland refused to see the writing on the wall, trying hard instead to mimic Germany in its grab for more land. I don't know how impressed the Poles were with that small piece of territory from

Czechoslovakia. I only know that in our part of Poland, the population, Jewish and non-Jewish alike, viewed it disdainfully.

With the onset of winter, something changed in the political air. It started with hints in the German press about Germany reclaiming the Free City of Danzig, and it quickly developed into a demand for the return of the entire Polish Corridor, the land between Germany and its territory of East Prussia that had been given to Poland after World War I. Poland began to mobilize its army in its primitive way.

That winter, the newspaper headlines proclaimed that Poland was hosting distinguished guests from Germany, like Göring. The guests were in Białowieża, taking part in a hunt. The next day, the same newspapers displayed on the front pages large photos of the successful hunt, including rows of dead animals and their exact numbers. Among them were over a hundred wild boars, several dozen deer and moose, and an assortment of other animals. Millions of Jews in Poland asked themselves the question: How naive could the Poles be?

In March 1939, the Polish government carried out the first mobilization. It consisted of last year's released men, who had completed their two-year compulsory military service. Among them were my uncle Eli and all his friends who had served at the same time. They were ordered to go to the railway station in Aranchytsy-Linovo, where further instructions would be given. My uncle later related that when he arrived at that railway station, everything was in chaos and panic because of the army's lack of organization and preparation.

In Shershev, and I am sure in all other towns and cities around Poland, the mobilization evoked fear and apprehension, despite the government's attempt to dispel the rumours of an imminent war.

In the spring, Germany demanded that Poland return Danzig to Germany, and Poland responded with continuous but small mobilizations and a feverish rearmament program. Except for a few hundred outdated tanks, the entire Polish army depended on horses. The army began to buy horses, and the only source was the farmers. Lack of money was no hindrance, as the government simply began to print more. The government paid exorbitant prices for horses, double and triple their value. Suddenly, the farmers had a lot of money to spend, and spend they did. They spent on clothing, footwear and bicycles. Some even removed their thatch roofs and replaced them with shingles, and for the time being, Jewish storekeepers and merchants were making a decent livelihood.

Hitler's Germany was now demanding not only Danzig, but also Pomerania, the strip of land connecting Poland to the Baltic Sea, but at the same time cutting East Prussia in half. The question of if there would be war was replaced by the question of when. The newspaper analysts predicted that it would start in the fall, right after the harvest, after the crops had been taken in, ensuring there would be a food supply for the army and the population.

At that time, many Jews already wanted to get out of Poland, although in their most horrible nightmares they could not have foreseen what the future held for them. Unfortunately, the doors of every country in the world were closed to them. The Jews who wrote to a foreign embassy in Warsaw for a visa received outright refusals. At best, they were informed that there was a long list of earlier applicants who were being considered, and therefore their application could not be accepted.

A continuous flow of news came via newspapers and radios, some of which we Jews saw as quite ironic. The Polish papers and radio complained that German youngsters were beating up Poles in the streets of Danzig, breaking windows and boycotting the Polish stores. These were the very same words that Jews had used to accuse the Poles. Now the Poles of Danzig had the experience of being persecuted instead of persecuting.

On those long summer days of 1939, we sat up till after midnight and talked. I had a premonition that this quiet lifestyle was not to last much longer, and the days became precious to me. I listened with intensity to my mother's beloved voice, her instructions, fables and parables. Some she had acquired from her own experience and others had their roots in the Talmud. One piece of advice my mother gave me, which she repeated to me several times, was that when you are making a deal with someone, always let the other person know that they are getting the better part of the deal or the bargain. I kept to this principle all my life. I doubt if this practice helped me financially—in fact, I know it did not—but it did wonders for my peace of mind. I knew that I had not wronged anybody or violated any moral standard, and I always slept with a clear conscience. My mother's instructions and traditional Jewish upbringing served me as a trustworthy moral guide in my most difficult times.

In the summer of 1939, a guest from the Land of Israel came to Shershev, Sonia Shemesh (née Pinsky). Sonia was the aunt of my two good friends, the brothers Rotenberg, and had married my father's cousin, Chaim Shemesh, in Palestine. She came to Shershev with a young daughter by the name of Lauma. The child was just beginning to talk, and the few dozen words she knew were all in Hebrew. In Shershev, that was quite a sensation. Imagine, a child only a year old, and she already speaks Hebrew! Sonia's arrival caused a commotion in the shtetl, and even more excitement for me. Despite the disparity in our ages, I felt close to her. There was a continuous rivalry between the Rotenberg brothers and me to hold the Israel-born baby. Sonia brought personal regards from over a dozen Shershev youths who had gone to the Land of Israel. She also gave a precise description and portrayal of the situation there in the third year of relentless Arab terror.

In the beginning of July, my uncle Eli, who had been mobilized in March, came home for a ten-day leave, which he had earned as a prize for taking first place in artillery exercises for hitting moving targets. My uncle arrived under a blanket of secrecy. Nothing about where he was stationed or what he did was to be mentioned. Local people, Jewish and non-Jewish, came to him to inquire about their sons, brothers and menfolk, but he was forbidden to answer them. He told us, his immediate family, that he and some others from the shtetl and the vicinity were posted near Mława, close to the border of East Prussia. Ever since the mobilization, they had been improving their trenches, in which they spent most of their time. Being under strict orders not to tell anything, he did not seek company and spent most of his time with his parents and with us. The days of his leave passed swiftly. We all accompanied him to the bus, the women with tears in their eyes.

To add to the sadness of Eli's departure, the political situation was getting worse. The non-Jewish population was busy taking in the harvest, but the Jewish tradesmen, artisans and storekeepers became apathetic and lost interest in everything, being fully consumed by the events of the day. Unable to sit at their work, they would congregate in the market square and talk politics.

Throughout the month of August, men were continuously called up to the army. The discussions revolved around the impending war and what to do when the front line would get closer. Nobody had any illusions about the might of the German army, especially in comparison to the Polish army, and everybody expected a Polish defeat if Poland's allies, England and France, didn't come to her rescue. Still, we expected that Poland would hold out alone against Germany for six months at least.

The self-appointed politicians of the shtetl were spending more and more time in our store. One of them turned to my father and asked, "What will we do when the front line reaches us?"

My father answered, "Then we will run to the Russians."

"But the Russians aren't letting anybody in even now," said the other.

"So we will go against the Soviet bayonets," answered my father.

A picture came to my mind of a row of Russian soldiers along the Polish border, standing shoulder to shoulder with one knee on the ground. Each held a rifle in his hand, a shining sharp bayonet attached to the gun barrel, pointing toward Poland, and thousands of Jews were running toward them, impaling themselves on those bayonets. But this thought did not stay with me long because, I reasoned, Russians are not animals and Communism is not Hitlerism. After all, the Communists represented the better human values, unlike Nazism, which represented the worst. The Russians would let us in and would protect us from the Nazis.

The end of August was approaching, and the media kept reporting that the German army was concentrated along the Polish border, and that the Germans were accusing Poland of all kinds of provocative violations. The Polish radio assured the public that Poland's allies would come to her rescue should Germany attack, and with the three of them united, Germany would be defeated in no time. The truth is that the population of eastern Poland, which consisted mostly of Belarusians, Ukrainians and Jews, did not have much confidence in the Polish army, but they had too much confidence in the two great powers, England and France.

BOOK TWO
World War II
(1939–1941)

9
War Breaks Out

ON THURSDAY, AUGUST 31, 1939, at about four in the afternoon, the local government plastered large announcements, proclaiming a total mobilization. Groups of people began to form around each proclamation, reading the large print carefully over and over, as if by rereading, they would get more information out of it. The groups of people seemed apathetic, devoid of energy. They just stood there, looking at the announcements in silence, or whispering to one another. Nobody seemed to want to go home. They stood there as if waiting for something or for somebody. My friend Laizer Rotenberg ran home and came back with a camera, wanting to take a picture of this important moment for posterity, he said. Eventually, we all dispersed home. I felt a fair measure of apprehension, but also excitement.

On the next morning, Friday, September 1, 1939, the sun shone brightly. Everyone went about their business, but the lack of enthusiasm was visible. The men who had been called up to the army were on their way to the railway station. I am sure that their families had not slept, and that now the women were sitting at home in tears. My father went to open the store as usual. My mother was busying herself in the kitchen, and Sheva was helping her. It was too early to start visiting my friends, so I walked out into the yard.

A few minutes later, I saw our neighbour's son, Leibel Feldman, pull up to his parents' house on a bicycle. Within minutes, our neighbour came over and told us that his son had just come from Białowieża, which had been bombarded earlier that morning. The police had confiscated all private vehicles for the army, so he came home by bicycle.

The population was edgy, particularly after the general mobilization of the previous days. People began to gather around the few radios in town. There were three radios in Jewish homes: one at the druggist's, one at the doctor's and one at my uncle Reuven's. The radios were put in front of the open windows for all to hear.

At ten o'clock on that memorable morning, President Mościcki addressed the nation in a patriotic speech. He officially announced that Germany had attacked Poland and that battles were being fought all along the Polish-German border. I still remember how he said, "We will fight for every Polish threshold and for every roadside crossing." As expected, he finished the speech with a promise of victory, "for God and justice are on our side."

One of the first acts of the Shershev police was to order my father to lock our store so that alcohol would not be available. The same applied to the four restaurants in town. They knew that alcoholic drinks were the best commodities to have during war. The townspeople remembered other things from World War I, like the fires that burned down houses, and the plundering by undisciplined and unscrupulous soldiers. People came up with all kinds of ideas to protect themselves. My family had two large trunks with forged metal straps. They must have belonged to my mother's parents. Sheva and I helped my parents fill these trunks with clothing, tablecloths, linen, underwear, silverware and other valuable and precious items. We also used a couple of large wooden crates that were ordinarily used for shipping vodka to pack other items. Kalman Kalbkauf's father had a horse and wagon, and he came and took everything to his large orchard, where we buried it all and concealed it so well that a stranger would not be able to tell that the ground had been touched. Every family in the shtetl did a similar thing.

My parents knew that our store, full of alcoholic drinks and cigarettes, made a tempting target for thieves. Soldiers would throw themselves at liquor sooner than at gold because they knew that liquor could get you just about anything in wartime. So, in the quiet of the night, my father and I made a few trips to the store, removing a few hundred bottles of liquor, including two dozen bottles of spirit 96 per cent pure alcohol, which was twice as strong as regular vodka and twice as valuable. We packed the spirit and half the vodka in sacks, wrapping them first in straw. Under cover of the night, we went into the garden and dug out some bean plants with the long stakes that they were wrapped around and carefully lowered the bags with the liquor. After covering the hole, we replanted the beans. The next morning, I went into the garden, and even I could not see anything suspicious.

The police advised the public to build bomb shelters—nothing elaborate, just a hole in the ground, covered with boards and piles of earth or stones. I tried to dig a hole in our yard but gave up because the ground was too rocky. The most impressive shelter I saw in the shtetl was Daniel Meister's, the blacksmith's. It was a large ditch dug in a U shape and was quite a roomy shelter. With so much room, they not only took in clothing and dishes, but even furniture.

As just about everyone had something buried, people worried about theft, so neighbours organized night watches. Every ten or fifteen neighbours got together and took turns patrolling the neighbourhood. In our family, we divided the night into two parts; I patrolled up to one or two in the morning, and my father took over after me, until daybreak. Apparently, nobody was sleeping very well, for instead of the expected two or three men on watch, there were always four, five or more. We patrolled the market square, walking into yards to look for anything suspicious. While walking, we would meet other groups from neighbouring areas, chat a bit and sit down for a rest. The nights were quiet and the moon was bright, and even the mosquitoes did not dare to buzz. A few times during those peaceful nights, I heard the distant drone of a single airplane, reminding us of the carnage that was taking place not too far away.

Who could have imagined how poorly the Polish army was doing in the first week of the war? Newspapers failed to appear, and the only news came from Pruzhany, which did not have more information than we did. The radio played patriotic and martial music, with constant interruptions of coded commands. One did not have to be a genius to know that things were not looking good.

On the third day of the war, our mood changed for the better. We heard that England and France had declared war on Germany. Those who had experience from World War I, including my father, warned that it would take months before England and France would be prepared to open another front. Their hope was that Poland would be able to hold Germany back for the next few months until England and France were ready.

The first ten days passed uneventfully. It was hard to believe that Poland was at war. One late afternoon, a plane appeared overhead. It did not look impressive or threatening. After a couple of circles above the shtetl, the plane opened fire. It lasted no more than ten seconds, but that was enough to send everyone running. There were no soldiers in or around Shershev, and nobody knew what the pilot was shooting at. He made another circle or two and flew away, leaving behind a subject of conversation for a day or two.

Then the first refugees began to appear. They were civilian Poles who were running away from the approaching Germans, and they were well dressed and looked prosperous. They travelled with their own cars, even limousines, despite the fact that all private vehicles in our part of the county had been mobilized. They paid good money for whatever they bought and were prepared to pay exorbitant sums for gasoline, which was not available in Shershev for any price. Among those refugees was the wife of the *voivode*, Kostek-Biernacki, the governor of our province, Polesie. She drove in her own car, and her daughter turned to the local police for help obtaining gasoline, but even they could not turn up any. Somebody suggested using rubbing alcohol instead of gasoline, and the chief of police ordered my father to give them all the rubbing alcohol he had in the store. The driver filled up the tank, and they drove away.

In the following days, more refugees arrived. They were mostly young Poles, and many had brand-new rifles that were in much better condition than those used by the army. Those refugees also behaved properly and paid for whatever they bought. To our surprise, there were no Jewish refugees among them.

A day or two later, we woke up to find out that the local police had disappeared. Shershev remained without a government or anyone to keep order. The Shershev Jewish community took the threat of a pogrom very seriously, especially when some Christians began to talk about it in the market square. Some of the prominent members of the Jewish community got together and decided to send a delegation to Pruzhany in the hope that there was still a government representative there. The delegation left at sunrise by horse and buggy, and they were back before sunset, bringing with them ten rifles and ten cartridges. The rifles were of a very old vintage, but still operational. What was to be kept strictly a secret was the number of cartridges that came with them. Would potential attackers have known the limited amount of ammunition, the weapons would not have stopped a pogrom.

Jewish men, former soldiers who had not been mobilized or who had come back because of lack of uniforms or rifles, volunteered to patrol the town square. That was where the bulk of the potential troublemakers gathered, especially in the evenings. The armed men conducted patrols of the Jewish streets and alleys in pairs so that there were always ten armed men in the streets, giving the Jewish population a certain degree of tranquility.

How long ten armed Jews with one cartridge per rifle could protect the entire shtetl was questionable. There were rumours that people in the nearby villages were organizing to join the local non-Jewish population in a pogrom. There was even an attempt to kill the most feared Jew in town, the blacksmith Srulkah Meister, who was both strong and fearless. On one of those lawless nights, he was sitting in his brother Daniel's house on Kamieniecka Street, which was a non-Jewish street except for a few houses, when somebody fired at him from the street. Srulkah had the presence of mind to slam his heavy callused hand down on the glass kerosene lamp, shattering it and throwing the room into darkness. Thus, he deprived his would-be assassin of another chance to fire at him. The people in the house could see a man running away but did not dare give chase to a man with a gun in his hand.

10

Under Soviet Control

FROM THE ONLY radio station in Warsaw that was still broadcasting intermittently, we could gather that there was not much of Poland left. Yet there was no sign of war in our parts. People began to listen to Radio Moscow as most understood Russian. On September 17, Radio Moscow announced that the Polish army had been destroyed and that the Red Army had crossed the Polish border. The Soviet foreign minister, Molotov, delivered a speech on the radio, stating that the Red Army marched into Poland in order to protect their brethren, the Ukrainians and Belarusians, in their time of need. A day or two later, Moscow announced that the artificial Polish government left the country, "leaving our brethren to their fate." The German army closed in around Warsaw.

One afternoon, a group of thirty or so peasants rode into Shershev on bicycles with an assortment of ancient rifles on their shoulders. They encountered the first two-man patrol, one of whom was my father's brother Reuven. The two men, finding themselves surrounded by a dozen armed men, gave up their rifles. Having disarmed the first patrol, those armed villagers proceeded to the market square, disarming the other patrols on the way. In the market square, they found a large crowd of people who did not know what to make of the situation.

They ordered the storekeepers to open the stores and to continue doing business. Our store remained closed because of what we were selling. Their spokesman announced to the growing crowd that they were part of an underground Communist organization, and they were taking control of the law and order in town until a representative of the Soviet Union arrived. The crowd sighed with relief that there would not be a pogrom.

The storekeepers opened their stores. Not being able to enter our store, I went over to see what was happening in my grandfather's hardware store. A short while later, some of the armed men came in. The one who seemed to be in charge told my grandfather to make sure to stay open until 6:00 p.m. and to open the next morning at 8:00 a.m. I watched with a keen eye the attitude of the group of armed men. They strode across the heavy wooden floor with confidence, walking over to the shelves, opening boxes, looking into every carton and corner. I heard one exclaiming "Eto nashe, eto vsio nashe"—*It is ours, it is all ours*. I felt that all it would take to transform this supposedly Communist defender of beautiful ideals into a troublemaker was a word or a nod from his superior. I saw how volatile these men were, and how easy it would be to turn from a human being into a beast.

That night, Jews did not patrol their streets nor did they sleep restfully. The next morning, the group of Communists attempted to organize a temporary governing body in the shtetl. They took over the police station and even recruited a few local young men into their ranks, among them a couple of Jews. A day or two later, rumours circulated that the Soviet army had entered Pruzhany. It took a few more days before we saw real representatives of the Soviet Union. A few truckloads of soldiers arrived and stopped in the market square. They were immediately surrounded by a mob of locals who bombarded them with all kinds of questions. Their looks and attire were not impressive. The uniforms were simple and devoid of any decoration. Their boots were well worn, Russian style, pushed down accordion-like. Their caps were unattractive, with a cloth point on top. Their rifles were long, and the unusually long bayonets had no sheaths, and dangled pitifully from the soldiers' belts, or were tied with a piece of cord to the gun barrel.

The soldiers smoked cigarettes rolled in newsprint. For tobacco they used what they called *koroshky*, chopped up tobacco stems. The whole picture evoked sympathy, even compassion, among us, but I admit to having also felt some smugness.

The soldiers conducted themselves decently, even politely, without using a single offensive or vulgar word. Yet looking at them closely, the crowd detected a hidden need and began to shower them with questions about the availability of all sorts of items in the Soviet Union. The answer was always the same: "U nas vsio yest"—*We have everything*. That answer became so automatic and common in the first few weeks after the Soviets arrived that it turned into a joke, which went as follows: A group of locals ask the Soviet soldiers the usual questions. Is there enough bread in the Soviet Union? Yes, their spokesman answers, plenty. What about butter? Plenty. And sugar? All you want. Vodka? You can get all you can drink. *Tsores* (troubles)? Yes, plenty. And we will send you ten carloads soon.

Still, on those first days, the Soviet soldiers were welcome guests. We realized that they represented a country and a government that had come to stay permanently. After all, they had controlled this area for several hundred years before, and under Bolshevik rule, Jews were not persecuted. So what could be wrong about it?

Now the only source of news was Radio Moscow, to which we listened regularly. On September 28, Radio Moscow announced that Warsaw had capitulated to the Germans. Moscow did not hide its joy and was gloating about the fall of the Polish capital. On October 5, Hitler reviewed his soldiers during a military parade in Warsaw, and Moscow Radio reported every move.

In the nearby town of Pruzhany, the Soviets had settled in. Besides the military, many civilians came, mostly Party members. They came to be named "Easterners" by the locals. Almost two weeks after the Red Army crossed the Polish border, some dozen Easterners came to Shershev and rented rooms from the locals. Those with families rented parts of homes and moved in with their meagre possessions. Then more and more started to arrive.

The experience of World War I had taught people that the two essential items needed in hard times were salt and kerosene. Being in an agrarian zone of the world, food could be obtained for money or bartered from the farmers. Salt and kerosene had to be brought from far away, making them at times unobtainable. The demand for salt and kerosene created a panic in town, and people began hoarding. The storekeepers were deprived of their sources of supply which were mostly in the western, industrialized part of Poland, now under German control. But even the bit of industry in the eastern part of Poland, now under Soviet control, came to a stop as all commerce ceased. Additionally, the Soviets devalued the Polish złoty to the value of their ruble. This made any article dirt cheap, particularly for the Easterners, who bought whatever was available and in quantities never seen before. The local population followed their example, sensing that not everything, if anything at all, was available in the Soviet Union, as the first soldiers or civilians had been saying. The stores were emptied in no time, and their doors closed.

That first month after the Soviets' arrival was the honeymoon period, and people felt free and liberated. Jews went to the synagogues on Shabbos, and Christians went to their churches. In general, an elated mood prevailed all around.

On a bright Saturday morning, while my father, my little brother and I were sitting in the synagogue, in walked my sister Sonia, who was then eight years old, and told us that the local police, or militiamen, were conducting a search of our house. We left the synagogue immediately. With pounding hearts we entered our house, finding my mother standing in the middle of the living room frightened and confused, with one arm around my seventeen-year-old sister, Sheva, and the other arm around Leiba, who was six. The house was filled with Soviet police who were searching, opening the drawers of every dresser, cupboard and closet. They were in every room, in the attic, and even in the woodsheds.

Though we had buried some of our liquor, we left some of it in the house in closets. They had found it all and displayed it on the floor.

Yet they continued the search. I went up to the attic to see what the militiamen were doing there. I saw the box containing stationery and stamps and the correspondence that I had kept up with the head office of Betar in Warsaw. I realized how ignorant the militiamen were, for they looked into that box several times and ignored its contents. Would they have understood what it meant, they would have had enough evidence to send us all to Siberia. To be a Zionist under the Soviets was tantamount to being a counter-revolutionary.

A couple of the men went out to our yard and began to prod the ground to see if it had been dug up lately. But the ground remained unyielding to them just as it had been to me when I tried to dig a bomb shelter. The one in command ordered his men to pack up the liquor they had found and they took it away.

It did not take long for us to find out what had happened. A couple of Jewish young men had gotten carried away with the enthusiasm of the new "liberators" and volunteered to cooperate with them. These men tried to prove their loyalty to the Soviets by squealing on someone, even a friend or relative. One of them, a young man with the ironic name of Tzadik, which means a pious or a righteous man, later had the insolence to brag about it.

My parents were very upset and uneasy about all this. By then, the authorities were well staffed with Easterners, who held all the major positions as managers, supervisors and militiamen. If they could come in the middle of the day to conduct a search for no reason at all and confiscate merchandise, who knew what else they could come up with? The next day, I dragged my box of Betar correspondence down from the attic and threw everything into the oven, watching as it slowly turned into ashes.

A couple of days went by, and we began to hope that the militia had forgotten about us, that being in possession of so much vodka they could not stand the temptation and drank it, thus annulling the whole affair, erasing it from paper and from their memory. We began to sleep more easily. A week or so later, after midnight, we were awakened from an uneasy slumber by a loud banging on the door. In a panic, we all jumped out of our beds and quickly got dressed. Opening the door, we were confronted by two militiamen who had come for our father. Without a word, they took him to the station.

My mother was confused and scared by the midnight awakening, and she remembered the ruthlessness of the Bolsheviks during their retreat in 1920, when soldiers had taken her wedding ring, almost taking her finger with it. My mother grabbed Sheva and me and with intensity said to us, "Run to the militia and don't let them shoot your father."

Her words left me stunned. The thought of my father being arrested was frightening enough, but to be shot? It had never entered my mind. The two of us set out immediately for the militia headquarters. On the way, many frightening thoughts went through my mind, which sped up our run.

When we arrived, breathless, at the station, a militiaman barred our way, telling us to wait outside. We remained outside, not knowing what to do. We figured that they would not shoot our father in the building but take him outside to the yard, in which case we would see him and could beg them to have mercy on him. With those dark thoughts, we remained standing on the sidewalk in front of the station. The long minutes turned into hours. About two hours later, the front door opened, and our father came out alone. We ran over and bombarded him with questions. He answered calmly that the chief of the militia said that, as the merchandise was not hidden, but simply in the house, he should come in the morning to pick it up and should sell it in the store on the following day. We were happy to have our father back alive, but it was difficult to fathom a system where even a positive or benign message had to be delivered in such a frightening way.

In the morning, my father hired a man with a horse and buggy to pick up the vodka and take it straight to our store. The news that there would be vodka on sale had spread around the town, and there was a long line in front of the store. Fortunately, a couple of militiamen appeared to keep order. In a matter of a couple of hours, our store was emptied, and we were left with a drawer full of nearly worthless rubles.

I believe that was the last time that liquor or tobacco of such quality was sold in Shershev. My parents looked around the empty shelves of the store with a heavy heart, locked the doors that guarded nothing behind them and went home in a depressed mood.

The Soviets wanted to show that everything was available in the Soviet Union, as they had stated. And as there was a great demand for salt and kerosene, they started to deliver the two items. First a fifty-ton carload of salt arrived in bulk, like gravel or sand. A hundred local farmers were ordered to go to the railway station with their horses and buggies to bring the salt to Shershev. The next day, from early morning, people lined up with containers for one kilo of salt. The fear of a shortage of salt drove people to line up again and again until all fifty tons of salt were gone. I looked at the salt and thought that nobody would have touched this coarse and lumpy stuff before the war. Now they were willing to stand in line for hours to buy fifty tons in a matter of a few hours, more than would be sold in Shershev in a whole year in normal times.

Shortly after the salt, a cistern of kerosene arrived. The militiamen went around the shtetl confiscating empty kerosene barrels from former storekeepers. Again, some of the local farmers and Jewish wagon drivers were sent with the empty barrels to the railway station, where they pumped the kerosene into the barrels and brought them home. At seven in the morning, an official knocked on our door and told my father that the kerosene would be sold from our store, and we would help with the distribution. I dressed quickly and went to our store. By that time everybody knew of the kerosene, and the line seemed to be a kilometre long, with men, women and children holding some kind of vessel, waiting for that litre of kerosene. As soon as they got it, they went back in line for another litre. By evening, all the kerosene was sold out. Some bureaucrats took the keys of the store and never returned.

The school year started late and was not coordinated with all the new Soviet-acquired territories. I went back to Brest-Litovsk, back to the dormitories. Substantial changes had been made in the school and in the dorms. The dorms, which had been under the management of the Jewish Organization for Rehabilitation through Training (ORT) and were kosher, became a government institution. The same happened to the school, and it was compelled to conform to Soviet whim. On the street where our dorms were located was a Polish technical school, which was known in the city and its environs as a hotbed of antisemitism, where a Jewish student would not dare set foot. The Soviet education department decided to unite the two schools.

The new director of our school was a Jew from central Poland, who had to be a Communist to get such a responsible job. He had become a Communist out of deep conviction and—which was rare—to improve the lot of the oppressed masses and create a better tomorrow for humanity. He was the sort of idealist who attained his belief through the highest intellect and boundless faith. He was also a good administrator. His most outstanding quality was the way in which he approached us students. He saw and understood each one of us and tried hard to do as much as he could for us. When I think of those days, I wonder what happened to that talented and dedicated man.

Some twenty-five non-Jews enrolled in the school. The new students were Polish high school students from western Poland who had escaped the Germans and now found themselves trapped under Soviet rule. They felt uncomfortable among a Jewish majority, but according to the Soviet law of equal minority rights, they had to put up with us. They weren't even allowed to utter the word "*Żyd*" or "Jew" in Polish but had to refer to a Jew as "*Yevrey*," which means "Hebrew" in Russian.

Up to then, in all the sixteen years of my life, I had never tasted *treyf*, non-kosher food. Pork, which was the staple food of the local non-Jewish population, intrigued and puzzled me. I did not know of any Jew in Shershev who had ever tasted it, except for those who had served in the army. Many Jews believed that pork fat was healthy because non-Jews applied it to sores and wounds to speed up healing.

Our breakfast in the dormitories consisted of bread and butter with tea or black coffee. When there was no butter, we each got a piece of cheese or sausage. One could have all the bread one desired, but the rest was allocated. With the Soviets, initially even the bread was rationed, and we received three slices of thinly buttered bread for breakfast and three dry slices of bread for lunch. Fortunately, my parents sent me cheese and honey from home. Slowly our food began to improve, and we started to receive cheese for breakfast.

One morning, we received a piece of sausage. Immediately, a rumour started circulating that the sausage was *treyf*. I looked around and saw that many ate it with gusto while others hesitated. Finally, unable to resist the temptation, they ate it too. Eventually everyone was eating the sausage. I bit into it as well. The taste was the same as last year's kosher sausage, and I consoled myself by telling myself that it may have been kosher. But that night, while lying in bed, I tormented myself with the thought that I had made myself unclean because of a piece of sausage. Was it worth it? I decided on that sleepless night not to eat it again. But within a couple of days, sausage was served again. This time I did not vacillate that much and ate it, realizing that sausage was going to become a frequent part of our diet. That night, I felt remorse, but I did sleep. When sausage was again served a couple of days later, I did not make a big deal of it, but I felt that I had lost something decent, something humane.

We spent eight hours at school, four in theoretical lessons and four in practical lessons. The theoretical lessons consisted of subjects like mathematics, geometry, physics, metallurgy and the Russian language. Most of the teachers and instructors were the same prewar Polish ones. Despite the reputation of the Polish technical school as antisemitic, the faculty behaved appropriately toward the Jewish students.

There were quite a few families in Shershev whose spirits were not lifted under Soviet rule—those whose husbands and sons had been mobilized into the Polish army and did not return. My uncle Eli was still not back. His absence affected all of us, his extended family. My grandmother Chinkah would putter around the house, crying all day.

My father and his brother Reuven visited their parents almost every day to encourage them and give them hope. Finally, my father decided to travel to Brest-Litovsk to see if he could find something out in the provincial capital.

When I met my father in Brest-Litovsk, I found him very discouraged. As we were leaving the restaurant where we met, I felt in my father's words a sense of resignation that I had never heard before. I felt a heaviness in my heart, bordering on anguish. This feeling was not strange to me, as I had felt it for my mother as I watched her busy in the kitchen and the house from early morning to late at night. She made sure that everything was in order and in place and that each of us was looked after. She exhibited so much tenderness and sympathy, not only for us, but also for strangers, whose troubles and suffering would move her to tears. My father, like most fathers in those days, must have learned to control his emotions, not only in relation to others, but even toward his own family. In those days, neither I, nor my friends or contemporaries, were ever hugged or kissed by our fathers or heard a statement of love—not even a compliment.

By the fall of 1939, the Jewish population of Brest-Litovsk had increased tremendously. Brest-Litovsk was now full of Jewish refugees who had escaped across the new border between Germany and the Soviet Union, which was close by. Many succeeded in finding accommodation, but others did not. They moved into synagogues, Jewish public buildings and into hallways of apartment buildings. The saddest sight for me when I went home by train was seeing those refugees packed together on the floor of the station. The sanitary conditions were appalling, and rumours of spreading diseases began to circulate. Their situation became so intolerable that some even decided to return home to live under Nazi rule.

While in the dorms, I got mail and parcels from home somewhat regularly. In fact, there was nothing regular about that time. There was no more transportation by bus from Shershev to Pruzhany as the buses had been mobilized at the outbreak of the war and were never replaced. All that was left were a couple of horse-and-buggy owners who were trying to eke out a living by driving people from Shershev to Pruzhany. At times, one could hitchhike a ride with a passing Soviet vehicle. If one managed finally to get to the railway station in Aranchytsy-Linovo, the train was never on time. The waiting time could be anywhere from six hours to a couple of days. It took many months till the trains became more dependable.

I corresponded often with my parents. One day I got a letter from them in which they informed me that the local officials had ordered them to vacate the house, giving them three days to move out. The law in the Soviet Union dictated how large a home could be, and as ours was bigger than required, and one of the most recently built, they decided to nationalize it—that is, to take it away without compensation. Besides, there were a few points stacked against us: my parents were merchants and capitalists, and my grandfather was the town mayor. Those points made our family undesirable in the eyes of the Soviets, and we could at any time expect a one-way ticket to Siberia. Not wanting to antagonize them, my family moved into the same three rooms at my grandparents' house that we had lived in when I took sick at the age of three. The local people had said that my father put his body, heart and soul into his house, as if he was going to live forever. And now total strangers had made him leave. In a way, I was glad that I was not there. To have to see my mother's tears would have hurt me more than the loss of the house. It was difficult for me to imagine what it would be like to go to Shershev now, and instead of going to our large and comfortable home, to walk up to my grandparents' house and be content with three rooms and a shared kitchen, but I slowly got used to the idea.

I later found out that the Soviets nationalized seven houses in town, six Jewish and one Christian. All were the nicest and biggest houses in the market square.

In November, I received the good news that my uncle Eli had

returned from German captivity and was home and well. A couple of weeks later, he came to Brest-Litovsk to complete some formalities, and I admired how quickly he adjusted to normal life.

During that early winter, a few of the students in the dorms were expelled. What happened was that a government commission appeared one evening to investigate everyone's "social background." They asked: What was your parents' occupation before the war? What are their holdings? How big is your house? Have you any relatives abroad? And so on. After that investigation, we were told to write home to get a statement of our family's "social background" from the local authorities and forward it to the director of the dorms.

When my turn came, I knew that it was not advisable to be a Zionist. All I told them was that my father had been a czarist soldier in the war, was badly wounded and is an invalid. They asked if I had relatives abroad, and for some unexplainable reason, the word "no" came from my mouth. The bigger problem was to get the letter on my social background from the authorities in Shershev. My father went to the local office, not expecting miracles. Entering the main room, where a few secretaries were sitting, he saw a familiar face. It was a local farmer's son who made violins in his spare time. My father had bought a violin from him when I was learning to play, paying him the full price without arguing. My father went straight to him and told him what he needed. The secretary, a bright young man, wrote as my father asked. The letter read, "Moisey [Russian for Moishe] Kantorowitz is the son of Isaac who has no home and who used to receive a war invalid's pension." I could not have dreamt of a better recommendation than that slip of paper. Later, when the commission concluded their work, and the rejected students were gone, we told each other how we had succeeded in obtaining a favourable report from the authorities. Most got it by bribery, which was prevalent in the Soviet Union.

Shortly before the new year of 1940, my father visited Brest-Litovsk, and I decided to go back to Shershev with him, as it was a day or two before the start of the winter vacation. It was so good to be back at home, even if it was our grandparents' house now, to be with my mother, to feel her love, her affection and tenderness. It must have been difficult for her to try to disguise her feelings about losing our house in front of us and to give us her full time and attention. Sheva also came home from Pruzhany. Eli was there, and we had the opportunity to hear about his experiences in the short Polish-German war and in the prisoner-of-war camp. During the Siege of Warsaw, a German shell had exploded where my uncle was stationed, wounding four soldiers. The other soldiers jumped out of the ditch and tried to find cover, abandoning their wounded comrades, but my uncle Eli went back to save all four wounded soldiers. His commanding officer shook his hand and promised him a medal for bravery at a more acceptable time, which never came.

During that winter vacation, a terrible sickness was spreading around. The Soviets called it *meningit* (meningitis), a plague none of us had ever heard of before. Children and teenagers were most susceptible, and those who caught it succumbed to it. A rumour spread that drinking vodka and smoking were a good protection against the sickness. We boys jokingly added playing cards as a remedy. That was the only time in my life that I tried to smoke. For some reason, the sickness was more prevalent among the non-Jewish population. In the middle of that winter, the epidemic subsided. But the sickness, the unusually cold winter and the shortage of all kinds of commodities were all blamed on the Soviets.

Over the winter, a few local families were exiled to Siberia. One of them was a Jewish family that was sent away for the sins of their oldest son, who had supposedly collaborated with the previous Polish government. Among the exiled Christian families was that of the former mayor of the shtetl, Szlykiewicz, who alternated with my grandfather as mayor of Shershev every second year. My grandparents were expecting the Soviet secret police to come for them any day. People thought that the only reason they were not taken was their advanced age. Both were in the seventies, and I doubt that they would have survived the trip. The fear of the Soviets among Jews and non-Jews alike was intense. All it took was a denouncement by anyone, and one would immediately become a candidate for a one-way ticket to Siberia. We had to be careful with criticism or remarks regarding government or its leaders.

The only one I knew who succeeded in getting out of the Soviet trap was Sonia Shemesh, who had been visiting her parents with her daughter and was allowed to return to Palestine on her Palestinian passport. It was from Sonia that we later found out that the great Zionist leader Jabotinsky had died. Her sister Raya received a letter from her in which she had written, "Our Velvl died." Velvl was the Yiddish first name of Jabotinsky, and we knew what she meant.

Under the Soviets, Jewish organizations were disbanded or stopped functioning. The Hebrew school was closed, and it was forbidden to learn Hebrew. Jews spoke Yiddish in the street and learned Yiddish in the former Hebrew school. The Jewish community bank was nationalized, and even such a charitable and beneficial institution as Linat Hatzedek, whose volunteers sat with sick people, was suspect and subsequently prohibited. The Yiddish library that a generation of young Jewish boys and girls had worked so hard to create was closed. The books disappeared. Jewish life ceased to exist. For some, the laws, such as those requiring them to work on Shabbos and holidays, were difficult to adjust to. It was something a Jew in Shershev had never done before.

At about the same time, two more Jewish homes were nationalized. One was turned into a restaurant and one a bank. The ancient *rond kromn* was converted into a huge warehouse. The thick walls separating the individual stores were broken through, forming a single unit. The warehouse had at its disposal two trucks that travelled almost daily to Brest-Litovsk for its allotted merchandise. One of the drivers was a Jewish man by the name of Eli Neibrief, and a load hand who travelled with them was a young Jewish man, Noah Hochman. My father was assigned to travel with them as well.

The Soviets started training people for the new jobs being created. They had opened many schools in the surrounding villages, and they needed teachers. My uncle Eli signed up for a course in bookkeeping that opened in the shtetl of Antopol and then got a job as a bookkeeper with my father's boss, a man by the name of Bobrov.

As there was no regular delivery of goods, tradesmen were left with no work and had to join the newly created artels, collective workshops. Some storekeepers managed to hide a bit of merchandise with friends and family for safekeeping, selling it on the quiet and living off the savings. Those in the grocery business were literally eating their merchandise. People hoarded leather, particularly for shoe soles, as it became exceedingly expensive and could be sold for exorbitant prices in an emergency. In general, people didn't dress up so as not to evoke envy among the Easterners, who referred to locals as capitalists.

Any sweet dreams about Soviet life soon evaporated. The Jewish tradesmen and artisans who had worked from early morning to late at night to eke out an austere livelihood might have dreamt about the Soviet Union before the war. True, they worked only eight hours in the collective workshops, but they had to work evenings at home or in the workshops on the quiet to supplement their income.

The varieties of bread, rolls and other baked items from before the war disappeared. Only one sort of bread was available. It was white and tasted like clay. There was a chronic shortage of even the most elementary articles like soap and sugar, not to mention clothing and footwear. The only place to get these items was the black market, where prices were tenfold the official rate. Unable to make ends meet, people resorted to cheating and outright stealing from the government.

Some farmers paid dearly. Any farmer possessing more than eight acres of land was considered a kulak, a rich farmer, and was looked upon by the Soviets with contempt and was persecuted. Some of them, hard-working, honest people, were sent to Siberia with their families, leaving behind their farms and everything they owned. Still, the farmers made out better than the Jewish population, as they could sell their produce to the town Jews, who by now were working in government workshops and were being paid government wages yet had to pay the farmers black-market prices for their produce.

Over the winter, more Easterners arrived from the Soviet Union. They took over the more important positions in offices and organizations first, and then lesser positions. They associated mostly with their own, and it seemed to me that they had an unwritten pact to help each other on the quiet.

After the winter vacation, I returned to Brest-Litovsk, where life continued on what seemed to be an even course. All sorts of promises were made for the young generation, above all a bright future. At times we did get carried away by the Soviet ideals. But the moment I looked at the reality, how carefully one had to step forward and how uncertain everyone's future was, I outright hated the Soviets. I would think about only a year earlier, when I had lived under a regime toward which I felt bitter aversion, yet I did not have to weigh every word or remark. Now, a word could get me expelled from school, and its ramifications could haunt me for the rest of my life. Under the antisemitic Polish, I could criticize the government among Jews and even among the general population. Now, in the so-called free Soviet Union, one had to be careful not only among strangers, but even among your townspeople and neighbours. While we youngsters sometimes permitted ourselves a frivolous joke about the government, a grown-up would not dare to.

What puzzled the Jewish population in the larger cities like Brest-Litovsk, Białystok, and Lvov was the arrest and expulsion to Siberia of the leadership of the Bund, the secular Jewish socialist organization. After all, the Bund was a socialist organization that even renounced any claim on the Land of Israel. So what was their sin? The bigger cities had richer inhabitants, bigger businesses and homes, which were nationalized by the Soviets, their owners unceremoniously sent to Siberia and their possessions appropriated.

That spring, the Soviets decided to solve the refugee problem in Brest-Litovsk and rounded up the refugees, locking them in cattle cars. After three days, the Soviets succeeded in emptying Brest-Litovsk of refugees. The Soviets' deportation of hundreds of thousands of innocent people to Siberia seemed so cruel at the time, but it turned out to be a favour for them. For despite their hardship and suffering in Siberia, the majority of them survived the war.

Passover was not the same that year. With difficulties, my mother got some hops and honey and stood in line for hours for sugar for her mead. Everyone had to show up to work on the holidays, and the only males to show up in the synagogues were men too old to work. A few people used all kinds of excuses to come to work a bit later, thus managing to go to the synagogue before going to work. These were trying times.

11
No More Idlers

IN LATE JUNE 1940, I returned home from school. There were no more young idlers in the shtetl. Every family needed all the financial help that was available, regardless of how small the pay, and the Easterners looked askance at young men who were walking around without work, repeating often one of the well-known Communist slogans: "One who doesn't work, doesn't eat." With my father's intervention, I got a job with the organization where my father and Uncle Eli were working. My work consisted of putting together the merchandise that arrived almost daily and dividing it into six different portions, according to the population of each group of villages. Each village group consisted of about twenty villages, each with a retail store. Each store had a manager and assistant. Both were government employees. In this way, the government created jobs. The employees were not bothered if there was nothing to sell, as they were paid regardless. Each village group had a manager and an assistant as well as a bookkeeper, thus creating more unnecessary government positions. It was a top-heavy bureaucracy that attached itself to the body of the masses like leeches.

The village group managers would come to the warehouse a few times a week to pick up their allotment of merchandise that had arrived from Brest-Litovsk. Bulk merchandise like salt, sugar, kerosene, vodka, cement, bricks and tiles came directly from the Soviet Union to the station at Aranchytsy-Linovo. Entire villages with their horses and buggies were sent out to the railway station to bring in those shipments. Even though some items arrived in huge quantities, the demand never ceased, and people bought whatever was for sale.

Food consumption had increased too. In Shershev, Jews were not drinkers. If a Jew had a small drink at a celebration, he was considered a drinker. In contrast, at Christian weddings, many people got drunk. On the other hand, Jews used a fair amount of sugar, while our Christian neighbours used almost none. But with the arrival of the Soviets things changed. Not only did the Christian population start using sugar on a large scale, but some Jews started quietly taking drink. Candy was a treat for children but only in the better-off families. During the Soviet era, it became accessible to all, as it was sold at government prices. Even though candy arrived in large quantities, enough to last for years in our district in prewar times, it was now sold out in a few hours.

Our work was physically demanding. The bulk merchandise was sent to its destination upon arrival, but the more valuable items were in part distributed and in part held back for the Easterners. By an unwritten law, and against the Soviet dogma, they received their supplies directly from the main storehouse. Among the officials receiving goods in this way were the first secretary of the Party, the judge, the chief of the militia, the mayor and the chief of the secret police, or the NKVD.

In the warehouse, we received crockery, dishes, utensils, notions, footwear with rubber soles, ready-made clothes, woollen underwear, gloves, hats, mitts, even dresses and men's suits. The products were of such poor quality that they would have never left the store shelves before the war. Still, people would line up in front of the government stores, sometimes even spending the night outside in the bitter cold.

From time to time, a few good products arrived with the shipments of merchandise, items unseen in the Soviet Union, like sewing machines, real fur coats, electric kettles, aluminum pots, even good wine or caviar. The Eastern big shots quietly got hold of them. In fact, it was part of my job to bring items to their living quarters, often dealing with their wives so that if they were exposed, they could deny any knowledge of the illegal dealings.

One day, the chief of the militia came in for vodka. I packed the bottles in an empty nail box, hammering the cover down so that it appeared unopened, and took it outside. There, in front of passersby, I called out to him, "Comrade chief, where shall I take the nails?"

He answered loudly, "Take it to the militia headquarters." Then, as if he had thought of something, he added, "You know what, I have to go to the station later. Take it to my house, and I will take it from there to the station myself."

That was one of the many faces of life in the Soviet Union.

My job was one of the best one could have in the shtetl. After all, the merchandise allocated for Shershev and its vicinity passed through our hands, and we benefited from it too. We took lessons from the big shots. When scarce merchandise arrived—and what was not scarce then?—the few of us would write out invoices to the retail stores and pay with rubles, taking the merchandise home. This was done in strict secrecy and within reason. When we brought home more than we needed, my parents would sell the leftovers. This too had to be done in strict secrecy through a trusted middleman. If I had been stopped on my way home from work by the militia, chances were that they would find something on me—a package of cigarettes or a piece of soap. That would be enough to send me to Siberia. But all of life under Soviet rule was steeped in fear. Considering the wages in those days, everybody had to improvise or literally starve. The saying then was that "Uncle Stalin gives enough to exist one week of the month, and for the other three weeks, one has to provide by himself."

I was the youngest worker in the warehouse. There was also Shalom Berenstein, a couple of Christian young men, and two retail store managers, Asher Pasmanic and Yosl Kiselew, who helped us conduct the illegal transfer of cash for merchandise that the big shots took from the warehouse. Our mutual fear of being caught held us together and helped cement our trust in each other. We would get together at the house of one of our Christian friends, drink and eat. Of course, the food was not kosher. As I used to go there straight from work, I would tell my mother that I wouldn't be home for supper. My mother did not object to my having a couple of drinks, knowing that I would not become a drunkard, but she made me promise not to eat non-kosher food. I promised her, knowing that I wouldn't keep my promise. Afterwards, I would reproach myself, not so much for eating non-kosher food as for not keeping my promise to my mother, whom I loved so much and would not want to hurt for anything in the world. What made me feel even guiltier was that Yosl did drink with us but ate only bread and cheese and no non-kosher meat.

In the middle of that summer vacation, I came home from work to find my parents upset. A few hours earlier, a member of the militia had come and told them to send me to their headquarters when I got home. At six-thirty I was there, reporting to the militiaman on duty. He pointed at a row of chairs and told me to sit down. All kinds of thoughts were going through my head, none of them good. Time passed by ever so slowly. It was already nine o'clock, then ten and eleven. Shortly before midnight, I was called into the chief's office. He sat behind a large desk that was covered with a loud red tablecloth. The first thought that came into my mind was, *What is the matter with these people? Don't they sleep at night?*

At first, the chief asked me seemingly innocent questions about my job. But when he asked me about the people who come into the warehouse, I became alert and careful with my answers. Then he asked, "What happened to the aluminum casseroles that arrived in the warehouse?"

For a moment, the directness of the question stunned me. In total, only four aluminum casseroles had arrived, and they had not seen the light of day, as they were "appropriated" by Easterners of high rank. Sitting there opposite him and looking straight into his eyes, I felt like saying, "Don't you know that your friends and comrades, the so-called liberators, as they liked to be called, have taken them?" But I did not dare. I decided to claim ignorance. He continued with questions about other goods and hard-to-get items. I waited for him to ask about the fur coat that I had personally taken to his home and handed to his wife, but he knew better.

To all his questions, I answered, "I don't know." He got so agitated that he said, "You know that your social background is not a good one," hinting to the fact that our house had been nationalized, and that my father was a merchant and my grandfather the mayor—all unforgivable sins. He then told me that it would be much better for me and my family if I cooperated with them.

I again repeated that I didn't know what he was talking about, that I finished working at five and had no idea what took place after I left.

"Keep your eyes open at work," he said. "See what is taking place, and quietly mark all transactions on a piece of paper. One of my assistants will come in, and you will slip that piece of paper to him."

I protested that I had nothing to write down, but he dismissed me, ordering me to go home and do what he had told me to.

I got home after two in the morning, and my parents were waiting up anxiously. I told them what happened, and my mother, not giving my father time to digest what I had just said, turned to me, emphasizing every word: "Moishele, remember, never be an informer, no matter what they will do to you or to us. Let them even send us all to Siberia, but an informer you should never be."

Those sacred words from my mother became my guide and moral motivator through all the years of my life.

A week later, one of the chief's assistants came into the warehouse and walked about looking around, passing by me several times. I am sure the others were wondering what he came for, but I knew and did not pay attention. After about ten minutes, he left. A week later he was back again and left empty-handed. Some days later, a militiaman came into the warehouse and asked everyone for their passports, which all residents had to have on them. All the workers had their passports except me. When the militiaman got to me, I told him that mine was at home. He told me to bring my passport to the militia headquarters during my lunch break. At the headquarters, I was received by no less than the chief of the department.

"Well," he asked, "you still do not know what happened to the aluminum casseroles?"

I was amused that four casseroles could stir up such a fuss. I had already made my decision about how to respond and knew that my parents would stand by me no matter what. So without hesitation I answered, "No."

The chief said, "Give me your passport." He opened it, wrote something in it, then handed it back to me, saying, "Now you can go."

When I got outside, I looked in my passport. There, in clear letters, was written: "This passport is issued according to paragraph 11 of the constitution...." This paragraph was known in the Soviet Union. It meant that the bearer of the passport was not a trustworthy person and must submit to certain restrictions. Among those restrictions was one that prohibits the bearer to enter a seven-kilometre-wide zone along the border. As Brest-Litovsk was within that zone, I could not return there, and that was the end of my education.

A short time later, my father was called to the passport department of the militia, where they wrote the same note in his passport. This prevented him from entering Brest-Litovsk and caused him to lose his job. Fortunately, he found a job as a bookkeeper with the shoemakers' artel.

The Bolsheviks were not finished with the Kantorowitzes yet. Stopping me from going back to school was not enough for them. They wanted to remove me from one of the best jobs in town, probably to replace me with someone who would cooperate with them. I found out later that my boss was under pressure to get rid of me. He refused, claiming that as there are always valuable items in the warehouse, he must have complete confidence in the workers. Having tested me several times, he had full trust in me and would not let me go. They gave in.

On a bright midsummer morning, a couple dozen young peasants appeared in front of the ancient burned-out synagogue. They had been sent to dismantle the ruins. The workers started to break down the four gigantic pillars of the facade that supported the large triangular pediment. Eventually the pillars collapsed, and the huge pediment came crashing down. Every Jewish heart in the shtetl grieved seeing the once beautiful synagogue—which represented the pride and glory of our shtetl's golden past, when our Jewish community numbered close to five thousand souls—come crashing to the ground. I, and I am sure many others, took it as a bad omen, although I never said it aloud. Many of us believed that God had already closed his doors and windows so as not to listen to his people's prayers.

It took the workers a couple of months to tear the walls down. The last standing wall, the eastern one, stood alone, as if in prayer, with the empty niche where the *orn-koydesh*, the holy ark, had been. The demolition team succeeded in toppling the eastern wall all at once. It fell straight, unbroken, face down over the mound of rubble from the previously demolished walls and the ceiling, like a tombstone over a desecrated grave. When the work was done, the walls and the thousands upon thousands of intact bricks were taken away. All that was left was a five-metre-high heap of rubble covering the entire space of the former synagogue.

As unbelievable as it sounds, the Soviets had the impudence to publish in their local paper that was printed in Brest-Litovsk that a brick kiln was operating in Shershev where twenty thousand bricks were being produced daily. People knew about the demolition of the synagogue. Yet nobody dared to question the authenticity of that article.

My prewar group of friends remained tightly knit. We trusted each other unflinchingly and shared impressions and the few remaining dreams that were slowly evaporating. By that time, we all came to realize that the Soviet Union was hermetically closed. There was no way in and no way out. With strangers, one spoke about the weather. The only safe political conversations were limited to heaping abuse on the capitalistic countries, especially Britain and the United States. Above all, one was cautious never to forget to praise the Soviet system and Comrade Stalin.

As the summer of 1940 came to an end, we entered the second year of Bolshevik domination. By winter, former merchants found their niches in the Soviet economy. Some got jobs with the government, and some managed to eke out a livelihood as middlemen. It was a precarious way for people to get by, as if they were sitting on a powder keg, under the constant threat of being sent to Siberia. In order to exist, everybody was breaking the law. It was only a question of how soon one would get caught.

The Soviets did not celebrate Christmas. Instead, they celebrated New Year's for three days. We spent those celebrations at our main office, drinking vodka but being careful not to overdo it so as not to let slip something we'd later regret. This is how we welcomed the year 1941. One could feel the unspoken change in the Soviet attitude toward Nazi Germany. The newspaper eased up on the praise of Germany and in general mentioned Germany less often. One could even hear, from time to time, a less than complimentary remark about Germany from an Easterner.

Some people from Shershev were sent to work in or around Brest-Litovsk. They were under orders not to say where exactly they worked and what they were doing. That in itself was no surprise, as everything was a secret in the Soviet Union. However, rumours were circulating that they were building fortifications, and some Shershev men who commuted there to work told us about the magnitude of the construction going on there. The Soviets were building two military air bases near Pruzhany, stationing an entire air force unit in the town. The airmen, the most privileged of the Soviet armed forces, quartered themselves with many Jewish families in Pruzhany, thereby helping them economically. The Soviets also brought in thousands of criminals from the Soviet Union to build the bases. We did not have to wait long before we understood why they were building air bases there.

In February 1941, I turned eighteen. I had considered myself grown up earlier, but now I was officially grown up. I recall lying in bed that night wondering what the future held for me. With all my naive thoughts and youthful dreams still intact, I made a resolution to dedicate my life to my people, the Jewish people. Considering my situation then and the events that followed, my dreams didn't last too long.

As the winter passed and the second Pesach under the Soviets approached, the preparations were harder. It became more difficult to get flour for matzos, and the baking was almost impossible to organize. Kosher butchers were being persecuted even more, as they were interfering with the government agents in buying up cattle. The procuring of hops and honey for making mead also became a problem. Somehow, everything got done, but under such conditions, the holidays lost much of their importance and holiness. Even though we had to be at work, we celebrated the seders on the two first nights of Pesach, and they were as kosher as they had been in the prewar years.

In June, Sheva came home from Pruzhany after graduating from her final year at the Soviet high school. That night, we had the traditional Friday night meal, not having the slightest inkling that this was to be our last real Shabbos meal. After dinner the next evening, I went out to visit my friends. First, I went to Kalman Kalbkauf's house, and together we went to Itzik Maletzky to see if he wanted to go for a walk with us. However, he had night duty at the power station. Not wanting to leave our friend alone in those boring three hours from nine to midnight, we decided to come along and spend the time competing with the huge motor to see who could be louder. Because of a shortage of replacement parts, the motor had become capricious lately, and that night, like some nights in the past, the motor would not start. Thus, on the night of June 21, 1941, several streets and lanes of Shershev were enveloped in darkness. All that was visible were the pale lights in the windows coming from kerosene lamps. For the Jews of Shershev and the Jews of the Soviet-annexed Polish territories, that was the last night they went to bed peacefully. For most of them, that night never ended.

BOOK THREE
German Occupation
(1941–1943)

12
Hoping for Miracles

SUNDAY, JUNE 22, 1941. The sun rose early, but being the only free day of the week, people were not in a hurry to get up and out. When I went into the street at nine, there were a couple of groups of people talking with interest but no concern about the workers who had been turned back from Pruzhany, even though they worked in the construction of the military airports. This calmness did not last long. A rumour spread that Pruzhany had been bombed the previous night. Nobody was willing to believe that. Soon, we could see the Soviet leaders gathering in their office, which was in the home of Joshua Pinsky, grandfather of my friend Laizer Rotenberg. While the meeting was taking place, militiamen were going from house to house, announcing that there would soon be a general meeting of the entire population in the market square. Everyone immediately started to gather.

At eleven that morning, all the big shots in the shtetl appeared on the podium. The first secretary began: "Today at the crack of dawn, the aggressive Nazi army attacked the peaceful Soviet Union. The Nazi beast stuck its swine snout in our Soviet garden." He continued by promising to pay Germany back for its aggression, saying how the Red Army would make ash and powder of them. His first two sentences stuck in my memory. The rest is a blur.

After the speech, the crowd slowly drifted away. Small groups remained to speculate as to what the near future would bring. For my friends and me, it was the second time in as many years that we were going through such upheaval. However, in contrast to the situation almost two years ago, this war was promising to be more balanced. We had heard of the ability of the German army, but we had also seen the huge numbers of Soviet tanks and army units that appeared to be a much better match than Poland had been. The general opinion in the shtetl was that in the worst scenario, the Red Army would have to retreat a bit. If and when that happened, we would have to decide what to do. But so far, we had nothing to worry about.

Later that morning and early afternoon, many planes flew over the skies of Shershev. Walking with my friends, I remarked that the Soviet flyers were paying back the people and the country for the good life they had in the Soviet Union. There was no doubt in our minds that those were Soviet planes going back and forth on bombing missions behind the front lines. It never dawned on us that those were German planes flying unchallenged over Soviet skies. The last couple of hours of that Sunday afternoon passed in suspense and expectation. Radio Moscow gave little information about the situation on the border, and we, so close to it, could not comprehend the unusual calmness.

In the early evening, as if carried by a whirlwind, the news spread that the Easterners were leaving town. I got to the market square in time to see the Easterners coming from all directions, either empty-handed or with small suitcases or knapsacks. They climbed in panic into overcrowded open trucks that looked ready to spill over. The local Jews stood by numbly. What was happening here? The huge Soviet Union with its mighty army was going down without a fight? Suddenly, the scorned and despised Soviet Union became beloved and dear to us. In an instant, we forgot the bad times. We would give everything to have them back. We waited for further developments, then dispersed and went home with heavy hearts to find protection and comfort in the nearness of our loved ones.

Before dark, my father sent me to his brother Reuven's house.

Reuven had not come home from his work in the military barracks near Pruzhany, and we were all worried about him. My aunt was alone at home with the children, Michla, Shalom and Shevach. As downhearted as we were, I found my aunt and children in a much greater despair, bordering on panic because of my uncle's absence. Suddenly, we heard a tremendous explosion, and every house in the shtetl shook. Looking out the window, I saw brightness like a ball of fire that reached high over the horizon in the direction of Pruzhany. We were all scared, but I, having been sent by my father to be the man in the house, tried hard to hide my fear and assure everybody that there was nothing to fear. When the second explosion was heard, my cousin Shalom begged his mother to lay down with him and the other children on the bed so that when a bomb struck, it would kill them all at once. We slowly moved to the bedroom. After the third explosion, all the children were crying, and they only stopped when the explosions did. We sat together by the light of a kerosene lamp until the two younger children, drained, fell asleep. It was midnight when my aunt told me to go home. I did not need much coaxing, as I wanted to be with my parents.

As I walked through the dark and silent streets, I had the eerie feeling that the street was already devoid of its inhabitants. At home, except for the younger children, everybody was up, sitting around the living room table. Their lips barely moving, they spoke in whispers, as if the Germans were already in the next room. The few hours of the night passed in anxiety. We were in the street early with other groups of Jewish men, hoping to hear some news. One prayer was on the lips of all the Jews—for a miracle that would bring back the Soviets, who would now be welcomed and appreciated.

That day began with a beautiful sunrise, but the mood of the shtetl Jews was weighted down, as if pulled by a heavy stone. One of the trucks that had left with the Soviet bureaucrats drove back into town later that morning. For a moment, the Jews of Shershev thought that their prayer had been answered. If the Messiah, for whom Jews had been waiting for millennia, had come, he would not have been welcomed with more joy than that truckload of Soviets. But they did not pay us any attention and just went into their office and shut the door behind them. After a few minutes, they sent a couple of their men for Srulkah the blacksmith and ordered him to break open the safe from which they needed to retrieve some documents. Apparently, in their rush to leave, they had lost the combination. They would be leaving again. Our exhilaration turned to despair.

While this was taking place, planes were continually flying overhead. That afternoon, we heard the clatter of metal over the cobblestone streets, and two Soviet tanks appeared in the market square. The tanks were covered with a thick layer of dust, and every available space on each tank was taken up by a crewmember who was covered with the same thick layer of dust. All that was visible from under the dust were pairs of eyes turned toward the sky, watching out for German planes. They looked helpless and scared. A few small groups of tanks passed through the shtetl, and from time to time, a single pitiful tank rumbled through.

Once the Easterners had the safe opened, they left in a greater hurry than the day before. The crowd slowly dispersed to their homes in search of imaginary security or at least some solace. Now, having seen the passage of the Soviet army, we all foresaw the downfall of the Soviet Union in a matter of days.

That evening, my father decided to reclaim our house after an absence of almost two years. The non-paying tenants had left the contents undisturbed. The storage was even full of assorted foodstuff that had never been seen in the main warehouse. Overwhelmed and frightened by all this, we withdrew, locked the door and went back to spend the night with my grandparents.

The next morning, Tuesday, my parents decided to move over to our house slowly and cautiously. Each of us carried something back home. My mother and Sheva began to straighten things out with little enthusiasm, making no progress and spending most of the time with the rest of us looking out the windows. We were expecting the Germans to arrive at any minute, and we were afraid. Together, we watched the market square, silent and empty as I had never seen or experienced it in all my life.

At exactly eleven o'clock, a few Germans on motorcycles pulled in from the south side of the market square, from Kamieniecka Street. Each motorcycle had a sidecar attached to it in which another German was sitting holding on to a heavy machine gun mounted on the sidecar. They stopped in the middle of the square just opposite our house, leaped off the motorcycles, forming a large circle around them, machine guns at the ready. The sight of the Germans did not disappoint our expectations at all. With hard, ruthless faces, they looked as we had imagined them, as if they had been born in their uniforms with machine guns in hand. They moved about with well-rehearsed precision and skill, taking in everything around them with their glances.

Within minutes, a few more motorcycles arrived and dispersed to every street and lane, and soon there were groups of Germans all around the outskirts of the shtetl. All this was accomplished without a loud order or even a single shot. It seemed that they knew in advance exactly where to go and what positions to take. They were impressive, outright frightening. Some young boys slowly tried to get closer to the Germans to challenge their tolerance, but a motion with their weapons was enough to stop the bravest. Every few minutes, more and more Germans arrived by truck and jeep, passing down Mostowa Street toward Pruzhany.

We postponed moving more of our things over to our home until the army passed. But, as the day progressed, the number of German soldiers increased. After a while, we had enough of looking at the Germans, and we locked the two front doors of the house and went outside to sit on the steps of the back entrance and analyze our situation. Suddenly, we were confronted by a group of German soldiers who had found their way through the lane that separated our house from our neighbour's. The one in charge asked my father if he was the owner of the house. Hearing the positive reply, the officer announced that they were taking over the house temporarily.

"But, sir, where should we go?"

"I cannot help you," was the reply.

"What about everything inside?" asked my father.

"Don't worry, everything will be looked after and will remain in its place. You can't touch anything and must leave now."

And so, we were expelled once more from our house and went back to my grandparents'.

At night, the trickle of military traffic turned into a flood. A steady flow of soldiers poured over the streets and sidewalks. We did not sleep much that night. There was no let-up to the motion of the Germans. On the second day, tanks and heavy artillery began to pass. Their mechanized cannons were pulled by tractors and had a mounted platform with four or five benches, four soldiers on each bench. When those vehicles passed by, the panes in the windows vibrated.

Groups of German soldiers began to break into Jewish homes, helping themselves to whatever they could carry, from a needle and thread to men's underwear, sweaters and shoes, even women's clothing. No one dared to protest. As we were not eager to go out in the street, we locked the front doors of the house and spent some time in the yard, which was quite spacious and had a high fence that made it inaccessible to prying eyes. The Germans were not deterred. They knocked or banged on the door with their rifles. Sometimes, after a few knocks, they would leave to go to another house, but if the knocking persisted, my grandmother or mother would open the door and let them in. Then they would help themselves to whatever they found of value.

On Thursday, I made my way to my friends Laizer and Litek Rotenberg via alleys and yards. Two of our friends, Kalman and Itzik, joined us a short time later. We dared to go outside, and we set out in the direction of Kamieniecka Street. On one side of the street was an old Russian Orthodox Church surrounded by a large yard, behind which was an orchard belonging to the priest. German soldiers took up the yard, the orchard and the yard of the priest's house. A few German soldiers got hold of us and directed us into the churchyard, where they had set up a mobile bakery. One soldier ordered us to use a power saw to cut a pile of quality timber into small pieces to be used as fuel for the bakery. The nearby German auto repair unit soon found out about us young Jews and made us pump the truck tires they were repairing. A truck tire needs four or five hundred pumps to fill it up, and that is not an easy task. Before night, a German escorted us home, for which we were grateful.

Apparently, I was tired after that day's work, for I fell asleep immediately, unlike the previous nights. Sometime in the middle of the night, I was awakened by a crash at the door and loud German voices. Suddenly, there were Germans in our living room and at the entrance to one of the bedrooms. By then we were all awake and almost fully dressed, for we had not gotten completely undressed since the war began. A couple of soldiers noticed Sheva and yelled, "Ein Mädchen!"—*A girl!*

I do not know how my mother managed to muster so much presence of mind. Within seconds, she was at the window, unlatching it and pushing it outward in one motion, opening it to its full extent. My mother yelled, "Jump out, Shevelah!" She did, and then my mother turned to me and said, "Go with her."

I was half asleep, and without fully realizing what was happening and how serious the moment was, I just jumped. Sheva and I ended up in a lane between my grandparents' and a neighbour's house. In one direction was the street, which was full of marching soldiers and German trucks. In the other direction, deeper in the lane, was a Jewish home, behind which were a few stalls and a large stable. We ran past the Jewish home, past the stalls, to an open and swampy meadow, which offered no place to hide. We turned back to the stalls and the barn, and I climbed onto the roof. Sheva followed me, and we flattened ourselves on that slanted roof as best we could. We heard shouting in German but did not know if it was coming from our grandparents' house or from the street. Our only solace was not hearing gunfire.

It felt like we were on that roof forever. Eventually, slowly and cautiously, in the dark, we climbed down and made our way back inside. We learned that the Germans had satisfied themselves with ransacking the house and left shortly after Sheva and I fled.

The sun was beginning to rise, and it was another beautiful morning.

Still the German soldiers kept marching. We began to think that the entire German army was passing through Shershev. That Friday morning passed as we silently prayed for an end to the constant marching of the Germans so that we could get a rest from them barging in and emptying the house of everything we owned.

Next door to my grandparents', in the direction of the market square, lived an elderly couple with a son named Baruch, a man of about thirty who was nicknamed "Ox" because of his size. He was built like a wrestler and looked as if he could carry a house on his shoulders. On that memorable Friday, June 27, 1941, the second day of the Hebrew month of Tammuz, in the early afternoon, our front door opened and in came Baruch. His face wore a twisted expression, his hair was dishevelled, his clothes dirty and he was soaked with sweat. Trembling, it was evident he wanted to say something, but all he could do was stutter. Words were stuck in his throat. Before he managed to get a word out, his parents come in with confusion and fear in their eyes. His father gestured in his son's direction, glanced at all of us but at no one in particular, and asked in a low voice, "*Nu*, what do you say to this?"

We looked at him, at his son and at each other as the unease grew in us. Finally, my father asked, "What are you talking about? What happened?"

A German soldier, Baruch's parents began, had entered their house, ordered their son to take a shovel, and led him to the large synagogue. There, in the yard of the synagogue, amid rubble, he and another dozen Jews watched as a number of German soldiers savagely beat a group of people. When their grisly work was done, the entire group lay on the ground unconscious. Then, the soldiers fired a bullet into each person's head. The Jewish onlookers were ordered to dig a hole in the middle of that yard, throw the bodies in and cover them up. There were nineteen bodies—eleven Jews and eight Christians. The largest number of victims were from the Chadricky family, who lived on that street.

Baruch's parents then told us the start of the story: the Germans had found a Soviet soldier hidden in a meadow and killed him after a short exchange of fire. Then the Germans rounded up the few men who were grazing their livestock in the meadow and began driving them into town. On the way, they stopped by some houses and took the males with them. The soldiers who surrounded the dozen Jews with the shovels mocked them and threatened to shoot them, beating them with their rifle butts to force them to dig faster. After covering the mass grave, the diggers were told to go to all the Jewish houses in the shtetl and tell everybody that if the Jews didn't turn in their weapons by four o'clock that afternoon, the entire Jewish population would be killed.

Those were the first few days of the German campaign in the Soviet Union. We had known that we wouldn't have it easy under German rule, but we never expected the Germans to slaughter more than a dozen human beings so savagely without any investigation. Now we understood who we were dealing with and what we could expect of them.

The German order to turn in the weapons was a problem. There was not a single weapon among the Jews of Shershev, and the Germans could see that as a refusal and use it as an excuse to kill us all. We were still naive enough to think that the Germans needed an excuse for slaughtering Jews.

The German ultimatum frightened everybody. It was now only an hour until the Germans would start going from house to house, collecting the men to be shot. The women were lucky, we thought, because who on earth would touch a woman? *God in heaven, what is happening? Is it a nightmare, a bad dream from which I will soon awaken? What should I do?* I looked helplessly at my parents and grandparents. The pain, the anguish set in, the fear that confuses common sense. I wanted to live, I wanted to run, but where to and how? The streets were full of Germans who had turned from robbers into bloodthirsty murderers.

No, they will not shoot me. I will kill myself. I will hang myself. But how and with what? And where? As I searched all through the house, nobody asked me what I was doing. I found a piece of cord, stuck it into my pocket and looked at the ceiling to see if I could throw it over something that would be strong enough to hold me. There was nothing, so I walked slowly out into the yard and into the outhouse. Yes, the thin beams on the ceiling there would do. I decided I would execute my plan as soon as the Germans knocked on the door. In the meantime, I went back to the house, where everybody was sitting deep in thought, hoping for a miracle.

The Germans marching in the street had been frightening enough, but now they were utterly terrifying. Every minute, I glanced at the old clock on the wall and listened to the seconds ticking off. At four o'clock, I looked out the closed windows. There was no let-up to the marching Germans. It felt as if the clock was moving a bit faster—soon it was five, then six. What were they waiting for, maybe nightfall? The sounds of the passing engines and the hobnailed boots continued. We sat until midnight, then after midnight. We tried to lie down, drained and exhausted from tension and fear, but nobody could sleep. We waited for dawn, knowing that it wouldn't bring deliverance. The unease and apprehension of those hours transformed into a constant fear. If in the first four nights of the German arrival, we managed to grab a couple hours of sleep, the events of that Friday robbed us of that possibility.

After Friday, June 27, Jews dared not go out into the streets, as they had, briefly, in the first few days after the Germans' arrival. Not even a woman would dare to go out. But on Sunday, June 29, two days after the slaughter of the nineteen men, Aunt Chashkah walked into my grandparents' house. Only a personal acquaintance would know that she was Jewish. She had a full head of thick light-blond hair, and the stocky build and sure gait that characterized the Pinsky family. She told us that my uncle Reuven had returned home three days after the outbreak of the war using back roads.

From then on, my aunt came to see us every couple of days. The Jews of the shtetl were sitting in their houses in constant fear, huddling together in the corners of their homes, expecting that the Germans would come for them to take them away or shoot them on the spot.

It was during one of my aunt's visits that I heard her saying, "I pray to God that I should lie down, fall asleep and not wake up."

My parents nodded their heads in agreement. I too started to hope for a miracle like that.

13
A State of Suspense

STILL THE NAZIS marched. We were getting by on whatever food we could scrape up in the house, but we could not do without water. Early in the morning, one of us would get out to the well with a couple pails for water. There we could meet a neighbour and exchange the latest news, like who had been beaten up or shot over the last twenty-four hours. Some poor souls did not understand the seriousness of the situation and would sneak out of their homes unnoticed by the other family members. The Germans shot them, including a young girl.

The constant marching through our shtetl lasted for three full weeks. On the last couple of days, we stopped seeing heavy equipment. All we saw were foot soldiers and horse-drawn wagons loaded with supplies. Then, as suddenly as they had appeared, they disappeared, and the streets fell silent. Jewish doors began to open slowly and carefully. First a head and then a person appeared. Neighbours began to gather in small groups to exchange experiences. Nobody dared to move far from their houses. When the night passed quietly and my parents didn't see any Germans around in the morning, they decided to check on our house in the market square. We found the doors open and entered carefully. The house was completely empty. Anything movable was gone, taken by the Germans. They had not left even an old rag.

That day, we carried a few things from our grandparents' back to our house, and my father and I spent that night there. Although we did not see or hear any Germans, the fear lingered. The next day, our wagon driver from before the war, the same man who had moved us out of our house two years earlier, moved us back in.

A couple of days later, half a dozen German soldiers and their officer arrived. They drove by every street and lane in the shtetl, stopping eventually in the market square. They walked around the square, eyeing every house before stopping in front of ours. After a short conversation among themselves, they came in. The officer told my father that they needed our house for an *Ortskommandantur*, the local military headquarters.

Were we going to experience an expulsion again? My father tried to speak to the officer in German. The officer asked my father how he spoke German so well. My father replied that just over twenty years earlier, the Germans had been here for three years. The Germans looked at each other knowingly, and I wondered what they were thinking. Did they think that they would have to leave this place like their ancestors, or that this time they had come to stay for good? The officer thought for a moment and then said, "Good, you can remain in the back part of the house, as long as the front part remains inaccessible to you."

My father thanked him for letting us remain in our house. The next day, the Germans hung up a big sign that read "*Ortskommandantur*" over one of the entrances to the house.

I do not know who arranged it, but within a couple of days, there was a provisional civilian administration in the shtetl. A police force was established consisting of a group of young local gentile ruffians who were showing off their newly acquired Soviet rifles. The first order of the day was the law that every Jewish person had to wear on their outer garment a round yellow circle no smaller than ten centimetres in diameter. Breaking the law was punishable by death. The Jewish population was ordered to elect from among them ten members to serve in the Judenrat, the Jewish Council. Nobody volunteered, but an appeal was made to those most suitable to join, and a number of men agreed to take on that heavy and responsible function, among them my uncle Reuven and my grandfather Yaakov Kopel. Officially, they were called Judenrat, but among us Jews they were referred to as "the Committee." Their first function was to submit a list of all the Jewish families and the number of members in them so that they could receive their bread rations. The next day, the Jews of Shershev realized that the ration was outright mockery, as the amount of bread allotted to each person could not sustain the life of an infant. People began to improvise, taking something from the house, like a dish or garment, to a Christian farmer to try to get something in exchange, like a bit of flour, barley or vegetables. A better item could sometimes fetch a few eggs or a piece of butter. The farmers became very choosy. Nobody wanted money. The Russian ruble was worthless, and the German mark was unavailable, and who knew its worth anyway. Whatever the Germans needed or wanted, they just took.

All able-bodied Jewish men were ordered to report to work every day at six in the morning. The order came from the local authority made up of local Christians. The only place where several hundred Jews could be put to work was on the highway. We were divided into groups of fifty. Our boss was a Christian who had been the road supervisor during the Polish and the Soviet eras. His job was to keep the highway between Shershev and Białowieża in good repair. Normally, he did it himself with a gang of temporary workers. Now he found himself in charge of several hundred Jews, and overnight this simple peasant became a general in his own eyes. He would ride on his bicycle from group to group, pointing out every hole or spot that needed repair. The holes had to be filled with sand, and cobblestones were placed on top. The military traffic on that stretch of road was quite heavy. Some of the soldiers passed by without paying attention to us, but others stopped to amuse themselves with the Jews. Many of us came home from the day's work beaten up badly and bleeding.

Along the highway and in the fields and meadows around Shershev, there were unmarked graves of Soviet soldiers who had been shot by the Germans. During the three-week-long German march through

Shershev, we often saw Soviet soldiers being led out of town, followed by the sound of gunfire. Soviet soldiers who had been separated from their retreating units found shelter in the heavy forests of our territories. But hunger drove them out.

On a hot day in late July, as I was working with my group on a stretch of road, two young men in Soviet military uniforms appeared from the forest. They looked as if they had slept in their uniforms on the ground for a long time and had eaten very little. Finding out that we were Jews and not any danger to them, they asked us which way was east and which side roads they should take to avoid Germans. They continued walking eastward along the narrow clearing between the road and the forest. No more than ten minutes later, a local policeman, Tolek, came along on a bicycle. We knew him to be a drunkard and scoundrel from a long time back. He was the sort of antisemite in whom a lust for dominance and disdain for the dignity and lives of a powerless enemy had taken root. Volunteering to join the local police under German supervision gave him the opportunity to express those sentiments. He fulfilled his job diligently, pedalling around us on his bicycle with his rifle on his shoulder, looking at us with an air of superiority and outright contempt. Tolek passed us and disappeared around the bend in the road where the two unarmed Soviet soldiers had gone. A couple minutes later, we heard two shots, and Tolek returned, passing us again slowly with a wide, satisfied grin on his face. We asked each other if it was possible that this despicable creature could have shot those two young men. Apparently, the road supervisor was also moved, for he got on his bicycle and rode in the direction the shots had come from. He was back with one comment: "A pity, such young men."

A day or two later, while working on the road, a long line of horse-driven buggies approached from the direction of Białowieża. As they got closer, we saw that the wagons were loaded with assorted household goods. We found out that they were from villages near the Białowieża Forest, where villagers had been ordered to load up their wagons with all they could take with them, leaving everything else behind. The Germans did not waste time in taking all their livestock and anything else they could use. Then the Germans set the villages on fire. The Germans escorting the wagons were on bicycles, and it was easy for them to stop and harass us.

The expulsion of entire villages became a daily occurrence. The Germans suspected villagers of giving food and shelter to the remnants of the Soviet army still hiding in the forests, mainly the Białowieża Forest, one of the largest forests in Europe. A few days later we heard that the Jews of Białowieża had been expelled to Pruzhany. We all questioned whether we too would be expelled, and everyone became even more depressed, wondering what would happen next.

The Gestapo headquarters for our district was in Biała Podlaska, west of the Bug River, a couple of hours away by car. But the immediate authority over us was the Nazi police force, the Schutzpolizei, in Białowieża, some thirty kilometres from Shershev. They would come by truck, unannounced, and park in front of a couple of Jewish homes. With the help of the local police, they would load everything from those homes onto the trucks, at the same time beating the inhabitants. They did not go systematically house by house, but picked houses at random in different streets, thus keeping everybody in a constant state of suspense and fear.

At times, the Nazi leadership from Biała Podlaska came along with many more police and trucks. They would round up as many Jews as they could in the market square, then go from house to house to make sure nobody stayed behind. Woe to those found hiding in their homes. In the market square, they picked out the men, tormenting and torturing them with exercise and what they called "gymnastics," kicking them with their boots and beating them with clubs and rifle butts, leaving them there, bleeding. I think the women and children suffered as much, if not more, than the men, having to watch their husbands, sons, fathers and siblings go through such torture. The herding of the Jewish population was accompanied by rifle shots that could be heard way out of town. For us working on the highway, not knowing what was taking place, it was very alarming.

The Nazi police never entered our house, assuming that there were no Jews living there because of the *Ortskommandantur* sign. Yet my mother would go out with the children into the square, not wanting to risk being discovered at home. My father, knowing what was awaiting him in the square, would hide in the woodshed. Working on the highway, I was spared this torment. One day, when I was not at work on the road and the Schutzpolizei showed up, I decided to run to the marshes that began behind Ostrowiecka Street and stretched for kilometres. My father decided to join me. Did he feel safer in the marshes, or did he want to keep an eye on me? In the confusion of running, yelling, beating and shooting, we managed to make our way through alleys to those swamps. There, lying submerged up to our necks in mud, we listened in fear to the constant shooting and screaming that came from the centre of town and imagined the worst. I prayed with devotion to God as I had never prayed before that he should bring my mother, brother and sisters safely home again. I even made a vow that if they all came home, I would say my morning prayers every day like a devout Jew.

Slowly the shooting subsided and finally ceased. A couple of hours later, seemingly an eternity, in mid-afternoon, my father and I started crawling closer to the centre of town. When we got to where the Jewish homes began, we found out that the Germans had left after a particularly savage visit. We ran home to see how my mother, sisters and brother had fared in this ordeal. From my mother, we found out that the Germans had not spared the women and children this time. They lined them up four to five in a row and threatened to shoot. My mother could not stop talking about my middle sister, Sonia, who was then nine years old. Sonia had pushed herself in front of my mother saying, "Mommy, I will stay in front of you. This way the Germans will kill me, and you will remain alive."

Dear, dear little sister of mine. You naive, innocent child of Israel. You evaded a cruel fate, but it caught up with you.

On that day, the Germans had singled out the rabbi and the older Jews of the community. They beat up the rabbi terribly and then ordered him to do all kinds of exercises. When they saw that his sweat was taking on the colour of blood, they put him under the water pump and ordered another elderly Jew to pump the cold water over him. After conducting searches in some of the nearby Jewish homes and helping themselves to everything of value, they departed, leaving the Jews wondering when they would be back.

We did not have to wait long. A day or two later they were back with a smaller escort. They immediately gathered the Judenrat, telling them that they would be back in five days, and that there had better be ready for them two hundred thousand rubles and a kilogram of gold. The raising of the rubles did not present a problem, as they had become worthless, but the kilogram of gold presented a big problem in a poor shtetl like Shershev. People made a great effort, giving up their jewellery. It was decided that the safest place in town to keep the money and gold was our house because the *Ortskommandantur* sign prevented the Germans from plundering it. And so it was that a suitcase full of rubles and gold was brought into our house, where it stayed under my parents' bed until two members of the Committee came to pick it up on the designated day. The Germans then left, satisfied with their haul.

Unable to get enough food, we were forced to fill our stomachs with anything that was available. On one of my free days, a couple of my friends and I decided to go to the forest to pick mushrooms. We had just entered the forest when we saw the first Soviet tank. Its heavy doors were wide open, and dozens of shell casings and unexploded shells lay about. It looked like the farmers had emptied the shell casings, helping themselves to the gunpowder. We concluded that the tanks had run out of fuel and that the crews must have realized that the road east was already in German hands, so they either surrendered or tried to make it on foot. Exploring around, we found over a dozen more undamaged tanks like the first one. It hurt us to see these tanks that had lost the battle without firing a shot. The words of King David came to me—"How the mighty have fallen."

This was our routine in August 1941: Most able-bodied Jewish men reported for work at six, bringing a shovel, axe or pickaxe, then marched out to the highway, worked till six and then went home. Nobody stood over us with a club, but passing Germans would amuse themselves by making us load a wheelbarrow with rocks or sand, then push it on the rough road while running as they beat us.

In the shtetl itself, the plundering and beatings continued. As the Germans were avoiding our house, it became a refuge for neighbours, friends and acquaintances, just as our store had been before the war. The very same men came, now dejected and struck with fear, and in quiet voices, almost in whispers, continued to talk politics. Discussions did not have the same character as before. The speculative assumptions of years gone by were replaced by wishful thinking. Hypotheses circulated around the shtetl, and by the time they came back to their source, they were unrecognizable. Even dreams were interpreted in countless ways to one's wish and liking. I am still not sure if our short-lived, optimistic interpretations were intended to give hope and encourage others, or is it human nature to fool oneself when in distress?

The only outspoken realist was my father's brother Eli, the veteran of the Polish-German campaign. For his gloomy predictions, he was branded a pessimist. Nobody could foresee the fast-approaching last days of the five-hundred-year Jewish history of Shershev. The Jews of Shershev tried to rationalize the expulsion of the Jews of Białowieża and Hajnówka by saying that they were living at the edge of the forest. Still, we began to take precautions, reasoning that if we were expelled, we would have to leave everything behind and it would be worthwhile to try and hide some things.

We had two big woodsheds in our yard. In one of them, we dug a large hole in which we buried two wooden chests full of clothing. Underneath the chests, I had dug a small hole in which I deposited a wooden box containing my personal mementoes, including my most precious possession—my stamp collection. After covering the chests with earth, we hid the spot with a high pile of wood. We did the same in the other woodshed, using the wooden crates vodka was shipped in to pack our silver cutlery, the good dishes and other valuable items. We hid clothing, leather and jewellery in other spots in the house and buried outside. There were still some items left in the house, but we did not want to dig up the sheds more because that would look suspicious. Besides, even if we had planned to hide more things, we suddenly ran out of time.

14
Fresh Graves

SUNDAY EVENING, AUGUST 24, 1941, right after sunset, a military vehicle parked in front of our house. Through the walls we could hear loud voices and commands in German. About half an hour later a group of civilians approached our house. It was the members of the Judenrat. They had been summoned and ordered to go around to every Jewish home with instructions that every Jewish male between the ages of sixteen and fifty, without exception, report at six in the morning for work. The little rest the Jews of Shershev might have gotten on that night was denied them. We sat up all night, trying unsuccessfully to guess what the Germans had in mind to do with us the next day.

At six in the morning, all the town's Jewish males were gathered near the shed of the volunteer fire brigade, a total of some four hundred men. We were surrounded by a detachment of Schutzpolizei. A Nazi called out in a loud voice, asking if anyone spoke German. The first to come forward was a Jew from Brest-Litovsk who had been brought by the Soviets to run the pharmacy in Shershev. To me he looked over fifty, yet he had showed up with us. The German spoke to him loud enough for all of us to hear. We also understood. The man repeated the command loud and clear in Yiddish with a German intonation, making sure that not only would we understand, but the Germans would too.

One Jew, not realizing the severity of the situation, interrupted the interpreter with a question. A German barked at him, "Hold your snout, cursed Jew!"

The German command was that we men go home and bring back with us our families—woman, children, young and old, healthy or sick. Anyone found at home would be shot. The women were to take with them food for two days; the men were to take only digging tools. All Jews were being taken to a labour camp where the men would work. In return, we would receive food and a roof over our heads.

The possibility of such a moment had been in the back of our minds, yet when it happened, it came as an unbearable shock. What was going to happen to us, and what conditions would we have in that camp? Would there be anybody to look after the old and sick or would the Germans let them expire without medication? What clothes should we take now that autumn was approaching?

Suddenly, the heavens fell on us. What was happening to us? Why and for what sins? What had we done to deserve such punishment? My two little sisters and brother could not comprehend what was going on. My mother looked at the children and wept. It grieved me deeply to see my mother cry, and my heart ached as much for her as from the misfortunes that befell us, maybe even more. We didn't even try to comfort one another. We just sat with heavy hearts.

There was no time to lose. The sun was up and it was warm already. My mother was the most practical of us, and she told us to put on a lot of clothing. I put on two suits, one on top of the other, over an extra couple of sets of underwear. On top of all that, I wore a three-quarter-length winter coat. My mother and Sheva helped the little ones get dressed.

The crowd was already gathering in the market square, right in front of our house. My mother prepared a small bundle for each of the children and for herself. My father and I did not dare take anything but our tools, as the Germans had ordered. My father took an axe, and I took a shovel. We left the house together, and my father locked the door and put the key in his pocket.

Outside, we gathered separately, the men each with an axe, shovel or pickaxe to one side, the women, children and old people to the other. The loud cries of the children and the subdued weeping of the women could be heard in the unusual silence. Nothing seemed real, for these Germans, who had plundered our houses several times a week, yelling and shooting, were now silent, as if they were ashamed of their unholy deed.

It was ten o'clock when the entire Jewish community was gathered. I saw sick old people lying stretched out on the cobblestone square. We took the German warning seriously. I looked around, and at that moment, I made a decision to stop being a boy and act like a man.

We heard a command to form a column, three abreast. Then we were led past an unused well and ordered to dispose of our tools, except for ten men who were told to carry shovels. The order to throw away our tools puzzled me. What good were we without tools, unless the place we were going to had better ones. I felt uneasy.

We were led out of the square onto Mostowa Street, followed by the sounds of the crying children and the wailing women who remained in the square. The main street of Shershev was empty. We marched in the middle of the street, escorted on either side by the Schutzpolizei. I looked around at the homes in which Jews had lived for generations. Nobody was looking out of the windows. Nobody was working in their gardens, as they usually did this time of the year. They were all marching now with me to an unknown future, leaving behind everything they had built and collected throughout their lifetimes.

We came to the end of Mostowa Street, to the beginning of Pruzhany Street, which was mostly a Christian street. This street too was empty. Here and there a pair of eyes looked out through a curtain. I wondered if it was the fear of the Germans that drove them behind the curtains, or were they hiding their smiles of contentment at our misfortune?

We left the shtetl behind. A few hundred metres farther, we were ordered to stop. The Germans picked out a couple dozen younger boys, taking them to the end of the column. They were told to lead the German bicycles by hand. The officer in charge loudly announced that if any one of us escaped or even attempted to escape, twenty-five of us would be shot. We took his word for it.

We heard a command to proceed. The Germans marched along us on either side. Some of them bent down and picked up heavy sticks, others were taking their rifles off their shoulders. We were ordered to march in step, and whoever did not, received blows with a stick or rifle butt. But how could we march in step when the German near us yelled "Right!" and the one two metres in front or behind us yelled "Left!"? The sticks, clubs and rifle butts started falling over us. The Germans were not particular where they hit—it could be the head, shoulder or back. Neither were they satisfied with hitting once. When they let go of us, we were already beaten to a pulp.

We were perplexed about what was happening. Had they brought us here to beat us senseless? How could they expect to get any work out of us? Another hour like this, and nobody would be in a condition to work. A thought came to me: Maybe they were not taking us to work at all. Maybe they just fooled us all in order to give us a good beating. If so, what would happen to the women, children and elderly we had left behind, the ones who were left lying half dead on the cobblestone square? I was not the only one with such thoughts. I could see them in other despairing faces. I heard others being beaten mercilessly, yelling, "Shema Yisroel!"—*Hear, O Israel!*—the last words Jewish martyrs utter before expiring. I too was in despair and mad at my God for letting this happen. The cries of "Shema Yisroel" came louder and more often. In my hopelessness I thought to myself, *Yes, yes, a lot of good it could do you now, the Shema Yisroel.*

Then we were ordered to sing. How does one make four hundred frightened, confused and beaten men sing? The beatings became more savage. We began to sing, each of us singing his own song. It was a horrible sound, carried from four hundred throats, that could have chilled the blood in any human vein or frightened Satan in his lair, but not the Nazi executioners.

How does one describe such a picture: several hundred men being forcibly driven out of their homes, torn from their families, led on a road to an unknown fate, yelling at the top of their voices and being mercilessly beaten by raging Germans?

At one point, a jeep passed us very slowly. The passengers were officers of the Schutzpolizei. The one who seemed to be in charge examined every face as the jeep moved along the line of men. Having passed in front of the column, the jeep turned around and came toward us again then stopped in front of Yaakov Meir Kabizetsky, a member of the Committee. The officer got out, and we were all ordered to stop. The officer loudly asked Yaakov Meir, "Have you got leather today?"

I heard whisperings that this was the big shot from Biała Podlaska. He had been in Shershev several days earlier, demanding leather, which the Committee could not deliver. Not waiting for an answer, he started beating Yaakov Meir. Yaakov Meir was a tall, strong man who could stand a beating, and the German kept hitting him until he ran out of steam. Yaakov Meir's neck was bleeding badly. He ran quickly back into the column and positioned himself between two tall men who pulled up his collar. When the German officer caught his second wind, he began looking for Yaakov Meir again. He drove up and down the column several times but did not find him. The jeep pulled away.

We resumed our march. Fifteen or twenty minutes later, we were ordered to stop and to sit down on the road cross-legged, looking straight ahead. Except for the screaming of the Germans or the thump of a stick over a Jewish back, there was a total silence on the road and in the surrounding fields. Suddenly, the silence was shattered by a single shot. The ten men with the shovels were called to the rear, and we could all hear the order to dig a hole. Now it became clear to us why ten men were ordered to take along shovels as we left Shershev.

The first victim of the march was a nineteen-year-old boy known by his nickname, "Kulie." He had been born with a deformed leg and had a noticeable limp. He could not keep up with us and so was disposed of in Nazi style. As soon as the diggers covered the grave, which was done under constant beating, we resumed the march. We did not march long before somebody else was unable to keep up with us and fell. He was shot, and the burial procedure repeated itself. While the marchers could catch our breaths during a burial, the ones with the shovels had no rest at all.

The day was sunny and hot, and we were dressed for winter. It seemed that even the heat of the day was against us, but nobody wanted to discard their outer clothes, as we all stuck desperately to the hope that we were being led to a work camp. We stopped a couple more times that morning to bury our dead. Shortly after midday came a sudden order to get off the road to one side. We were to sit on the embankment with our backs to the road and not look behind us. A minute or two later, we heard passing trucks from which ear-piercing screams from women and children could be heard. They were coming from our families—our mothers, grandmothers, sisters and little brothers. They cried out to us, but we were not permitted to look at them.

As soon as the trucks passed, we continued the march, stopping only to bury our dead every half-hour or so. I wondered who would tire sooner—would it be us from receiving so many blows, or would it be them from constantly hitting us? How could they go all day long beating and shooting people they had never known? In mid-afternoon we reached Pruzhany. At the outskirts of town, we collapsed on a green meadow, broken physically and mentally. The Germans left several soldiers to guard us while the others went to eat.

Jews from Pruzhany came to see us but were not permitted to get close. My father's brother and sister came out to look at us, no more than that. After an hour or so, we continued our march. Until now, we had all hung on to the extra clothing we were wearing, but in the afternoon, battered, exhausted, thirsty and at the end of any hope, some began to discard some of their clothing. During those hopeless hours, when I turned my head and looked back, I could see items of clothing strewn along the road. To an uninformed passerby, it might have looked as if the column of marching Jews were deliberately leaving behind markers so that they could find their way back home.

The march was not getting any easier. Anyone who fell and could not get up, or who got up to join the march only to fall again, was shot. The men with shovels soon realized that they wouldn't be able to keep it up for much longer, and when the Germans were not looking, they dropped them and continued marching. The Germans did not make much of it, just pointed a finger at the one nearest to the shovel, barking, "Pick it up!"

At about six in the evening, we were led off the main road into a farmer's large homestead. In the middle of the yard was a well, and we were ordered to form a single line for water. Then we were told to empty our pockets and warned that whoever hid anything would be shot. We had no doubt that they meant it, and we gave them everything, including any money we had hidden or sewn into our clothes. As we each approached the well for a drink, the Germans searched us.

One of the diggers passed by me, and noticing that no German was watching, he inconspicuously let his shovel drop. A German nearby saw the shovel and, looking at me, hissed, "Pick it up."

No sooner did I pick up the shovel than another German motioned to me to follow him, and six of us were taken behind a farm building where we were told to dig a pit. What made us very uneasy was that there was no body to bury. For whom then were we digging the grave? Now I also felt the taste of being a digger. The three Germans lowered their rifle butts over any back that tried to straighten up. I don't know if it was due to the hard labour, the extra clothing or the fear that I was digging my own grave, but I perspired so much that even my winter coat was wet. I noticed that the others were just as wet.

When we finished digging the pit, we were ordered to lie in a row, face down next to it. I was sure that those were my last seconds, and I thought to myself that death was not so terrible. Soon, I would get a bullet in my head, and my world with its suffering would end. But should I be spared for some reason, I would never fear death anymore. With such lofty thoughts, I became aware of other voices. I heard the command, "Throw him in," then, "Get lost," followed by a shot.

The diggers were ordered to get up and fill the hole. I looked down and saw an acquaintance, Moishe Gleser, who had married a year earlier and had an infant. He had fallen at the entrance to the farm, and his fate was sealed. He died instantly, for the bullet that entered below his right eye tore off a piece of cheek, though the torn cheek and the hanging part of the face was not bleeding. We covered him quickly, and one of the Germans led us straight to the head of the line to drink.

The sun had begun to set, and the Germans forced us into the barn. There wasn't enough room to sit, so most spent the night on their feet. As they closed the barn door behind us, my father said to me, "If they want to get rid of us now, all they need is one match."

He was right; the thatched roof would have caught fire like a tinderbox.

At daybreak, the Germans took us outside in the pouring rain, lined us up like on the previous day and ordered us to march. Apparently, the idea of marching along a column of Jews in the rain did not appeal to the Germans, so we were ordered to get off the road and march in the ditch alongside it. By then, the ditch was filling up, and we were marching in water that was ankle- to knee-deep. It turned out to be a blessing, for the Germans marching on the road could not reach us with their clubs or rifle butts. But it did not last. At noon, the rain stopped and our luck ran out. We were ordered back on the road.

The Germans seemed to want to make up for lost time because they lined themselves up on both sides of the road for a kilometre or so and ordered us to run the gauntlet of clubs and rifle butts. There were some casualties, either from a disabling blow or because of age, exhaustion and the effects of standing up all night; some were simply unable to run that far. We sat cross-legged in the deep mud until the victims were buried. As soon as we got up from the ground, we saw the Germans lining up as before. We ran again, and then again. With each run, the number of casualties increased. It got to the point that the Germans did not stop us to bury only two men; we were making stops for no less than four or five. Those who fell were grabbed by their arms and legs by four men and carried along until the stop. They were fully conscious and knew what was going to happen to them.

Sometimes, when one person fell, those behind tripped and piled up into a heap. The Germans had a ball with those in the heaps, trashing them with all their might. If there was a pileup ahead of us, we could avoid it by running around it, but then we were exposed to additional blows. Those on the bottom of such a heap were often so trampled that they were unable to get up, thereby sealing their fate. It suddenly dawned on me that my father, at forty-eight, was one of the older men and might fall or trip over someone. I made my way to the rear of the column so that I could see if he was in trouble. My decision was a timely one. People were soon falling one on top of the other in a pile-up. My father was almost at the bottom of the heap. I do not know where I found the strength, but I stopped in the middle of the running column, anchored my feet into the muddy ground and lifted my father. I put his left arm over my shoulder and wrapped my right arm around his waist. Holding my father, I could not move with as much agility as before, so I could not avoid the blows to the degree I could earlier.

I saw a German delivering a blow to a young man, who fell. The German was not satisfied and continued to hit him. The victim was a young man named Motl Shocherman. When we got to Motl, he was already lying motionless by the side of the road. His tormentor took him for dead or half dead, left him, and joined the others chasing us. Suddenly, Motl made an attempt to get up. He succeeded in pushing his upper body up, and from his throat he uttered a horrible cry. Then, another German came along and delivered a blow to his neck with a thick club. Motl fell with his face to the ground. That German left him and continued to run after the column. As Motl tried a second time to prop himself up, a third German came along, stopped, raised his rifle and pulled the trigger. It was the first time that I saw a man being shot from such a close distance. His entire skull was torn off, spraying those around with drops of blood.

We continued running for another couple hundred metres before we stopped to bury our dead. As soon as we stopped and lined up, Moishe Shocherman, Motl's father, stepped out of the line. He walked over to the nearest German and said to him, "You have just killed my son. Kill me too."

He did not have to ask twice; the German immediately obliged.

I wondered if the Germans planned to finish us all this way. During the next run, I felt that my father was weakening. As we sat down on the muddy road to bury our dead, a German asked if any of us were ready to dispose of our coats. A farmer was stopped, and we were told that whoever wanted could put his coat in the buggy. In no time, the buggy was full. The farmer could not believe his luck.

While a pit was being dug for the latest victims, some Germans counted us and others looked for visibly bleeding men. If the wound was obvious, that man was taken to join the others waiting to be shot. My best friend, Laizer Rotenberg, had received a blow to the left side of his head and was bleeding noticeably. A German ordered him to get up and pointed him toward a group of men waiting to be shot. Laizer was twenty years old and in excellent shape, always considered a hero among us. If anybody would try anything, it would be Laizer. Following the German's order, Laizer began to run toward the condemned group. But on reaching them, he did not slow down. He jumped over the ditch alongside the road and ran into a potato field. He covered several dozen metres before the Germans realized that he was running away. Several of them raised their rifles and began to shoot. We all looked, praying that he would make it. He fell. The Germans lowered their rifles and turned their attention to us. At that moment, Laizer jumped up and began to run again. The Germans lost several precious seconds before they saw that he was running again and started shooting. He fell again, and again, when they lowered their rifles he started to run. For the third time, they opened fire, but by then he was on the other side of the field and had disappeared into the adjoining forest.

The officer in command announced in a loud and clear voice that twenty-five men would be shot. But first they had to count us for the umpteenth time that day. As we sat three in a row, two Germans on either side of us walked along the column, hitting the men sitting on either side with a club over the head, counting aloud for all to hear. I do not know if it was deliberate or not, but every time they came to the end of the column, the number did not match the previous count, and they started counting again, still clubbing us over the head.

It was late in the afternoon when the diggers started digging a large grave, and the Germans picked the victims from the rear of the column. We were told not to look back at the unfortunate ones. All we could hear was, "You, you..." and blows and cursing falling on the condemned. I could not resist my curiosity, so I lowered my head and turned around for a few seconds. I saw that they were picking the older men among us. I was worried for my father, but they stopped two or three rows behind us.

Although the Germans had said they would shoot twenty-five men, they picked only fifteen. Ordering the first five to enter the pit, they told them to lay face down shoulder to shoulder. Five Germans fired at the same time into the hole. The next five men were told to lay face down on top of the five just shot, but in the opposite direction. Another volley of gunshots, and for another five innocent Jewish souls, the suffering ended. The same was done to the last five.

By the time the diggers finished covering the grave, the sun was setting. We were sitting on the ground wondering what would become of us. The officer in charge positioned himself in front of us so that we could all see him. He yelled, "Judenrat, step forward!"

My father whispered to me, "Now they will finish off the Committee."

The members of the Committee who were still alive stepped forward. The officer asked, "Can any of you read a map?"

One Committee member, a doctor, hesitantly took a step forward. The officer took a map out of his pouch, showed the doctor a point on the map and said, "You are here. Seven kilometres down the road is a place called Antopol. There you will find your women and children. From here on you can continue on your own."

With those words, the Germans took the bicycles from the boys who were holding them, mounted them, and, without looking back, pedalled back the way we came. For a moment, we thought that this was another German trick, but the bicycles soon disappeared in the distance, and we realized that we were free. Our first impulse was to fall into each other's arms with the joy that we were alive. But that joy lasted only for seconds, for the events of the last thirty-six hours and the dozens of unmarked graves we left behind quickly sunk in.

Exactly how many were slain in those two days nobody knew, but we figured it was somewhere between seventy-five and a hundred men.

Some knew this road and confirmed that it led to Antopol. Antopol was about the same size as Shershev but with a somewhat larger Jewish population. Maybe they were still in their homes undisturbed. If so, they would take us in and let us catch our breath and be among Jews in a Jewish home, even for a moment.

Our group, beaten and crushed, dragged itself forward. We were afraid and spoke in whispers. Rumours and assumptions were mixed with despair and tears. It was dark all around us—not a light to be seen, not a sign of human presence. I was walking with my father and my uncles Reuven and Eli, each of us burdened with our own dark thoughts.

We finally made it to Antopol. The street was dark. The first men we stumbled across told us to be quiet, for there was great tension in the shtetl because the Germans had come into the town that day, collected two hundred Jewish men and marched them away. There were rumours that they were shot as soon as they were out of town. Nobody knew if those Germans were still in town or if they had left to do their gruesome work somewhere else. It was not safe to remain in the street. My father and uncles and I spent the rest of the night in the corner of a barn.

At dawn, we left the barn and saw others crawl out from all kinds of hiding places. We all headed to the town centre where, among the Jewish homes, were two synagogues close to each other. To our astonishment, we saw our Shershev women and children in the synagogue yards. Everybody looked feverishly for their own, the women with expectation and fear for their men, as they had heard rumours of our two-day march and its consequences. Nobody was in a hurry to tell the newly made widows or bereaved mothers of their losses.

Not finding my mother outside, I ran into one of the synagogues, where women, children and elderly people were tightly packed. Some were sitting on their pitiful bundles, while others were sitting on the floor with bundles in their laps. Among this group of unfortunates, I found my mother and the children. My mother's face brightened for a second when she saw us, but only for a second because the reality was too much to bear. We looked at each other, petrified, not daring to ask one another about the events of the past two days. There was so much crying and so much despair. Raya Rotenberg heard from her son Litek how the Germans had shot after Laizer as he was escaping, and she started to lament and mourn him. We tried to quiet her down, especially my mother, who heard from me that he had run into the forest. Raya only got quieter after I swore on my life that he was alive.

It is impossible to describe the mourning of dozens upon dozens of women who suddenly found out that their husbands or sons were killed or the cries of hundreds of freshly created orphans. There was no time for niceties, and when a woman asked with apprehension and fear about her husband, one did not hesitate to tell her the truth, regardless of how heartbreaking it was when that woman broke down.

In our hopeless situation, we did not immediately notice the absence of local Jews or offers for help. From our experiences over the past two days, we felt that the whole world had rejected us. We soon heard that a fresh grave containing the two hundred local men was discovered not far from shtetl. The Jews of Antopol had their losses and their mourning to do as well.

Before we had a chance to have a good look at each other or exchange a few words of compassion, members of the local Ukrainian police appeared. They were of the same category of ruffians who had made up the local police in Shershev. They ordered us to leave town immediately. But where should we go? The answer was short: "Out!! You may go eastward."

Besides the seven of us—my father, mother and five children—we left together with my grandparents, my uncles Eli and Reuven, my aunt Chashkah and my three young cousins, Michla, Shalom and Shevach. We picked ourselves up and joined the throng in the street, all barely dragging their feet. My aunt Chashkah disappeared behind a house and came back a couple of minutes later with a loaf of bread under her coat. She had smelled freshly baked bread and followed the smell to a bakery, where, half begging and half by force, she got the loaf of bread. This was the only food that my entire extended family had for the next two days.

15
Khomsk

TWO DAYS AFTER we had been expelled from our hometown, the majority of the remaining Jewish community of Shershev left Antopol. The local Jews hid in their homes and sat shiva for the two hundred men who had been murdered. We were escorted by the local Ukrainian police, still in civilian clothes with their Soviet rifles and light machine guns, who rode alongside us on bicycles. Others passed us and stopped at every farmhouse along the way, warning the farmers not to give us any food, not even a drink of water. Some of us were on the verge of fainting from hunger or thirst. But anyone who knocked on a door was refused and sent away. Those farmsteads had wells that never ran out of water, so it maddened us that they refused us even a drink of water. I tried hard not to think how my parents must be feeling. Our family walked or dragged itself along. Some ten kilometres past Antopol, our police escort turned back, and the farmers farther along the road began to show us more compassion, permitting us to fetch water from their wells. I even saw a couple of farmers cutting up a loaf of bread and handing the pieces to the children.

As the day progressed, our hunger intensified, and some parents began to accompany their children in begging for a piece of bread. I looked on with pain as my uncle Reuven went with his son Shalom to a farmer's house. The door opened and the farmer's wife came out to the porch holding a loaf of bread and a knife. She cut up the bread and began distributing it among the surrounding mob of children. My cousin Shalom, not being an aggressive child, was pushed aside by other boys. My uncle pointed at his son and said to the woman, "Please give him a piece of bread."

I knew those words were not easy for my uncle to say, for there was a tear rolling down his cheek. I thought to myself, *How can it be that my uncle Reuven, the richest man in Shershev, now stands begging for a piece of bread?*

Our progress on the road was slow, and when the sun began to set, we were in the middle of a road surrounded by fields. We couldn't go back, but we did not know what was waiting for us ahead. Night was falling, and an entire destitute community stood under the open sky with nobody to turn to. We had no choice. We stopped at the embankment along the road and sat or lay down on the ground. Maybe some dozed off for a moment now and again, but most did not shut their eyes. There was no conversation. Everybody was engrossed in their own dark thoughts. Now and then, a German vehicle passed by, slowing down to look at the scene.

With daybreak, we were on our feet and dragging onward. Those who knew the road said that we were going toward Drohitchin, and indeed, we reached it that afternoon. Drohitchin was thus far untouched by the Germans, although the Jewish population of some neighbouring shtetls, like Khomsk, had been slaughtered completely earlier that month. In other towns, the men had been executed, like in the town of Pinsk, where eight thousand men were slaughtered on August 5, 1941. There was a rumour that the priest in Drohitchin had intervened with the Germans on behalf of the Jews. How much substance there was to this rumour, I cannot say.

We suddenly found ourselves among Jews, and despite their own concerns and fears, they responded to us very warmly. They saw to it that each family got some bread and found us all accommodations with local families. It grieves me that I cannot remember the name of the family to whom we were assigned. Not only did they empty two rooms for us, but they also provided beds and bedding, making us feel as if we were family. They were a family of four, a husband and wife, with a daughter of about thirteen and the wife's sister. The house was not new but quite large with a big garden in the back. The garden had all kinds of vegetables, and the potato bed was over an acre in size. Wanting to make myself useful, I volunteered to dig potatoes for them, but they would not hear of it. They finally agreed to let me dig only for our needs, pointing out where the good potatoes grew.

A couple of days later, a few Shershev families quietly moved back to Antopol, as they had family there. Meanwhile, the Drohitchin Committee was looking for a place to settle the Shershev families. Eighteen kilometres north of Drohitchin was Khomsk, whose Jewish inhabitants had been massacred earlier that month by the Einsatzgruppen, the Nazi death squads. The local Christians collaborated with the Nazis, and after the slaughter, they plundered everything the Jews left behind. Now they needed the Jewish skilled tradesmen and artisans to make their clothes and shoes, or to refit the plundered Jewish clothes that did not fit properly. Being almost exclusively farmers, they needed blacksmiths and carpenters. They agreed to let in between eighty and a hundred Jewish families from Shershev. A number of families moved to other nearby shtetls. The rest of us remained in Drohitchin for the time being.

Not wanting to overstay our welcome with our generous hosts, my parents decided to go to Khomsk. Before going there with the children, my mother and I wanted to take a look at the place. So on a warm September day, my mother and I left Drohitchin for Khomsk. The road ran between fields and swamps and was in poor condition. We walked with apprehension, afraid of encountering Germans or local police, who would easily recognize us as Jews. After walking about half the way, I asked my mother if she would like to sit down. My mother answered with a question—Was I tired? I said yes, which was a blatant lie. But I was worried that my mother might be tired, and this was the only way I could make her sit down. We sat at the side of the road.

After a short time, my mother said to me, "I am grateful to God that my legs can still carry me. You, an eighteen-year-old young man, are already tired and I could still go on."

I too was grateful to God that my mother could go on, but I said nothing. We did not sit for long and carried on walking. At about five in the afternoon, we got to Khomsk. As in most Eastern European shtetls in those days, Christian farmers inhabited Khomsk's outskirts, and we found ourselves on a Christian street. The few Christians we saw in the street gazed at us in a way that told us everything that we did, or did not, want to know. Their glances expressed less compassion than the kind of look one would favour a stray dog with. With fear and dread, we continued. The Christian part of the street was short, and we soon entered what had been the Jewish part only weeks earlier. The most obvious sign that these were Jewish homes was the open doors and windows. The windows with their dark backgrounds were like big holes from which eyes had been torn out, and the light was gone. The doors were like big wide mouths that screamed into the street to every passerby: *Where are the Jews that lived for generations within my walls? The ones that kept me warm and illuminated, that rejoiced and grieved, laughed and cried? What have you done to them? Why?*

There was not a living soul in the street. Even the Christian neighbours who had helped the Germans do their gruesome work with so much enthusiasm did not take over the Jewish houses. They had taken everything that was removable, and now there was nothing left to take. We walked slowly and carefully along a dead street among dead houses, as if to avoid waking the dead. Then we noticed a man huddled between the houses. He was from Shershev and had arrived two days earlier but was afraid to be out in the streets. We asked him about Yosl and Brina Pomerantz, my parents' friends who we had heard went to Khomsk. The man pointed to a house farther down the road. We found Yosl and Brina, and they talked us into settling in Khomsk. They were two lonely people, had no children and wanted to be among friends. I looked around. The small house was completely empty except for a small table that wobbled so badly that even the plunderers would not take it. The couple had been in Khomsk for two days and ate potatoes from the garden. We were invited to partake in the supper. We spent the evening in the dark, speaking in subdued voices about our helpless situation. The bare wooden floor did not seem inviting, so we sat up till late in the night.

In the morning, after a breakfast similar to the supper—that is, a few potatoes—Yosl and Brina took us to see the resting place of the Jews of Khomsk. We continued along the same street, at the end of which were two large mounds, one on either side of the road, in a lush green meadow. Despite the green grass around, there was not a single blade of grass on either of the mounds, as if the grass refused to grow on the mass graves of innocent victims as a protest to God and a reminder for humanity of the Nazis' cruelty and barbarism.

Out of the 1,700 Jews of Khomsk, a dozen or so boys and girls had managed to save themselves from that slaughter and returned only after the Jews of Shershev arrived. Even then, they tried not to be seen by local Christians, who were not interested in having witnesses to their cooperation with the Nazis in the slaughter of the local Jews.

Our first impression of Khomsk the previous day, our walk through the Jewish part of the street, the long and depressing conversation with Yosl and Brina, the few hours on the bare floor with sinister thoughts and now the sight of the two gigantic mass graves was too much for my mother, and she broke down in a heart-rending lament. As I looked at those two mass graves, I tried to imagine what must have happened there but in no way could. The mind could not grasp the event; it defied comprehension.

We left Khomsk, hardly exchanging words the whole way back. The images of the dead shtetl and the two mass graves pressed hard on our minds. When we arrived in Drohitchin, we shared our experience with my father and Sheva. I don't know if the younger ones understood any of it. I know that they experienced fear; I saw it in their eyes. A decision had to be made, and my parents decided on Khomsk. Our grandparents Yaakov Kopel and Chinkah, my uncle Eli, and my uncle Reuven and his family stayed behind in Drohitchin.

A couple of days later, we left Drohitchin for Khomsk. We walked into a former Jewish house on the same street where most of the Shershev refugees had settled, the street with the mass graves at one end. We had to settle for one of the last houses on the street, closest to the graves. The house was small, with two rooms and a kitchen, and completely empty. Fortunately, the door and windows had been left intact. The little shed in the yard had hay and firewood that the owner had prepared for the winter. There was a garden behind the barn with potatoes still in the ground. We brought in some hay and spread it on the floor along a wall in one room, converting it into a sleeping room. The next morning, I explored the last few empty Jewish houses and returned with two old tin cans, a couple of twisted spoons and a knife with half the handle gone. I used the larger can as a pail for water I got from the well a couple of times a day, and my mother used the smaller one as a pot for boiling potatoes three times a day. A day or two later, I found a rusty bowl that we used for washing, although we had no soap.

My mother's foresight to wear extra underwear and clothing before leaving Shershev proved to be a blessing. We could put on another set of clothing while my mother and Sheva tried to wash the dirty ones in water mixed with ashes. After such a wash, the clothing looked a bit cleaner. We dug up all the potatoes in the garden and stored them in the house. Eating only potatoes three times a day, we knew that we would run out before spring.

Several days after settling in Khomsk, my uncle Reuven came to see if it would be worthwhile for him and his family to move too. Like us, he came on foot, as this was the only means of movement for a Jew, and this too was very risky. Like us, he slept on the floor with a bit of hay underneath him. In the morning, I took him to the two mass graves. I stood near him and watched his face. For a moment, he remained speechless and motionless, then I heard a barely audible murmur coming from his lips: "God in heaven, make them pay for it!"

With this picture in his mind, my uncle turned around to go back to Drohitchin. That was the last time any of us saw Uncle Reuven.

During their rule, the Soviets had established a brickyard near Khomsk. Now, the local authority was in charge of it, and they turned to the Jews for free labour. My turn came once a week. There, in the middle of the fields, we helped ourselves to potatoes and baked them over a fire. They were delicious. We were also sent to work in a dairy, where we operated a huge churn. The manager generously rewarded us for that day's work with a litre of buttermilk. That was a real treat after a diet of unsalted potatoes, but we were not destined to enjoy this treat more than a couple of times. There were more aggressive boys who became permanent churn operators for such a highly paying job as a litre of buttermilk a day.

Among the Shershev Jews who came to Khomsk were tradespeople and artisans, and they had it much easier. All a tailor or dressmaker needed was a needle and thread. Some procured a pair of scissors or even a press iron. The tools were in such condition that even the local plunderers did not want them, but in professional hands, they served their purpose. These tradespeople, including blacksmiths and carpenters, worked for the surrounding population and local farmers. As there was no money in circulation, they were paid in flour, potatoes, cereals or sometimes with a few eggs, some cheese or even a piece of butter.

A week or so after our arrival, my friend Laizer Rotenberg, whom I had watched run away from the Germans when we were marching, came to his family, who were also in Khomsk. He had suffered bullet wounds to the fleshy part of his legs, but within a month he was back to himself.

One task others and I felt duty-bound to do was to cover the partly dug-up mass graves from time to time. The local gentiles would dig up the graves at night to search the decomposing bodies for valuables that might have been overlooked by the Germans.

In the later part of September, when the days grew noticeably shorter and the evenings longer, we burned kindling in the open door of the brick oven, not wanting to sit in total darkness. There wasn't a need for much light in a house consisting of two rooms. We had nothing to read, and besides, our strained nerves would not permit us to sit down for long. We would pace around the house from window to window, looking out into the dark street or yard for a suspicious shadow which would signal the arrival of the Nazis or local police. At about midnight, we would go to sleep on the hay-covered floor. If one could call it sleep is questionable, as we jumped up at every sound and every distant bark of a dog, running to the window to look for a motion that would betray the dreaded murderers. Before sunrise, we were up, knowing that an *Aktion* usually started at this hour of the morning. In such an atmosphere of tension and fear, we spent our days in Khomsk.

On Saturdays, some of us youngsters would get together with one of the survivors of the Khomsk slaughter, listening to their stories of escape. We would just talk and even tell jokes that made everybody laugh. In those rare moments of laughter, I looked at those young people of Khomsk, trying to understand how they were able to laugh after what they had seen and lost. I thought that in their place I would not even want to listen to jokes, certainly not laugh. I did not yet understand the extent of human endurance or the strength of the human spirit and its ability to recover.

With fall, the weather changed, and the streets and lanes became muddy from rain. On such a day, me and several others my age were tasked with moving piles of *sforim*, Jewish religious books, from one former Jewish home to another. We walked through a muddy lane to a house in which we found *sforim* heaped on the floor halfway to the ceiling. It pained me terribly to think that their owners were all in the ground and that their holy books—which they would have treated so gently and respectfully, not letting them out of their hand without a kiss—were lying there, desecrated by the Nazis and their collaborators. Our task was to take the books to a nearby house, where we found more books, piled from floor to ceiling in every room. What hurt even more than seeing the books was seeing the number of *tfiln* that were scattered in the mud over the lane. The local gentiles had torn off the *retsues*, the leather straps of the *tfiln*, and broken open the boxes containing the parchment, looking for hidden valuables. Not content with murder alone, they had to desecrate our sacred objects. My mind went to the part of the Yom Kippur prayer about the martyrdom of the ten sages, when Rabbi Yishmael lifted the head of Rabbi Shimon and cried out, "How is the tongue, skilled in the words of God, brought low to lick the dust?" Dispirited and sad, we finished our task and went back to our families.

Not all Shershev families wanted to stay in Khomsk because reminders of what had happened to the local Jews stared them in the face daily, and they knew that the same could happen to them at any time. Some moved from shtetl to shtetl, wherever there were Jews, to try to find a place. Some got to Pruzhany. There was a rumour circulating that Pruzhany was becoming a Jewish town. My grandparents and uncle Eli in Drohitchin decided to go to Pruzhany to join the rest of the family and found a farmer to drive them there. Why my uncle Reuven and his family did not do the same will remain a mystery.

At the beginning of October, my parents started talking about going to Pruzhany. There was no other choice, as our potatoes would not last the winter. At least my father had his brothers Joshua, Hershel and Eli, and his sister, Sheindl, in Pruzhany. My parents decided that before we made such a move, my father and I should go and take a look for ourselves.

A couple of days later, the two of us set out for Pruzhany. The distance of the eighty odd kilometres led through forests and fields along a dirt road that turned muddy in the rain. We removed our yellow badges but we still had to be on guard, not so much from fear of the Germans as of the local police who could tell more easily who was a Jew and who was not. Before entering a village, we would ask farmers in the fields if there were any policemen in the village. If the answer was positive, we would circle the village, adding extra kilometres to our journey.

At night, we came to a village and went straight to the village elder, who personally led us to a farmer, with whom we stayed overnight on hay spread on his kitchen floor. The farmer would not let us leave without a breakfast of boiled potatoes washed down with milk.

Before nightfall the next day, we reached Malch, a small shtetl of eight hundred Jewish souls. My father's two first cousins Joshua and Zalman Nisselbaum lived there. Malch was a typical Polesie shtetl, with small Jewish houses and muddy little streets and alleys, where Jews had lived for many generations. We asked for directions to my father's cousin Joshua's house. As we were sitting and talking about our situation, the chief of the local police entered and was greeted warmly by Joshua, who introduced my father to the chief. It turned out that this man had been the chief of police in Malch before the war, when Joshua was the *sołtys*, village elder. My father told the chief about the experiences of the Jews of Shershev and Khomsk in the last couple of months. As expected for a chief of police under German rule who was still friendly with a Jew, he did not make any comment and just nodded slightly. When he left, Joshua said to my father, "Actually, he is not a bad sort."

The next morning, we left for Pruzhany, which was twenty kilometres away. About halfway there was a railway track that had been turned into a border between the newly formed German administrative territories of East Prussia and Ukraine. There was no permanent border guard, but from time to time a German patrol passed along the tracks. We passed it without incident.

Near Pruzhany, we saw a large group of Jews returning to town from work. We joined them and got into Pruzhany without a problem. The Jews of Pruzhany had been forced to live in the area of town that had become the ghetto, though many had homes inside the ghetto perimeter and were allowed to remain there. Jews from many places were being brought into the Pruzhany ghetto or came by their own accord. They came from places like Białowieża and Hajnówka, where Jews were expelled from their homes and towns even before Shershev. Half of the Jews of Kamenets Litovsk went to Pruzhany. Jews from small shtetls left their homes and places of birth voluntarily before being ordered to move. They were looking for security and safety in numbers. Jews also arrived from Aranchytsy-Linovo, Malch and Sielec and other nearby villages. To add to this multitude, five thousand Jews from Białystok were being sent to Pruzhany. The expulsion of the few Christian families from the ghetto area and the huge influx of Jews gave the impression that Pruzhany was indeed being made into a Jewish town.

As soon as we were in Pruzhany, we went straight to my father's sister Sheindl. We found her with her husband and children, my grandparents and my uncle Eli. My father's brother Hershel, from Kamenets Litovsk, was also there with his wife. After spending a couple of days talking and listening, our relatives advised us to move to Pruzhany, and my father agreed. We left Pruzhany on a Friday afternoon, arriving in Malch just before dark. This time we stayed with a different relative of my father's, Tzalkah the baker. That Friday night, Tzalkah's wife gave us a piece of challah. It was the first time that I had tasted challah in over two years. It would also be my last piece of challah for the next four years.

When the first shot woke me, it was just past five. It seemed to me that I had just fallen asleep. We jumped out of bed and dressed in seconds. It was still dark outside, but out of the still darker room I could see two men running with rifles, shooting at random into the street. The last two months in Khomsk had prepared us for such moments. Not losing a second, my father and I ran to the door, opened it with one kick and ran out. We did not slow down as we crossed the street and somebody's yard, jumped over a fence and found ourselves in an open meadow. Then we started to run in earnest, away from Malch. It was dawn and I could make out a few more people running in the meadow. My father, panting, said to me, "This is the rabbi, his son and the *shames* [the beadle]." Farther on our right, I recognized a girl named Symah, who had been my sister's classmate in the gymnasium.

Our objective was to get away as far and as fast as we could. I turned to see if we were being chased and saw several men behind the fence we had just climbed, their rifles resting on the fence, firing in our direction.

I saw Symah fall to the ground, and I prayed and pleaded that the bullets aimed at us miss their target. When we finally stopped to catch our breath, we could still hear the shooting but not as continuously as before. In our imaginations, we could already see the Jews of Malch being driven to the slaughter like the Khomsk Jews.

The only road left for us was to Khomsk, to my mother, sisters and brother. As we walked along that road, we encountered a tall farmer coming in our direction. When we came face to face with him, he asked in Yiddish, "Jews?" We were taken aback. He continued, "I am a Jew too. I spent all my life in that nearby village. This morning, the Germans came and ordered me to leave everything behind and go to Malch." We told him what had happened that morning in Malch. This only added to his confusion, but still he continued in the direction of Malch, perhaps not having anywhere else to go or anyone to turn to. We could not understand why this Jew, in his farmer's attire and with his farmer's looks, went on to Malch. How sad it was that a Jew who had lived his entire lifetime among Christians could not turn to anyone for help in his time of need.

As we continued walking, I saw two Germans coming in our direction. My father was looking down at the road to avoid a deep puddle and had not seen them yet. Just ahead of us was a homestead without any sign of life in the yard. I grabbed my father by the sleeve and pulled him off the road, leading him behind the house to a well, telling him that I was very thirsty. From where we stood, we could not see the road or the passing Germans. Not wanting to worry my father unnecessarily, I lowered the pail slowly into the well, bringing it back up at an even slower speed. Putting the pail on the rim of the well, I drank very slowly. When I could not drink anymore, I still held my face in the pail pretending to drink. My father finally asked me, "How much can you drink?"

I only stopped pretending to drink when I felt that the Germans had passed the house. I talked my father into taking a drink himself, and then we emerged from behind the house onto the road. By then the Germans were a fair distance away. I did not say anything to my father, just nodded in their direction. My father said nothing, but I knew he understood the reason for how I was acting.

We kept plodding along the muddy road toward Khomsk. Before dark, we entered the village of Minki and went straight to the village elder. Soon some farmers arrived from Malch. They did not know much of what was going on there. All they said to us was, "The Germans are shooting ours and yours, but yours more."

Where could we go on a dark and rainy October night? The elder took us to a farmer, and we spent the night on a hay-covered floor. We did not have any nightmares simply because we could not sleep after the experiences of that day. The escape from Malch, the fear of being shot, the tension in every step affected us. Behind us, Malch was being massacred. The road to Pruzhany was closed. Death loomed in every village where either Germans or local police were present. And when we got to Khomsk, what then? For how long would Khomsk be left alone?

Everybody was up before daylight. The farmer's wife gave us boiled potatoes with some milk. The rain had stopped overnight, and the road began to dry up, but most of our walk took place across fields and forests as we had to avoid the villages. Around noon we stumbled upon a homestead somewhere near a forest. We entered the little house and asked for a piece of bread. The farmer's wife took a crust of dry bread out of the cupboard and handed it to us. As she offered it, I noticed her looking critically at the bread. She must have seen that the bread was too small for two men, so she went back to the cupboard, took out a fresh loaf of bread, sliced off another piece and gave it to us. We left the house, my father holding the two pieces of bread. He handed me the bigger piece, the fresh one. Without thinking, I gulped it down. It was after I finished my piece that I looked at my father, who was struggling with the piece of dry crust. I hated myself for being so thoughtless about the bread. But it was too late. I had eaten it.

In mid-afternoon we entered a little village. In another hour and a half, we would be in Khomsk. Not that we had any good news or were safe in Khomsk, but after the last two days, just to be with the rest of the family, no matter for how long, would be a relief. Suddenly, a few farmers' children appeared and started mocking us, yelling, "Hey Jews! Where are you going? To Khomsk? There are no more Jews in Khomsk. They were all slaughtered."

In that moment, our entire world collapsed. We were numb and unable to think while the village children jumped around, shouting and laughing. Dimly aware of our actions, we left the village, if only to escape the laughing children. Just outside the village, we stopped. The two of us were now alone in the world, had nowhere to go and nobody to go to. Why did we abandon our family? We should have stayed to be with them in their final moments, to hold my little sisters' hands at the edge of the ditch. Why did we have to go to Pruzhany exactly now? God in heaven, why?

In the distance, a horse and buggy were approaching. A farmer pulled up next to us. He was dressed like all farmers but in cleaner and better-fitting clothing. With a friendly face and encouraging smile, he offered us a ride. We wondered if he was making fun of us. We told him what we had just heard from the village children, and he listened with a serious but critical expression on his face. When we finished, he said, "I am a village elder from a nearby village. If something had happened in Khomsk, I would have known. The children were most likely referring to the original slaughter. Do not be afraid. Get on the wagon and let us get closer to Khomsk."

We had nothing to lose and got on the wagon. As we spoke, the man pointed to a sewing machine in his wagon and said, "This used to belong to a Jew. A friend of mine plundered it from a Jewish home. I borrowed it from him, as my wife needed to do some sewing." He expressed sympathy with our plight. We entered Khomsk while listening for the first time to expressions of compassion coming from Christian lips. The lanes were empty and quiet in Khomsk at dusk. We thanked the good Christian. With great emotion and relief, we greeted and hugged my mother and the children.

Within a week, the events in Malch became fully known to us. The Germans had come to Malch to inform the local Jews that they were being transferred to the town of Bereza Kartuska. Before daybreak, they had started to assemble the Jews, screaming and shooting in the air. When Jews panicked and began running away, the Germans shot at them. The local police followed suit. A couple dozen lives were taken. On the next day, the Jews of Malch left their centuries-old homes. A few families took the chance and moved to Pruzhany instead of to Bereza Kartuska. Among them were my father's cousins Joshua and Zalman Nisselbaum and their families.

After we recovered from the experience in Malch, my parents again discussed going to Pruzhany. We would be dependent on help from the family there, for whatever money my father and I had with us had been taken from us during the march from Shershev. The little money my mother succeeded in hiding from the Germans was insignificant, even though it was in US dollars. Our jewellery and gold coins were buried in Shershev. To go and get it was out of the question, even if it was still there and had not been found by the local gentiles. My parents came to the decision that we would remain in Khomsk for as long as the potatoes lasted and then go to Pruzhany.

Late fall was always a rainy season in our part of the world. That fall was no exception. The mud in Khomsk's streets and alleys was harder to deal with than in Shershev, where at least the streets were cobblestone. To go to a neighbour was a problem, especially since we didn't have proper footwear or attire. So that fall, we sat on the only piece of furniture we had, a broken bench, or on the hay on the floor in the dimly lit room. The only light came from the burning kindling in the brick oven. In the semi-darkness of the room, we could not see the soot floating around in the air, but in the morning, we saw each other's black soot-filled nostrils. The adults were able to wash the soot out ourselves, but my little brother and sisters needed help, poor dear sweet children.

We attributed exaggerated significance to rumours and sometimes even to dreams. Some of the circulating rumours were well founded, some were just rumours, and none were encouraging. One rumour was that in some places the Germans killed only the men and that the women were being left alone and were safe. In other places, it was the opposite. In our desperation, we failed to see the reality at which we stared every day—the two mass graves in which men, women and children, young and old, lay shoulder to shoulder, without regard or compassion for sex or age. Every day brought its quota of rumours, and these upset us to the limits of our already agitated nerves.

From all my friends at home, the only ones I had in Khomsk were the two Rotenberg brothers, with whom I spent a fair amount of time. My friend Laizer, who had escaped during our march, decided to marry a girl from Khomsk. She was one of the dozen young people who had managed to escape the slaughter. To say that the wedding was a modest one would be a great exaggeration. It took place without a rabbi, without the blessing over the wine, just in the presence of two witnesses. The wedding was befitting the times.

With November came the winds, cold and snow. Fortunately, it was warm in the house. The previous owner had provided himself ahead of time with wood for the winter he did not live to see. One November day, I was given the job of cutting wood in the schoolyard for the school, which was now attended by Christian children only, as the Jewish children were lying in the mass graves. We had to saw and split the logs outside and bring them in by the armful. As I was coming into the school with the wood, I passed through the corridor where the pupils' coats were hanging. I froze on the spot. Only a Jew who grew up in that part of the world could have noticed and understood: There in front of me, on hook after hook, hung Jewish children's coats. While farmers' coats were made of homespun wool, Jewish ones were made from manufactured fabrics. There, in front of me, was a row of coats that had been owned by Jewish children only a short time ago. The true owners of those coats were now decomposing in the ground, while the children of those men who had diligently helped the Nazis in their atrocious and savage act were wearing their victims' clothing. Looking at those Jewish children's coats, I wanted to scream, "Not only did you murder, you have also plundered!" But what good was the cry when the murderers were the law, the judge and the enforcer?

My parents were soon talking about Pruzhany in earnest. The potatoes in the corner of the room were disappearing fast. But Pruzhany was at the end of eighty kilometres of frozen and snow-covered road, on which there might be local police, Germans or both. For a Jew to be caught by either of them spelled death. We could not delay the trip either, for the moment we finished the last pot of potatoes, we would have nothing left to eat. One day, in the second half of December, my mother boiled the last few potatoes and divided them among us. We put on all the clothing we had, and with nothing to carry we left the house that had sheltered us for three months.

After covering a couple of kilometres on the road, we reached a forest, proceeding under the trees that protected us from the falling snow. From a distance we saw an approaching horse and buggy. When it came closer, my father and I recognized the village elder who had given us a lift to Khomsk when we were running from Malch, the one who had expressed so much sympathy and compassion for us Jews. Seeing this friendly Christian, we came out of the forest to greet him. He recognized us too. As we were talking, several local policemen with rifles over their shoulders approached on bicycles. Seeing them at a distance, the village elder said, as if to himself, "What are they doing here?" Turning to us he asked, "Did anybody see you leave Khomsk this morning?" We said we did not know. He nodded knowingly and said, "Go on your way but stay close to the forest, and may God be with you." He pulled the reins and started out toward the approaching policemen. From behind the tree branches, we watched as they met and talked to one another. We looked on with relief as the policemen turned and headed back to Khomsk on their bicycles. I want to believe that the good Christian was sent to us at that moment as if from heaven.

At noon, the weather changed. It cleared and turned frosty, and the snow began to crackle under our feet. My two little sisters, Sonia, who was going on ten, and Leiba, who was not yet eight, were struggling in the deep snow. So was my brother, Leibel, barely eleven. Their little faces were red from the wind and cold, their eyes teary from exposure to the hostile weather, and they held on to my parents' hands with their bare ones. My father still had his worn winter coat. My mother was wrapped only in a shawl. That sight pained me terribly, and I tried to imagine how my parents felt, especially my mother, who had always been so protective of us.

Every hour or so, we were forced to knock on the door of a homestead. Out of compassion, those ordinary farmers let us in to warm up. Some even gave us pieces of bread for the children. Coming into one house on that same afternoon, we must have presented a pathetic picture, for the farmer and his wife started begging my parents to leave the three children with them. They were quite outspoken and said openly to my parents, "You know what will eventually happen to you. With you, the children stand no chance. Leave them with us. We will look after them as if they were our own."

My parents, Sheva and I knew that they were telling the truth. But how do you leave your own children, your own flesh and blood, with total strangers? How do you tell your own children, "Dear children, from now on you are no more ours, you will never see us again nor hear from us. These total strangers will from now on be your guardians. They will feed you and look after you for better or for worse"? The scene would be unimaginable: children begging, pleading with parents not to be left behind with total strangers, children telling parents that they would rather die with them than live without them!

And who were these people? Was it a normal reaction of decent people to a heartbreaking scene that moved them for a moment? What would their reaction be an hour or two later when they realized that they had committed themselves to feed three more mouths? Would they still feel the same way, or would their altruism evaporate? A spark of hope still smouldered in our hearts, no matter how vague or naive, that we would be safer in Pruzhany.

As for me, I could not have parted with my little brother and sisters.

Looking at their teary swollen eyes for fear of having to remain, I could not even dream of it. I guess my parents felt the same way. We thanked the good people and left.

Before dark, we got to another village and asked to be taken to the village elder. We asked him if he could put us up for the night, and without a single question, he took us to a farmer's house, where we spent the night on the kitchen floor.

In the late afternoon of the next day, we approached Malch with great apprehension. Even if there were no Germans in town, there was a local police force, and they were as dangerous. But it was out of the question to go around Malch this late in the afternoon; we would get stuck in the open field, deep in snow, and perish for sure. Having no alternative, we entered Malch. We came face to face with two local policemen. They smirked as they led us to the police station, right into the chief's office. I remember the surprise on the policemen's faces when they saw the chief get up from his seat, stretch out his hand to my father and say in a friendly voice, "Mr. Kantorowitz, how are you?" It was the chief of police we had met at my father's cousin's house on our way to Pruzhany in October.

The two policemen immediately changed their attitude toward us. They reported to the chief that they had met "these people"—not "Jews"—in the street. My father told the chief the reason for our being in Malch and asked if he could find us a place to spend the night. The chief said that we would have to break up into two groups, as we were too many for one household. He also mentioned that there was a man in Malch whom we might know. My mother and siblings went one way, and my father and I went to the person the chief said we might know. It was my former boss Pietrukiewicz, the manager of the Soviet warehouse where I had worked for a year. We spent the night there, reminiscing with him until late about the good times in Shershev.

In the morning, we set out on our last leg to Pruzhany. The crossing of the railway track passed uneventfully, and we entered Pruzhany via Seltzer Street, where Jews occupied the first houses.

16

The Pruzhany Ghetto

PRUZHANY WAS A haven not only for the local Jews, but also for Jews from the nearby shtetls who had miraculously managed to save themselves from the slaughter of their respective shtetls. Credit for the order and organization in Pruzhany must be given to the leadership of the community, which followed the tradition of previous generations, guiding the community with justice, compassion and honesty.

A day after our arrival, the Committee assigned us accommodations in a house that had belonged to a Christian who had to vacate it, as it was within the perimeter of the ghetto area. It consisted of two small rooms and a kitchen that we would share with two women who lived in the same small house. The two women, a mother and her daughter, who was a teacher by profession, had been brought to Pruzhany from Białystok. My father's sister Sheindl and his brother Joshua gave us a double bed, a couch, a table and a couple of chairs. We already had more than we had in Khomsk.

The allotted portion of bread per person was distributed under the supervision of the Judenrat at a minimal price. There were some who could not afford to pay anything, and they received their bread for free. Thus, the Committee made sure that every inhabitant of the ghetto was provided with a roof overhead, a piece of bread and a few potatoes.

For some unknown reason, Pruzhany enjoyed certain privileges that no other shtetl in the district did. For example, the Germans allowed market days; every Monday and Thursday, the farmers from the surrounding villages came to town to sell their produce and buy other necessities. Market days were a very old tradition that the Soviets had abolished. In the old days, the farmers could bring the items they wanted to sell to the market, and then they would go to the stores, many of them Jewish owned, and buy whatever they needed. There were no Jewish stores now. Still, some former storekeepers had managed to hold on to some of their merchandise and could barter with the farmers. But most of the local Jews bartered some of their household items or clothing for food. The farmers had restrictions. They were permitted to bring in potatoes, cabbage, beets and carrots, but no meat, butter, eggs or cheese. Yet some of these forbidden products found their way into the ghetto hidden inside sacks of potatoes. The ghetto was still accessible in many ways, which made food prices reasonable.

All this does not mean that Jews in Pruzhany knew no hunger. Many of the Jewish tradesmen, artisans and even merchants had always lived hand to mouth, and many had no savings to rely on or merchandise to sell. However, as long as Christians could get in and bring with them work in the form of raw material for Jewish tradesmen and Jews could go out and work in Christian homes, survival was possible.

Despite the tension and uncertainty, the ghetto pulsated with life. There were still assets and materials to fulfill the German demands and to pay bribes when needed. Everything was done to postpone the inevitable, hoping upon hope for a miracle.

Some of the Jews from Białystok and Kamenets Litovsk who had been transported to Pruzhany by the Germans quietly began to move back. Others remained, among them my uncle Hershel and his wife, Sheine. My uncle believed there was safety in numbers and that the fact that Pruzhany was incorporated in East Prussia made us German citizens, and therefore privileged Jews. How naive he was!

The Germans had a constant demand for workers. One group worked for the Schutzpolizei, the German police force. Work there meant hell on earth. Men returned from that work beaten and bloodied and had to be replaced almost daily. Another place of work was the *Ortskommandantur*, where soldiers from the Eastern Front came for a rest. Other work required physical labour, like cleaning snow off the streets. Any kind of work done for the Germans and their Polish pawns was done without any compensation. We were grateful if we got away without a beating.

For me, Pruzhany was a change for the better. No more did I walk among the dead like in Khomsk. Here I was among the living, who dared to hope. And I found two of my closest friends in Pruzhany, Kalman Kalbkauf and Itzik Maletzky.

Despite my experiences in Khomsk, I still did not understand the importance of helping my father in providing the most elementary items for our survival. I left it all to him, taking it for granted that he would somehow manage. I don't know what my father did while I was at work outside the ghetto. Nor do I really know to what extent my uncles and aunts helped us. I know that they did help us, especially my father's sister Sheindl. It is quite possible that my father dabbled a bit in buying and selling small items. I will never know the truth of what happened.

Among the many regrets that I have had to carry throughout my life, this is one for which I cannot forgive myself even today. How could I have been so unfeeling as to not understand what was going on? After all, I was going on nineteen! When I worked outside the ghetto, I would get a quarter of a kilo of bread, which I greedily ate up. I never stopped to think that maybe I should bring it back home. Coming back from work, my mother always had a piece of bread and a bowl of soup for me. I never thought of asking my mother how she managed it or if she had eaten. I never saw my little brother and sister emaciated, but my mother, who was always a heavier woman, had been slowly losing weight since our expulsion from Shershev. Why didn't I think of asking my mother or father if they had eaten or if they were hungry? These thoughts haunt me and gnaw at me even today.

On one cold day in February, the Gestapo ordered the Judenrat to deliver five hundred Jews, preferably entire families, for deportation east. The Committee was given three days to deliver, or the Germans would do it themselves. Everyone in the ghetto knew that if the Germans took over, many more lives would be lost. The Committee was faced with the task of annulling the decree if possible, and if that was not possible, making the selection themselves. How do you tell someone that he and his family must die? The inhabitants of the ghetto lived in a state of tension and outright fear. The out-of-town refugees knew that any list would not consist of the locals, so we were doubly concerned.

The Committee tried hard to annul the decree. The intermediary was Zalman Segal, a member of the community. In the ghetto, he was called "the foreign minister." He was born in Pruzhany and spent many years in Danzig, where he learned the German language. A tall man with a military gait, he looked German, and apparently he understood their approach, psychology and attitude toward Jews. He could at times anticipate their next move or intentions. In the hours before the deadline, when the Committee was supposed to deliver five hundred Jews, it felt like messianic times. Zalman Segal sent a messenger from the Gestapo bureau, where he had been sitting all evening in difficult negotiations with the chief of the Gestapo, to the office of the Committee. It consisted of three words: "It is good." These three words spread throughout the ghetto within minutes, despite the late hour. That day was the happiest in my short life in the Pruzhany ghetto. When does a pauper rejoice? When he finds the nickel he has just lost.

The success of those negotiations could have been due to two factors: the talent of the negotiator and the susceptibility of the Gestapo bigwigs to bribery. Sometimes money was sufficient, sometimes leather boots and coats were required, or fur coats for their wives, or liquor, and sometimes all those things together. It depended on the severity of the decree.

From the refugees' point of view, the local Jews of Pruzhany had it much better than them. After all, the locals remained in their homes and could always find something to barter with, no matter how difficult it was to part with. The refugees had nothing to sell. A few Shershev Jews now living in Pruzhany would sneak into Shershev at night and try to collect things that they had given their Christian neighbours for safekeeping, or simply try to get some food by begging. Others did not dare go to Shershev, and they sent messages to their Christian friends to come out to Pruzhany on market days. Some asked their Christian confidants to dig up something in their yard or hiding place and bring it to them. In rare cases something could be retrieved, but most of the time those attempts were futile. As soon as the Jews had left the shtetl, the local gentiles threw themselves at the Jewish possessions and searched their yards. Hardly anything escaped detection.

My father did succeed in recovering some leather, which we had hidden in the double floor of our house. The couple who had lived in our house before the war, when half of the house served as a health clinic, had helped. Some weeks later, my father asked the same man to retrieve several pairs of new shoes we had hidden elsewhere, but he claimed that there were none to be found. That was our last attempt to recover anything from our house or yard in Shershev.

Throughout the winter, a trickle of Jewish refugees kept coming to the ghetto. Among them were Shershev families who were really starving. Having no other choice, they were compelled to take the risk to get to Pruzhany, where, despite all the difficulties, they were welcomed. The allotted bread and potato ration alone could not fill one's stomach, and those who were not able to obtain extra food were forced to stretch out a hand, which was never sent back empty. Some refugees, most of them from Shershev, took awful chances to avoid becoming a burden on the Committee or on anyone else. Men travelled the long distance to Drohitchin on foot, carrying saccharin in knapsacks to exchange for tobacco. A couple even procured a horse and sled for this purpose. The Christians along the route they used soon found out and would ambush them, taking away the merchandise, the horse and the sled.

Having no alternative, those men had to go on foot by a different route every time. In such a way, some Shershev families survived the winter.

Shortly before Passover in the spring of 1942, the Germans reduced the size of the ghetto. We had to move out and were assigned a room on Nowa Street, in a big house belonging to a tailor by the name of Beryl Zukerman. He appeared to be close to sixty and was a bit stooped from spending a lifetime over a sewing machine. He was a socialist by conviction, and like many old-time idealists was well informed about politics, a worthy and formidable opponent in a discussion or debate. His wife was a quiet, easygoing woman. Their oldest daughter had recently married a refugee from Białystok. A young intelligent couple by the name of Eisenstein from Białystok already occupied one room in the house. The husband was the assistant chief of the ghetto police and was always busy, and his wife would come into our room to chat with my mother. The room we were given was small, especially for the seven of us. Sheva had to move to my uncle Joshua's, which was on the same street a few houses away. We were in the heart of the Jewish part of Pruzhany, where Jews could move about out of sight from prying German eyes.

At that time, the Germans had an exact count of how many Jews were living in the ghetto and so did the Committee. With spring, the demand for workers outside the ghetto increased, and it became difficult to dodge it. I now had to appear every day to be assigned to different tasks. Outside Pruzhany, the Soviets had started building two military airports along with a row of wooden barracks and several two-storey brick buildings to house the military. The German Schutzpolizei had moved into the brick buildings. They decided to dismantle the wooden barracks, and a large group of us came every day to do the job. The work could have progressed quietly and quickly, but the Schutzpolizei liked to come over to have some fun with the Jews. The work became a torture chamber.

The barracks were built on sandy ground, supported by large posts dug into the ground. After dismantling the roof and the wall, the heavy posts had to come out. Once, I saw a German supervising a small group of men digging out a post. He ordered them to dig around the post and let it fall in whichever direction. When the post fell halfway, he ordered them to pull it out of the hole. It was never an easy job, but this one got jammed and would not budge. The German was standing over them with a heavy club, beating them continuously. I do not know where I suddenly got the nerve to do what I did. I ran over and jumped into the hole and quickly dug to one side of it, then jumped out and pushed the post in that direction. I nodded to two other men, and we put our hands around the post and pulled it out. Without stopping to straighten my back, fearing the German's reaction to my intervention, I ran to the next post, quickly digging a narrow ditch on one side of the post. I pushed the post in that direction. The post fell promptly along the intended path. With a couple more men, we quickly pulled the post out. It was only then that I chanced to look at the German. To my surprise, he was looking at me approvingly. The group around me soon caught on and started doing it my way to avoid further beating. The German came over to me, put the stick in my hand and said, "You take care of them." As soon as he turned away, I let the stick slide from my hand. He noticed, came over and picked it up, and I got ready to receive a good thrashing. Instead, he simply handed it to me without a word. Again, as soon as he turned away, I let the stick drop from my hand. This time, the German just sighed in resignation and turned and walked away. I believed then, and still believe now, that on that day I saved some of my co-workers from a lot of blows, and I am proud of myself for daring to throw the stick away.

The next day, I was assigned to another task. The Schutzpolizei showed up too. I could never understand why. Was it sheer idleness? Was it for amusement? Or was it plain sadism that made them come torture us? Within two weeks, we finished that job, and I began to work in a different place every day.

There were two jails in Pruzhany from way back. One was built of bricks and was referred to as the red jail, the other was covered with plaster and was called the white jail. Under the Soviets, those two jails served mostly as holding places for criminal and political offenders before they were sent to Siberia. Under the Germans, the two jails served as a gathering point from where arrested people were dealt with in the Nazi manner, that is to say, sent to their eternal rest. Those arrested were former Soviet collaborators, Communists, employees of the Communist Party, militia members, Soviet sympathizers and suspected sympathizers. When the activities of the pro-Soviet partisans intensified in the spring of 1942, their sympathizers and supporters were arrested. The Germans did not need any proof of guilt to arrest anybody. All they needed was a name. And so, it became a time for revenge, for settling old misunderstandings, rivalries and resentments. All one needed to do was tell the Germans that so-and-so supports the partisans. Within twenty-four hours that person would be arrested and brought to one of the jails. The jails filled up quickly, and to make room for new prisoners, the old ones had to be disposed of. A couple of Gestapo men would arrive from Biała Podlaska to look over the cases of the detained. There was no interrogation, no hearing, and everything followed the whim of the Gestapo representative. The two jails would be almost entirely emptied after such a Gestapo visit.

Between Pruzhany and the railway station at Aranchytsy was a birch forest surrounded by sandy terrain, overgrown with bushes in spots. Near those bushes, the Germans decided to make a resting place for the condemned. First, a mass grave had to be prepared, and it was the Jewish Committee that had to send diggers, so the ghetto was forewarned about impending executions and the number of people to be shot. The Nazis calculated the size of the grave depending on that. The pit was dug a couple of days before the execution, and on the day of the execution a group of thirty men waited there for the burial at six in the morning. Of course, nobody wanted to volunteer for this job, but as these events took place about once a month, many didn't have a choice, and one spring day, it was my ill luck to be in that group.

In the early morning, we received about a quarter of a kilogram of bread and marched out of the ghetto to our destination. After a six-kilometre march, we turned off the road and reached a large clearing.

A pit had been dug in the sandy soil. Judging by its length, we figured that 150 prisoners would be executed. Steps had been dug into the ground, reaching to the bottom of the pit. It must have rained at night, for the steps were partly washed away. The leader of the group told us to fix the steps. While we were busy fixing the steps, a German police officer pulled up on a motorcycle. He inspected our work and gave our foreman some instructions. As soon as we finished, the German told us to get behind the bushes some fifty metres away and not to look in the direction of the pit. Our group leader, Beryl, turned to us and said, "Fellows, if you have something to eat, eat it now, for later you will not feel like it." We took his advice and ate our bread.

Soon we heard approaching vehicles. Not being able to conquer our curiosity, we looked through the bushes. Half a dozen military police on motorcycles and in other vehicles and covered trucks pulled up. From behind the bushes, we could see one truck backing up almost to the rim of the pit. Two Germans opened the back door of the truck and yelled, "Raus!"—*Out!* and people started jumping to the ground.

They were driven down into the pit, using the steps that we had fixed an hour earlier. As soon as the first truck was empty, a second and third followed. Then, some of the police threw something into the hole, and a second or two later, we heard explosions. "Those are grenades," Beryl whispered to us.

Then the Germans approached the pit and began to shoot into it. We understood that they were finishing off the ones who had survived the explosions. They hung around the pit for several more minutes, firing from time to time, making sure that nobody was alive.

Finally, they picked up the shovels we had left near the pit and began filling it in. Their shovelling lasted a minute or two, and then they dropped the shovels, got into the vehicles and pulled away. The remaining German yelled to us to come over. This time we did not walk but ran. For a moment, I was thankful to the Germans for throwing a few shovels of sand over the slaughtered bodies. The just-murdered mass of humanity with torn bodies lay under a thin layer of sand. Each of us grabbed a shovel and shovelled the sand into the pit. Some of the sand was beginning to change colour, absorbing blood. A terrible thought came to me: *If so much blood was being absorbed by the sand on top, what must it be like down below?* We worked quickly, and apparently the German was satisfied with our progress. He got on his motorcycle and drove away. We straightened our backs and tried to relax our nerves. We wanted to get away from there as soon as we could, but we had to stop to collect our thoughts. Even though almost half the pit was taken up with bodies, there was not enough sand to fill the pit. We had to scrounge around for pieces of wood and even tree stumps to fill up the grave.

A day or two later, I was assigned to a group of close to a hundred men whose job it was to dispose of Soviet bombs. We were marched along an unfinished railway embankment built by the Soviets and then into a forest, where there were three huge craters filled with water. The foreman told me that where the craters were had been three large Soviet warehouses filled with aviation bombs, which the Soviets blew up before they withdrew. I recalled the three tremendous explosions I had heard in Shershev on that memorable Sunday night of June 22, 1941. However, not all the bombs had exploded then, and live bombs were spread throughout the forest.

Two German airmen were waiting for us. They ordered us to collect the strewn around bombs and stock them in piles. While they were preparing the blast, we ran to the nearest farmstead, half a kilometre away. Then the airmen lit a delayed-action fuse, giving them enough time to run to shelter. After the explosion, we had to run back and collect more bombs. The work was not only dangerous but very hard. We carried the fifty-kilogram bombs on our shoulders, and the hundred-kilogram bombs were carried by two men on two hammered-together boards. The larger bombs were loaded on a horse-drawn buggy. But even to carry a fifty-kilogram bomb on one's shoulders several hundred metres through a thick forest is no easy task. The two Germans were willing to use their sticks generously. One of them was a non-commissioned officer who carried a submachine gun. At midday, one of them suddenly pointed at me and said, "You, come here." I wondered what I had done now. The German took off his machine gun and put it over my shoulder, saying, "Take care of it and go to the shelter where we keep the explosives, timers and detonators."

The shelter was in a ditch at the main road that was covered with branches and earth that had been dumped on top. I spent the afternoon walking back and forth along the ditch. Compared to the others, I got off easily that day. The next morning, I was given the same job to guard the shelter. As I was walking back and forth on the road, I wondered what the farmers were thinking, seeing a young Jew with big yellow patches on the front and back of his shirt, walking back and forth without fear and without interest in them.

Going to work and back, we talked among ourselves about the number of bombs the Germans were now destroying, about the waste of material, and what's more, about the effort that was put into producing all this that was now being destroyed — all without the loss of a single Nazi's life.

Between jobs, I got away with spending a day or two at home. I would meet with my friends, our conversations focusing on rumours of German defeats and recent slaughters of Jews. Unfortunately, the rumours about the slaughters of Jews were always proven to be correct, whereas the rumours of German defeats were not.

During that spring of 1942, I was one of many called upon to work on the ghetto fence. We had to dig posts into the ground and then fasten a net of barbed wire on them. I happened to work on a stretch of fence behind Rezki Street, where there was a large meadow. Our foreman said, "Look, fellows, nobody is here to supervise now. Let's take in a bit more of the meadow so that the ghetto children will have somewhere to play." When the fence was erected and the German commission came to inspect it, they decided that the ghetto had too much space. They ordered us to move the fence right behind the houses, depriving the ghetto of its only bit of green grass and empty space.

The Committee was informed that the Germans were planning to construct a work camp near Białowieża, and they were required to deliver two hundred able-bodied men. To go out daily from the ghetto to work for the Germans and to come back at night was one thing, but to be away for a month or two under the constant supervision of the Schutzpolizei was something else. Understandably, nobody wanted to go. The Committee appointed representatives from all the shtetls whose residents were now in the Pruzhany ghetto and asked the representatives to give names of people to send to the work camp. From Shershev, they appointed my grandfather Yaakov Kopel. My grandfather told them, "I can give you only one name," and that was the name of his youngest son, my uncle Eli. I do not know if it was due to spitefulness or perhaps helplessness, but they put Eli's name on top of the list, and he was sent to the Białowieża camp.

During the two months of the camp's existence, the workers who got sick from overwork or from beatings were sent back to the ghetto and were replaced by others. The Judenrat did everything in their power to ease the conditions in that camp. With the help of bribes, they sent out several horse-drawn wagons with food every week, and when it was necessary, even with a German escort. No wonder that when those two hundred men returned, they had nothing but praise for the Committee.

A few more Shershev families succeeded in making their way from Drohitchin and Khomsk to Pruzhany, driven by hunger and fear. With the warm weather, the killings of Jews by the Nazi squads and their helpers intensified, and the news the newcomers brought was depressing and shocking. Moving to and from other towns became practically impossible by the summer. Villagers could stop Jews on the road and hand them over to the Germans or local police. Or they would force Jews to dig their own graves before shooting them. Some villagers satisfied themselves with robbing Jews on the road and letting them go. It was rare for a villager not to rob a Jew, and even rarer for a villager to let Jews in overnight and give them something to eat.

The Jews in the Pruzhany ghetto wondered how much longer our luck would hold. We had our share of foolish optimists who found all kinds of reasons that the Germans would leave us alone. The Germans had opened a tannery, where good quality leather was produced. The Germans, especially the Gestapo, craved leather. These optimists pointed out that a workshop was to be opened in the ghetto in which several dozen Jews would sew leather and felt boots to be sent to the army on the Soviet front. It was no secret that the German army had suffered from the bitter cold on the front the previous winter. For those naive optimists, there was no question that the Germans saw their solution to the cold Russian winter in the couple dozen Jews sewing leather and felt boots. This does not mean that the majority of Jews in Pruzhany were foolish enough to believe that they would be spared the fate of other Jewish communities. On the contrary, Pruzhany had many intelligent, realistic and lucid Jews who were active in the Judenrat and the other social and communal organizations in the ghetto. Maybe they felt that this was all that could be done. After all, thus far they had managed to steer the ghetto clear of catastrophe. Pruzhany was unscathed while the Jewish communities all around had disappeared. Every day that we survived could bring us closer to an Allied victory. But for us refugees, who had already tasted real Nazi atrocities, the future was very bleak. All we could hope for was a miracle.

In the late spring of 1942, we found out from a Shershev Jew who had made it from Drohitchin to Pruzhany that the Germans had demanded from the Drohitchin Committee two hundred men for a labour camp. As was usual in such cases, the Drohitchin Committee picked the outsiders. One of those taken was my uncle Reuven. The two hundred men were led away from Drohitchin, never to be seen or heard from again. Peasants from nearby villages had said that they saw those men being led into a nearby forest and killed.

From those scarce wanderers, we were told that the ghettos were being divided into two separate categories, Ghetto A and Ghetto B. In Ghetto A lived the members of the Committee, the ghetto police and employees of the Committee, all those needed for the functioning of the ghetto and those employed by the Germans and their cronies. Those in Ghetto B qualified as unproductive and thus not needed. If ever Jews, in their long history of persecution, did not need division of any kind it was in those days. The Germans understood this perfectly and took advantage of it to the fullest, turning Jew against Jew. Lifelong friends became bitter enemies. Everyone understood that the first victims in case of a Nazi slaughter would be those in Ghetto B. The ghettos were like drowning passenger boats that didn't have enough lifeboats. After the division of the ghettos, the inhabitants of Ghetto B knew that it was only a matter of time before the Germans would come for them. The Jews of Shershev found themselves mostly in Ghetto B because they were refugees. Having nothing to lose, they tried to get out of the ghettos and make their way to Pruzhany. The local Ukrainian police caught and shot most of them. Only a few made it. It was from one who made it that we found out that my aunt Chashkah and her three children were let into Ghetto A as compensation for her husband being killed.

Pruzhany as a whole, including the ghetto, was administrated by a Nazi party member who held the title *Bürgermeister*, or mayor. There was also an *Ortskommandantur*, a military district command. It was housed in several brick buildings and had a fenced-in yard on Pocztowa Street, which led to Pruzhany's main street, Pacewicz or "Negidish Gas" (Rich Man's Street) as it was called in the old days. In the *Ortskommandantur*, the bulk of the buildings held soldiers who had come back from the front for a week or two of rest. A group of Jews went there daily to clean and put things in order. In the beginning, it was a large group. As things began to fall in place and the rooms were equipped with beds, tables and chairs, less help was needed. In the end, they employed only six men. I was one of them. Our work consisted of sawing and splitting wood, pumping water into a water tower, peeling potatoes for the kitchen and cleaning. Nobody was eager to work there. There were too many Germans around, too many eyes watching. As long as they did not beat us, I did not mind them watching.

The six of us made primitive knapsacks in which we could place a few chips of wood to take back to the ghetto. This was significant in the ghetto; at least we became independent as far as wood was concerned. When I came home from work, my mother would heat up some soup for me, using the wood chips I had brought the previous day. I felt that I was contributing something and wished I could do more.

At work, after the noon meal was cooked, the Germans gave us the large pots and kettles to clean. There was always something left in them. As we divided it among us, I would feel twangs of conscience for having eaten the piece of bread I got at the exit from the ghetto. After all, I could have saved it and brought it home. We had two lucky days, once when an unpleasant smelling salted and dried codfish went uneaten by many soldiers, and another time, when a wooden barrel full of fresh milk was left uncovered in the middle of the yard and turned sour. We were told to move the barrel behind some distant buildings, but before going home we looked at it and noticed a transparent liquid on top and a white cheese-like substance on the bottom. Pouring out the water, we emptied the white substance into our knapsacks, which served as sieves, and brought it back to the ghetto.

Leaving and entering the Pruzhany ghetto was less restricted than in other ghettos I was told about or later read about. In agreement with the Germans, the ghetto Committee issued a permit to any Jew to leave and come back into the ghetto. A foreman, called a "column leader," accompanied groups leaving the ghetto and carried a permit stating the number of people he had with him. In our case, six men did not warrant a column leader, so we received individual permits. It meant that each of us could get in or out of the ghetto at will. We preferred to enter as a group, hoping that would discourage the Germans at the gate from searching us. We were not always completely innocent. Working around a kitchen, we sometimes succeeded in hiding a couple of raw potatoes, or a carrot or beet in a pocket, or we would hide the vegetables under the wood chips. We were lucky that the guards never discovered our hidden food.

There were often extensive searches conducted not only by the

Schutzpolizei, but also by a group of soldiers referred to in the ghetto as the "Lehman Gang." They were not satisfied with beating up Jews outside the ghetto but liked to come in and beat up anyone at random. Together with the Schutzpolizei, they would stop entire columns of people on their way to the ghetto, lead them into a yard and order them to get undressed. Those found with even one potato paid for it dearly.

At the gate of the *Ortskommandantur*, where the guard stood, the Germans affixed a billboard on which they attached one or two daily newspapers every morning. Before going in or on our way out, we would glance quickly at these papers. The headlines proclaimed German victories and gave the numbers of prisoners they had taken, which ran in the hundreds of thousands, and predicted their imminent takeover of Stalingrad. We knew that some reports and numbers were a bit inflated, but we also knew that the Germans were advancing deeper into the Soviet Union.

I spent many of those long summer evenings with Kalman Kalbkauf at Itzik Maletzky's, in a small one-room house where other young men from Shershev would gather. Besides the news from the front and the constant slaughter of Jews, a new topic arose, the topic of partisans. By that time, there were a few single men from Shershev and neighbouring towns who had left their families to come to Pruzhany, the imaginary safe heaven. Only a single young person could undertake such a dangerous journey. Passing through or around unfriendly villages and avoiding the local Ukrainian police took youthful strength, agility and courage.

Among those who gathered at the Maletzkys were two friends of Itzik's older brother. They had left their families in Khomsk and made their way to Pruzhany. It was they who brought me the news that my close friend Laizer Rotenberg, who had gotten married the previous fall in Khomsk, had become a father. The Maletzky's small house offered us complete privacy, which none of us refugees had. Our conversations were usually down to earth, but at times they were characterized by wishful thinking, allowing us to distract our strained nerves from the hopeless reality for a moment. During those moments of hope, we spoke of joining the partisans in the forests. When I asked the young men who had come to Pruzhany alone why they didn't go into the forest, they answered that if I joined them, they would go. I was the youngest among them; they all were a year to three years older than I was. I argued that I still had my parents, sisters and brother, not to mention other relatives, in the ghetto, while they had nobody here to leave behind. They responded that I most likely knew that it was safe to remain in the ghetto for the time being. It dawned on me that because my grandfather was officially representing Shershev in the Committee, they thought that I knew more than they. How foolish and naive we all were.

Groups of Jewish men were taken daily from the Pruzhany ghetto to work at the railway station, Aranchytsy, which serviced the entire district of Pruzhany, carrying news in either direction. One July day, a group returned from the station and brought the sad news of the slaughter of the Jewish population of Linovo that morning. The entire Jewish population had been taken to the nearby petrol depot, lined up in small groups at the edge of a pit and shot. Because of its proximity and the close relations between Pruzhany and Linovo, the news shocked us and made a lasting impression on the community. The outpouring of grief surpassed the combined sadness that Pruzhany had shown for all other communities slaughtered thus far. This event was too close to home. It gave the impetus for young men to think seriously of going into the forests and joining the partisans.

That summer, the activities of some partisan groups became quite daring. Their exaggerated heroic deeds assumed legendary proportions among the villagers and even more so among the Jews closed in the ghetto. Nazi revenge, however, was swift and merciless. If a German was killed in or near a village, on the following day, the village was flooded with Germans who rounded up the men and simply shot them. This reaction of the Germans became so predictable that, after a German was killed, the nearby male villagers immediately ran away to more distant villages or to the forest, returning home after a day or two.

On a late July afternoon, the ghetto gates were opened and a large number of Germans started passing through. We estimated them to be a thousand strong. We had not seen such a number of executioners before, and their appearance caused panic in the ghetto. Many speculated that they had come for us. The next day, when the six of us who worked at the *Ortskommandantur* showed up to work, a non-commissioned officer led us to a warehouse and pointed to some buckets with lime, trowels, crude paint brushes, and bags of cement and sand. He ordered us to load it all on a truck and then get on it ourselves. Two soldiers accompanied us on the truck, and we were driven on the highway to Brest-Litovsk. From the road, we could see an entire village in flames some two kilometres off the road. Then we passed another village in flames, and there were more in the distance. All together, we counted six villages. The two soldiers also looked at those villages with surprise. A little later, we came to a guardhouse that held a dozen or so soldiers, two of whom were guarding a wooden bridge that spanned a river. We were told to cover the walls of the guardhouse with a new layer of cement and whitewash it, as there were bedbugs in the cracks of the walls. By mid-afternoon, we were heading back to Pruzhany. We again passed the burning villages, over which heavy smoke was hanging. Near one village, by the roadside, we saw two women sitting and crying. As we drove by, we called to them, "Which village was it?"

They yelled back, "Rudnicky!"

The truck kept on driving.

Back in the ghetto, we found out what had happened. The impenetrable swamps and dense forests in the area had become a haven for partisans, whose numbers kept on growing. Many of those partisans were local peasants who knew passages through those swamps, which they crossed at night to carry out attacks on the Germans. The Germans, unfamiliar with the terrain, were unable to chase them, so they fortified individual houses in certain villages, converting them into defence positions. This gave the partisans an immobile target to attack. And attack they did. Crossing the swamps at night, they attacked the fortified house in the village of Rudnicky. The Germans resisted stubbornly. The partisans, unable to overcome them, set the wooden house on fire and retreated the way they came. However, the Germans had prepared for such an eventuality by building a fireproof cellar in the house. When the house became engulfed in flames, they went into the cellar, and most of them survived. Before daybreak, all able-bodied men left the village, fearing immediate German retribution. To their surprise, no Germans came on that day or the following day. Slowly they all came back to their families and homesteads. It was a week later, before daybreak, that not only the village of Rudnicky, but five nearby villages, were surrounded. The Germans picked up every male from sixteen to sixty and shot every one of them. They ordered the women to load their wagons, drove them out of the villages and set all the buildings on fire.

The Germans we had seen passing through the ghetto committed this crime, and those were the fires that we saw from the road. Having accomplished their horrible retribution, the Germans did not come back to Pruzhany. Most likely there was another such crime waiting to be committed somewhere else.

Every day of the summer of 1942 brought heart-rending news about the Jewish settlements in our area. From the few individuals who miraculously survived and managed to sneak into the Pruzhany ghetto, we heard stories of slaughter and partial or total annihilation of centuries-old Jewish communities. In some places, a few individuals managed to hide, at times for a week or two without food, and then got away at night. Most of them fell victim to non-Jewish "friends" or other characters. After being robbed of whatever they had left, they were killed or handed over to the Germans or local police. From a couple of those who managed to get into our ghetto, we heard that somewhere along the way, the Ukrainian police had apprehended them, taken everything of value and then let them go. Most likely they did not want to waste time and effort on rounding up locals to bury them. From these escapees, we in Pruzhany learned about the annihilation of the ghetto in Neshviz on July 21, 1942. My father's sister Pesl lived in Neshviz. She was married to Zelig Remez, and they had a five-year-old son, Max, and younger children I had never met. We never heard from them again.

The names of the destroyed shtetls are so familiar to me that as I read them, they sound like a litany, a lament so full of pain that it should shatter the heavens. These names include Bereza, Kosov, Yanov, Horodets, Drohitchin, Olshan, Luninitz, Slonim, Baranovich, Neshviz, Steibtz and many more. All were within a stone's throw of Shershev. We knew nothing about what took place in the countless other Jewish communities from which not a single soul escaped, but we imagined the worst. Unfortunately, our imaginings were proven to be correct.

17

Who Will Live and Who Will Die

WITH THE APPROACH of the Days of Awe—the Jewish New Year and Yom Kippur of 1942—the final phase of the slaughter of Jews intensified. This time it was aimed at the remnants of the A sections of the ghettos, those seen by the Germans as "useful Jews"—Jewish tradesmen and artisans who worked for the Nazis. The Nazis' plan to annihilate these Jews meant that even their desperate need for Jewish artisans for the war effort could not save their lives.

In one of the sheds in the *Ortskommandantur* yard, I found a German map of our district. I could not get over the accuracy of that map. It covered a territory from Pinsk in the east to Brest-Litovsk in the west, from Novogrudok in the north to Rovno in the south. I found on that map every trail and every footpath in every field, town and village. A steeple signified an Eastern Orthodox Church and two steeples a Catholic one. I hid the map on me and brought it into the ghetto. I shared my find with my friend Kalman, and a couple of days later, he asked me to lend it to him, as an acquaintance of his wanted to copy it. A few days later, Kalman told me that his acquaintance had left the ghetto with a group of young men who were heading to the forest to join the partisans, taking with him the original map. This was the first group of young people who left our ghetto to join the partisans and fight the Germans.

In September, we got the news that the Jews in Khomsk—the eighty families from Shershev who had settled there—were killed. Among those families was my good friend Laizer Rotenberg, his wife and newborn child, as well as his brother Litek, their parents, Yosef and Raya, and their three daughters—Pola, Lisa and Minah—plus my friends' grandparents Joshua and Bluma Pinsky.

The month of October in 1942 was particularly vicious for the remainder of the Jews in our part of the world. The final liquidation of the ghetto in Brest-Litovsk began on October 15, 1942. Those who were not killed were deported. Two men succeeded in getting away and making their way to Pruzhany, bringing the sad news with them. On the same day, Ghetto A of Drohitchin, including the family of my uncle Reuven, was annihilated. On the very same day, 1,800 Jews of Ghetto A in Bereza Kartuska were killed, as were the remaining Jews in the ghetto in Antopol. These were places close to my birthplace, which I had become emotionally connected to during those dark days. But places farther away shared the same fate, often not a single soul surviving to tell the stories.

A few Shershev Jews in Drohitchin took the risk and ran for their lives, despite the next-to-zero chance of succeeding, and a few days after the slaughter of Drohitchin, six Shershev men and two women made their way into the Pruzhany ghetto. They had walked over a hundred kilometres through forests and fields where Jews were being hunted down like wild animals.

As for what happened next, I do not want to dwell on the moral aspect of the event. I neither accuse nor justify it. Who am I to judge? Apparently, someone from outside the ghetto had seen these eight Jews crawling under the wires. The next day, the Germans came to the Committee, demanding the eight Jews. The usual negotiations took place between the Committee and the Germans, but this time, no amount of bribery could change their minds.

That unforgettable morning, the Committee, being compelled to hand over the eight Shershev Jews, ordered the Jewish ghetto police to collect them. As far as I know, this was the first time the Pruzhany ghetto Committee was compelled to perform such a repulsive job like handing Jews into German hands, and the Jewish ghetto police were not prepared to perform such a task. They were accompanied by several members of the Committee, led by the president himself, Itzik Janowicz, who was respected and admired by all citizens of the ghetto. A crowd of onlookers followed them. They approached the house in which Gottel Wiener lived. His younger brother, eighteen-year-old Pinchas, had just escaped Drohitchin. Gottel stepped out the door, approached the chief of police and said, "I am ready; we can go."

The chief answered, "We did not come for you but for your brother."

But Gottel insisted on going with them instead of his brother. The members of the Committee got closer and so did the crowd. Gottel tried to reason with the president, saying, "The Germans want a Jew, but they do not know who he is or what he looks like. Let me go instead and let my brother stay alive. He is only eighteen years old."

We could all see the tears in his eyes as he pleaded for his brother's life. The moment Gottel uttered those words, the charade was over. Up to now, the Committee had been talking of the eight men being put in jail as negotiations for their release continued. But everybody knew that this time the Germans had something else in mind. Now, with those words, everybody realized that there was no need to pretend.

In a trembling voice, Janowicz said, "Gottel, I am not God. I cannot decide who shall live and who shall die. The Germans want the one who sneaked into the ghetto. I cannot change that. It is up to God, and he made the decision."

The eight people were gathered, wretched souls who already had nobody in the world to shed a tear for them, except for Pinchas, whose brother was willing to die for him. The Germans put them in jail. For several days, the Committee continued to negotiate their release. Meanwhile, the two jails in Pruzhany were filling up, and the time had come to empty them in the usual Nazi manner. They ordered the Committee to send men to dig a pit. A couple of days later, they ordered a group of men to be the grave coverers. When the men showed up the next morning, a German told them to go back to the ghetto. All kinds of rumours began to circulate in the ghetto, for instance, that the Germans decided to stop executions or that the Allies had cautioned the Nazis against killing civilians, and more. All the rumours stopped when it became known that the Germans wanted those men back the next day. On the next day, when the men returned from their gruesome work, they told of the killing of three truckloads of people, among them the eight Shershev souls.

Several days later, we learned that a couple of days earlier, a car full of Germans had driven into Shershev and stopped in front of the house in which Avreml Kwelman had lived. Among the Germans was Avreml, who carried a shovel. He led them to a spot near the fence and dug up a small metal box. They all got back into the car and drove away. Two former members of the Shershev Jewish Committee told us that when they had collected the rubles and gold that the Nazis had demanded from us, it amounted to almost twice as much as was needed, so the Committee kept the extra for an emergency. They divided the extra gold into three parts, and three Committee members—one of whom was Avreml Kwelman—were entrusted to hide the parts in safe places unknown to the others. We believed that when the jail inmates were being loaded on the trucks, Avreml had cried out to the Germans that he would give them gold if they let the Jews live. After the Germans had Avreml retrieve the gold, they drove him to the jail in Pruzhany, and he was executed with the rest the next day.

As far as we knew, the Pruzhany ghetto was an island in a sea of gentiles, with the nearest Jewish community in Białystok, about a hundred kilometres away. No more could one find Jewish shtetls every ten to fifteen kilometres apart, or the numerous Jewish settlements even closer in between. The constant question lay heavily on our minds: How much longer would they let us stay alive?

A partial answer came on November 1, 1942. As I approached the gate of the ghetto to leave for work in the morning, I noticed a large crowd. Getting closer, I saw a detachment of Schutzpolizei outside the ghetto and others patrolling the perimeter around the barbed-wire fence of the ghetto. Without an explanation, we were told that nobody was allowed to leave. The crowd continued to grow in front of that main gate as more and more workers tried to go to work, and people began to assemble in front of the Committee office across from the gate, hoping to find out what was happening. Inside, the Committee was having an emergency meeting, which was interrupted by the arrival of some Gestapo men. The Nazi in charge announced that as of that moment, the ghetto was in a transitional state, meaning that it could be transferred at any time. He commanded the Committee to provide the files of every person in the ghetto and to load the files into his car. Meanwhile, the crowd in front of the Committee office had grown, and people were speculating and predicting conceivable and inconceivable things.

The first to appear outdoors from the meeting was Zalman Segal, the so-called foreign minister of the ghetto. His tall, slim figure towered over the crowd. A thousand throats cried out, "What does it mean? Have they come for us?" Zalman raised his hand, gesturing for silence. From his grief-stricken face and twisted lips came a quiet answer, as if he were talking to himself, yet he was heard across the entire crowd: "What makes us better than the Jews of Brisk or Pinsk or Kobrin? Have we got more *skhus oves* [ancestral merit] than they? Have we earned it more than they?"

His words immediately caused an outbreak of laments and cries, and it was impossible to hear him anymore, nor did it make any difference to me. I went to find my parents, sisters and brother to spend the last few hours of our lives together.

The news had already reached them and every corner of the ghetto before I got to them. To get to our room, I had to pass the house owner's living room. It was usually a noisy place. Now there was total silence. The owner and his family were sitting in a corner of that big room, and my entry made no impression on them; they glanced at me without a sign of recognition. I walked into our room and found my parents, sisters and brother all sitting on the double bed and couch. They had the same empty gaze in their eyes as those in the other room. Without saying a word, I sat down near them, sinking into my thoughts. I was aware of how imminent and unavoidable death was, and of a desperate desire to live. I admit, shamefully, that I was thinking of saving myself without thinking of saving my dear ones. Everyone was quiet, and if somebody did say something it was without meaning or value. Words were of no importance anymore.

I decided to watch, observe and remember as much as possible all that happened around me. If this was my fate and destiny in what would be left of my life, then I wanted to look at it clearly, discerningly and lucidly, for this was all there was.

18
A Perilous Existence

WE SAT UNTIL noon, listening. The streets were as silent as a cemetery. I imagined that after surrounding the ghetto, the Germans would enter with shouts and shooting, herding all the inhabitants into the street and from there outside the town to be shot. But we did not hear any shots. It was my mother getting up to announce that she was going to prepare something to eat that interrupted the silence. Nobody was thinking about food, but it gave her something to do. The lunch consisted of dry potatoes, which went down with difficulty. I decided to see what was going on in the streets and at our relatives. Outside, there were still a lot of Germans at the main ghetto gate but none of the Jews who were there earlier that morning. From a few passersby, I found out that the Committee had made several attempts to communicate with the Germans but to no avail.

At my relatives, the mood was the same as in our place, but there was a larger crowd, and they tried to be more preoccupied with daily chores. It felt as though time was passing faster there. I returned home to find everybody sitting in the same places as when I had left them. They looked at me with a glimmer of hope that disappeared instantly without me saying a word as they saw my face. After a while, we decided to join our relatives, hoping to find some comfort in dying together.

And so, my immediate and extended family sat together, waiting for death, not knowing when and in what form it would come. We sat there together without sleep and without getting undressed all night. If someone did lie down and doze off, it was only to awaken after a minute from a nightmare. Unable to sit all night in one spot, some got up and looked out the windows or walked nervously around from room to room.

If now, so many decades later, I have difficulty recollecting my thoughts at that time, how can I attempt to describe the thoughts and comments uttered by members of my family in those desperate and hopeless hours? It is my belief that I was the only one who had any thought of attempting to save himself, and for my parents, sisters and brother, for all my extended family, there was no hope. What was going on in their minds?

And so the night passed. At dawn we saw someone sneaking by with a *tales* under his arm—a Jew on his way to the synagogue. With my mother's encouragement, I too went to a nearby synagogue. To my surprise, the synagogue was full. The crowd started to pray, and after the daily Shemoneh Esrei prayer, we recited the penitential Avinu Malkeinu prayer said on special days. If I ever recited that prayer and paid attention to it, it was on that morning. Never in my life had I seen a congregation saying this prayer with so much commitment, with so much dedication, with so much devotion and heaven-splitting weeping, crying "Our Father, Our King…." Leaving the synagogue, I thought that God was surely watching and listening to those fervent prayers. How could he not answer?

And so, the second day passed in tension and fear. We could not understand the game the Nazis were playing. What were they waiting for? Some suggested that gentiles were digging mass graves for us outside of town.

The next morning, the synagogues were even more crowded and the prayers more fervent. During the day, more people appeared in the side streets and alleys. And so, another day went by. Rumours began to circulate that the Committee had succeeded in making contact with the Germans, that the Germans had requested some things and were satisfied with the response.

Finally, on the fourth day, a couple of Gestapo men showed up at the Committee office and announced that the ghetto would temporarily remain in place. There was, however, a new list of restrictions, including a reduction of rations and the total abolition of exit permits from the ghetto. From now on, no Jew was permitted to leave the ghetto unless accompanied by a German guard. The large number of Germans at the three ghetto entrances left, and one guard remained at each gate. The cordon of guards around the fence was replaced by patrols.

To make their patrolling of the ghetto fence easier, the Germans straightened the fence by cutting away parts of the ghetto, thus squeezing the population in tighter. One of the ghetto's main streets, Kobriner, was partly cut off, including the building housing the Committee. The Committee office, which had taken up an entire building, was forced to move. They picked my uncle Leibel and aunt Sheindl Pinsky's house, giving them in return a big house on Rezki Street to accommodate not only my uncle's family, but the rest of my extended family.

The ghetto sighed with temporary relief. We went back to our room feeling somewhat better but also with an increased awareness of our perilous situation. Our exit permits were no longer valid, and the six of us workers at the *Ortskommandantur* had to wait for a soldier to accompany us there daily. We no longer dared to leave the yard where we worked to read the newspapers plastered on the wall. We needed an escort even to go from the *Ortskommandantur* to the yard where we cut wood. Because of that, we missed the leftovers from the soldiers' kitchen. I missed that very much because whatever the soldiers would not eat was still much better than what we had in the ghetto. It was only then that I began to wonder if my parents, sisters and brother were getting enough food to fill their stomachs. With the new regulations and the constant patrols around the fence, it became much more difficult to smuggle in extra food.

With me worked Shalom Berenstein, who had worked with me in the Soviet warehouse in Shershev. He was a former Soviet soldier and a runaway German prisoner of war, and he was responsible for providing for his mother and younger brother and sisters, as his father had died shortly before the war. Necessity drove him to look for additional sources of income.

In those weeks, we spent more and more time cutting wood at the yard, which was at the outskirts of town. The entrance to the yard was a wide gate with a guardhouse manned by two soldiers who rarely ventured outside, preferring to sit inside, where it was heated. There really was no need for them to go outside, as nobody came in or out except for us. Not that there was nothing to guard. The Soviets had left these warehouses full of spare parts for tanks and other machinery. Many of those warehouses were under lock and key.

The two soldiers at the gate paid little attention to us, spending most of the time sleeping on the bed in the guardhouse and keeping the fire going in the cast-iron stove. So Shalom Berenstein attempted to go out to the street and came back unnoticed. Perhaps the two soldiers saw him but didn't care. He started doing it regularly. He made contact with a non-Jew down the road who became an intermediary, buying food from farmers and selling it to Berenstein. Then we divided the produce, hiding it so as not to look suspicious at the gate, and brought it into the ghetto, where Berenstein sold it. Soon we were taking turns crossing the street to pick up the food. Smuggling potatoes was not a profitable venture, so we concentrated on barley, porridge, beans, peas, even cheese, butter and a couple times, whole frozen fish from the river. There were a few Jews in the ghetto who could permit themselves such a luxury, but very few, and only from time to time. We, the risk takers, could only look at this food and dream. The following morning, Berenstein would bring the money to work where we would divide the profit among the six of us, retaining the original investment for further transactions. Not every day could our supplier provide us with products and not every day were we sent to cut wood in that yard. Those days were lean days for our families and us.

The events of November 1 had put the ghetto on notice and shaken it out of its complacency. The inhabitants, particularly the young people, understood how dangerous the situation was and started to discuss how the only place where a Jew had any chance of survival was in the forest with the partisans. But partisans did not accept unarmed men, nor was it easy to find them. They were constantly on the move, being hunted by Germans, local police, local Nazi sympathizers and other partisan groups of other persuasions, such as the Polish and Ukrainian nationalistic groups. Those groups were fighting the Germans and fighting each other. The only thing they had in common was deep-rooted antisemitism, and they killed Jews as efficiently as they killed Nazis. The only partisans who accepted Jews were the pro-Soviet ones. But even among them, there was no shortage of antisemites who made life for Jews, even those in their own ranks, unbearable. A Jewish partisan group found it even harder to survive because of the antisemitism that was so deeply rooted in the population, which hated the Germans but did not object to the Nazi dogma that declared Jews subhuman and targeted them for total annihilation. It was only when Jewish groups had proven themselves as equal or better fighters than non-Jews that they began to be accepted by non-Jewish partisan groups.

Surviving in the forest in winter would be extremely difficult—all a hunter had to do was follow the footprints of the hunted. Wild animals were created to blend into their environment or to outrun their hunters, but humans cannot. And what of spending night after night under open skies, cold, scared and hungry? The previous summer, I had naively argued that I preferred a night in bed in the ghetto rather than wandering about in the forest. Others had the same opinion. After November 1, many claimed that we had to prepare ourselves for the forest, but as long as we could remain under a roof, why not? There were, however, those who understood that we might miss our chance. The Germans could surprise us at any time by surrounding the ghetto and taking all of us away.

The insurmountable problem was the procurement of weapons. From time to time, one of the workers employed at clearing the former Soviet military barracks would stumble upon a damaged rifle or revolver, a few cartridges or a grenade. Not enough to arm even one group of men, and one could never be sure if they were functional. If we wanted to join the partisans, we would have to intensify our efforts of procuring weapons, and this required organization and time, which we knew we might not have. It was possible that the Germans would come for us in the middle of the winter, and that we would run to the forest no matter the consequences because we were going to die anyway. However, we would first have to hide during the evacuation of Jews from the ghetto. The Germans would search high and low to make sure that not a single Jew was left. Only after they were sure that there were no more Jews, would they call off the guards around the ghetto fence, which would give those who survived the searches a chance to sneak out into the forests.

Some of the hiding places people prepared were quite ingenious, but their preparation depended on space, availability, materials and finances. Refugee families were at a disadvantage here, living in somebody else's home, a whole family crowded in one room. However, a few refugee families lived in former Christian homes that were now included in the ghetto—including the Maletzky family. The house consisted of a small room and a hallway that served as a windbreak and storage place for the turf that they used for heating and cooking. The house looked very inconspicuous, with no way to hide in it. The three Maletzky brothers, Kalman and I decided to dig a hideout there, in the evenings after work. We moved the loose turf away from the hallway's back wall and started digging before the frost set in. After filling a sack with earth, one of us would take it and walk around the nearby alleys, letting the earth spill out slowly on the muddy ground. Not having materials to support the walls or ceiling of the hideout, it was nothing but a hole in the ground, narrow on top and wider at the bottom. We covered it with short pieces of wood and spread some turf over it, but we knew it could only pass a superficial search. We were counting on the simplicity and the innocuousness of that little house more than on the security of the hideout itself. We assumed that it was one of the most primitive hideouts in the ghetto, but with our resources what else could we do?

How the ghetto continued with its "normal" existence is difficult now to understand and impossible to describe. At night, my thoughts would race as I tried to imagine the last hours of my life, the very last minutes before my death. I listened to the regular, innocent breathing of my little brother and sisters, and the constant turning and twisting of my parents. I knew that they too were awake and haunted by the same thoughts and nightmares. Now that I am a parent and a grandparent, I can understand how dark and desperate their thoughts must have been. How could I have understood then, my parents' concern for their children? Lying on that narrow couch, I deliberated and wondered if digging a hideout was such a good idea. If by some miracle I would manage to survive the slaughter of the entire ghetto, what would my life be worth without my mother, the dearest and most precious person in the world to me? I could not imagine life without her. Eventually the weariness of the day's work would take over, and I would fall asleep for a few hours, only to be awakened to a daylong nightmare.

In the short November and December days, I was the first to rise. My mother usually prepared breakfast—three or four potatoes and a piece of beet for colour—the night before. She would cook on the small cast-iron stove with the wood splinters that I brought from work as fuel. While in use, that stove made our room unbearably hot in the summer, but it turned ice cold in the winter when the fire was out. At five in the morning, I would throw a few splinters of wood in it to warm up the potatoes, at the same time taking the chill out of the room so that the rest of the family would not find it as cold when they got up.

One morning, as I was sitting down to eat the few potatoes, my sister Sonia, who was not quite eleven years old, said to me, "Moishe, give me a potato."

Before I grasped what she had said, my father responded, "Do not take the potatoes from him. He is on his way to work for the rest of the day, and we are soon going to have breakfast."

Here I committed a sin, which I have tried to atone ever since, but in vain. I did not give her the potato. All the years since then, I've tried to find an excuse for my behaviour. All I could come up with in my defence was the knowledge that throughout our time in ghetto, we never experienced a shortage of potatoes.

At the beginning of December, we stopped going to the *Ortskommandantur* and spent the entire day cutting wood at the yard. Two of the men from our original group of six were registered as mechanics and repaired trucks in the same yard. Their work took them into the warehouses where the abandoned Soviet machinery and dysfunctional Soviet weapons were. When they needed machine parts from a padlocked warehouse, one of the two soldiers from the guardhouse would go with them. The two mechanics began to eye the discarded weapons in the warehouse and looked for a way to get a few rifles out. An occasion arose sooner than expected through a man by the name of Yitzchak Hydamak, a locksmith and a plumber who had owned a bicycle repair shop in Pruzhany. In the ghetto, he did all kinds of repairs for the Germans, and once, when he needed a certain part, he came to the yard. Our guard took him to the warehouses, including the one with the weapons. Finding the needed piece of machinery, Hydamak left with his guard.

Before the week was over, he was back with another soldier, needing something that was, of course, in the warehouses where the weapons were stored. This time he came prepared, pulling behind him a sled stacked high with tin stovepipes. Coming into the guardhouse with his guard, he pulled a bottle of vodka out of his pocket and proposed to have a drink with them. One drink led to a second, and once the three soldiers began to feel comfortable, Hydamak offered to go for the needed part by himself while they finished the bottle. Without hesitation, one of the soldiers gave him the keys. Hydamak went straight to the warehouse, grabbed a couple of rifles and shoved them into the empty pipes outside, pinching both ends. Then Hydamak turned to us and said, "Take them, fellows. Now is your chance." We followed his lead and grabbed rifles too, but in the great excitement, all we did was stand in the middle of the yard with the rifles in our hands, not knowing what to do. Hydamak harnessed himself to the sled and started out in the direction of the gate and guardhouse. We quickly pushed the weapons under a pile of wood.

The two mechanics became the leaders of our group of six, and I, being the youngest, followed the rest. The mechanics told us that they were in contact with a well-organized partisan group in the ghetto who were in need of weapons. For the price of eight rifles, the group would accept all six of us. But how would we do that? The partisans, one of whom was a young man named Shmerl Helman who worked for the mayor's wife, worked out a plan. The plan was to get a sled made with a double bottom, and Helman would come looking for wood for the mayor's wife. Some of us would distract the German guard, and the others would hide the eight rifles in the false bottom of the sled and pile wood on top. Then, we would hope for a miracle that we didn't get caught at the ghetto gate. Not only did Shmerl put his life on the line, but the lives of his family, as well as our lives, the lives of our families and perhaps the lives of other ghetto dwellers.

One day, Shmerl appeared at the gate of the yard harnessed to a fairly large sled made in the ghetto by a young carpenter, Hershel Morawsky. A rifle-toting soldier accompanied him. They approached us, the soldier looked around, and, I do not know if it was because of the cold or sheer boredom, he turned around, walked back to the guardhouse and disappeared inside. Now we were alone. We quickly took off the top covering of the sled, put the rifles in the hidden compartment, replaced the cover and piled on some wood. We still had time to exchange a few words and wish each other good luck. The soldier came out of the guardhouse. Shmerl hitched himself up to the sled, and they left the yard. We continued our work but constantly glanced in the direction of the gate, expecting a bunch of Germans to come for us at any minute. Finally, the workday came to an end. Our guard appeared to lead us back to the ghetto. Only after passing the gate did we realize that our fear had been a bit exaggerated. Why would a German soldier stop to search a single Jew who was constantly under guard and apparently had permission to take along with him a sled filled with pitiful wood splinters?

The barometer of our safety was the factory in the ghetto where workers put leather soles on felt boots for the German army. Like clockwork, a big military truck would bring raw material and take back the completed boots. It was said that as long as the Germans were bringing material, we were safe. Should they stop the delivery of the raw material, that would be a bad omen.

One of the first days of January 1943 happened to be a beautiful day, and the two soldiers from the guardhouse came out for a stroll in the yard. A couple of the Schutzpolizei strolled over to the soldiers for a chat. They spoke loudly, and I could overhear their conversation. After exchanging a few polite words, their conversation turned to the topic of the Jews. I clearly heard one police officer saying that if the Jews weren't taken away by the end of the month, they would have to remain until spring. I had a bad premonition all that day. When I got home, I shared the news with my parents.

A few days later, part of our supposedly future partisan group held a meeting. I told them what I overheard at work, hoping to add some urgency to our plans. Everyone had his own interpretation and expressed his opinion, but nobody was in a hurry to rush into the forests in January. To be honest, neither was I. By the end of the meeting, we hadn't made any decisions, and we returned home via back alleys.

19
Abandoned

IN THE MIDDLE of January, I had a dream. I was on a train that was stopping at a railway station. The station was a nondescript, one-storey building plastered in a light grey colour. I did not know why, but that building was repugnant to me, yet in my dream I knew that I had to get off there. I woke up feeling distressed, with a bitter taste in my mouth.

When the military truck came in the third week of January to pick up the felted boots that were made in the ghetto, they did not bring any raw material. That was the bad omen. There were those who made nothing of it and shrugged their shoulders. I am sure that among them were many who saw the unavoidable, impending catastrophe, but did not want to say it aloud so as not to make the atmosphere in the ghetto even more depressing.

We were hearing that the few groups of partisans that had left the ghetto for the forests were having a hard time. While some had been accepted into established partisan groups, others had to fend for themselves, always on the move between attacking and escaping the Germans. When they needed more clothes and new footwear, the best and safest place to get it was from the Judenrat, which had to have leather and leather boots on hand in case they needed to pacify the Germans. Nobody in the Judenrat was surprised when during their late-night meetings, a couple of Jewish partisans would appear, asking for good clothing and footwear. They usually got what they needed and left the ghetto on the same night under the cover of darkness. Of course, such transactions were conducted in total secrecy, because the existence of the ghetto and the lives of its approximately ten thousand inhabitants depended on that.

Tuesday, January 26, was, according to the Jewish calendar, the twentieth day of Shvat, and my twentieth birthday. My loving and devoted mother never failed to remind me of my Jewish birthday even in the darkest last days of the ghetto.

The next day, our group of six held a meeting with some members of the group of future partisans. We gathered in a house across the street from the offices of the Judenrat. The meeting did not last long because nobody had any new plans or ideas, and we did not want to walk in the street late at night, as it was prohibited to be outside after dark. Nobody cherished the idea of coming face to face with a German at night. Even though we started our meetings after dark, one could claim that he was coming from work up to seven o'clock, but not later. The meeting was over at eight-thirty, and as soon as we arrived at the gate leading out from the yard, we heard a car stop in front of the Judenrat office. In the deathly quiet, there was the sound of car doors opening and a voice saying, "Willy, keep guard," then steps ascending the porch, a loud opening of a door and a few seconds later, several shots. We remained frozen to the spot. Until then, we had not heard a single shot fired in the ghetto. Two minutes later, we heard the Germans come out of the Judenrat, get into the car and pull away.

Immediately, there was talking and yelling in Yiddish coming from out in the street. Opening the little door in the gate, we saw a crowd gathered in front of the Judenrat. It did not take long to find out what happened. When the Gestapo had entered the Judenrat office, they found two armed partisans who had come from the forest. As the partisans jumped up and ran out the back door, the Germans pulled out their handguns and fired indiscriminately, killing one member of the Judenrat and the night watchman, and wounding several others.

The Gestapo men didn't say why they had come. Whatever the reason, all they said was that they wanted the partisans by 11:00 p.m. that very night. Otherwise, they had their own method of dealing with the situation.

The Judenrat had but a couple of hours. Those two partisans had family in the ghetto, and on their way out, they had stopped and taken with them two of their brothers. They escaped through the barbed-wire fence minutes before the Nazis reinforced the guards around the ghetto. Whoever tried to follow them just a few minutes later was shot at the fence. The Judenrat called a hasty meeting. It was decided that they would arrest a man from each of the partisan families, hoping to pacify the Nazis for the time being and negotiate with them later. In the worst-case scenario, they would sacrifice the two men as supposedly the two partisans, though everyone in the ghetto knew that the Germans would not let us off with the delivery of two substitute partisans.

After hanging around the Judenrat for an hour, I went home. This time I did not have to be careful walking the dark ghetto streets. The ghetto was not asleep. It was swarming like a beehive. The reinforced Nazi guards around the ghetto could plainly see it but did not react. No one in the house was sleeping. My parents were too upset and nervous to even sit down, so they stood in the middle of the room looking at each other and at the children, unable to say anything. I revealed to them for the first time that I belonged to a group that was planning to run to the forest and join the partisans. The expression on their faces did not change. My mother turned to me and said, "If there is a chance to save yourself, you must try it. May God help you."

I went out to see if there were any new developments. Kobriner Street, where the Judenrat was, was filled with people. At about 10:30, half an hour before the deadline, the main ghetto gate opened and a German car drove in and stopped in front of the Judenrat. Although it was night and Jews were not allowed to be outside after dark, nobody made a move. Had we suddenly become brave, or were we resigned to our fate? Two Germans walked into the Judenrat. Everyone waited in tension, wondering what calamity would befall us now. What new decree? A minute later they were out, proud and arrogant as if they had just conquered the world. In a precise military gait, they stepped down to the car, the driver opened the door and saluted smartly, and they pulled away.

Before anyone had a chance to ascend the steps of the porch, the door of the Judenrat opened. One member appeared and announced that the Germans had revoked the demand for the two partisans, for, in any case, the ghetto would be evacuated—the German euphemism for slaughtered or killed, though some believed we would be taken to a labour camp—starting in the morning. The evacuation would last four days, during which 2,500 people would be taken away daily. They even left behind a map showing which part of the ghetto would be emptied each day.

Immediately, assumptions and accusations circulated—that the two Jewish partisans had been betrayed, or that if they were good Jewish boys, they would have stayed home and it would not have come to this, or that they should have stayed in the forest and not put the ghetto in jeopardy.

The arguments were resolved the next morning. At nine o'clock on January 28, four hundred sleds entered the ghetto. The drivers were peasants from the surrounding villages who told us that they had been ordered at noon the day before to show up at the ghetto fence. That was long before the incident with the partisans. It became clear to all that the event with the partisans had not caused the impending evacuation.

We, living on Nowa Street, were supposed to leave the ghetto on the first day, January 28, 1943. My father's brother Joshua, his wife, Freda, and their three children lived on the same short street, along with my sister Sheva. The rest of my father's family—my grandparents; my father's sister Sheindl and her husband, Leibel, and their two children; my father's brother Hershel and his wife, Sheine; my father's youngest brother, Eli; and my father's two cousins from Malch, Joshua and Zalman Nisselbaum, and their families—all lived in one big house on Rezki Street, which was not to be evacuated on the first day. During that despairing night, my parents decided to go over to Rezki Street in the morning so that we could spend our last hours together.

How can one describe our feelings, sitting there in despair and fear of our impending deaths? My thoughts were again preoccupied with saving myself. I reasoned that if any one of us had a chance to save ourselves it was me, with my group of young men who had been preparing to go into the forest. What chance had my parents, sisters and brother? What went through their minds that night?

At daybreak, as we were getting ready to go over to Rezki Street. My mother turned to me and said, "Run over to your uncle Joshua and find Sheva. Let us be together before we die." At that moment, I glanced out the window and saw my sister approaching. She was walking slowly and calmly. Her face was pensive, I would say serene, as if she had already made peace with her fate. Even though I had struggled with the idea of having to die all that night, I felt a shudder that would not leave me. As soon as Sheva entered, each of us picked up the little bundle my mother had prepared, and we walked out into the cold January dawn.

Walking along that cold windy street, my thoughts went back thirteen months to December 1941, when we had dragged ourselves for three days from Khomsk to Pruzhany. That journey, in that bitter cold and in fear, was a sweet memory in comparison to this moment. Then, despite the fear of being caught and the cold and hunger, we could look forward to eventually getting to Pruzhany. Now, looking at my brother and sisters, watching as their little cheeks were turning red from the wind and cold, my heart was crying out to God—*Why?* I looked at my mother and tried to tell myself that the dampness on her face was from the blowing flurries and not her tears. My father walked silently, trying to keep the little ones together, as if to make sure that death did not miss them.

The ghetto streets were quiet. One could not hear a yell or scream, or a shot. There was not a single German in the ghetto, but we could see many around the fence. Here and there one could see a person running across the street. Though everyone knew when they would be "evacuated" and could postpone it for a day or two by just crossing the street, hardly anyone did it.

Entering my uncle's living quarters, we found the family all sitting together in one room. Their mood was like ours. Attempts to make conversation were difficult. Unimportant remarks or statements exhausted themselves quickly. Nobody said much, and everyone was engrossed in their own thoughts. There were futile attempts to keep away from morbid speculations as to whether the Germans had already dug graves for us or if we would have to do it ourselves, whether the graves were nearby or we would be taken to Bronna Góra, where many of the Jews of Bereza Kartuska, Ruzhany, Antopol and other places were buried. I asked my uncle Eli how long a person would go on suffering before death if a bullet struck the body and not the head. "It depends where it strikes," he answered. "If the bullet strikes the heart, death is almost instantaneous. If it strikes a major organ like the lungs or stomach, one might lose consciousness. However, if the bullet does not strike a major organ, a person might lie in a mass grave in horrible pain for hours or even days."

Such was the theme of our conversations during that depressing Thursday morning of January 28, 1943, when two and a half thousand souls were to be taken out of the ghetto. My brother and sisters listened attentively to that conversation but did not participate. I watched as my aunt Sheindl tried to explain to her fifteen-year-old deaf son Shalom—an exceptionally bright, strong, red-headed boy—what was happening in the ghetto and what would happen to us. I could see that he understood everything his mother told him, but his face expressed one question that none of us could answer—*Why?*

At about three in the afternoon, people began to appear in the street. My father, uncles and I went outside to find out what had taken place during these few hours. People were eager to listen and share their experience. The horror of the reality shook the ghetto population, especially the young ones, some of whom still believed that the Germans had been bluffing. Now, with a quarter of the population gone, no further proof as to what would happen to us was needed.

And so, the second night of siege began for the remaining citizens of the ghetto, who sat in a cold sweat, counting the diminishing hours of their lives. There was an atmosphere of extreme agitation and confusion. Young people looked for a way out, trying to get closer to the barbed-wire fence and hoping to find a less guarded stretch of it. Unfortunately, the Germans knew only too well how to keep Jews confined. At every fifty-metre interval, two men—one gendarme and one local volunteer policeman—walked back and forth from the two opposite sides toward each other, thus keeping their assigned fifty metres always in sight. With electric lights on each fence post and pistol flares that they fired at any sound, the ghetto was tightly closed in. After a few brave young men were killed at the wire while trying to get out, hundreds of others began to lose courage and hope. As a result, collaboration and contact between the semi-organized groups ceased. Those who had the weapons whispered and schemed on their own and for themselves, forgetting their commitment to those who had procured the weapons. I don't blame them for acting that way. It was obvious that a group would never make it outside of the ghetto. Only an individual, or maybe a few people, had any chance at all.

I spent that Thursday night near the ghetto fence, hoping against hope that a watchman would get distracted long enough for me to get out. Now and then, I came in the house to try and persuade my uncles Hershel and Eli to join me at the fence, hanging on to the hope that maybe a chance would present itself for us to get out of the trap and make it to the forest. I was not even thinking of the difficulties that would await us should we make it out. My thoughts were on how to avoid imminent death. But my uncle Hershel had recently developed severe back pain, and he felt that he would not be able to run any distance. My uncle Eli, at twenty-nine, was a healthy man who had gone through the Polish-German campaign with distinction. However, he would not abandon his parents.

That night, too, nobody slept. The outside door of my uncle's house was unlocked, and I came in from time to time to find them all sitting up, exhausted from lack of sleep but even more from despair. If someone lay down and dozed off for a moment, they woke up with a startling scream or cry.

Later that night, I heard that several small groups had succeeded in escaping. Apparently, a group of armed men managed to bribe a local policeman who let them through while his German partner was looking away. At one point, another armed group was sneaking out and others started to follow them. Then the German turned around, and the local policeman fired and instantly killed a young man. The others retreated into the ghetto. Still, thirty odd young men had made it out, among them my friend Itzik Maletzky and his two brothers. This event took place at the end of Rezki Street, where my family was spending their last hours together, but at that moment, I was at another spot along the fence.

Near the former Polish gymnasium, another group succeeded in making it out. Among them was my cousin Lisa Pinsky and her boyfriend, Yudel Ruben. I heard about this on Friday morning after spending the night running along the ghetto fence in a futile attempt to get out. At my uncle's house, everybody had been talking about Lisa's successful escape. I asked my aunt Sheindl, who was in the kitchen, if she knew any details. She answered that no bodies had been found where the group got out. Then she turned back half-heartedly to busy herself at the stove, as if to make breakfast, which was the furthest thing from anyone's mind.

It is impossible to describe the mood, the morbidity, the anguish that existed wherever I turned, the pain of seeing my father, mother, sisters, brother, grandfather, grandmother, uncles, aunts and cousins, who, only hours from now, would be dead. Their bullet-riddled bodies would fall into the gigantic pits waiting for them, some dead, others half-dead. The dead would be the lucky ones. The half-dead would expire in pain and prolonged suffering, either from bleeding to death, or from suffocating under the bodies on top, which would bury them alive.

At nine o'clock on Friday morning, like the previous day, the Germans escorted another four hundred sleds into the ghetto. This time they parked along Seltzer Street and Holender Street and in all the smaller streets and alleys in between. Some of the younger men conversed with the peasant sled owners and found out that on the previous day the sleds had taken the Jews to the railway station in Aranchytsy-Linovo, where they were loaded into cattle cars. What happened to them later they did not know. Some of the peasants mentioned that on the way to the ghetto that morning, they had seen a few dozen dead Jews scattered along a section of the road a few kilometres from Pruzhany. They even described the victims' attire. Hearing this news, the young men slowly melted into the side streets and spread the story in the ghetto. The description of clothing was so precise that some of the families could identify their sons and daughters. In that confusion, I found out that among the dead were the three Maletzky brothers. Of course, the whole story could not be verified, but neither I nor anyone I knew ever heard from the Maletzky brothers, or from the others who were with them, again.

Friday's evacuation took place with the same precision and efficiency as the day before. I do not recall any shooting. The Germans were doing a thorough and clean job. It was much easier to handle a living Jew than a dead Jew. A dead one does not obey commands. As soon as the last sled of the convoy left with two and a half thousand souls and the Germans shut the gate, people appeared in the street. Despite all indications of the last two days, there were still some who dared to hope that we were being taken to labour camps and stubbornly refused to believe that we were being led to the slaughter. Such is the human desire for life. The locals were among those adhering to this belief. It is possible that the comparative tranquility of the Pruzhany ghetto instilled a false hope in some, or maybe the belief was the result of a desperate desire for life in conjunction with a disbelief in what was happening.

Among the young people still in the ghetto, new groups were being formed. Some groups were trying to entice new, more dependable members by claiming possession of weapons. A young man approached me and showed me an impressive handgun. I took it from him and pulled out the magazine in which there were two cartridges. Without a word, I handed it back to him. With such an arsenal I would not feel much safer than with my bare hands.

Of my very close friends, the only one I had left was Kalman Kalbkauf. Kalman and I decided to make an attempt to get out by ourselves that night. The next day, Saturday, the Germans would be coming for us. The sleds would drive into Rezki Street, and some would stop in front of the house in which my entire family was now living, and they would take us all to our deaths. We were hoping to remain another day, until Sunday. However, there were not enough people left in the assigned streets to make up 2,500 people, so it seemed that the Germans would also take Rezki, Brisker or the new Shershev Street, and the small alleys in between. When I said this to my family out loud, my voice sounded like thunder, even though I was whispering. Still louder was the silence that followed. Maybe their hearts and feelings were so numb from pain and despair that they were unable to cry. Whatever the reason, none of them made a sound. They just remained standing, avoiding each other's glances. A little while later, they turned away from each other so as not to look in each other's faces. Looking at a corner, a wall, or a window was better than looking at your family members in their pain and suffering. Most difficult for me was to see Liova, Sonia and Leiba huddled against my mother as if she could protect them. Their eyes looked up to her, saying all that their lips could not utter.

Having arranged to meet my friend Kalman, I told my mother that I was going again to try my luck at the fence. As if knowing in advance that I would not succeed, I did not say goodbye to anyone. I took an improvised knapsack I had made from an old sack and some rope in which my mother had put my few pitiful possessions of underwear and clothes. The lanes and alleys were teeming with young people who were even more desperate to find a way out than they had been the two previous nights. Kalman and I became part of the crowd that was constantly moving from spot to spot along the barbed-wire fence. The more aggressive we became, the more alert the Germans were, and quicker on the trigger. And so, I spent the third night at the fence in helplessness and despair. I felt completely exhausted—physically from not sleeping for three nights and being constantly on my feet, psychologically from the tension of the last three days. At times I felt like going back to my parents, throwing myself in a corner for a couple hours of sleep and then perishing with them. I was ready for anything, as long as there would be an end to it. With daybreak, I returned to my parents and family. As on the previous couple of days, they were fully dressed and looked completely exhausted.

Later, I would see many walking dead, but that was the first time, and they were my father, mother, sisters, brother, grandparents, uncles and aunts and their children. They walked mechanically from room to room as if in a trance. They were supposedly getting ready. According to the German instructions, everyone could take along a small suitcase or a knapsack. These were the horrible yet precious last minutes in the ghetto. I stood there not knowing what to do or say. Indeed, what could I have said? What was there to say? In one room was my uncle Hershel, bent over a small valise, arranging things in it. In the other corner, over another valise, was my uncle Eli, preparing it for his parents, my grandparents, Yaakov Kopel and Chinkah. Suddenly my uncle Hershel, still packing, started to sing, "Eli, Eli, lama azavtani?"—*My God, my God, why have you abandoned me?* Those words from Psalms had been made into a Yiddish song with heart-rending words regarding the centuries-old persecution of Jews, befitting many dark periods in Jewish history. If there was ever an appropriate time to say these words, it was then. If God did not respond, he must have been in a deep, deep sleep that lasted a long time. Through the entire German occupation and Nazi horror, I had not cried. The closest I came to crying was at that moment.

I slowly turned around to leave the room when I heard my grandmother say, "They are taking us to the slaughter, and he is singing."

My poor grandmother, the last few days and nights had affected her badly. She failed to recognize that this was my uncle's prayer, a cry to heaven.

I left the room and wandered aimlessly around the house until I came to a door that I had failed to notice previously. The door led into two large rooms that had served as a hiding place for all the medicine in the ghetto. The jars of medicine were piled knee-deep on the floor, trampled into powder and mixed with the crumbled glass of the jars. This damage had been done by a few young men who had been tipped off by the Judenrat of its whereabouts, with instructions to make the medicine unusable to the Germans. Those young men had done a good job.

The image of the destroyed medicine, on which so many lives in the ghetto had depended, lives that had hoped that with their help they might overcome the difficult times, shook me out of the delirium into which I had momentarily sunk and gave me the push into reality that I needed. I had to make a final decision, whether to stay here with my loved ones and share their fate or hide out for a few hours and try once more to get out at night. The decision was made by my mother who came quietly over to me and said, "Moishele, time to go and hide. The Germans will soon be here. Then it will be too late."

I wanted to start saying goodbye but did not know where to begin. So far, nobody had cried aloud, even though everyone's heart was breaking and crying beyond imagination. I knew that if I started saying goodbye, the ready-to-burst well of tears would not shut off. My mother noticed my hesitation and understood. She took me gently by my hand and said quietly, "Come, I will accompany you to the porch."

Since my early years, I had always felt that I was my mother's favourite child, if there is such a thing. How did my mother feel when she took me by my hand for the first time in years, knowing that it would be the last time in her life that she would hold my hand? Did she think of the times that she had held my baby hand when I tried to take my first step? Did she think of the times when I was two or three years old and she held my hand to make sure I did not run into the road, or when I was four or five and she led me to the cheder or to kindergarten? One thing I was certain of, that in her heart she was praying so ardently, so passionately on my behalf, that it moved heaven and earth. Otherwise, I would not have survived.

On the porch, my mother stood calmly and said, "Remember my child, you have two uncles in America, my brothers Shloime and Pesach.

If, God willing, you will survive, go to them and tell them how we lived and how we perished. Remember my brother Shloime's address: 2133 Daly Avenue, Bronx, New York."

I did not mark it down. I had very little faith in my chance of surviving.

Then my mother said to me, "*Nu*, Moishele, go my child."

I was waiting for my mother to take me in her arms and kiss me, expecting a flood of tears. To my astonishment she made no move in my direction. She stood there as if petrified, motionless, looking ahead into the street and not at me. Seeing that I was not moving, she added, "Try to get out tonight. Should you not succeed, you will be leaving tomorrow with the last group. I am sure the Germans will let us live near the pits for a day or two before they shoot us, and we will see each other tomorrow evening."

I agreed with my mother, adding, "Yes, we will most likely see each other tomorrow night," knowing only too well that, by that time, my dear ones would all be dead. I understood that my holy and loving mother was trying to make my leaving easier. We were fooling each other to ease the terrible pain of parting.

Still my mother did not make a move. Realizing that she feared an uncontrollable outpouring, I decided to go. I was standing by her side, and I bent down a bit and kissed her on the cheek. My mother did not move. Without another word, I started down the steps of the porch. Before walking too far, I stopped and turned back to take another look at my mother, whom I loved more than anybody in the world. She was wearing a dark skirt and my aunt Sheindl's sweater. I noted that my aunt's sweater fitted her nicely although my aunt was a slim woman whereas my mother had been on the stout side. I thought about how my mother must have been hungry many times in the last year and a half, and I had not realized it. I also thought that my mother might catch a cold standing outside without a coat at the end of January and that as long as she could see me, she would stand there. I forced myself to turn and walked quickly away.

My mother's strangely numb behaviour during our parting puzzled me for many years. I understood that her heart was so full of pain that it could not bear an emotional parting. But my mother was an exceptionally warm, affectionate and sympathetic person. How could she control herself so well? Many years later, I read a book by the American rabbi David Wolpe, *In Speech and in Silence: The Jewish Quest for God*. He wrote that in times of colossal emotion, only silence suffices, quoting the Kotzker Rebbe: "The cry one holds back is the most powerful one of all." How befitting of my mother's behaviour then.

My legs carried me down Rezki Street, toward the little Maletzky house where we had dug a hiding place. Seeing some men running by, looking for a place to hide, I offered them ours. Soon there were so many people, we could barely fit in. Brina Maletzky, the mother of the three Maletzky boys, covered the opening with small boards and spread turf over it. The space was cramped, and we were very uncomfortable. There was no fresh air, and the ceiling, that is, the few boards over our heads, was too low. We sat one on top of the other, bent down as far as we could. Suddenly, we heard somebody shovelling away the turf overhead and then removing the boards. I looked up and saw my father with my little brother, Liova. Pushing some people aside, I stood up and asked him what had happened. My father spoke to me in a voice I didn't recognize. My father's voice had always been strong and confident, even authoritative. Now he spoke to me with a voice full of anguish, as if all Jews under Nazi Germany's control were speaking through him: "Your mother thinks it would be a good idea if both of you hide. Maybe one of you will manage to get away through the wires and, who knows, maybe survive."

I looked at my brother. He was still a little boy, tucked under my father's arm. Before I managed to say a word, a flood of voices came from underneath, a chorus of protests and screams that turned into a jumble of words and shouting: "There is no more room here for anyone! We are already suffocating. What are we going to do with a little boy at the wires? And should we get out, do you think we can look after him? He will only be a hindrance." Somebody even yelled at my father, "How dare you expose our hiding place!"

I was thunderstruck. These were the same people to whom I had offered a hiding place, which they had been desperate for, no more than half an hour earlier. Now they were turning against me, against my father and brother. But what about me? Here I committed the greatest sin in my life, one that still haunts me today. I listened to the others complaining and yelling and did not say a word. True, I was not the boss there, but at least I should have told them off. After all, it was my hiding place that I had dug with my own hands, and I had invited them in. But I kept quiet. For keeping quiet then, I have so far not asked God for forgiveness. I do not dare, for in my book I do not deserve it.

We heard the sound of horses approaching. At any minute, the gate would open, and the Germans with the farmers' sleds would come in. My father took my little brother's hand and said, "Let's go."

There was barely room enough in that narrow hallway for them to turn around. I stood in the hole, watching them walk out, hand in hand, never to see them again.

I squeezed myself back into the hole, and Brina Maletzky covered the opening with the small board, dumped some turf over it, and we remained in the dark. Soon we heard the voices of the Jewish inhabitants, the peasants commanding the horses, and, above it all, the voices of the accursed Germans driving the Jews out of their homes to their deaths. Brina and her blind mother must have left their little house on time and quietly, for we did not hear the usual abuse, swearing and curses from the Germans inside. However, every fifteen minutes, we could hear a German coming in to make sure that there was nobody left. The reverberations of their booted steps shook the floor of that little house.

At around two o'clock on that Saturday afternoon, there was a dead silence in the ghetto. We moved away the boards and crawled out into the daylight. There was no sign of the Germans, and a few Jews began to appear in the street. Many seemed to wander, lost and bewildered, not knowing what to do or where to turn. Several times, I passed by the house from which my entire family had been taken away. I did not dare to enter.

I wandered around that part of the ghetto and felt so removed from it, without a person I loved or cared for in it. The nightmare of thoughts revolved around how my dear ones would perish, and I conjured up the most horrible visions that only the reality we were in could trigger. Then I found myself back near the Maletzky's house where I had been hiding a couple hours earlier. I saw some people through the little low window, and I went inside. There were a few Shershev Jews, speaking about those who had been taken and about the chances of getting out that night. The conversation was confusing. Everyone wanted to talk, and nobody had patience to listen as they tried to ease their own state of mind and the heaviness on their hearts. In the middle of that tumult, the door opened and Isser Gichman walked in. Like the rest of them, he was a man in his early forties, and a close friend of one of the other men, Moishe Tuchmacher. On that day, both their wives and children had been sent to the slaughter. The two friends fell in each other's arms. For a split second their faces lit up but then instantly twisted into a heart-rending cry. Even though everyone was in deep grief and ached over their own losses, it was difficult to watch two middle-aged men crying in each other's arms. Like the others in that little room, they had parted with their families forever, deciding to spend the last night in the ghetto in an attempt to get out.

One man banged his fist on the table and declared, "Now I feel better. Let them know what it is like to be without a wife and children as I have been in this ghetto for the past four months ever since I lost mine in Drohitchin."

I looked at the man in astonishment, not believing what I had just heard and wondering how anyone could even think such a thing, never mind say it. No one bothered to answer him. Everyone felt too dejected and tired and maybe already indifferent to what they saw and heard.

We remained in the Maletzky house till after dark when we went outside to try, once again, to escape. The Germans understood only too well the mentality of the Jews still remaining in the ghetto—that their attempts to escape on the previous three nights had been frustrated, and that they would be more aggressive on the last night. And so, as soon as it got dark, the Germans started shooting into the ghetto. Unlike the previous nights, when they shot at visible targets, this time they fired for no apparent reason, not even aiming at real or imaginary targets. It became dangerous to cross a street. Many believed that the best place to make a break was at Old Shershev Street, which was partly in the ghetto, with Christians living just on the other side of the barbed-wire fence. Once you made it to the other side, you could disappear into the alleys between the Christian houses. And indeed, many attempts to escape were made along that street. That night, one could find a group of young people behind almost every house, waiting for a chance to get out.

Despite the danger, we continued to wander from place to place, exhausted, half asleep, hoping for a miracle. And so, the last night in the ghetto passed in prolonged anguish. With daybreak, everyone hurried to make decisions. The gathering point became Rezki Street, where one could hear all kinds of suggestions. One proposed resisting, as there were still a few rifles stashed in a hiding place. Somebody asked how many cartridges we had. "Sixty" was the answer. Someone pointed out the fifty armed Germans who had just arrived at the main gate and said, "With the two rifles and sixty cartridges, do you want to take them on?"

Not only the men, but also a lot of women were in the street, many of them mothers. Hearing talk about resistance, many started crying, accusing the proponents of resistance of trying to provoke the Germans to kill us. Some of my acquaintances were still talking about hiding another night and trying again to get out. Others suggested searching for food in the empty houses. I could not remember when or what little I had eaten in the past few days. We ran into a few nearby empty houses and found some potatoes, carrots, beets, uncooked cereal, nothing ready to eat. In a couple of houses, we found food that really surprised me, like sugar, fat and oil. It was food that I had not seen since leaving Shershev. In one house we found a stock of czarist silver rubles. We started to fill our pockets but realized that they would weigh us down and make a jingling sound. In my pocket I had twenty or thirty marks that my father had given me and twice as many dollars from my uncle Hershel. I took a few silver coins and left the house. Outside, I met my friend Kalman and asked him if he had made a decision. He had decided to go to a hideout in his house, although people claimed that there was no room. I had no wish to hide alone in the previous place. Besides, there was nobody to cover it with turf this time.

And so, with daylight, the farmers' sleds arrived, and I watched as all the men who had spent the last four nights with me around the ghetto fence settled down into the sleds under the club-swinging watchful Germans. Everyone was trying to sit near family, friends and acquaintances to spend their last hours on this earth together. There were many single men like me, whose families had been taken earlier. To me it made no difference who shared the sled with me. Still, when I saw Shalom Berenstein, whom I had worked with outside the ghetto, approaching my sled, I reacted. He sat down to my right, and I found myself in the middle on the three-seat board.

The sight of entire families trying desperately to sit together made me feel painfully guilty. At this time yesterday, my family was being loaded on these sleds. They too had wanted to sit together. Had they? Or had they been torn apart and put in different sleds for that last trip? My efforts to get out of the ghetto had failed. I should have been with them; instead, I had abandoned them when they needed me most. At the same time, I felt some relief at not having to witness my loved ones being herded by the accursed Germans, who would have showered them with curses, swearing, name-calling and, above all, blows.

On the first two days, Thursday and Friday, the expulsion had taken place on streets we could not see. On Saturday, when my family was taken away, I was hiding in a hole from which I could hear little and see nothing. Now, on Sunday morning, January 31, 1943, the gruesome picture revealed itself in its full horror.

Who could imagine, an entire family being led to the slaughter—grandfather, grandmother, father, mother, children and grandchildren? Poor, broken Jews, exhausted after years of persecution, accompanied by beasts in the image of men who were treating them as if they were the scum of the earth. Who could imagine, who could comprehend and who could describe?

20

From Pruzhany to Auschwitz

IT WAS A couple of hours before the caravan started to move. The sleds moved slowly, one close to the next. Interspersed among them were sleds filled with Germans, who kept a watchful eye on the sleds ahead of them. We reached the ghetto gate, passed it and then left the ghetto behind. Suddenly, I was overwhelmed by an immense longing for the ghetto. Everything in it assumed bright colours, and even the German guards at the gates seemed tolerable.

Once we were in the Christian part of town, I am sure that, like me, many had the idea of jumping off the sled and disappearing among the Christian houses. I looked back and saw a sled of Germans three or four sleds behind me, their rifles ready. We were approaching the edge of town, where snow-covered fields stretched for kilometres. The last building was Krucel's flour mill. As we slowly passed the wide-open gate of its yard, Shalom Berenstein poked me with his elbow and asked, "Are you coming?"

Before I had time to digest his words, he swung his feet out, jumped off the slow-moving sled, and without looking around, walked straight through the gate of the flour mill, where a few peasants stood, looking at the Jews passing by. I watched in astonishment as he walked straight past the peasants into the yard. Not only did the Germans not see him, but it seemed that neither did the peasants, as if all were afflicted with blindness. At that moment and many times afterwards, I called myself by the worst names in my vocabulary for passing up such a chance. It was not just an ordinary loss—my life was at stake, and I lost a chance to save it.

I later heard from a former partisan from Pruzhany that Shalom had joined the partisans and fallen in the Battle of Berlin just a few days before the end of the war. Among other words of praise about Shalom, he said, "He killed more Germans than you have hairs on your head." I know an exaggeration when I hear one, but there is no doubt in my mind that he was a brave partisan. Honour to his memory.

We left Pruzhany and were in an open field. Farmsteads were scattered across the seemingly endless landscape, and the wide space appeared so undisturbed, so tranquil. My eyes wandered from the long line of sleds to the serene farmhouses in which the inhabitants went about their routine household chores, indifferent to the fact that just outside, two and a half thousand Jews were being led to their deaths. Some of them were probably even happy.

It was a frosty day with no wind, and the sky was blue and clear. I wondered why the sun shone so brightly given what was taking place on the ground. Why didn't the sun blot out her light and envelop the earth in darkness?

Soon, we were passing through a small village, and suddenly eight or ten men jumped off the sleds and ran into the village. The column of sleds stopped, and guards instantly took up positions around us. A few of them chased the escapees inside the village, where the doors were shut tight against them. A few tried to run into the snow-covered fields, but they were picked off easily by German rifles. The others were rounded up and ordered to go back to the sleds. As soon as they turned around, they were shot in their backs.

We moved on. Roughly halfway between Pruzhany and the railway station, Aranchytsy-Linovo, the Germans had created their German-Ukrainian border. German border guards were stationed there by the roadside in a fortified dugout for fear of attacks by partisans. Passing by, all one could see were four little windows from which machine guns stuck out. Behind the dugout was a pine forest. It was not an old forest, or a thick one. As soon as the first scores of sleds passed the dugout, several dozen men jumped off and began to run into the forest. Again, the Germans formed a chain around us while others shot at the fleeing men. Their dark figures were clearly visible against the white snow, and they became easy targets. But their fate was really decided when the border guards opened fire with their machine guns. We watched with pain in our hearts as one after the other they fell to the ground. The Germans went over to each one to make sure that they were all dead before the caravan continued.

An hour or so later, we arrived at the station and were driven past it, out of sight of the local population. There, on the sidetracks, stood about twenty-five cattle cars with their small windows boarded up. Local Ukrainian police surrounded the entire place, supervised by German soldiers. Those Ukrainian volunteers fulfilled their duty with fervour, surpassing the Germans in cruelty. As the line of sleds pulled up to the empty cattle cars, the Ukrainian police chased the Jews off the sleds. If a suitcase or a knapsack caught a Ukrainian's eye, he ordered the owner to leave it right there. The peasants, the owners of the sleds, also tried to benefit from the Jews' misfortune. Older Jews, after having sat immobile on the sleds for four hours, were stiff and had difficulties getting off. As soon as they managed to straighten their backs or regain mobility in their limbs, the farmers whipped their horses and quickly drove away with the meagre possessions still on the sleds. Who would pay attention to the screaming Jews amid all the crying, the laments of the women and the swearing, cursing and beating of the Germans?

As I approached the cattle cars, I kept an eye open for familiar faces, especially for people from Shershev. Apparently, others had the same idea, for in the blink of an eye, we were almost a dozen men from Shershev standing together. Some of them I still remember, like the two brothers Shepsl and Itzel Pomerantz, their brother-in-law Beryl Tenenbaum, Leibel Feldman and Gottel Wiener. I looked closely at what was going on around me and saw that the Germans were loading five cattle cars at a time and counting heads. As the doors of the cars were about a metre above ground, some of us were told to put long boards leading from the ground to the floor of the cars to serve as ramps. People were walking up the ramps and filling the cars to capacity. The Germans were not particular about who got in as long as the required number of people were inside. Then they slid the doors shut and sealed them. There was chaos and confusion all around. Having forced a certain number of people into a cattle car, the Nazis would stop the flow and divert it to the next car. In that desperate moment, families wanted to be together and indeed die together. How tragic it was when the Germans stopped the flow of people and divided up a family. No amount of begging, pleading or imploring helped. The doors were shut behind small children while their parents remained outside, or vice versa. Elderly and infirm people were separated from their families or caretakers. I looked with wide eyes at the barbaric treatment of innocent souls being taken to the slaughter, three- and four-generation families who were going to die together.

As the loading progressed, some people were pushing their way into the cars. I could not understand it then nor can I now. It seemed that the Germans were surprised too, for one yelled out, "Crazy Jews, what are you pushing for? Do you think that we will leave you here?" I know that the prospect of remaining behind and being killed on the spot did not appeal to me. I knew that the end would be the same, but I still preferred to be buried with all the others. Is it possible that those who pushed to get inside the cattle cars had the same thoughts and could not control themselves? Or perhaps they were trying to secure a place together for their families in the same car.

Eventually my turn came to enter a car. At twenty, I was agile and quick, and I was one of the first to make my way to a window. Although the windows were boarded up, there were narrow spaces between the boards, enough to tell if it was day or night, even to see some movement or objects from a distance. I positioned myself at the window and was surrounded by the other Shershev men. The car filled up in no time. The sliding door was pushed into place, locked and sealed, and we remained pressed together in the dark. Coming in from the bright outdoors, it took a while to get used to the dark. Slowly we began to distinguish and recognize faces. Whoever had family, friends or acquaintances called out for them. Between the calling out of names, the screaming of children, the crying of infants and women, the groans and moans of the elderly and the sighs of those who had been beaten up, it was difficult to talk. Besides, what was there to say? We all knew what was awaiting us. Since the Germans had not killed us right outside Pruzhany, they were taking us to Bronna Góra, where they had slaughtered thousands of the Jews of Bereza Kartuska, Ruzhany, Pinsk and other neighbouring places.

And so we stood in the cattle car, leaning on each other, exhausted spiritually and physically. It had been four nights since I last slept. I had spent those nights along the ghetto fence, barely eating anything, possessed with one thought: How to get out. Now everything was lost. There was nobody left of my family, and I was sealed in a cattle car that would take me to the same place, maybe to the same ditch, in which my family was already sleeping their eternal sleep. The noises from outside were getting quieter and soon stopped. Inside the car, it became quieter, too. When an infant was not crying, one could hear the footsteps of the guards around the train, interrupted by commands in German. It was now dark outside, and in the car it was pitch black. Once the train started moving, every minute would bring us closer to our eternal resting place, but what kind of living was it to stand pressed together like herrings in a barrel? We were barely on our feet, inhaling the continuously more suffocating air that was heavy with the smell of people relieving themselves as they stood.

Finally, at one in the morning, the train began to move, heading westward. We were too exhausted and resigned to our fate to wonder why the train was going west instead of east toward Bronna Góra. The train dragged slowly. At times it would speed up, but not for long. We made stops, sometimes short ones and sometimes longer. And so, early Monday morning, we passed Brest-Litovsk and continued farther west. In some, a spark of hope began to awaken that perhaps we really were going to work camps in Germany. The reasoning was that had the Germans wanted to murder us, they would not be dragging us so far from home but would have killed us on the spot, as they had done with the surrounding shtetls and towns.

In the past couple of months, a rumour had been circulating in our ghetto that something very bad was taking place near the Małkinia railway station on the line from Brest-Litovsk to Warsaw. Most Jews in the ghetto did not even know where Małkinia was, and if something bad was taking place there, could it be worse than what was happening around us? We knew that Pruzhany was like an island in the middle of the sea, that there were no more Jewish settlements around us, so what could be worse? And so, the rumour had died down. But on that day, as we stopped at a station some fifty kilometres before Warsaw, a travelling salesman who was familiar with the rail routes looked out through a crack in the boarded-up window and said, "If our train starts moving again and turns right, we will be going to Małkinia. It won't be a good sign. But if we continue straight, we will be going toward Warsaw." And so it was that our train went straight ahead toward Warsaw. None of us knew yet of the existence of Treblinka, which was just past Małkinia.

We did not go far before we entered a city with a large railway yard. Through the crack between the boards, I saw many railway lines. Looking across to the other end of the station, I saw a line of men, all of them with their backs to us, and on each back was a yellow Star of David. I saw a tall young man, and next to him a shorter, older and somewhat stooped man. The tall man made a motion with his head toward the older one, as if to point us out, but did not turn toward us. The older one lowered his head even more, nodding as if to say, "Yes, another trainload of our brothers to the slaughter." This image lasted only a few seconds, but it engraved itself on my memory forever.

Between us and the line of the Jewish men, freight trains and cars were being shuffled back and forth. After a while, a freight train parked alongside us. Its locomotive was unhooked, and the cars remained motionless. Through a crack in the window, I saw somebody crawling underneath the freight train and coming up almost in front of our car.

The man threw darting glances in all directions and said, "*Yidden*, save yourselves. You are being led to the slaughter. Break out of the cattle cars and run wherever you can. We were thousands of Jews here in Mińsk Mazowiecki, and now only a couple hundred are left, working on the railroad tracks and expecting any day to be murdered by the Nazis." Then the man disappeared.

These words evoked a tumult in the car. Should we or should we not? At least we would die trying to escape. Getting out from the car was not the biggest obstacle. The boards over the little windows could be beaten out, and jumping off a running train seemed feasible. More dangerous were the Germans who stood on the elevated platforms behind each car. We could hear the lament of older people and mothers of small children, crying that they would be shot in retaliation for our escape. The truth is that their complaints were not the reason for our remaining in the car. The real reason was that we all knew that our attempt to escape would be like jumping from the frying pan into the fire—that even if we escaped the Germans, we would fall into Polish hands. So we stayed.

As we were leaving Mińsk Mazowiecki, a group of Polish railway men got on our train, positioning themselves on the buffers between the cars. It was from them that we found out that we were going to a place called Oświęcim. The Poles tried to do business with us, to sell us bread and water, claiming that where we were going, we would not need money or jewellery. Their prices were a hundred dollars and up for a slice of bread, and even more for a bottle of water. Others simply asked for our money, saying we would not have any need of it where we were going. There were no transactions with them in our car, but we were left wondering: What kind of place were we going to, and why wouldn't we need money and jewellery but bread and water?

In the evening, we passed Warsaw. From my spot at the windows, I could see rows of tall buildings. Again, the always-present question hit me with intensity: *Why? What had we done to deserve this?* Here in front of me lived a million Poles. I imagined them to be continuously celebrating, whereas our destiny, our fate, was to be led to the slaughter.

In deep despair and with an aching heart, I turned from the window, thinking to myself that it wouldn't make any difference if I saw a couple more kilometres of the city or not. In any case, I would soon be dead. And so, I spent the second night leaning against the car wall. I became indifferent to what the next few hours might bring. I was too exhausted from the last several days and nights. With no feeling, simply numb both physically and mentally, I stood there, unable and unwilling to move or to look out through the crack for a familiar name of a station or town.

At midday the next day, the train stopped in the middle of nowhere. Through the crack, I could see a young pine forest along the railway tracks. The ground was covered with pure and untouched white snow, and it seemed to me that shadows were moving about in the forest. Sure enough, seconds later, human forms took shape. The crack in the window could accommodate three pairs of eyes, and three of us looked on as some men in British uniforms appeared at the edge of the forest. They were close enough that we could see the insignia on their shoulders. With unbelieving eyes, we read "Palestine."

Instantly, the news spread through the car, and whoever had strength left tried to push their way to the cracks to see the miracle with their own eyes. We yelled to them in Hebrew that we were being led to the slaughter. Without getting closer, they kept yelling to us, "Lo, lo, atem holchim lichyot velo lamut!"—*No, no, you are going to live and not to die!* Suddenly, one of them left the safety of the woods, ran across the ten metres of snow-covered ground, pulled out from his pocket a chocolate bar and shoved it through the crack in our window. Then he swiftly ran back into the forest. A minute later the train started moving, and the Hebrew-speaking soldiers in British army uniforms quickly disappeared from our sight. The man who stood by my side unwrapped the chocolate bar that our benefactor had shoved into the car. The bar consisted of forty-eight little squares, and those by the window decided to divide it among us, a square each. Needless to say, more than half of us in the car did not get any, but everyone understood that it was impossible to cut the tiny squares.

This event with the British, Hebrew-speaking soldiers is still vivid before my eyes. It was not always like that. There was a time when I began to doubt it had really happened, and I wondered if I might have not been fully conscious, or perhaps I was even hallucinating. But deep down I knew that it had happened. Many years later, while attending an *azkara*, a memorial service for the Pruzhany ghetto that took place in Israel, I met a man from Pruzhany by the name of Kalman Grossman, who was living in Jerusalem. During our conversation he mentioned that he too had left Pruzhany with the last transport on Sunday, January 31, 1943. I asked him if he remembered something unusual that happened a few hours before our arrival in Auschwitz. He thought for a moment, and then said, "The only striking event that I can remember was the appearance of the Jewish soldiers who were prisoners of war."

It turned out that he was with me in the same cattle car and remembered even the chocolate bar. I said to him, "Kalman, you have just returned my sanity to me."[1]

The event with the Hebrew-speaking British prisoners momentarily lifted our spirits, but not for long. The complete exhaustion, the feeling of being closed in a coffin-like railway car, the suffocating air and the apathy that comes with total resignation contributed to a delirious state. Most of us were in a stupor when the train started to slow down, giving the impression that it was going to stop again. I looked through the crack and awakened with a start. I saw before my eyes a low building and a slanted roof. The building was plastered in a grey-beige colour. I saw before me the very same building I had seen in my dream two weeks earlier while still in the ghetto. The sign on the building read "Auschwitz."

The train did not stop but just passed by and picked up speed. I thought to myself, *How can it be that I saw that very building in my*

1 In late January 1943, about six hundred Palestinian Jews who had volunteered for the British army and were captured by the Germans were brought to the prisoner-of-war camps in Jaworzno and Libiąż, Poland, towns close to the route the trains took from Aranchytsy to Auschwitz (Dr. Piotr Setkiewicz, head of the Research Centre, Auschwitz-Birkenau Memorial and Museum).

dream? What sinister omen was it? My despair came back with greater intensity than before. I had a premonition of things so gruesome, so appalling, that the fear of that unknown transcended the fear of death itself. Fortunately, I was not allowed to stew in my nightmare. I felt the train slowing down, and then it came to a sudden stop.

BOOK FOUR
The Camps
(1943–1945)

21
Auschwitz-Birkenau

BEFORE I HAD a chance to put my eyes to the window crack, I heard yelling and commands given in German and the barking of dogs. The door of our car slid open with momentum, and a rough voice shouted, "*Raus!* Everybody out!" The cramped and tired bodies started moving. The Germans hurried us with screaming and yelling. In their hands were leashes, at the end of which were vicious dogs baring their teeth. Before I reached the opening, I decided for the umpteenth time to pay attention to see and hear all that was taking place around me, not so that I should be able to talk about it later. No, for this I held out no hope. But I wanted to be fully conscious to the last moment. This was my life. This was what life had to offer me, and I had to accept it.

Despite the perilous situation I was in, I ventured to glance around. The platform below me was swarming with SS men running from car to car yelling and beating anyone who did not move fast enough. At a distance opposite our train, there was a high barbed-wire fence, the beginning and end of which I could not see. Beyond the fence, there were rows of barracks, and in the distance, many watchtowers.

As soon as I jumped off the cattle car, I found myself between two SS men with clubs in their hands, yelling, "Able-bodied men on the other side!" and pointing in the direction of the long barbed-wire fence. Anyone who did not react immediately received a paralyzing blow from the club.

It is impossible to describe what took place there, the fear, the panic, the confusion and the tragedies that took place before my eyes. Men were torn away from their families, sons from their parents, mothers from their children. Everything was happening at once. Wherever I turned, I saw heart-rending scenes. I had nobody to say goodbye to, though I would not have had a chance even if I did. The SS chased the men to the other side of the platform, and our group kept growing as more men joined us. As our group grew, the SS men ordered us to fall in line, five to a row. No matter how we did it, it was not good enough for them, and with the help of their clubs, we repeated the drill over and over. It occurred to me that the SS were trying deliberately to keep us men busy so that we should not see too much of what was taking place all around. This reinforced my decision to keep my eyes open.

Looking around as I was running back and forth, I was thinking of what it would have been like the day before, when my entire family had arrived—how my little brother and even littler sisters would have huddled up to my mother, if they had found each other at all in this confusion. How they could have used me when they needed me so badly! I felt a terrible guilt. Yet in a strange way I was grateful that I did not have to see them being tortured this way.

Those who could get off the cattle cars by themselves did so in a hurry. Others, like children and older people, were helped. Still others had to be carried off. The little suitcases or knapsacks that each had taken along from Pruzhany had to be left right there on the platform. The mass of humanity that had just descended from the cattle cars was facing the SS and was being pushed back against the cars along the length of the train while the able-bodied men were sent to the fence where I stood. A huge SS man appeared. He was almost two metres tall and almost as thick around his middle. In his hand, he held a bullwhip, at least four metres long. He went back and forth along the crowd of women, children and old people, whipping them mercilessly. I thought, *How can you, beast, although you are in the image of man, be so cruel as to torture helpless, innocent people before their deaths? Why can't you leave them alone in the last minutes before they die?*

A tarp was spread on the frozen ground, and I watch in horror as SS men walked along the mass of women and children and tore infants out of their mothers' arms and threw them onto the tarp. The infants flew ten metres in the air before landing, falling one on top of the other. Some hit the tarp with an ear-splitting scream. Some hit their little heads on the hard, frozen ground and were either knocked out or killed instantaneously. As those infants were being thrown, their mothers tried to run after them but were held back and beaten with heavy clubs. They were beaten to the ground and dragged back to the others. I watched and understood how cruel death could be, and I no longer asked myself why we deserved such punishment. I asked only how many forms death could take and why it did not come easier.

I then saw SS women striding along the group of women, picking out younger women and leading them to one side. The group of able-bodied men that I was in was made to form a line. At the head of the line, there was an SS man who exchanged a few words with each man who stepped forward. The SS man then made a slight, effortless motion with his finger: To the right, you joined the group that was forming along the wire fence; to the left, you went back to the mass of humanity alongside the train. The fate of that group was clear to us. Some men, seeing that they were being sent to the women and children and realizing what it meant, tried to go in the opposite direction. Unfortunately, they could not escape the watchful eyes of the SS men, who chased those poor souls with hard blows of their clubs.

With unbelieving eyes, I saw SS men selecting a number of old Jews with long grey beards and telling them to pick up the four corners of the tarp on which lay the innocent and holy Jewish infants, some of whose pure souls had already left their tiny bodies. With blows and curses they forced the old grandfathers and great-grandfathers to tie the four corners together and make it into a bundle. I can still hear the whimpers of those holy little souls and the thud of the blows that fell on the backs of the old men. I wondered how God could look upon the scene and not react. Yet nothing happened. The murderers went on with their grisly work. The clouds became heavier and darker on that late Tuesday afternoon of February 2, 1943.

A truck pulled up. It turned around and backed up toward the bundle of dead and dying infants. The back door was lowered, and the SS men ordered the old Jews to lift the bundle of infants onto the truck. The old men strained under the blows of the SS men and managed to put the bundle on the truck. The back door was closed, and the truck pulled away. As soon as that truck was gone, another one appeared. Some of the old men were instructed to bring a stepladder over to the rear of the truck, and the women, children, old people and those rejected at the selection started to get on. Within seconds, the truck was full, and the old men closed the rear door and the truck pulled away, only to be replaced by the next truck. Again, the process was repeated—truck after truck.

I was slowly getting closer to the SS man at the head of the column. The closer I got to him, the more preoccupied I was with my situation. I knew that my life, or at least my immediate survival, was in the hands of that SS man. It all depended on his whim. A couple more men ahead of me went through, and then I was standing in front of the creature who held my destiny in his hands. He glanced at me with an expression of indifference, even boredom. I meant nothing to him, and with the slightest motion, he could send me to my death. Fortunately, he did not keep me waiting and asked, "How old are you and what is your trade?"

I answered, "Twenty years old and a locksmith by trade."

He made a motion with his hand, indicating the area where the fittest were being gathered. With a dozen long strides, I found myself among the group chosen for the camp. They were being drilled by some SS men. One SS man stretched his arm out and told us to fall in. Then he turned, and we had to do it all over again. Our group kept growing, and the lines were getting longer. A few more SS men joined the others to keep us moving. Avoiding the blows became more difficult.

I was aware that trucks kept coming and going, taking the women, children and others away. We were all very tired and wondered how long this would go on. Suddenly, the SS man stopped and waited till we had all lined up five in a row. A few more SS men and officers arrived. The one in command gave an order, and they started counting us, once, twice and again. We stayed in line, not even daring to whisper a word. The SS men were in conversation.

I used the quiet break of that moment to glance across to the cattle cars in which we had arrived an hour and a half earlier, and I froze in horror. I did not see a living soul. The cattle cars were there with their sliding doors wide open. The bundles that the passengers had brought with them were scattered on the ground in front of the train. But where were the over two thousand living souls who had stood there an hour and a half earlier? How could they have gone so quickly? They had all disappeared. They had disappeared, and with them, their screams, their cries and their lament. All that was left along the empty train was a frightening and deadly silence.

22

What a Concentration Camp Is

FIVE ABREAST WE were led into the camp. The entry gate was quite unassuming, and we were counted again as we passed it. I remembered my decision to try and see everything, to record it in my memory. As soon as we entered the camp, I saw a well-fed man dressed in a striped jacket and pants with a club in his hand mercilessly beating another man dressed in the same striped attire. The victim looked like he had not eaten in months. He was like an emaciated caricature of a man as he attempted to protect himself from the blows with his weak, clumsy arms. The helpless soul did not even try to run. Instead, he held on to an empty wagon and moved with difficulty around it, falling every few steps. That poor man was still being hit even when he was lying on the ground. The unfortunate victim made a couple of attempts to get up, only to fall again under the blows. As we were passing, I looked back to see what would happen. I saw that poor soul lying on the ground, the well-fed man still hitting him. It was clear that he intended to finish him off.

That was the picture that played out before my eyes in the first two minutes after entering Birkenau, or Auschwitz II, or Hell itself. As we proceeded, I saw a wagon approaching, pulled by two horses. The horses looked well fed, and the two young men on the seat looked even better.

They seemed to be content, for they conversed and laughed heartily. I took notice of this contradictory observation.

Soon, we found ourselves in front of one of the countless barracks. Its doors were like a gate and just as wide, open in both directions, as if eager to take us in. The barracks was about ten metres wide and forty metres long. There was no floor, so the ground served as one. In the middle, along the barracks' length, was a brick partition that looked like a horizontal chimney. I later found out that indeed it was meant to act as both a stove and a chimney, though it never worked. This chimney duct served as a partition in the barracks. Along one side of the partition were two rows of desks. Behind each desk sat a man dressed in the striped concentration camp attire. Some SS men were walking back and forth behind those men, keeping an eye on them and on us.

We were ordered to stand on the other side of the partition. There, for the first time, we came face to face with kapos. These kapos were Polish inmates, and their task was to supervise the other inmates, using SS methods. They hit us using clubs, shovels, pickaxes or anything that was handy, and if nothing was available, they used their hands and feet to hit and kick. The SS men were there to make sure that the kapos were doing their jobs satisfactorily.

Someone announced that everyone whose family name began with the letter *A* should step over the partition and present themselves in front of a desk. The people behind the desks were asking questions and writing things down on forms. So it continued, letter after letter, until they got to the letter *K*. I stepped over the partition and positioned myself in front of a desk. Behind the desk sat a young Jewish man a couple of years older than me. He did not look emaciated, but his face was pale, actually white. He picked up a form from a pile, and looking up at me with visible compassion, he told me to empty my pockets. I had on me the dollars my uncle Hershel had given me on the last Saturday, before I went to hide, an hour or two before he and my entire family were taken away, plus the few marks from my father. As I reached into my pocket, I felt the few rubles I had taken from an empty

Jewish home on Sunday morning, shortly before I got into the sled. I put it all on the table. An SS man saw the money and moved closer.

The man behind the desks asked, "Is this all?"

"This is all," I answered.

While the SS man picked up the money and threw it in a nearby basket, the young man picked up a pen and asked me my name, age, vocation and a couple more questions. Then he asked one question that stunned me, "What is the reason for your arrest?"

It sounded to me so preposterous that I suspected some trap behind the question. It seemed to me that my interrogator deliberately let me think for a few seconds. Maybe he did that to emphasize the absurdity of the whole process—the form, the questions and everything else. In a place like this, what purpose did all these questions serve?

The young man looked around, and seeing the SS man walk away, he said to me quietly, "I know the answer, but I am ordered to ask regardless." He filled in the line on the form, asked me one or two more questions, put the form in another pile, then gave me a small piece of paper and said, "Step to the desk behind me and give him this scrap of paper."

Behind that desk was another young Jewish man, about the same age as the first, with the same white face of a dead man. He took the piece of paper from my hand and told me to roll my left sleeve up to the elbow. He dipped a needle in an inkwell, and, glancing at the piece of paper, made a tattoo on my forearm, with the numbers 99347. In normal times, getting a tattoo with such a crude tool would be painful, but at that moment I was not paying attention. It was only the next day that my forearm swelled, but then I was confronted with so many other problems that I could not even pay attention to it. As soon as I received my number, I joined the other prisoners. From that time on, I was only a number and was always referred to as such by the Nazis and camp administration.

The registration process took several hours. How many exactly I did not know, for our watches were left on the desks together with the rest of our possessions, but it seemed late in the evening by the time it was over. A group of prisoners accompanied by several SS men entered, carrying bags, which they began to fill with everything that had been taken from us—money, rings, watches and even documents. Then they left, followed by the SS men.

We were then led to a nearby barracks and told to get completely undressed. We were shaved from the tops of our heads to our toes. As soon as one person was shaved, a man who stood near a barrel full of liquid disinfected him. The man wore a thick mitten, which he dipped in the liquid and smeared over our bodies. The liquid made the skin red and itchy. After being shaved and disinfected, we were led into an adjoining barracks, which was the bathhouse, leaving behind all our clothes except our shoes and belts, which we were permitted to hold on to. As soon as the water started running from the showerheads, many of us drank it, as we hadn't had any water in the last days. The attendants of the bathhouse, prisoners like us, cautioned us to stop drinking the water as it was contaminated. They told us that there had been a typhus epidemic in the camp that had caused the death of tens of thousands of inmates.

The bathhouse attendants were the first Jews from France who were brought to Auschwitz. They were immigrants who had moved from Poland between the two world wars, and as foreigners, they were the first to be deported from France. They had received numbers starting from late 41,000 up to about 42,500. In the camp they were pegged "the forty-two thousands." They spoke excellent Yiddish and Polish, but among themselves they spoke French. I suspected that speaking French gave them a feeling of cultural superiority over their former countrymen in camp, the Jews of Poland.

After the shower, wearing nothing but our shoes and belts, we were led to the next barracks, where we found piles of clothing on long tables. Several prisoners were standing behind the tables. As we were passing by in a single line, they threw at each one of us a pair of underwear, an undershirt, a jacket and a pair of pants. Besides the few SS men who were there, several kapos and their helpers with their clubs were present, making sure that we moved quickly. Each person received the opposite of what he needed—a big man received a small pair of pants, while a slim one had to pull up his pants constantly; a tall one received pants reaching halfway to his knees, whereas a short one had to roll his up. There was no such thing as asking for an exchange, so we tried to exchange our clothing with one another while getting dressed under the blows of the supervisors. The caricatures into which we were suddenly transformed would have been comical if not for the tragedy that brought us there.

And so, outfitted, we were led on that bitter cold night into an empty barracks. Before we were told to lie down on the bare bunks, we were ordered to take off our shoes or boots and line up our footwear along the flue that ran almost the full length of the barracks. Then they ordered us to get on the three-tier bunks and go to sleep.

Despite our exhaustion, none of us could sleep on the hard boards. An hour or so later, a group of kapos came in with their assistants. They examined our footwear, picked out the best pairs and threw the rest in a pile. As they were going out, one yelled, "Get your shoes!"

I had arrived in Auschwitz in a pair of high leather boots given to me by my uncle Eli at the beginning of the ghetto's evacuation. As soon as the kapo yelled, "Get your shoes!" everyone jumped to get his, knowing that some would remain without any. I grabbed a pair of boots that looked very much like mine. I pulled on one boot, and it fit perfectly. I felt lucky that I got my boots back. But when I pulled on the second boot, my foot did not get in all the way. I looked around for another boot, but the pile of footwear had disappeared. I was stuck with a boot in which my heel did not get fully inside, and I had to tiptoe on one foot.

We did not even bother to lie down on the hard bunks. We remained standing, bracing ourselves for the next surprise. We did not have to wait long. Before sunrise, we were driven outside. Despite the darkness, the camp was brightly lit, and one could see as clearly as if it were midday. We were lined up five abreast and ordered to march. It seemed to me that we were not going in any particular direction. We turned right, then left, right again, and back and forth several times.

We finally stopped some distance from the barracks and were told to remain standing in line. We stood there exposed to the sub-zero wind with our freshly shaved heads, our feet in shoes with no socks, dressed in underwear, undershirt, jacket and pants—no hat, no sweater, no coat, scarf or gloves. Our heads and ears took the brunt of the wind and cold. Dawn came, and we did not move. From a distance we could see detachment after detachment of inmates marching out to work. Meanwhile, we were numb from the cold.

Eventually, a couple of SS men approached us. The kapo stood to attention and reported to them. We were told to march and were led from one area of fenced-in barracks to another. The entrance was simply a hole in the wires, and we were between two rows of barracks that were unoccupied. We marched between the rows until the last few barracks, where groups of inmates were standing. A rumour spread quickly among us that some of them were from Pruzhany, but nobody was sure. We turned left and then stopped and were lined up. The ground was pure mud, and it felt as if we were sinking into it. The new man who was going to be in charge here had an armband on which was written *Blockältester*, block elder. He was a tall, well-fed man in his late twenties. We did not know at that time what the armband meant, but we recognized him to be a big shot of sorts by the size of the club in his hand. He spoke to us in German with a noticeable Polish accent. I wondered why he didn't speak to us in Polish, since he knew that we were all former Polish citizens. Then it dawned on me that he did it for the benefit of the SS men around.

When we were finally standing in a straight line to their liking, we were suddenly ordered to squat. This was not difficult for a young person to do for a short period. It was quite a different story to remain in that position for an hour or two. The lower part of my legs became numb, my knees cried out in pain and my desire to stretch my legs became urgent. The older men began to do just that, and it was then that the *Blockältester* came into play. Standing behind us, he and his assistants, the *Stubendienste*, or room orderlies, began to beat anyone who tried to stretch a leg. There were some who fainted in that position and were beaten mercilessly while they were lying on the ground.

While we were squatting and being beaten, an SS man delivered a speech. All I remember of that short speech was that he compared the concentration camp to a military camp, which was based on discipline. If we obeyed all the rules, he said, we would be fine. Most of us did not understand what he said. This was obvious from our faces, so the SS man turned to the *Blockältester* and told him to repeat it in Polish. After the *Blockältester* repeated some of the SS man's words, he added in a question: "Well, now do you know what a concentration camp is?"

We answered naively, "No."

The *Blockältester*, with a smile on his face, said, "Then you will find out."

We took this as a warning but couldn't imagine what was to come.

While all this was taking place during our welcome speeches—hours-long squatting and other so-called sports, in the camp language—a group of inmates gathered near us. They were not the ordinary camp inmates. The ordinary inmates were working all over the perimeter of Auschwitz-Birkenau. Those near us were the prominent internees, as they were known. They were the kapos, *Blockälteste*, *Stubendienste* and their cronies—a bunch of sadists and murderers who at times made the SS men look almost human. In short, they were the scum of humanity. Those prominent prisoners stood there watching as our immediate supervisors were making sport with us, as they called beating us mercilessly. They encouraged the ones beating us, advising them how to deal with us. From time to time, some of them waded in between us with their sticks. The few SS men became bored with all of this and walked away, leaving us at the mercy of these murderers.

In late afternoon, a group of men approached us. In front walked a short man in civilian clothes marked with red stripes on his jacket and pants, just like some of our supervisors. His armband read *Lagerältester*, senior camp prisoner. Judging by the respect that the other big shots showed him, we understood that he was a very big fish. We watched him walking by slowly in his riding pants and polished boots, stepping nonchalantly on the muddy ground. He looked at us with so much scorn, with such contempt, that it made our blood congeal in our veins. So this was the man, supposedly an inmate like all of us, in whose hands lay the destiny of all the inmates. As if to confirm our thoughts, he ordered us to straighten our lines and slowly walked by the first row of five, looking each man directly in his eyes. He stopped in front of a tall man and ordered him to step forward. I quietly asked those around me and found out that this inmate was one of a group of Dutch Jews who had joined us that morning.

The *Lagerältester* stood close to the Dutch Jew, menacingly holding a club in his hand, and asked him, "What is your profession?"

"I am a salesman," came the answer.

Poor unfortunate soul. He did not realize that this was exactly what the Germans were looking for, to stereotype a Jew as a salesman. The club in the *Lagerältester*'s hand came up high and then came down with force on the Jew's head. Blood started running over his face, but he remained standing. This infuriated not only the *Lagerältester* but also those who were with him, and with his nod they surrounded the man, hitting him repeatedly. In a minute, his head and face became a mass of blood, and he fell. It was clear that he was unconscious, but the beating went on. When they finally stopped hitting him, they kicked him with their boots. They left the motionless body only when it came time to go to the barracks. The double doors opened, and we were herded inside, accompanied by blows and curses. There was tremendous confusion in the barracks among the mixed-up, beaten, bruised and panicked inmates.

We were some three or four hundred men in a barracks that was exactly like the one in which we had been registered and the one in which we spent the previous night. We looked around. It had the same flue and along the length of both walls were three-tier bunks. The bunks were bare and damp. I do not know if it was because the wood was still fresh or if the rain or melting snow came in through the roof. Near the entrance of the barracks, there was a small room with a closed door, and I wondered what was behind it.

We were broken up into groups of ten and assigned bunks. Mine was the middle one. It was better than the bottom bunk, but I had to sit bent over because of the bunk above mine. After a while, my back was aching.

The *Blockältester* announced that we were going to get bread, and we were told to get on one side of the flue. Some assistants, the *Stubendienste*, positioned themselves on top of the flue to make sure that no one tried to sneak across it to get another piece of bread. The clubs in their hands discouraged anyone from trying. From one side of the barracks, we advanced to the end of the flue, received a quarter of a loaf of bread and then went over to the other side. This process took about an hour, and then we returned to our bunks. I looked at the piece of bread and concluded that I might survive on it. Even though I had not eaten for several days, I wasn't hungry, yet I started to eat. It was after I finished the bread that I felt how thirsty I was.

We were told to go to sleep. The shoes went under the bottom bunk, and the jacket with the pants went under our heads. We were not permitted to sleep with our clothes on and were given one blanket for the ten of us. As soon as we took our jackets and pants off, we were shivering. We tried to lie down on the hard and damp boards, only to discover that there was not enough room for the ten of us. After pushing, shoving and wrangling, we finally succeeded in fitting on the bunk lying on our sides pressed tightly together. No matter how we positioned the blanket, it could in no way cover the ten of us, and a struggle began between the two men at the ends. The name-calling, swearing and berating went on until one after another we started complaining of pain in our arms, hips and sides from lying on the hard boards. We could not turn individually to the other side, so we decided to turn over all at the same time.

Despite our exhaustion, nobody slept. In the middle of the night, the door of the barracks opened and several men of the kind that had welcomed us some hours earlier with their clubs and blows came in. They approached a couple of bunks and pulled down the blankets, revealing some of the occupants in pants and jackets, and a hail of clubs fell on them. Their screams were unbearable. Others began to take off their jackets and pants under the blankets, but the men noticed and ran along the rows of bunks beating everybody, not even bothering to pull the blankets down. Having satisfied their desire to inflict pain and having impressed the SS men who came with them, they warned us against putting on our clothes and walked out. And so, lying on the bunks and shivering from cold, we survived until February 4, 1943, before dawn, when the wide doors of the barracks opened, and the *Blockältester* and a couple of *Stubendienste*, their inseparable clubs in hand, stood there. A couple more were at the rear of the barracks, swinging clubs and chasing everyone toward the exit. In the blink of an eye, we pulled on our pants, jackets and shoes and joined the pushing and shoving crowd that was trying to dodge the blows.

We were finally outside. It was dark but well lit. All around, in a large circle that surrounded the few nearby barracks, stood SS men with rifles at the ready. It occurred to me that they had guarded us all night and were in a bad mood. The *Blockältester* and *Stubendienste* wanted to placate the SS men by beating us continuously. They were trying to line us up five in a row, just so, but it was not easy with people who had gone through what we had in the last couple of days. The ground that was soft yesterday was now frozen and uneven. It must have taken an hour before they got us standing to their liking. We were told to remain standing at attention.

How long could a man remain standing still after what we had endured? Something was bound to happen, somebody had to be the first to move a hand or a foot. The *Blockältester* and *Stubendienste* noticed every move, and the guilty ones got beaten up. The longer we stood, the more of us committed the crime of stirring or making a move, and clubs fell over our heads and backs. Two SS men approached, and the guards assumed a more dignified stance. Our *Blockältester* warned us to obey his command properly, or else.... As soon as the two SS men were near us, the *Blockältester* yelled, "Attention!" We raised our heads and stretched our necks out like string instruments. One of the two SS men came closer and started counting us. He made sure there were five in each row, said a few words to the other SS man who wrote something down in his notebook, and then they left in the direction they had come from.

By then it was daylight, and we were told that breakfast would soon be served. When it finally arrived in metal barrels, we were still standing five in a row. The first in each row got a red bowl containing boiled water with blueberry leaves, a liquid they called tea, and was told to share it with the other four in his row. We were all thirsty and noticed that the first guy seemed to hold the red bowl to his mouth for too long. The man behind him was not worried. He knew that there would be enough liquid for him too. But the fourth in line was worried that it might not be enough, and the fifth was sure that there would not be anything left for him. He yelled, "*Nu!* Enough already, leave some for others!"

Some listened to such an appeal and passed the bowl to the one behind him. Others continued to slurp. The last one or two in line moved forward to take the bowl by force. A struggle ensued in some of the lines, and liquid spilled on the ground.

After the so-called breakfast, we were dismissed to remain outdoors in the space between our barracks and the next. Some braver men stuck their heads out from behind the barracks to have a better look around and found out that in the next barracks were the men from Pruzhany who had left the day before us. The more courageous ran over there when our overseers were preoccupied. We found out that barracks numbers 15, 16, 17 and ours, 18, housed the men from the Pruzhany ghetto who had been selected for the camp, with each transport from the ghetto in a separate barracks. I was sure that my uncle Eli would be there, but I could not find him. After a long search, an inmate told me that my uncle had voluntarily gone with his parents, my grandparents, refusing to join those selected for the camp. Our overseer eventually noticed our transgression and quickly put a stop to it.

We were forced to remain outside without hats on our shaven heads, without coats or sweaters. To get a bit warmer, we huddled up to the wall of the barracks and to one another, ten or twenty men deep.

Several hours later, we were driven back into the barracks. Standing in line, one by one, we approached the end of the flue, where each of us received a red enamel cup that could hold no more than a third of a litre of liquid. A *Stubendienst* standing near two large wooden barrels filled with soup put the ladle in the barrel and filled the cup. After receiving the soup, we went over to the other side of the barracks. Some of the *Stubendienste* were standing on the flue, watching and making sure that nobody stepped over it and joined those who had not received their soup yet. Woe to him who tried and got caught. After we finished eating, we were told to hang our enamel cups on our belts for use the next day. As there was no water, the cups remained unwashed. Then we were driven outside.

All day long we saw countless groups of prisoners going to and from work. Where to and where from we did not know—the camp was too immense—but their appearance gave us the shivers. From where we stood, we could see that we were at the edge of a huge camp and that work was taking place to extend the camp—from digging ditches, to levelling the ground, building roads, digging in fence posts, stringing barbed wires and erecting barracks. There, before our eyes, a gigantic camp was rising, the extent of which we could not see. Beside our barracks, number 18, was one more barracks, which was empty. In the other direction, past the four barracks occupied by inmates from Pruzhany, over a dozen barracks were empty and inmates were working inside, erecting bunks. Opposite the last few barracks in that row, some fifty metres away, stood a low brick building with a tall square chimney. This brick building was surrounded by an extra fence with its own guard towers. Between the building and the fence surrounding it were thinly spaced pine trees.

On our first morning in that part of the camp, there was no chance to start a conversation with the veteran inmates. In the afternoon, when they passed by our barracks on their way back from work, some of us succeeded in exchanging a few words. Understandably, our first question was about our families and where they were. Even though I did not understand the answer I received at that time, I would use the same answer myself later when asked the question by newly arrived prisoners. A young man not much older than me pointed with his finger, which was attached to an emaciated forearm. He said, "Do you see that fire and smoke? That is how your family went to heaven."[2]

I looked at him, not understanding what he said or what he meant. I thought that he had lost his mind.

Before dark, our supervisors appeared. They came out from the barracks where they sat in the small, heated partition. The morning drill repeated itself. We were chilled to the bone and our bodies were numb, but the club was an effective instrument, and the drilling continued. During the day, the muddy soil had softened, and it was difficult to lift one's feet, but the *Blockältester* and *Stubendienst* were generous with their clubs. We stood in rows of five and did not dare move unless ordered to. In the cold, the wind cut through our jackets and undershirts.

Finally, a few SS men arrived to count us. The roll call, or the *Appell*, was over, and the wide door of the barracks opened. We were told to get in. But nothing was easy in Birkenau. A couple of the *Stubendienste* stayed behind and more were at the door. The ones behind were hitting and driving us inside while those at the door were hitting the stampeding prisoners indiscriminately over their heads and backs. The nearby SS men who would form the first shift on guard did not stand idly by and hit us with their rifle butts.

We were finally inside, driven to one side of the barracks, and as on the previous evening, one by one we crossed over to the other side for our bread ration. As soon as the bread was distributed, we were told to go to the bunks. Everybody ran to the bunks. It was not important

2 The four gas chambers and crematoria in Auschwitz-Birkenau went into operation between March 22 and June 25–26, 1943. Before that time, people were gassed in two houses at the perimeter of the camp that were sealed off for that purpose, and the bodies were burned in burning pits. In February 1943, the time Moishe is writing about, inmates of Birkenau would have seen the smoke from the burning pits (Dr. Piotr Setkiewicz, Auschwitz-Birkenau Memorial and Museum).

who lay where, as long as we had a space to lie down. Let it be on a damp and hard board, I just wanted to lie down out of the wind and the cold. I did not know anybody on the bunk, but I didn't care. We ate the bread and shared our experiences of the day in whispers. I found out that some from our barracks had made it to the fourth barracks that held the people who had left the ghetto on the first day, Thursday, January 28.

A few people managed to have a lengthier conversation with inmates who had been there for weeks or even months, and from them they heard stories that did not make any sense, stories that I would have been embarrassed to repeat for fear of being ridiculed. I had gone through the two-day march from Shershev. I had seen with my own eyes the two mass graves in Khomsk, and I had spoken to individual Jews who had saved themselves from slaughters in places like Drohitchin, Kobrin, Antopol and Brest-Litovsk and who had brought with them stories of horror. I, and the rest of us in Auschwitz-Birkenau, knew only too well what the Nazis were capable of doing. And still, my mind could not grasp, could not understand what was taking place here. Nor could I comprehend the reason why the Nazis dragged us halfway across Europe to kill us here. Was there not enough space for burial around Pruzhany? Why should they use railway cars for Jews when they were needed more urgently for supplying the Eastern Front? Was it possible that they wanted to obliterate any trace of their crime? Nonsense! They were leaving behind mass graves of Jews near every shtetl and city in eastern Poland and in the conquered Soviet territories. Had we been told by the other inmates that our families were shot, we would have believed it, but to come up with a bizarre story of people being gassed and their bodies burned was unacceptable. Finally, we settled in our bunks with the conviction that the stories were made up by our tormentors to make our lives more miserable.

The night went by with aches and pains. We were visited again by our tormentors, who again pulled off the blankets to make sure that we were not sleeping in our clothes. Again, the bitter cold had forced many to put on their pants and jackets. Those who were found out were left beaten up and bleeding. Few of us slept and none rested that night.

The next day, we went through the same routine—the same long time standing in line and the same supervisors with their clubs. We got acquainted with a few more abusive words in German. All the supervisors yelled and cursed in German, and I began to wonder if the German language consisted of only abuses and curses. The same disorder occurred when they served the tea, and we stayed outside, leaning against the barracks wall, huddled against one another.

As I lay down on the hard bunk that night, I felt a terrible thirst. I had not had water to drink since January 31. All of us were thirsty, but where did one get water? We knew that there was plenty of snow on the roof of the barracks and that the little windows above could be opened, but that was prohibited. Apparently, my thirst overcame my fear of being caught, for I got to the window and came back with a handful of snow, which I slowly let melt in my mouth. Regretfully, it made me even thirstier than before.

On the morning of February 6, I turned twenty according to the Gregorian calendar. The day started as usual. I do not remember if I got a mouthful of the tea or not, but right after its distribution, the *Blockältester* showed up with a list and called out some numbers. They were the numbers of several fourteen-year-old boys who had been selected for the camp when we arrived. It seemed that the Germans realized that such young boys would be of little use to them and decided to get rid of them. They were told that they were being taken to another part of the camp where they would receive better nourishment. There were about half a dozen boys in my barracks, and some more in each of the other three barracks. These two dozen or so boys were led straight to their deaths.

One of the boys taken from my barracks left behind his father. As soon as the father understood what had happened, he broke down in a heart-rending lament. It so happened that the *Lagerältester*, the camp elder, passed by a few minutes later. To everyone's surprise, he stopped to find out why the man was crying. When he heard the answer, this man, the very same man who had welcomed us upon our entry into that part of the camp by demonstrating extreme barbarism when he and his companions beat the Dutch man to death, walked over to the crying father and with as much compassion as such a brute could muster said to him, "Too bad they took your son away. I will soon need some *Blockälteste* and will appoint you as one."

I doubt if his words were of any consolation to the crying father. But when the large transports of Roma inmates arrived a few weeks later, this man indeed became a *Blockältester*.

Ironically, this event with the fourteen-year-old boys eased my conscience somewhat. In the first days in Auschwitz, despite my own hopeless situation, I was gnawed at by guilty feelings for not standing up more insistently to the men in my hiding place in the ghetto when they refused to let in my thirteen-year-old brother, Leibel. Now I knew that he would have been sent to his death for sure. Now I knew that my brother did not have to confront death alone as he would have if he had been with me. At least he was with his parents and sisters when they clung to each other with their last breath.

The *Lagerältester* likely saved the life of that father in my barracks. By promoting him to *Blockältester*, he raised him to the highest position an inmate could achieve in camp, second only to himself, ensuring he would have all the food he wanted and protection from other inmates. I found out after the war that this man came out alive from that hell. This was an accomplishment in itself, especially for a man his age. Many times, I have wondered what moved that murderer to have compassion for that unfortunate father. Why did he want to relieve that father's pain in a place and a time when thousands of lives were being put out daily?

And so my twentieth birthday began.

Our midday meal was the same cup of soup. Every other day we would get half a cup of soup and two or three boiled potatoes. As the number of inmates in our part of the camp increased, the soup and potatoes were delivered in wooden barrels loaded on a wagon and pulled by inmates. Because of the muddy ground, the wagon would stop a hundred metres from the barracks, and we had to carry the barrels the rest of the way. Four men were needed to carry a barrel of hot soup, making sure that it did not spill. For constantly starving men this was hard work, but it had benefits too. Somehow many of us managed to get spoons, and while carrying the soup, one could hold the bottom of the barrel with one hand, while with the other try to skim off some scalding hot soup and gulp it down, providing the *Stubendienst* was not watching.

For the men who were picked to carry the barrels on the days we got potatoes, the situation was better. It was much easier to throw a potato in your mouth, even a hot one, than to try to bring a spoonful of liquid to your mouth while carrying a heavy barrel across treacherous terrain. One could also put a couple of potatoes in one's pocket and hope not to be searched when bringing the barrel into the barracks. Unfortunately, I was only picked a couple of times to carry the barrels, but I succeeded in slipping some potatoes in my pocket when I did. By that time, my thirst had been replaced by a gnawing hunger, and the few potatoes did not satisfy it.

Slowly we got used to the surroundings. Some ventured away a bit farther, trying to exchange a few words with the inmates passing by. Their kapos and foremen, the *Vorarbeiter*, interfered in our attempt to start conversations with them and took out their anger on their underlings—dozens of emaciated, wasted-away inmates—by hitting them ruthlessly. I looked at the clubs falling on the starved bodies and wondered how those bundles of bones held together. They too were looking for a chance to sneak away from the hard labour and constant beating for a moment's respite by hiding behind our barracks or among us. When they managed to slip among us, we could converse with them. Again, we heard the story about our families. We could see the sincerity in their emaciated faces, which reflected bitterness, pain, desperation and a cry to be believed. One of those walking skeletons saw the doubt in my face, grabbed me by my sleeve and pulled me out from behind the barracks to have a better look. Pointing to a crowd of Jews behind a fence in the distance, he said, "You better have a good look at them, for you will never see them again."

With those words he left me there, staring at the multitude with the yellow stars on their garments, while he went back to join his group. I looked, but it was not possible to count them from the distance I was at. However, I could see an overwhelming number of children, women and old people.

Before dark, we again went through the barbaric act of being counted and driven into the barracks. On the bunk, exchanging information of the day, we found out that the group of Jews we saw that day was from Białystok.

One morning, a week or so after our arrival, right after receiving our morning tea, we were told to remain standing in line. After a long wait, we were approached by a small group of inmates accompanied by two SS men. The inmates were dressed in standard camp uniform, but it looked much better on them, as if it had been made to their specifications. We were told to open our mouths and stick our tongues out. The well-dressed inmates walked by us, looking at our tongues, one of them marking down the numbers of the men pointed out by the others. After they left, the *Blockältester* called out the written-down numbers, gathered those men together and led them away.

We soon found out that those well-dressed inmates were Polish doctors who worked in the *Krankenbau*, the hospital barracks. Part of their job was to identify anyone suspected of being sick, which they did by glancing at our tongues. Two hours later we found out that those ten men had been killed. The group of doctors and SS men returned twice a week, never leaving empty-handed.[3]

3 Doctors who were Polish inmates in Auschwitz did not have the authority to send other inmates to their deaths. They could, however, select people to be sent to the hospital barracks, and the SS made the decisions about who would be killed (Dr. Piotr Setkiewicz, Auschwitz-Birkenau Memorial and Museum).

As difficult as it was to put up with the hunger, cold and beatings, the blatant stealing of our food by our overseers was particularly unbearable. We watched with envy as they filled up bowls of soup for themselves. When cutting the bread into quarters, they would take out a thick slice from the middle of each loaf. While we had to share one blanket among ten inmates, the *Stubendienste* who slept in the barracks with us had several blankets each.

A few daring young men in our barracks managed to get hold of one of their blankets. They cut it into pieces and wrapped those pieces around the upper part of their bodies, pulling their undershirts down over them. It did not take long for our overseers to discover the theft, and a search began. A couple of men managed to discard the blanket pieces before the searchers got to them, but those who were caught were beaten; their wrists were tied behind their backs, a rope was passed over that tie and they were pulled up and left hanging from a beam in the ceiling. They screamed, cried and begged until they fainted. Only then they were taken down. What happened to them afterwards I do not remember.

One morning, we were driven out in a downpour. It was so bad that the SS men who conducted the twice daily *Appell* told us to get back inside. The half a dozen or so men from Shershev in our barracks tried to keep together. These were the same men who had travelled with me in the cattle car. During the *Appell*, we had gotten soaked through, and we stood in the barracks dripping, grateful that we didn't have to stay outside.

Suddenly I heard a subdued voice saying, "Moishe."

I turned around and saw Gottel Wiener. He motioned with his head for me to follow him, and we came to a bunk where the few Shershev men sat, staring at a red bowl. I bent closer in the dim light and saw that the bowl was full of potato peels, the thin skin that comes off boiled potatoes. Gottel nodded, and everybody's hand reached into the bowl. The potato peels had been lying on the ground overnight in the rain, and Gottel had grabbed them when the *Stubendienst* was looking the other way. The peels had absorbed the rainwater and the tiny little stones from the ground, which cracked between our teeth, but we ate them anyway. We were grateful for the treat.

In mid-February we were all moved to the neighbouring barracks. So were the other three barracks that held the men from Pruzhany. I made sure that I got a bunk not too close to the rear of the barracks, where there were two large wooden containers that were used as toilets during the night. The containers were open, and because of the many cases of dysentery and the general state of the inmates, the rear part of the barracks smelled terribly. Every morning, those who slept near the containers had the job of carrying them out and emptying them in the public outhouse. Still, those who spent a couple of nights in the vicinity got used to it and did not mind the offensive smell. In fact, it had an advantage. As the *Stubendienste* were not anxious to visit that part of the barracks, the inmates in that corner were left alone and were beaten less. I never visited that corner. I urinated outdoors, as most of us did, and the only time I had a bowel movement in the six weeks I spent in Birkenau, I managed to do it outdoors.

After the middle of February, the frequent snow squalls turned into light rain, which softened the ground around the barracks even more. A couple of days after we were moved to the new barracks, after the *Appell*, we were ordered to remain in line. Our *Stubendienst* lined us up single file and led us to a mound of bricks. We were told to stack five bricks one on top of the other, pick them up from the bottom and walk in a single line holding them in front of us. Eventually we formed a large oval. There was no beating or yelling. We just continued to walk. At first it was not difficult, though it made no sense. By the time lunch came around, it had become tiring. We halted for our cup of soup and then continued with the bricks. By the end of the day, we were good and tired. After we carried the bricks, we were made to carry sand. We were told to put our jackets on backwards, forming a kind of apron in front, and were led to a mound of sand, where we held out the bottom of our jackets and sand was dumped in them. We walked with the sand all day long.

Because of the rain, the ground around the barracks, especially where we did the *Appell*, became a swamp. We had to stand a foot deep in it twice a day, morning and night, for an average of two hours each time. It occurred to our *Blockältester* that if a hole was dug in the middle of the *Appell* grounds, the water would drain into the hole and the place would dry up. There was never a shortage of shovels in Auschwitz. The *Blockältester* picked some men, and a large hole was dug. However, he failed to take into consideration that water does not flow freely through muddy ground. The *Lagerältester* came to examine the situation. He called together the three *Blockälteste* from the nearby blocks who had the same problem. They all decided that instead of us walking around all day with sand, which served no useful purpose, we should dump the sand on the *Appell* grounds.

The next morning, right after the *Appell*, we were told to bring the sand to the *Appell* grounds and dump it. The *Blockältester* said that he wanted it finished by two o'clock. Nobody hurried us or chased us, so we continued at the speed of the day before, which was relatively slow. Two o'clock came, and we were far from finished. It seemed that in the last few days we had been lulled into a state of complacency, from which we were to be brutally awakened that afternoon. The *Lagerältester* appeared. He looked at the *Appell* grounds and said something to our *Blockältester*, who in turn called together his assistants and gave them an order. They dispersed over the camp and were back shortly with kapos, *Vorarbeiter* and *Stubendienste*. This group had an ominous look about them, and they spoke among themselves with anticipation, looking at us with contempt as they started to break the handles off the shovels. We wondered why they were breaking perfectly good shovels. It became clear to us as soon as they started swinging the long shovel handles. They lined up along both sides of the muddy road from our barracks to the sand mound and impatiently swung the sticks. We were ordered to squat.

The *Blockältester* said, "I told you to have it finished by two o'clock, and you did not, so now you will get your punishment." He ordered the first line of men to stand up and yelled, "Run for sand!"

The approximately seventy men in the first row set off between the two rows of overseers, who stood with their sticks held high. They ran with bent heads and shoulders over which sticks fell relentlessly. At the sand mound, they received one or two shovels full of sand and ran back with much more difficulty—the path was narrow, strewn with piles of sand, heaps of bricks and stones and other discarded building materials. Those who spilled the sand or fell were beaten. But even those who did not fall got beaten just the same.

I squatted and thought to myself: *Considering that the seventy men have to run approximately a hundred metres in each direction while being beaten by several dozen overseers who do not care where their sticks fall, how long can this go on?* The answer came soon. Some men were bleeding from their heads and faces, and from their knees and legs from falling over heaps of bricks, sharp rocks or pieces of construction wood with protruding nails. Quite a few were already limping but kept running out of fear that falling might spell death. This lasted for about half an hour, and it was obvious that at any moment the men would start falling and would not get up. The *Blockältester* called a halt. The men were a beaten, sweaty, blood-soaked mass, and they collapsed, unable to catch their breath. Then the *Blockältester* commanded the second line to stand up from their squatting position and take their place. They got the same treatment as the first group. I wondered how long the overseers could keep it up. Did they not get tired? It occurred to me that I would not be able to take it, and I shivered. The hours of squatting would not be of any help in running. My legs were already numb. Some who had just gone through it were lying motionless.

The second line had finished, and they fell down in the same state as the others. The *Blockältester* stepped in front of us, and I braced myself for his command to the third line. I was in the fourth line, and I knew that by the time they got to me, I would not be able to move. But, instead, he said to us, "Look at your comrades and remember that if you do not obey orders, this is only a taste of what will happen to you. Now get up and finish your work." Two hours later, when we were lining up for the *Appell*, we stood on a dry sandy ground.

The next morning, when we were driven out to the *Appell* and tea, we carried out the bodies of those who had died overnight, as was done every morning. Usually, there were one or two dead, never more than five. On that morning, we carried out twenty-eight bodies, the result of the previous day's treatment.

Even though the number of inmates in our barracks kept getting smaller because of indescribable hunger, malnutrition, cold, beatings and unsanitary facilities, the camp administration did not bring in new inmates. We found out that they intended to keep our group of four barracks quarantined for six weeks and then send us to another camp to work.

In the later part of February, one of the *Stubendienste* in our barracks announced that we were going to get washed. We had not washed since the first day of our arrival. In fact, we had not even seen water except for the camp tea, the rain and the dirty puddles on the ground. We were led to the first two barracks in our row of twenty barracks. These barracks contained two long wooden boxes with rows of evenly spaced round holes. On the long walls of the barracks, about a metre off the ground, were fastened wooden troughs that held cold water. We were divided into groups of fifty and ordered to remove our jackets and undershirts and get washed, of course without soap. I was in the third or fourth group, and when I got to the troughs, the water in it was so cloudy that I could not see the bottom. Before I even stuck my hands in the water, I asked someone about the meaning of the long wooden box with the holes in it. The man just said, "Look in there."

I walked over, and before I even got to it, I smelled it. Still, I looked in and saw a deep trench in the ground and boards that held the earth from falling in. I estimated that there were about seventy holes, and

I wondered how many prisoners the Nazis intended to squeeze into this part of the camp.

I still remember how disgusting it felt to stick my hands into the trough after examining the public toilet. But I did and even splashed some of the murky water on my face. There were no towels, so I wiped my face with my lice-infested undershirt and then pulled it on. I was cold, and the shirt would dry on me sooner. I remarked to someone near me that I felt dirtier now than I had before. After about three weeks in Birkenau, we were all louse-ridden. It is a miracle that nobody contracted typhus, which would have meant the end of most of us.

A couple of days later, right after the morning *Appell*, as soon as the SS men left us to the supervision of our overseers, we were surrounded by the *Stubendienste*, who conducted a thorough search of everyone. What they were looking for we did not know. Before dark, when we were finishing with the evening *Appell*, the *Blockältester* called out a young man from Pruzhany by the name of Laizer K. He placed him with his back to the rim of the hole that we had dug for the water to run off into a week or so earlier. Then the *Blockältester* announced, "I will not kill you today. I will drag it out for several days." The *Blockältester* then hit him on the face. The blow was delivered with such force that the young man was lifted off the ground before falling into the hole. The deep hole was half full of water, and when Laizer fell in, he was submerged. When he stood up, the *Blockältester* ordered others to get him out. He stood with his back to the hole, dripping with ice-cold water from head to toe. The *Blockältester* delivered another blow, and when Laizer got out, he hit him again. After the third blow and dunking, we were driven into the barracks. The next morning, that young man went through the same three immersions and again in the evening. We were beginning to admire his fortitude. The same happened on the third day. That evening at the *Appell*, we could see that his strength was decreasing, and we began to wonder if he would survive another day. Not that death distressed us anymore; by then we had seen enough of it. But this case was different. Here, a young man had been unable to resist the incomprehensible hunger and had knowingly risked his life by stealing two cubes of margarine from the *Blockältester*, who had himself stolen them from us starving inmates. Of course, our sympathy was with the young man who had taken from the *Blockältester* that which was rightly ours. We also admired his bravery, which bordered on madness.

That night, we were aware of some activity in the *Blockältester*'s partitioned-off corner. In the early morning, we had a new *Blockältester*. After the *Appell*, we found out that the previous *Blockältester* had been dismissed and sent to another camp. The new *Blockältester* knew nothing of the crime committed by young Laizer, and as a result, his life was spared. Laizer survived the camp and became a successful businessman in Philadelphia.

Our new *Blockältester* was a German with a green triangle, which categorized him as a *Berufsverbrecher*—BV, a criminal. Every inmate in Auschwitz-Birkenau was obliged to have the number they received marked on a piece of white material and sewn onto their jackets and pants. In front of the number was a downward pointing, coloured triangle. The colours of the triangles identified the reason the internee had been arrested.[4] All political internees had printed on their triangles a single letter that identified their country of origin. Poles had a letter *P*, Frenchmen an *F*, Dutchmen an *H* and so on, except for Germans and, of course, Jews. The Jewish country of origin made no difference to the Nazis. By far the most common triangles in Auschwitz-Birkenau were the Jewish triangles, which consisted of two triangles: the red political triangle and a yellow one that was superimposed over the red one but pointing up, thus forming a two-coloured Star of David.

4 According to the Auschwitz-Birkenau State Museum, prisoners in Auschwitz were classified and identified by a system of triangles: red for *Schutzhäftlinge*—Sch., political internees, mostly Poles; black for *Asoziale*—Aso, asocials, a loose concept that included prostitutes and Roma; green for *Berufsverbrecher*—BV, criminals, mostly German; purple for *Internationale Bibelforscher-Vereinigung*—IBV, Jehovah's Witnesses; pink for homosexuals.

Shortly after taking over the block and settling in, our new *Blockältester* dismissed a couple of *Stubendienste* and appointed new ones, men from our block, and so from Pruzhany. To be a *Stubendienst* meant an end to the constant nagging hunger, thirst and exposure to cold, and protection from everything that could lead to a horrible death. In return, however, in most cases the person had to renounce all the human principles according to which he had lived until then. The *Stubendienste* had to forget friends, neighbours and acquaintances, even family, by turning against them in order to prolong their lives a little, helping the SS make the camp into the hell that it was. I do not know if those people found it difficult to change, or maybe they were creatures of low character to begin with. Maybe I am being too harsh on them with my judgment. Maybe they were too weak to endure the hunger and beatings and gave in to temptation. How can one understand now what it was like in those times? In any case, we were happier with the new *Stubendienste* from among us than with the non-Jewish strangers who had treated us with such cruelty.

Among the *Stubendienste* in the three neighbouring barracks, which housed the other inmates from Pruzhany, were two Jews from France, one by the name of Freiheit, the second by the name of Zulty. If they were any better than the non-Jewish *Stubendienste* I do not know. But their being *Stubendienste* was enough to instill fear. Tall and well fed, they always kept each other company and did not associate too much with the non-Jewish *Stubendienste*. I once found myself near a neighbouring barracks where the two of them were sitting on a bench having a conversation. They were totally oblivious to me and spoke quite loudly. Even though many of them preferred to speak French, when it came to conversing about everyday events, they spoke Polish or Yiddish. As I got close, I heard one say to the other, "Ale ten wladek ma wspanialy cios"—*One can admire Wladek for his magnificent punch*.

This remark was made regarding a Polish *Blockältester* in one of our four blocks. After almost a month in Birkenau, I had heard many unpleasant, offending and repulsive words or statements, but that remark horrified and stunned me. I could not imagine how a Jew could admire a non-Jewish *Blockältester* for his talent in hurting and killing people. But before I had the time to digest what I just heard, the other man replying in Yiddish: "You son of a bitch, he killed many Jews in one night. Is that what you are praising him for? Is that what you are glorifying him for?"

At least one of the two Jewish *Stubendienste* still had in him some decency and morality.

At the end of February, as the days became longer, no longer did we huddle to the barracks wall or to each other, and we began to explore the layout of the parts of the camp that were accessible to us. In our barracks, the crowded bunks had long disappeared. Now there was room for everybody. We waited impatiently for the end of the six weeks that we were supposed to spend in quarantine to weed out the sick and the weak. The Nazis had gotten rid of the weak and sick, but they had also managed to make many healthy men sick. There was talk that in the camps where we would be working, the food will be more plentiful. Even the new *Blockschreiber* (block clerk) confirmed this. He was from the French transport, the so-called forty-two thousands, and was tall, handsome, cleanly dressed and never raised his voice. He was always polite, even though he outranked everyone in the barracks except the *Blockälteste*. He did not fit in with the crude, vulgar and murderous bunch of overseers around him.

The days stretched like years, with constant beatings, hunger, filth and lice that crawled leisurely over us. One day, as we were driven into the barracks for the cup of soup, we were told to remain inside. We remained in the barracks for the rest of the day. It was only the next morning when we went outside for roll call that we noticed that some barracks across from us were occupied. We were not permitted to get closer. Nevertheless, during the day we found out that the new arrivals were Roma. Unlike us Jews, they did not go through any kind of selection. They were simply taken from the train, entire families—men, women, children and baggage—led to the barracks and assigned a family per bunk.

Blockälteste were sent in from the older part of the camp, but the *Stubendienste* were chosen from among the newly arrived Roma. In the first couple of days, they were confined to the barracks and were not even counted. They were left alone, and nobody raised a hand or even a voice to them. They had come from their homes with their possessions, bulging suitcases, money and food. In the first few days, they looked with contempt at the camp soup that was brought to them and refused to eat it. We, barely existing on our starvation diet for a month, slowly moved closer to their barracks, hoping to gain something, although we were chased and beaten by the overseers. Still, the hunger overcame the fear, and I was able to get close to a barracks. Suddenly, the barracks door opened and out came the *Blockältester*. Before I could take one step backwards, he saw me, called me over and told me to stand at the door and not to let anyone in or out. Without another word, he walked away. I knew that no manna would fall from heaven while I was standing outside, so I took a chance and opened the door, slid in and closed it behind me. I walked slowly along one side of the bunks on which entire families sat with heaps of luggage. About halfway down, I saw an old Roma woman sitting on a bunk among a pile of suitcases and bags. She winked at me and nodded. I stopped and looked at the old, wrinkled face that projected so much life experience and understanding. She pulled out from under an old blanket a red camp bowl half-full of yesterday's soup, now congealed, and said to me in German, "I need the bowl."

My spoon was always at hand, and I unpretentiously stuck it into the congealed soup. The tasteless, cold and lumpy soup slid down my throat with difficulty, and I wondered how clean it was after being uncovered all night under her bunk. But the hunger conquered all. Still, I remembered thinking: *Look at you and see what you have turned into. Did you ever imagine that you would eat something like that in your entire life?*

I was almost at my last spoonful when the door opened and in marched the *Blockältester*. I gulped down what was in my mouth, put the spoon in my pocket and ran toward him and the door behind him, my only means of escape and salvation. His curses and club fell on me simultaneously and followed me a good part of the way. When he finally let me off and turned back to the barracks, I stopped to wonder whether the half bowl of yesterday's soup was worth the beating I had just received.

Among the Roma inmates were musicians who had brought their instruments—violins, guitars, mandolins and accordions. As the weather got warmer, they would give concerts in the afternoons. The men with long hair and clean-shaven faces would dress in their Sunday best and try to go for walks on the muddy road, trying hard not to dirty their shoes, an impossible task. Some of the women tried to do the same in high-heeled shoes but quickly gave up. A couple of days after their arrival, not only did the camp bread become precious to them, but the soup did too. We started to wonder how long it would take before they looked like us.

In mid-March, right after the evening roll call, we were ordered to remain standing outside. Soon we were joined by the men from the other three barracks—all the men from Pruzhany who had been selected to enter the camp. We were lined up, five in a row. A detachment of SS officers arrived, and we were counted. I looked around at those in my barracks and noted how many were missing. The SS men were counting us over and over. There were barely eight hundred of us in total, from over twelve hundred from Pruzhany and the few hundred men who had joined us as we entered this part of the camp. My mind did not want to accept it. Was it possible that almost half of us had perished in a period of six weeks? What was the reasoning in keeping us in quarantine while half of us died from beatings, hunger and disease? And the other half of us were in such a state that we would not be able to put in a day's work. It all seemed so senseless, so ludicrous.

The SS officers finally got their numbers straight, and we were surrounded by SS men with rifles at the ready and ordered to march. We marched through our part of the camp and then along a dirt road. It had been a couple of hours since sunset, but the road was so lit up that even a fly could not hide. After less than a half-hour's walk, we found ourselves between what seemed to be stables. As we emerged from behind those buildings, there was in front of us a tall, well-lit metal gate over which was a sign in black metal lettering that read "Arbeit Macht Frei" (Work Makes You Free).

We stopped in front of the gate. I was in the first row, and while we waited for the others to catch up, I looked around. The camp was surrounded by an electrified double-barbed-wire fence. Outside of that was a solid cement wall, about two-and-a-half metres high. It would have been humanly impossible to get through the electrified fences and past the SS men in the guard towers all around, so I thought that the cement wall must have been built to stop others from looking in. I looked up again at the sign that read "Arbeit Macht Frei" and thought to myself, *What a mockery! Aren't they ashamed to put up such a flagrantly dishonest sign?* In the last six weeks in Birkenau, I had become only too well acquainted with the Nazi promises, with their respect for human life.

Through the gate, I saw large buildings looming inside. They appeared even bigger behind the lampposts that illuminated the camp. I wondered what this camp would hold for us.

23

The Auschwitz Routine

SEVERAL SS MEN appeared from the nearby guardhouse. Two of them opened the wide gate, and we marched in while being counted carefully. We were being led between rows of two-storey brick buildings to a building at the very end next to the fence. As soon as we entered the building, I could smell the unmistakable odour of disinfectant, which reminded me of a shower, for which I had been longing. The filth on our lice-ridden skin was a centimetre thick. In groups of two hundred, we were shaved completely, disinfected and showered. We received a set of underwear, a pair of pants, a jacket, a cap in the shape of a beret and a coat. The coat was made of the same material as the camp uniform, that is, the striped pyjama-like style, and it had no lining nor did it give any warmth.

By the time we went through the entire process, it was daylight. We were driven outside and watched as work groups were being formed. As soon as they left, we were taken to the *Appellplatz*, the roll-call square, which was in front of the kitchen. There we were divided in specialized work groups by the overseers who were under the supervision of the SS. There were a lot of tradesmen or artisans among us who were needed for the rapidly growing camp and the industry that was being developed in the vicinity. During the process of assigning work, the

SS did not miss an opportunity to have their bit of fun with us. One of them announced that they needed typists. There were a few typists among us, but many figured that they could assure themselves an easy job and claimed to be typists. After a good deal of mockery, the SS guards sent them all to work unloading trainloads of bricks, stones and sand, which turned out to be one of the worst kinds of work. When they called for locksmiths, I stepped forward. We were a group of some twenty men and were taken to block 18, opposite the kitchen.

Unlike in Birkenau, where the buildings were wooden barracks, in Auschwitz I, the buildings, referred to as blocks, were two-storey brick buildings divided into two sections. The first floor and basement were under one *Blockältester*'s jurisdiction; in our case that was block number 18. Another *Blockältester* oversaw the second floor and attic; that was 18A. Block 18 used the front entrance, and block 18A used the side one.

We were led through the front door into a long hallway with several doors leading off it, then to a door with a number four over it. We were welcomed by a stout man of about thirty. His name was Kazik and his triangle was red with the letter *P* for Polish. He asked where we were from, and when we told him, we could see the blank look in his eyes. While this almost cordial conversation went on, he mentioned that he was the *Stubendienst* in this *Stube*, or room. Then the *Blockältester* who had led us into the building appeared holding four or five loaves of bread and explained to us that this bread did not represent our usual ration. This was a personal present from him to us. He stood and watched as the *Stubendienst* cut and divided the loaves among us. We exchanged glances, and I wondered if we were not dreaming, thinking about the reception we had received in Birkenau six weeks earlier.

The *Stubendienst* assigned us bunks. I was assigned bunk number 64. From there I had a chance to look around the room. It was filled with three-tier bunks, with a couple of tables and a narrow passage, just wide enough for the emaciated bodies to squeeze through to get to their bunks. The bunks were individual, narrower than our previous ones, and were surrounded by low boards so one could not roll off.

On each bunk there was a straw sack and two blankets, one to sleep on, the other to cover oneself with.

The *Stubendienst* told us to take off our shirts, turn them inside out and look for lice. We were sure that we had no lice, as only a few hours ago we had been shaved, disinfected and well scrubbed under a hot shower. How could we have lice? The *Stubendienst* insisted, and we obeyed. Lo and behold! We found lice in our undershirts. Where did they come from? The *Stubendienst* told us that we would not be able to rid ourselves of lice with one disinfectant treatment and a shower. They bit into the skin and laid eggs. So we continued our hunt for lice, squashing them between our thumbnails.

At noon we received a red enamel bowl and lined up for our lunch, a full litre of soup. Even though it was three times as much as we got in Birkenau, it did not satisfy our hunger. We spent the afternoon with the *Stubendienst*, who acquainted us with the regulations of the room, the block and camp, how to make the bed (it should be straight as an arrow), where the toilets were with their individual enamel seats, where the washroom was with its several long troughs over which there was a constant flow of water day and night. The walls of the washroom, the troughs and floor were tiled. One was not allowed to enter the washroom with his shirt on, and the punishment was severe for violating this rule. The longer the *Stubendienst* spoke, the more threatening his voice became. His attitude, which had been almost fatherly in the morning, was slowly being replaced by that characteristic Birkenau air. Without exchanging a word between us, we began to understand that it would be advisable not to underestimate his unfinished sentences, which ended mostly with "if not..."

In the early evening, the work groups, or *Kommandos*, began to return. Our *Stubendienst* led us outside and had us line up with those from our block who had just returned from work. The *Blockältester* knew that his twenty new arrivals, *Zugänge* in camp language, were unfamiliar with the *Appell* procedure. All six hundred men in our block lined up ten deep in straight lines like soldiers, and an SS man came over to do the counting.

The *Blockältester* yelled, "Achtung!"—*Attention!*

We pulled in our empty stomachs and puffed out our bony chests.

Then he yelled, "Mützen!"—*Hats!* and everybody grabbed their caps with their right hands like we were a perfectly synchronized machine.

"Ab!"—*Off!* and everyone pulled their caps off and brought them down with a loud slap to their thighs.

The SS man walked slowly by the front row, making sure there were nine more behind the one in front. He counted the front row, gave a nod to the *Blockältester* and walked to the centre of the *Appellplatz* to report his findings to the *Rapportführer*, the reporting officer.

We heard again, "Mützen!" and we brought our hats to our heads, "Auf!"—*On!* and, leaving the caps as they landed on our heads, we brought our hands down to our thighs with a loud slap. If one was late by a split second, it would be heard immediately, and the culprit would get a good thrashing from the *Stubendienste*.

After a few dozen tries and many blows, we responded to the commands like old pros. From where we were, I could see those assembled in front of blocks 14 to 17. They were all going through the same exercise. The SS man who counted us went to the centre of the *Appellplatz*, where a small portable stand had appeared, seemingly from nowhere. An SS officer stood nearby with a book in hand. The SS man saluted the officer and reported the number of prisoners he had just counted in his assigned block. The officer marked the numbers down and added them up. By the time this was done, the chief officer of the camp, the *Lagerkommandant*, showed up. As he was approaching the stand, we could hear the command "Mützen ab!"—*Hats off!*

This time the entire camp did it simultaneously. The officer who did the adding and summation, the camp *Rapportführer*, quickly marched over to the camp commandant, saluted and reported the number of prisoners. As soon as this was over, we heard the command "Mützen auf!"—*Hats on!* and were dismissed.

Some of us went back to the *Stube*. Others looked around the nearby blocks for inmates from Pruzhany. We did not remain outside for long, as we had to be back in the *Stube* at 8:30 p.m. If we expected something to eat that evening, we were disappointed. All we got was a few mouthfuls of the bitter camp tea. At exactly 8:30 p.m., the sound of a gong was heard all over camp.

Our *Stubendienst* yelled, "Stubensperre!"—*Room curfew!* Nobody was allowed outside the room except to use the washroom, which was across the hallway almost opposite our room. We heard his voice again: "Läuseappell!"—*Lice roll call!* Everyone took off their shirts, turned them inside out and looked for lice.

My bunk was the middle one. On the bottom one sat a man in his mid-thirties, his number exactly 42000, so I knew that he was from France. He was of medium height, broad-shouldered and not emaciated. I quickly calculated: He was from the French transport, and we had already met a couple of his compatriots in Birkenau. But he was not hungry. He had a friendly face and was not hostile. Who was he? I spoke a few words to him, and he seemed interested in having a conversation. His name was Fish, and he was trying to help me by sharing his camp experience. As we were talking, a man came over. His red triangle told me that he was a political internee, and the letter *P* told me that he was a Pole. Fish welcomed him with a polite, "Good evening, Mr. Leon." The other answered just as politely, adding, "I see we have a new neighbour." With those words, he stepped onto the bottom bunks and propelled himself onto the top bunk.

Not having slept the previous night and knowing that there was a straw sack and a blanket waiting for me, I could not wait to lie down. Another gong, and I heard the *Stubendienst* say, "Lights out," and then everything was concealed in darkness. A bit of light coming from the washroom across the hall entered through the two little windows in the doors. It seemed that I had just shut my eyes when I heard the gong again, and immediately, the light in the room came on and the thundering voice of the *Stubendienst* called, "Aufstehen!"—*Get up!*

He had told us yesterday that we get up at 5:30. Was it already 5:30? Had the night already gone? Everyone jumped off their bunks, pulled on their clothing then quickly pulled off their shirts. We had forgotten that we were supposed to wash in the morning but were not allowed in the washroom with our shirts on. I stuck my hands under the rapidly flowing water in the washroom and my fingers became numb from the cold. I splashed some water over my face and neck and realized that I had nothing to dry myself with. All other inmates had some sort of towel, but the newly arrived had none, so we used our shirts. We got dressed and lined up near the table in the back of the room where the *Stubendienst* was handing out a quarter of a loaf of bread and a tiny piece of sausage to each of us.

At the other table in the front part of the room, the prominent inmates were sitting. They were a kapo and about half a dozen of his assistants, the *Vorarbeiter*. I recognized among them the Pole who slept on the third bunk above me. A Pole in his twenties was serving them and sliced bread for them, not from quarters but from a whole loaf, spreading margarine over the slices, and covered them with pieces of sausage that were thicker than the ones we got. They sat calmly, ate slowly and washed the meal down with the camp tea. I waited patiently in line for my piece of bread and the tiny piece of sausage. I got my bread, and it seemed to me that the man before me got a bigger piece. I was upset at how fate had shortchanged me. I glanced once more at the piece of bread in that other man's hand, and I was not so sure anymore that his piece was bigger than mine. I got the thin slice of sausage, and we then went outside to line up for the *Appell*.

We practised the exercise with our caps several more times and heard the *Blockältester* announce that the new arrivals should line up with the DAW (Deutsche Ausrüstungswerke; German equipment works) group after the *Appell* was over. When we heard the command, "Kommando antreten"—*Fall into work groups*, everyone ran to his *Kommando*. Our *Kommando* was the largest in the camp, numbering twelve hundred men. We were divided into groups of hundreds, five rows, twenty rows for each hundred. In charge of each group of a hundred men was a kapo who appointed ten men of his hundred to be in charge of each ten. The ones in charge of the ten marked down their numbers and passed them on to the kapo. I could hear an orchestra playing and see groups of prisoners marching toward the gate. It was not day yet, but everything around was well lit.

We were one of the first groups to leave the camp. After all, we were twelve hundred men and very important to the German war industry. I saw the first hundreds already marching ahead in military fashion, and I prepared myself to do the same. Then we were marching, past the camp kitchen with its tall chimneys to our left, then a green lawn with rows of chairs on which sat several dozen musicians in striped camp uniforms that looked freshly cleaned and pressed. A conductor conducted the orchestra from a pedestal. We turned toward the gate, and I tried hard to walk alongside the other four men in my line to the beat of the march the musicians were playing. At the gate, several SS men of different ranks stood. They counted us but did not interfere with our march. Out of the gate, I felt better. I could even turn my head and look around. The inmates around me were all from my block, most of them Poles. They saw that I was a newcomer and asked where I was from. Receiving the answer that I was from the Polish province of Podlasie, their curiosity was satisfied, and they did not ask anything more. I thought to myself: *one country, and I couldn't be more than five hundred kilometres away from them, yet they do not even know what to ask, as if not only are we not from the same country but not even the same world.* Most of the Christian Belarusian population in our part of the country considered the Poles strangers, and the feeling was mutual, so it was not surprising that even now the Poles did not care about what was happening in those eastern parts of former Poland.

We marched on for about a kilometre and turned into the yard of a factory, a large four-storey building painted in white and five large wooden barracks. I heard again the command, "Kommando antreten!" Everybody ran to his assigned place except for the twenty locksmiths from our *Stube* and fifty carpenters who had been assigned to block 18A. A few kapos and *Vorarbeiter* approached us. They read out everyone's number. They already knew everyone's trade and where to take him. We were broken up into smaller groups, and the carpenters were led to the two large barracks, which were being referred to as "halls," and to the large building. The locksmiths were divided into two groups and taken into the third and fourth hall. I was taken to the third hall, in which there were prisoners working around rows of dismantled and damaged ammunition wagons. Along the walls of that large barracks were inmates at workbenches.

The kapo, a short, broad-shouldered man with a thin, twisted face and the green triangle of a criminal offered me a skeptical glance, fastened a piece of metal in the vise and handed me a file. I took the file, not understanding precisely what the test was. At school in Brest-Litovsk, I had done more complicated work than this, but I still did not consider myself to be a tradesman. The moment I applied the file to the metal, I could tell that the metal had too much give and that to file it properly it had to sit deeper in the vise, but I did not dare do it. After all, the kapo had put it this way, and who was I to correct it? So I started to file. The kapo looked at my filing approvingly, then asked me why I did not lower the piece of metal deeper into the vise. I responded that he had put it there and told me to file. Without a word, he and his foreman turned away and marched off toward another new arrival. One of the foremen took me to a workbench around which eight or ten men were working. Turning to one of them, he said, "Here is your new man," and walked away. The nearby workers looked at me inquisitively, and I returned the look. We were looking at each other's triangles, and I did not see a single Jewish star. What I saw was dissatisfaction and outright hostility in their faces. They turned around as if I was not there and went back to work.

My new boss showed me where to find the needed tools. He pointed at a demolished ammunition wagon and told me to start taking it apart. The wagons were made entirely of metal, and most of the joints were welded together, with many nuts and bolts to strengthen them. Because of the damage and the design, it was difficult to get to many of the screws, and one was forced to crawl into the narrow and tight compartments of the wagons.

At my workbench were a couple of Poles, three or four Czechs and as many Soviet inmates. The Czechs and Poles wore red triangles, the Soviet prisoners black. The work was strenuous, but nobody was standing over me with a stick. Exactly at noon we heard a loud whistle. Everybody dropped their tools where they stood and ran outside. In the middle of the factory yard, five long lines of prisoners were being formed, supervised by kapos, and at the head stood the *Oberkapo*, or head kapo. With their yelling, and at times with a stick, they kept our lines in order.

Among the kapos was a large man who, for Auschwitz, was very old, between fifty and sixty. He walked along the rows of prisoners without a stick or a sound. I concluded that he must have such a reputation that he had no need for a stick or a yell. When he turned around, I saw the two triangles, red and yellow superimposed over each other, indicating that he was Jewish. A few days later I found out that this man, Rosen, was originally from Berlin. By profession he was an engineer, and before the war he had designed and manufactured all the machinery that was now in this plant. He kept the entire plant running, as he was the only person who understood the complexity of the machines. He had a couple of dozen mechanics at his disposal and had been appointed kapo over them. I also found out that this man never raised his voice to anybody and certainly not a stick. Every morning, he gathered a *minyan*, the ritually required quorum of ten men, so that they could pray together. If caught, he would most likely have paid with his life.

I got my litre of soup and relished every spoonful. Before I knew it, the soup was gone, and I scraped the empty bowl with my spoon until it was as clean as if I had washed it. I thought how nice it would be to have another litre. Everyone hid their empty bowls around the workbench, and I did the same. The spoon remained in my pocket, never to be parted with. Who knew when an occasion might arise when I would need it?

At six o'clock the whistle blew. The workers tidied up in a hurry. The foreman made sure that the tools were back in place, and everybody ran outside to fall into line with the same groups they had come with in the morning. We were counted by the kapos and started the march back to camp. As we passed the camp gate, we were again counted closely. We marched on. To the right, the orchestra played. We turned right, passing the kitchen, and then we were in front of block 18. Again, we lined up like well-trained soldiers and went through the same procedure as in the morning with the hats on and off. Then we were dismissed.

I could now move around freely, but my hunger muffled all feelings and occupied all thoughts. I was unable to think of anything other than food and started wandering among the barracks, thinking that maybe some would come my way. But none did. The inmates were a diversity of human suffering beyond imagination. Yes, I saw some well-fed prisoners. These were the privileged ones and the prominent ones in the camp—the *Blockälteste*, kapos, *Stubendienste*, *Blockschreiber* and others without rank who were given good positions. They were well dressed in clean and freshly pressed uniforms and walked erect, almost with a military gait and with noticeable aloofness. Most of them wore the green triangle as if it were a badge of honour, even though it identified them as criminals. There were others in this elite group besides the German criminals. Some were Polish inmates, mostly with red triangles, political prisoners. Many belonged to the Polish intelligentsia. Some of them managed to get themselves comfortable positions. But by far, the majority of the inmates were emaciated, starving skeletons. The term *Muselmann* applied almost entirely to Jews, except for some Soviet prisoners and Roma, who were barely noticeable among the multitude of Jewish walking skeletons. Their deep-set eyes, their sunken, almost transparent cheeks, protruding jaws, and dry lips that could not shut over teeth, expressed so much suffering and hunger that for a moment I felt more fortunate than they. But then I thought, *How long will it be before I look like them?* Depressed and in shock, I returned to my *Stube* where I took off my shirt. Turning it inside out, I began to look for lice.

At nine o'clock the lights went out, and everybody lay down to sleep. Compared to the bunks in Birkenau, the bunks in Auschwitz were comfortable. The hunger, however, was so intense that I could not shut my eyes. I thought about the food I had eaten at home before the war, about the food that I did not like and had refused to eat, or that I had left on my plate to be thrown away. I thought of home, my dead parents, sisters, brother and grandparents, and I scolded myself for becoming so unfeeling, so morally degraded that instead of grieving and mourning the loss of my family, I thought of food. Eventually the exhaustion of the twelve-hour workday took its toll, and I fell asleep.

The days fell into a routine. To my surprise, a couple of days after arriving in Auschwitz I, right after returning from work and after the *Appell*, we lined up, block after block, on the *Appellplatz*, and each one of us inmates received half a loaf of bread and a slice of sausage. I found out that this extra half a loaf and the slice of sausage, which was called in camp *Zulage*, meaning extra, was a twice-a-week occurrence.

A few days passed with working and continuously thinking about food. On Sunday, we slept an extra half-hour. After the *Appell*, we received the regular quarter loaf of bread and a small piece of cheese that smelled terrible. I held the piece of cheese for no more than two minutes before it was gone, yet during the day I washed my hands several times and could still smell it on my hands the next day.

The *Stubendienst* ordered everyone to shave, not only our faces but our heads too. We had a professional barber in our *Stube*, a Jewish man from France, referred to as the "block barber." There were a hundred men in our *Stube*, so it was an impossible job for one man. He shaved only the big shot prisoners, and he picked three men from among us to shave the ordinary inmates. In return, the three men would receive an extra litre of soup at noon. The three chosen were not barbers and were as handy with a razor as I was. When the job was done, quite a few men had cuts on their faces or heads as if after a brawl.

I downed my litre of soup in seconds, and my stomach felt as empty as before. I looked with envy at those who were still eating theirs, savouring every spoonful, and I was mad at myself for having eaten so fast. A couple of us were ordered to collect the bowls and take them to the washroom to wash them. It was one o'clock on Sunday afternoon when the *Stubendienst* yelled, "Bettruhe!"—*Bedrest!* and all had to lie down for two hours. *The accursed Nazis*, I thought to myself, *they are killing thousands of innocent people daily and make us work until we fall dead, yet they give us two hours of bedrest every Sunday afternoon, for which we will repay them by working twice as hard tomorrow*. After the two-hour rest, the prisoners were told to write letters home, except of course for the Jews, who had nobody to write to, and the Soviet prisoners, I presume for security reasons.

That Sunday was unfortunately the last quiet Sunday for us Jews for a long time. The following Sunday, right after the *Appell*, the kapos rounded up "volunteer" workers to unload building material from railcars: bricks, stones, sand, cement, planks, entire logs and the like. The supervisors were a mixed lot from all blocks, consisting of kapos, foremen and their cronies who were eager to please the many SS men around by beating the emaciated bodies of starving inmates. The SS men delighted in watching Jews being beaten, and they doubled over with laughter and pleasure. After six hours of such work, we returned to the *Stube* at noon, beaten, bleeding, barely dragging our feet, and we got our litre of soup.

Hunger became a constant companion and did not leave me for a moment. All my plans to satisfy it remained a dream. While I was at work in the factory, I noticed that the Soviet inmates were stringing potatoes on a piece of wire and lowering them into the tin ovens that heated the room. I asked them where they got the potatoes, but I got no answer. The hunger was driving me to despair, so I approached the pile of garbage in front of the kitchen. It consisted of rotten vegetables and potatoes that even the SS men saw as unfit for the prisoners. One morning before lining up for work, I went over and rummaged in that garbage heap. Someone appeared from nowhere with a stick and drove me away. It occurred to me to get up before the gong, which entailed risking my life, for it was forbidden to leave the block before the gong sounded. Nevertheless, I got dressed in the dark *Stube* while lying on my bunk, and I sneaked outside to the pile of garbage. There I filled my pant pockets with rotten, oozing potatoes. Entering the block, I did not dare to enter the *Stube*, where I might be seen. I went into the toilet and spent the next few minutes in fear of being found. As soon as the gong sounded, the entire block came to life. In the tumult, I entered the room, quickly taking off my jacket and shirt. I went to the washroom and mixed with the crowd.

The rotten potatoes were an oozing mass, and they filtered through my pant pockets as if through a strainer, dripping down my legs and pants onto my shoes. Once at work, I strung them on a piece of wire and baked them in the oven. While the Soviet inmates used good potatoes, which came out nicely baked, mine came out of the fire as pieces of an undistinguishable burned substance. I knew that those burned pieces of rotten potatoes had no nourishing value. Just the opposite, I could get sick from them. But, for the moment, there was something in my stomach, and I felt as if I had eaten.

24
Penalty and Salvation

ONE MORNING, AFTER I had been working in the factory for about two weeks, our kapo passed by and noticed the pieces of wire hanging out from under the tin plate covering the stove. Lifting the cover, he saw the strings of potatoes. His face looked angrier than usual, and he thundered, "Whose is it?!"

I was astonished to see the four Soviet inmates, whose potatoes the kapo had discovered, pointing their fingers at me. I was also hurt and offended, knowing that they hailed from deep Russia, where fellowship was a virtue and antisemitism was officially prohibited. Since I had been working with them, I had succeeded in establishing a rapport of sorts, speaking their language and relating to them as a former citizen of the Soviet Union. I thought that they had accepted me as one of their own.

Without a word, the kapo handed me over to one of his *Vorarbeiter*, who told me to follow him. Arriving at the edge of a huge lumber yard, or *Holzplatz*, he led me through stacks of timber and planks of assorted lengths, thicknesses and widths to a group of working inmates. The foreman came over, and my escort said to him, "Here is one more for you," and then turned around and left.

My new supervisor barely offered me a glance and, pointing

with his long stick at the nearby group, barked his order, "Go to them!"

Before my eyes were several dozen young Jews like me — confused, bewildered, battered, with emaciated bodies and protruding bones wrapped by a greyish colourless skin. They were bending over and straining to lift boards that were thicker than them, loading them onto a wagon. I suddenly felt a terrible pain in my back. The foreman had delivered a blow with his stick. He yelled, "Did you come to observe?!" I ran at once and started lifting a board. It was much heavier than I expected, as it had been lying outdoors for months and had absorbed a lot of water. I strained and lifted one side of the board. Someone at the other end did the same, and we threw the heavy board into the wagon. We were working with all our strength, but the foreman hit us continuously. I would have liked to ask him why, but I didn't dare. I saw the others working with their last gasp, and he was even harder on them. *What kind of a creature are you?* I thought to myself. *Do you require of us work, or do you hit us for no reason?* It turned out that the answer to both questions was yes.

When the wagon was filled with thick and heavy boards, we harnessed ourselves onto it, with others taking up positions around it. With encouragement from the foreman's stick, the wagon began to move slowly forward. I could see the others straining with their last ounce of strength, and the stick kept on coming down on us. We reached a piece of road where the ground was a bit firmer and the wagon moved more easily. The foreman disappeared for a moment and was back with a long stick. He shoved the stick in between the spokes of the front wheels, and the wagon came to a stop. Then, in an uncontrollable rage, he started hitting us indiscriminately over our heads, shoulders and backs. He stopped in front of a young man, now the ghost of a young man, and started hitting him mercilessly. The young man was trying hard to stay on his feet, but the heavy blows were too much for that exhausted soul to withstand, and he fell. The foreman delivered more blows to his head, immobilizing him. With his boot, he delivered a few kicks to turn him around, face up. Then we watched in horror as the foreman put his stick across the poor young man's throat, stepped with one foot on one end of the stick and brought the other foot down on the other end. The skinny neck could not resist the weight of the well-fed foreman. We looked on with sympathy and fear as the tortured soul expired before our eyes. The foreman then picked up his stick and without missing a beat started swinging it at us. Then, he pulled out the long stick from between the wheel spokes and the wagon moved again.

We stopped in front of another group of workers. Their foreman was a tall man with a red triangle and a *P*, and he didn't have a left arm. In front of him was a little stand on which there were some papers. The men under his command were measuring and stacking the planks according to size, while he wrote the details down. I envied those workers and felt sorry for myself. We unloaded the wagon and went for another load. Again, the pummelling, the beating, the back breaking under the heavy timber, and I wondered how long I could survive here.

The midday whistle was like the coming of the Messiah. On the way to lining up, I saw a red camp bowl stuck in a timber pile. I picked it up and went to line up for the soup. During the break, I conversed with the others in the group, a sorry lot of beaten, broken young Jews. They told me that the group I worked with was called *Kommando Holzplatz*, and it was a *Strafkommando*, or penal company. Anyone who committed a transgression in this factory was sent here. The group consisted of fifty to sixty men, depending on the mortality rate, which was on average five or six men per day. The foreman whose acquaintance I had the misfortune to make that morning was called Pilarek. Pilarek had an assistant, a Polish prisoner who was not much better than he was. There was a kapo, a German prisoner with a green triangle who left it up to Pilarek to do the grisly work, and there was a *Schreiber*, or registrar.

The same hell continued after the break. I thought, *What crime have I committed that I deserve such an end?* We carried the boards between two of us in a long line with Pilarek at our side, hitting us constantly. He concentrated on the legs between the knee and the ankle. We could hear the stick landing on the bony legs of the unfortunate ones, who, because of the heavy weight of the boards and the fear of dropping them, could not even attempt to avoid the blow.

Pilarek found his next victim, an unfortunate young boy who fell with the boards. He did not get a chance to get up. Pilarek's heavy stick hit him without stopping. At first, the boy covered himself with his hands and arms, but soon he could not move them fast enough. Then they ceased moving, and the boy lay helpless under Pilarek's blows. With a few more blows, the boy was motionless, and Pilarek was placing his stick across his throat. I watched the macabre scene with horror and imagined myself under the stick. In that moment, I felt grief for not having left the ghetto with my family. I could have spent two more days on the train with them and died together. For what did I have to suffer the past two months? The hunger, the cold, the beating, the anguish, the agony, the pain—what for?

With such disheartening and dark thoughts, my first day on the *Holzplatz* passed. At six o'clock, the whistle blew, and we ran to line up in our group. The man in charge of our group was a Pole in his thirties. Unlike the others in my group, he behaved humbly and spoke to me, the only Jew, decently. The others ignored me as if I were not there, which suited me fine. As we were lining up, I turned around and saw at the end of the last group of a hundred, a covered wagon that was being pulled by prisoners, and I knew that it held the bodies of those who had died that day.

Back in the camp, after the *Appell*, I sat on my bunk and took off the soggy shoes I had received on arriving in Auschwitz I from Birkenau. My feet were swollen, and I wondered what they would look like the next day after work, if I survived the day. I was totally exhausted and morally broken. I stretched out on my bunk, asking God why I deserved this. With dark thoughts on my mind, I fell asleep. When the gong awakened me, I asked God again why he had not taken me to him. Why was he exposing me to another day? How nice would it have been to fall asleep and not to get up!

Again, after getting to the factory, we heard the command, "Kommando antreten!" and everyone ran to his group. The morning before, I was running to fall in with factory number 3, but now I had to go to the penal *Kommando*. I felt that that day would be my last on earth, but worse than the idea of death itself was the way I had to part with the world, by being beaten and throttled by the murderer Pilarek. We fell in. The *Schreiber* checked all the numbers. A few were missing, and we all knew that their tortured souls had expired overnight in the block. The group who measured and stacked the planks was separated from us and led away by the one-armed Pole. The remaining men were divided into two groups, one under the supervision of Pilarek, the other under the supervision of his Polish assistant.

I was with the assistant. The work was the same, and the Polish foreman yelled and hit us too, but not as much as Pilarek. He would hit and beat someone if he did not move fast enough, or if he tried to pick up a lighter plank or log instead of the one closest to him, but at least he did not stop the wagon wheels from turning. The two Poles who had joined us the day before were not with us today. I asked the others why. I was told that Poles or even Soviets did not remain to work on the *Holzplatz*. It was only Jews who were condemned to remain here in this *Kommando* and to end their short lives in suffering.

Even though there was less beating under the Polish assistant than under Pilarek, the work was not easier. With a sigh of relief, we welcomed the noon whistle. I found the red bowl that I had hid the previous day, stayed in line and got my soup. I ate quickly, for I was told that the kapo took some men to Kanada, the place where the belongings of the Jews brought to Auschwitz were sorted. There was often extra soup there, and our kapo arranged to distribute it among us. It was not for our benefit that he made this arrangement. As our kapo escorted the soup carriers out of that fenced and guarded place, he succeeded in making friends with the kapo of the group working inside, and I am sure he befriended a few SS men. They would search the soup carriers on their way out, even put a stick into the soup containers, mixing it around to make sure there was nothing in it other than soup. Still, my kapo, a German with a green triangle, knew how to fool the SS men, and succeeded in smuggling out a fortune's worth of Jewish possessions during those trips.

And so, after we finished our soup, all the workers of the timber yard lined up among the piles of timber and received some additional soup. This time, I ate slowly and savoured every spoonful. I had barely swallowed half a dozen spoonfuls when we heard the whistle that signalled the end of the midday break. Before I had a chance to take another spoonful, the foreman was near me and with his large hand grabbed the bowl, saying, "Daj mi to!"—*Give it to me!* I still wanted to salvage another spoonful, but he screamed "Zostaw lyzke!"—*Leave the spoon!* He took the bowl, spoon and the bit of precious soup from me and handed it to a passing Polish inmate. The bowl was a loss, but not as great a loss as that last bit of soup. The spoon, too, was a loss, for spoons were not supplied in the camp.

That same afternoon, I overheard my Polish foreman saying to a couple of Polish inmates who passed by, "I do not like to supervise Poles. I cannot beat them, and yelling at them does not work. But I do not mind beating Jews." Still, the second day in the penal *Kommando* was easier than the first, and under the Pole's supervision nobody was killed.

Later that day, when I entered the *Stube*, I was called over by a French Jew of the forty-two thousands, who said to me, "I saw you working under the supervision of Pilarek. I too worked on the *Holzplatz* but under the supervision of the tall Pole with the one arm. I want to give you one piece of advice. If you want to live a bit longer, do not attempt to bribe Pilarek. Tomorrow is when they distribute the *Zulage*, the extra half a loaf of bread and piece of sausage. Pilarek will expect you to bribe him with it so he goes easier on you. Give him nothing, for if you do, he will expect it every time, and without this extra food, you will not last more than a few days, even if he does not hit you."

I took this man's advice seriously. The next day, I had Pilarek as my foreman, and it was as bad as it had been the first day. The only brief escape was in the toilet. That little building served as a short-lasting refuge where we would catch our breath. The only problem was that there was a sort of supervisor appointed by Pilarek whose job it was to make sure that nobody overstayed his allotted couple of minutes. That man fulfilled his duty to the letter. If he hadn't, he too would have become Pilarek's victim.

That third day I barely survived. Returning to camp, we received the *Zulage*. I exchanged the piece of sausage with a Pole for a quarter loaf of bread, and I exchanged the piece of bread for a little cloth pouch in which I put my ration of bread for the next day. I ate the remaining half a loaf but remained hungry. The following day, I came to work with a piece of bread in my pouch, dangling on my belt for all to see, including Pilarek. Others had done the same.

I expected a rough day, but not as rough as it turned out to be. It made the previous day seem like child's play. I could not understand where that beast got the strength to hit so much without a break. He did not forget me either. As two of us were carrying two heavy boards, Pilarek got hold of me. After a few blows on the back, he hit me on my legs, as was his usual style. I no longer felt the blows, for the part of my leg between the knee and ankle was in unbearable pain. Just as suddenly, he let go of me and started on someone else.

How I survived that day, I do not know, but I managed to get back to my bunk. My legs were swollen and covered with bruises of all conceivable colours. I took off my shoes, which were oozing with mud from walking all day in the rain. Taking off my jacket and shirt, I entered the washroom and placed my legs under the constantly running cold water. After a while, my feet began to feel better, or maybe they stopped having any feeling. They were like ice to the touch. In this condition, I stretched out on my bunk and was asleep in minutes.

The next morning at the *Holzplatz*, we were carrying planks into the main factory building. On the way out, I asked an inmate for directions to the toilet. He directed me to the basement. I sneaked away from my group and made my way there. The toilets there were individual, and in a tiled and heated room. To my surprise, the person responsible for looking after the room and making sure the inmates did not overstay was the humble Pole in charge of my group of ten. I asked him if I was permitted to use the toilet, and he nodded. I did not feel like leaving that warm place where I had no fear of a blow from a stick. Yet I did not want to take advantage of his hospitality or impose on him, so I thanked him and left quickly. That day after work, when we lined up to go back to camp, he asked me where I worked. When I told him, he said that I could come to the toilets whenever I wanted.

A couple more days passed, and it was Sunday again, when "volunteers" were rounded up to unload trainloads of bricks, stones, sand, cement, logs and train rails. I looked for a way to get out of it. The recruiters were already in the *Stube* and were driving Jews out, pushing and hitting them. I slid under the bunks. It was a tight place, with barely enough room for my head to squeeze under. I lay quietly and hoped that nobody would notice me. From my position on the floor, I could see many shoes passing by me. I knew who they belonged to—the shiny boots to the SS men, the polished almost-new leather shoes to the *Blockältester*, kapos and their assistants, and the worn-out shoes with the wooden soles to us, the dejected, exhausted, hungry, hopeless Jews.

Nobody noticed me sliding under the bunk. They were not looking for me. It was quiet now. I slid out and looked around. Nobody even noticed me getting up. I looked at the faces of those who remained in the *Stube*. There was the *Stubendienst* Kazik and his assistant, the kapo, along with half a dozen of his foremen, among them the man who slept on the bunk above me, number 805. *Well, let it be so,* I thought to myself. They are big shots, but I also see ordinary Poles who work alongside the Jews in DAW. Why have they been left alone while every Jew in the *Stube* was taken? A few Poles looked at me, smiling mildly as if to say, "You managed to wiggle out of it," but there was no malice in their expression.

I felt uncomfortable by myself, the only Jew in the *Stube*. The Poles stretched out on their bunks for a nap, but I was uneasy because they might come again for more volunteers. Nobody came. There was an unreal silence. No Jews to yell at or to beat up. The *Stubendienst* did not yell at Poles. There was a moment of tranquility in hell.

Noon was approaching. The *Stubendienst* ordered me to take the red bowls from the cupboards and place them on the table. Some prisoners brought in a large wooden barrel with hot soup. It would stay hot until the other inmates returned, when it would be distributed. I was told to sweep the passages between the bunks and to throw the bit of dirt into the tile stove that warmed our room. I finished my job just before the others returned. They came in dirty and covered with dust. Many were beaten up and injured from the sharp objects they handled. I could see they'd had a hard morning. They scraped as much dirt as possible off their clothes and lined up for their litre of soup. Kazik dished out everybody's soup and ordered me to collect the empty bowls and wash them. After I had put them back in the cupboards, he handed me a bowl with soup.

The following week, work was no different. I was amazed at how much I could take. I think that Pilarek realized that he would not get anything from me and eased up on the beatings. The work wasn't any easier, but there was something that helped me. I started to go more frequently to the toilet in the factory. There I could sit for ten or even fifteen minutes at a time. Once when that timekeeper told a young Pole to leave, the young man turned to him and said, "Why do you let that Jew sit here? He was here when I came in."

The humble Pole answered, "He works on the *Holzplatz* the entire day, in the cold and in the rain. You work under a roof where it is warm. Besides you do not overwork yourself anyway." I saw how noble he was and how high the standard of his morality was.

Without medical attention, dysentery can exhaust a healthy and well-nourished person in a matter of days, but it can kill a hungry, emaciated and exhausted body within the same length of time, and indeed it did. In our group, those that Pilarek did not finish off perished this way. The only known and available medicine at the time was charcoal pills. The instructions were as follows: Don't eat or drink anything for forty-eight hours, and take two charcoal pills three times daily. Not following these instructions to the letter meant that the entire effort would be in vain. If it was difficult to stand hunger, the thirst was worse. Some were strong enough to resist temptation, others could not resist taking just one sip of water, and that spelled death. Those charcoal pills were not always available, so as a substitute, some gnawed on a piece of partially burned wood that could be easily found around. Chewing the pills would blacken the teeth, mouth and lips, but the piece of wood would blacken the face and hand that held it to the mouth as well. In our group of fifty-six men, almost half always had blackened faces. They were candidates to die within the next four or five days. I too could not remain immune to dysentery and one day was stricken with it. I made many trips to the toilet, but just before the workday was over, I was unable to get there in time and dirtied my underpants. This was something I had never done, and I was in a panic.

Coming into the *Stube* after the *Appell*, I asked the French inmate, the one who had advised me not to bribe Pilarek, where I could get a pair of underpants. I could get it for a ration of bread, he replied. My morning ration was available, as I was not eating, trying to cure my dysentery on my own. I gave it to him, wondering where he would get a pair of underwear. He stuck his hand in the straw sack on which he slept and pulled out a pair of well-worn underwear covered with bits of straw. I thought to myself, *Learn boy, learn. The man arrived in this camp six months before you, and look how much he learned during that time, even to have the foresight to provide a pair of underwear for any contingency.* Taking the pair of underwear, I went into the washroom, washed in the ice-cold water and got dressed again, leaving the dirty underwear behind. As I lay on my bunk, I suddenly understood the blunder I had committed. I had just given away an entire ration of bread, a day's worth of bread, the worth of a human life—for I had seen men killed for less—for a pair of underwear. I could have washed my own dirty ones and still had my bread ration. What was the hurry? The underwear would have dried out on me, and besides, it was only coloured liquid that stained them. However, I was also aware that the *Blockältester* could have come in while I was washing them, and, if in a bad mood, he would have left me dead.

From carrying the heavy boards, my bony shoulders became red and then erupted in blisters that cracked and turned into sores that would not heal. I put my cap on my shoulder under the jacket to create a cushion. It helped, but not enough, so I picked up some dirty old rags to add more cushioning.

After another week, I was an old-timer in the lumberyard, and Pilarek eased up on me a bit. He stopped hitting with the intention of killing me outright but only so as not to leave me out. The Polish foreman was even speaking to me from time to time but nevertheless continued hitting me, apparently to remind me who he was and who I was.

I thought that I had no more weight to lose. Yet on Sundays, when we were shaved, I could feel my bare bones touching the seat of the wooden stool, and with each passing Sunday, it got worse until I could no longer sit on the stool. But the worst part was the constant nagging hunger, which would not leave me for a second. The most trying time was coming back from work, right after the *Appell*, when we had an hour before we searched for lice in our shirts. I spent that time walking all over the camp looking for something to eat, knowing that I would not find anything. The hunger drove me to unreal thoughts like wishing to have teeth of steel so that I could bite into the brick walls. After the hour of searching, I would return to the *Stube* more tired and hungrier than before, if that was at all possible. Taking off my shirt, I would look for lice, which to my surprise, I almost always found.

The *Stubendienst* inspected our shirts himself. He would pick half a dozen or so of us at random and examine our shirts, and of course he found lice. One evening, he picked me for inspection and found a louse. The following evening, after the *Appell*, he took four of us to the bathhouse to be disinfected. My *Stubendienst* wanted to have his fun, so he asked the Polish prisoner who worked there to aim a powerful hose at us. The water was ice-cold, and it knocked us down and pushed us along the slippery boards up to the wall. Then he changed the direction of the hose, and the water pushed us to the opposite wall. When he finished, I could not catch my breath. Now the bundles of bruised bones had to pick themselves up and stand under the hot water of the shower.

If we suffered from the plague of lice, that was nothing in comparison to the swarms of fleas that inhabited the entire camp. When we got up in the morning, our bodies were covered in countless tiny red dots from their bites. Not having a mirror, I could only see the faces of others and imagine what I looked like. Showering or individual disinfecting did not work against the fleas. They were everywhere—in our bunks, in the cracks in the wood, in the straw sacks we slept on, in the blankets we covered ourselves with and on the floor.

Surprisingly, time did not stand still. Somehow, I was still alive, which must have been a great surprise to my overseers and was an even greater surprise to me. I felt, however, that my strength was ebbing and my time was running out. There was nothing left of me but skin and bones. I could collapse at any moment, if not from Pilarek's beating, then from hunger. Which of the two would come first, I did not want to know.

In early May 1943, I felt that my end was near. I had a second bout with dysentery, and I'd had three hellish months of Auschwitz experience behind me and knew exactly where I stood. I didn't think that I would make it through the week.

One Sunday evening, as I sat with my shirt in my hands looking for lice, Leon Kulowski, Polish inmate number 805, who was sleeping on the bunk above me, was making his way through the congested hallway to his bunk. Apparently, I was in his way, for he asked me to let him pass. As a rule, he would spend the hour or hour and a half between the evening *Appell* and lights out with the other prominent inmates around the front table where no Jew dared to sit. He was only among us when on his way to the bunk. This time he noticed me and asked, "Where do you work?"

"In the *Holzplatz*," I answered.

"Under whose supervision?"

"Under Pilarek's."

"How long have you been working there?"

"Six weeks."

"You survived there under Pilarek for six weeks?" he asked with astonishment. Without a word, he turned to the kapo Janek G., who was his supervisor but also his friend, and in a loud voice so that the kapo should hear him over the noise in the *Stube*, he said, "Janek, take him to you in the factory."

Janek was the kapo in factory number 1 of the DAW complex, a carpenter shop where 150 prisoners worked. The kapo answered, "You know, Leon, that I cannot take him from there without his kapo's permission."

I never expected that someone would intervene on my behalf in this hell. Suddenly, I saw a tiny spark of hope. I grabbed the opportunity and said, "My kapo said that he has no more use of me, and I could leave whenever I want."

"If that is the case," said the kapo, "tomorrow morning when we all get to the factory, line up with my people."

The next morning, as we got to the yard of DAW, and I heard the call, "Kommandos fall in!" I ran to the group of factory number 1. Before going into the factory to work, the factory *Schreiber* went by with a list and checked off every worker. He got to me and asked, "What are you doing here?"

With apprehension, I answered, "Ask the kapo."

The registrar turned to the kapo, who was some twenty metres away and yelled, "Mr. Kapo, what about him?" pointing to me.

The kapo looked at me and said, "Write him down."

In the factory, the kapo led me to a workbench where a French Jew by the name of Itzik was working. "Here is your helper," he said.

The man was so busy at his work that he didn't even look at me. As soon as the kapo walked away, Itzik said to me, "Do you see what I am doing?"

In the two minutes I had stood near him, he had managed to fit four L-shaped metal brackets into a window's wooden corners and attach it to a window frame with the help of four hinges. I had never in my life seen a craftsman working with such speed. I nodded, not really understanding his hurry.

"I can work by myself," he said. "You will just be in my way. Do you see the line of people over there?" he pointed at a few men standing in line near a wall. "You stand in that line. When an unfinished wooden window is ready, bring it to me."

I went over to the line and stood behind the six or eight men ahead of me, each waiting for a wooden window that was being glued together from prefabricated pieces. As soon as one was ready, the first in line took it to his master craftsman. It was obvious to me that I would have to wait in line for some ten minutes, so I used the time to look around and strike up a conversation with the others in line. They told me that there was no beating in the factory. The kapo used a carrot instead of a stick. As a reward for producing the greatest amount of work in each department, the kapo would give that inmate an additional litre of soup. It was for those litres of soup that those craftsmen worked harder than they had ever worked in their lives.

How lucky I was, I thought to myself, to be here instead of in the *Holzplatz*, where I spent the twelve-hour workday outdoors, exposed to the cold and rain under Pilarek's constant beating, with the knowledge that within a few days, I would succumb to his stick. Standing here, under a roof and in comparative warmth, without the beatings, I simply did not believe my good fortune.

I was next in line. I grabbed the window and ran to my boss. As soon as I put it on the workbench, he said to me, "Run for another one."

I was back in line in a couple of seconds, where I waited another ten or fifteen minutes to get a window. I wondered if this was a sweet dream in the middle of a nightmare. I looked around, and I was delighted to see a couple more young men from Shershev. They were older than me and carpenters by trade.

The morning went by quickly. The whistle told us that it was noon, and we got the bowl of soup. I sat with my townspeople and had just finished my soup when I saw my boss, the French Jew, passing by. He said to me, "Come." Without a question, I followed him to the office. Near the door there was a small barrel of soup surrounded by the kapo, a couple of foremen, the *Schreiber* and the Pole who attended the kapo and the foremen. The *Schreiber* called out the numbers of those who had produced the most in each stage of the production. I looked on as every well-performing worker approached and got a litre of soup. I saw my boss walking over and getting his. He looked around and saw me standing at a distance and said loudly and indignantly, "*Nu?* What are you waiting for?"

I walked over slowly, hesitatingly, wondering if I would get a litre of soup or a blow over the head with the ladle. When the fellow poured me a ladleful of soup, I could not believe my eyes. Was I dreaming?

After the break, everybody went back to his job. A short while later, as I was placing a window on the workbench, which was not far from the door through which all planks and timber were brought in, the wide door opened and in came my former co-workers from the lumberyard with heavy boards on their shoulders. Leading them was the murderous Pilarek. He noticed me immediately and asked, "What are you doing here?"

Out of sheer fear, I could not open my mouth, not that I had something to tell him, anyway. Pilarek knew that he had no authority in the factory. As soon as his men dumped their loads, they all left.

A few minutes later, the kapo from the *Holzplatz* marched into the factory and went straight to the office of my new kapo, Janek G. I knew it was a bad sign for me. As a rule, kapos in DAW did not visit departments under the authority of other kapos, so when this kapo entered, everyone took note. A couple of minutes after he entered the office, I was called in, and as soon as I closed the door behind me, my new kapo said, "You lied to me. You told me that you have his permission to change jobs. He is here to take you back."

It was true that I had lied to him, but was it such a big crime to save my life, even if temporarily? I knew whom I was facing. Janek had taken me to his factory because of the intervention of his friend Leon Kulowski. He did not owe me anything, nor did I mean anything to him. I was just another Jew, one of thousands who died daily in this kingdom of death. He would not jeopardize his friendship or even acquaintance with another kapo, especially a German kapo, for the sake of a Jew. And then there was my former kapo, the German with the green triangle under whose supervision half a dozen Jews died daily due to hard work and beatings, and whose authority was now being challenged by a half-dead Jew whom he had come to claim in order to make an example of him.

If I had something to say in my defence, I do not remember what it was, but I do remember that before I had a chance to open my mouth, Janek gave me a slap in the face. I do not remember feeling the slap, but I remember the floor coming toward me and suddenly realizing that I was lying on the floor, hearing my new kapo say, "Pick yourself up and get out of here."

It was too good to last, I thought. Was it worthwhile to taste a couple hours of rest only to be beaten to death by Pilarek? I left the office knowing that when I walked out through the factory door, Pilarek would be waiting to finish me with his stick. I barely managed to walk two or three steps when Leon Kulowski, the one who got me the new job to begin with, confronted me. Like everybody else in the factory, he had seen my former kapo going into the kapo's office. When he saw me being called into the office, he had guessed what it was all about and knew how it would end. He grabbed me by my shoulders, pushed me to the wall next to the office and said, "Stay here; do not move from here." He stepped into the office. Five or so minutes later, he was out. He gave me a friendly slap on the back and said, "Go back to your job."

How I felt at that moment, is now, over fifty years later, difficult to describe. I knew that Leon Kulowski had just saved my life. That episode is still vivid in my memory as though it is happening before my eyes. Through all those years, my gratitude toward that man, my benefactor, did not diminish by an iota.

When the production of windows was finished, we started making walls of barracks, the same as those in Birkenau. They were the Pferdestall barracks OKH 260/9, which were prefab horse stables, 40.76 metres long, 9.5 metres wide and 2.65 metres in height. As building the barracks parts required several men, the competition for speedy production could not be implemented, and I stopped getting the extra litre of soup. The gnawing hunger did not let up for a moment and was worst between the evening *Appell* and lice checking.

From the moment that Leon Kulowski intervened on my behalf and saved my life, I began looking for a way to thank him for his deed. But the only tangible item in camp was food, and I was the starving one, not him. He was a big shot, a foreman under the protection of a powerful kapo, his close friend. How could I reciprocate? All the big-shot inmates had enough food and wore well-fitting clothing.

I decided to ask my benefactor, Leon Kulowski, whether I could polish his shoes. He agreed. After several evenings of polishing his shoes, the attendant, a young Pole named Zygmund, asked me to do the shoes of the other big shots. I accepted his proposition gladly. First, I wanted to be on their good side, and I did not hold anything against the kapo for the slap on the face in his office. I knew that he could not have acted any other way. And most importantly, I hoped for a reward. It came on Sunday, when we received our soup in the *Stube*. The prominent inmates rarely ate the soup. They would take a couple of spoonfuls, turn up their noses and leave it. Zygmund used to find a hungry Pole to give it to. That Sunday, however, he gave it to me.

If anybody thinks that with a couple of extra bowls of soup one can fill up a hungry stomach that had been empty continuously for three months, one is grossly mistaken — in any case, not the kind of hunger we knew in Auschwitz. That Sunday was a good day for me. I do not know if I realized then how low I had sunk morally if a couple of bowls of soup could bring the heavens down to me. But then again, who can understand Auschwitz except the ones who were there?

Shortly after becoming the overseers' shoe polisher, I started to wash their laundry. Their shoes had to be polished almost every day as the grounds of the factory turned muddy after the frequent rains. In the beginning, their attendant gave me a piece of soap to wash their laundry with, for the small piece of soap we received once a month did not produce suds. One could never wash a shirt with it and hope to make it look white or clean. The soap was small, the size of a matchbox, and on either side of it were imprinted three letters, R.J.F., which gave credence to the rumours circulating in camp that it was made from the fat of Jewish bodies burned in the crematoriums, as we believed then that the three letters stood for *Reichs Juden Fett* (state Jewish fat).[5] That the Nazis were capable of doing it we knew only too well. We also suspected that they were deliberately imprinting those three letters on the soap to laugh in our faces, showing us how lawless their world could be and how wanton, immoral and merciless they were, how abandoned we were by an indifferent and uncaring world.

However, the soap that Zygmund gave me had found its way into camp from the continuous trainloads of Jews who were being brought to Auschwitz from German-occupied Europe. Thousands of the newly arriving Jews were being led straight to the gas chambers, and their belongings were being sorted to be shipped to Germany, but the inmates who sorted their belongings would sometimes risk their lives to sneak some soap or shoe polish into the camp to help a relative or friend. The inmates who had the job of sorting the luggage of the Jews were considered better off than others in camp. If any Jews dared to hope they would survive, it had to be them. Still, they took risks to help their friends and relatives, and that is a testament to their devotion.

A couple of weeks later, Zygmund told me that he had no more soap. He handed me half a loaf of bread and told me to go buy soap somewhere. Fortunately, I knew a man in our *Stube* who, seeing me washing the laundry, had asked if I needed soap. This time, I approached him and bought a piece of soap for half a loaf of bread. During the entire year that I did laundry for the overseers and was buying soap, I never

5 Scholars of the Holocaust have concluded that there is no evidence that the Nazis manufactured soap from human bodies. The letters on the soap were R.I.F., standing for *Reichsstelle für Industrielle Fettversorgung* (National Center for Industrial Fat Provisioning), the government agency that procured soap products during the war, rather than R.J.F.

got an extra bite of that bread. Those big shots paid me with the soup that they seldom ate anyway, while the nagging hunger kept gnawing at my insides without respite.

25
Struggle for Survival

THE SPRING OF 1943 was very difficult. All my thoughts were about food, and there was no way to satisfy my hunger. How I regretted the times when my mother had put food in front of me and I refused to eat. Those thoughts alternated with thoughts of my family who had perished in the very place I was being held, and I reproved and chastised myself for thinking about food. Even on Sundays, when, besides my ration of soup, I got another litre for collecting and washing the bowls in our *Stube*, in addition to a couple of litres that the attendant, Zygmund, gave me for doing the laundry and polishing the shoes, I never felt full, not even temporarily satisfied.

Once, while marching to work, we passed a line of empty freight cars that must have contained raw turnips, for there were tiny turnips scattered nearby. They were shrivelled, pitiful things not even fit for camp consumption. The cars were no more than ten metres from us, but leaving the line was prohibited. Getting caught meant at least a beating, or worse. But I could not stand the temptation. I ran out and grabbed a few little turnips. Luck was with me. None of the kapos or SS men noticed. A few days later, passing the same way, I saw tiny beets. Again, I ran out and grabbed a few without being seen.

The Jews from across German-occupied Europe who came in trainloads did not only bring with them their valuables and attire, but also provisions for the trip. Many did not finish their food, and in the state of mind they were in, others did not eat at all. As most of them were taken straight to the gas chambers and their eternal rest, all they brought was left for the living. The camp administration used the assortment of baked goods that arrived to make a sort of soup called *chlebówka* from the Polish word *chleb* (bread). This soup sometimes contained pieces of cake, which gave it a sweet taste. There was not enough soup to go around the entire camp, so every evening a different block received it. On the evenings when we got that soup, I received extra from my superiors whose laundry I did. On a few occasions, when I'd had what I thought to be enough from a moral standpoint, I shared my good fortune with a young man from Shershev who was in block 18A.

Behind the last row of blocks, blocks 1 to 11, was a long walkway, part of which had young birch trees on either side. That walkway served as a gathering place for many inmates, especially Jews, on Sunday mornings. One could hear there many European languages, like French, Flemish, German, Polish, Czech, Slovak and Greek. But it seemed to me that the prevalent language was Yiddish. On one early Sunday morning, I met a friend from my childhood days in Shershev, Hershel Schneider, on the walkway. We were delighted to see each other, like long-lost friends. Although my stomach growled from hunger, and I am sure his did too, we did not want to part and walked around for a couple of hours, oblivious to those around us. We met on a couple of consecutive Sundays. He was the only childhood friend that I saw in Auschwitz and spent a few hours with, talking about home and family. How dear those hours were. I do not even know how, when and under what circumstances he perished.

The increasing arrival of trainloads of Jews meant an increase in the distribution of bread soup to twice a week. While eating or sipping that soup, I could not push out of my mind the thought that I was sipping Jewish lifeblood. The Jews who brought the bread were being burned now in the crematorium, and I was eating their bread. I am sure that the same thought occurred to the hundreds and thousands of other Jewish inmates while eating that soup. Yet I looked forward to the days when we got that soup. I cannot really say whether we had a moral justification for eating it, but I do believe that only those who were there and tried to extend their miserable existences for an extra few days have a right to answer that question.

I continued to work as a carpenter's assistant at different jobs and in different places. I learned to use carpenter's tools and was able to do some of the work. In our factory, of the 150 carpenters, 125 were Jews. Of them, 25 came from the Pruzhany ghetto, and among them were half a dozen men from Shershev.

At the end of May or beginning of June, the kapo's attendant, Zygmund, called me into the office and gave me a tin of canned meat to bring into camp. I was not happy with this mission, for quite often the SS conducted searches at the entrance of the camp. But I did not have a choice. To refuse would not only mean losing the extra bit of soup I got from him, but also expulsion from the factory back to the *Holzplatz*. Fortunately, there were no searches on that day, and I passed safely. From then on, I seldom returned from work without carrying something illegal. To my daily problem of trying to procure a bit of extra soup was added the fear of being caught entering the camp with forbidden goods. Usually it was a small item, like a tin of sardines, fish or meat that I would put in the pouch in which I had carried the extra piece of bread from the *Zulage* to eat at work. On the way back, it was empty, and I would tie the cords of the pouch to my belt and slide it inside my pants, letting it dangle between my legs. With the masses of inmates marching in from work, searches could not be thorough. On an emaciated inmate, one was not likely to find something of value anyway, so the searcher was satisfied by feeling the pockets and protruding lumps of the loosely hanging jackets on our skinny bodies.

To make the searches more thorough, the SS men ordered the marchers to continue into the camp and line up on the *Appellplatz*, where the inmates were surrounded and searched. One day, Zygmund called me into the office and gave me a round tin with fish or meat to take into the camp. It must have weighed a kilogram. I put it into the pouch and tied it to my belt. When I looked down, there was an immense bulge. I knew that if there would be a search on that day, it would spell my end. I wanted to say no, that I could not take it, but I did not dare. My only hope was that they would not search that day. But even without a search, the tin was very noticeable, and I would be stopped at the gate. We marched to the camp, and my fear got more intense. We passed the gate and marched into the camp. I was ready to start breathing easier when suddenly we were encircled by SS men and *Blockälteste* and led to the *Appellplatz* to be searched. *Now*, I thought, *I will pay for everything*. We stood in rows of five and were searched by five men. They stood in front of us, and we approached them five at a time. I knew that the searcher would immediately notice the bulge under my stomach. I spread my legs apart and put my hand deep in my pocket, pushing the can behind me and bringing my legs together. The bulge disappeared, but what it looked from the back I do not know. I approached the SS man, keeping my feet close together. He slid his hands over my pockets and around my waist and said, "Go." With my first normal step, the heavy tin in the pouch swung forward and was back in its previous position, where it could not be seen from the back. Walking quickly, I went to the block. After the *Appell*, when I gave the tin to Zygmund, he was astonished. "How did you do it?" he asked.

I just shrugged my shoulders. What could I say? Deep inside, I still believed in miracles, and in a hidden corner of my heart I believed that my mother's soul watched over me.

Among the few prominent inmates in my *Stube* were two *Vorarbeiter* with black triangles, a rarity among Polish prisoners. Both were in their mid-twenties. One of them was Lutek, a well-fed man who had been a petty thief. Like many in his profession, he was mischievous. But he was also fraternal and sympathized with the underdog and the oppressed, which included Jews. No wonder he was liked among the Jewish workers in the factory. With his reputation as a criminal, he was also respected among his own people, the Poles. Quite often the big shots would sit around the table in the evening telling stories about life before the war. I recall Lutek's story about his city, Krakow, and how in his early career he would break into Jewish homes on Yom Kippur eve, knowing that no Jews would be at home as they were all in the synagogues. He even knew how long the Kol Nidre prayer took and at what time the worshippers returned home. I never heard him utter a contemptuous word about Jews. I had the feeling that he yearned for the Jewish Krakow that he had known, which by that time did not exist anymore.

When Lutek left our *Stube*, his bunk, which was in an honourable place right near the table around which all the big shots slept, was given to Leon Kulowski, my benefactor. Leon's bunk was taken over by a newly arrived Pole, Szewczyk, who was somewhere between fifty and sixty years old, the oldest inmate in our *Stube*. Thanks to the many and ample parcels that he got from home, this man managed to survive, at least until we parted in 1944. Those parcels opened doors for him. Even the well-fed *Stubendienst*, who assigned him the bunk on the third tier, looked up to him like a dog waiting for something to be thrown to him while the old man sat on his bunk opening his just-arrived parcel. There was usually something for the *Stubendienst*, a piece of cake or sweets.

We Jewish inmates considered Szewczyk an angel, and for good reason. While most non-Jewish inmates looked upon us Jews with scorn, he showed us compassion, supplemented by action. His parcels always contained two loaves of bread, and he would spread his jacket on his bunk and slice the two loaves. He would then hand me the jacket full of bread, climb down from his bunk and take the jacket from me, saying, "You do not need it as badly as those poor souls," motioning with his hand in the direction of the other Jews in the *Stube*. Then he would hand out a piece of bread to every Jew in the *Stube*. I was the only Jew who did not get a slice of bread, and God only knew that I could use it. But that did not diminish my respect or lessen my deference for that saintly man. In the hell of Auschwitz, he proved to me there were still moral people with principles who could rise above the multitudes to give hope and, yes, life—for bread was life.

Sometime in June, the camp bakery needed some carpentry work done. The SS chief of the bakery asked my kapo to send over some men, among whom was Hershel Morawsky from the Pruzhany ghetto. He was a top-notch carpenter whom the kapo would send to do work where something could be acquired in exchange. Understandably, everybody wanted to work in the bakery because, despite the many watchful eyes, one could swipe some bread and eat it quietly, or even hide a piece on oneself. The bakery made the regular bread for the entire camp, as well as a special white bread that the doctors prescribed for the prominent sick inmates. It was that white bread that my kapo and his buddies craved. Hershel found a way to obtain that bread and bring it safely to the factory, but it was up to me to get it into the camp. Every day, before leaving the factory, I would go to the office, where Zygmund would give me a loaf of white bread. I would stick it under the belt of my pants, and it could not be detected beneath my jacket. During the frequent searches, I pushed out my chest and pulled in my stomach, if one could call it a stomach, and the cavity could have hidden two loaves. Once in the *Stube*, I would pull the bread out from under my jacket, careful not to be seen by anybody. Of course, the French Jew who slept below me and the saintly elderly Pole, Szewczyk, could not help but see it. A couple of times, Szewczyk warned me, saying, "You should not do it for them, for you might pay for it with your life."

How could that venerable Pole understand that I was risking my life daily so that the big shots would pay me off with a couple litres of soup a week? I believe that without that extra soup, I would not have survived and lived to write about it.

Up to now, I have depicted most Poles in a negative way, even with scorn, with very few exceptions. One exception was the Polish bathroom attendant who permitted me to spend an extra ten or fifteen minutes under a roof and in the warmth to escape the murderous blows of Pilarek's stick. That Pole did not owe me anything, nor did he know me, except for my number. He did not even know my name, nor did I know his.

There was the elderly Pole Szewczyk, who used to divide seventy slices of bread among the seventy Jews in my *Stube*, at a time when thousands of starving Jews paid with their lives while trying to procure a mouthful of bread or a couple of potatoes, when one hour or one day could be decisive in turning a life upside down. If that piece of bread helped a particular inmate to survive a day, then it's possible it saved his life.

There was the Pole Leon Kulowski, who got me the job in the carpenter shop and protected me from being thrown out when my former kapo came to claim me back, which would have spelled my doom. Even when Leon moved to the more prestigious bunk next to the table, he kept protesting to the *Stubendienst* about his assistant, Wladek, who constantly beat the Jews for no reason. Even after Leon was moved to a different block, he kept giving me his soup on Sundays and his bread soup once or twice a week.

One day in the middle of June 1943, right after the evening *Appell*, we passed a strict selection during which several Jewish young men from my *Stube* were marked down. They were fine and intelligent young men, no more than boys, who had arrived in Auschwitz from the Netherlands and Belgium three months before me. By June, they were completely exhausted, literally skin and bones, *Muselmänner*. In them I saw the reflection of myself and wondered how long it would be until I was in their place.

As far as I could tell, selections were conducted only on Jews.[6] The process went as follows: When the evening *Appell* was over, Jews were ordered to remain in place while all other inmates were told to go into their blocks and were locked in. The Jews were then ordered to get completely undressed. Carrying our bundles of clothes under one arm, we were marched five abreast to the front of the kitchen. There, among a group of SS men, stood a dreaded Nazi doctor. Surrounded by SS men, *Blockälteste* and other overseers, we lined up in a single file to march by him. Before approaching him, many would puff out their chests, taking in as much air as possible to expand their stomachs and appear a bit heftier than they were. With a hardened prayer in our hearts, we confronted our destiny. It was then that our prayers were most sincere. With the thought that only God could help, we passed by the doctor. Not every prayer was answered. All it took was the pointing of his finger or the slight motion of his hand to send you to your death. The moment you were pointed out, a *Blockältester* or kapo immediately wrote down your number and sent you to your block. The next morning, the block *Schreiber* would come into the *Stube* and read out the numbers of those unfortunates who were marked down. He collected them and led them out to the *Appell*, where they stood separately, as if they were already dead. After the others had gone to work, the poor souls were gathered and led on foot the three-and-a-half kilometres to the Birkenau gas chambers.

After one such selection was over, the mood was so heavy that it even reflected on some of the non-Jewish faces. Even the sight of bread soup waiting for us when we returned to the *Stube* did not improve our

6 Until August 1943, non-Jewish prisoners, mainly Poles, were also subject to selections, although the criteria applied to them were less restrictive than for Jewish prisoners (Dr. Piotr Setkiewicz, Auschwitz-Birkenau Memorial and Museum).

mood. I stood near my bunk with my elbows resting on it, supporting my chin with the palms of my hands, trying to recover from the experience of the last hour and shake it off. Leon Kulowski approached me, and asked in a quiet, worried voice, "Did they mark you down?"

Just as quietly, I answered, "No."

He turned around, walked back to his place at the table, picked up his bowl of soup, brought it over to me and said, "Here, try to put on some weight."

By this time, I was well acquainted with the layout of the camp, from the bathhouse near block 1 to the infirmary, or *Krankenbau*, in block 28. In block 24, there was a brothel frequented by privileged non-Jewish inmates. The *Paketstelle*, where parcels for inmates arrived and were inspected, was near block 25. In block 10, the Nazis kept young Jewish women on whom they performed all kinds of terrible operations and experiments. These women were kept inside the block and no inmate was allowed in, but from time to time, SS men escorted them on a walk around the camp. We would sometimes see them on a Sunday, walking in slow steps like they were at a funeral, which in this case was their own.

Next to block 10 was block 11, which was better known by its fearsome name, the "Bunker." It was famous for its *Stehzelle*, standing cells, where inmates were crammed in groups of four with no room to sit down all night, after which they had to do a twelve-hour shift of work. Of course, many died. For a lesser crime, an inmate could receive twenty-five or fifty lashes. Not many survived fifty. There was a brick wall between blocks 10 and 11, in front of which inmates were executed.

Poles, especially, feared the Bunker. Some Poles had been brought from jails, others straight from homes or streets, arrested for imaginary or real crimes. Many were accused of anti-German activities. Some offenders were taken to the execution wall and shot, but the great majority were kept in the camp. Jews feared the Bunker less, as our fate was to die no matter what. Still, Jews were also sent to the Bunker for transgressions in camp. Some got out after a few days, others not at all. In my *Stube* there was a young man from Pruzhany, Yankl, who was caught at a gate search with a small tin of shoe polish and was taken to the Bunker. We never heard of him again.

The SS man in charge of the Bunker was a tall and husky redhead who harboured a special animosity toward Soviet prisoners. When he walked through the camp on his way to the Bunker, he never missed the opportunity to kick the Soviet prisoners in his way. In such a time and place, it was strange to see him kicking non-Jews while there were so many Jews around.

In late June or the beginning of July 1943, as we stood block by block in front of the kitchen to receive our extra half loaf of bread and sausage, two men approached. One of them was the tall red-headed SS man in charge of the Bunker. The other was dressed in camp attire but had a hefty build and was taller than the SS man. I had never seen such a well-built prisoner in Auschwitz. As they got closer, my astonishment became greater, for I saw from his triangle that he was a Jew. As they passed us, the large inmate put out his hand—in which he carried a whole loaf of bread and two pieces of sausage—and said, "Here, have it and share it with your comrades."

It took me several seconds to absorb what had happened. A total stranger had just handed me a whole loaf of bread. Excited, I cut it into four pieces and gave three quarters of the loaf to three nearby inmates. After I had done it, the other inmates poked fun at me saying, "You fool. You had a whole loaf of bread in your hands and gave it away." Other inmates told me that the man was Yakov Kozalchik, a Jewish strongman and wrestler. I found out later that Kozalchik sometimes entertained the SS and the prominent inmates of the camp by showing off his extraordinary strength. The big shots in my *Stube* would return from his performances marvelling at his strength.

That summer, the camp management organized a few Sunday afternoon entertainment sessions for the entire camp. They erected a temporary arena on the *Appellplatz* for wrestling or boxing competitions. I recall a clown act performed by two German inmates who were professional entertainers as well as criminals. Their performances were excellent. This was the contradiction of Auschwitz. For those big shots it was the best place to spend the war years, while for others, there was not even a place for burial, so they were burned, and their ashes were thrown into the Vistula or scattered over the surrounding fields.

In time, a loose circle was created among the former inmates of the Pruzhany ghetto who worked in our factory. During the noon break, when we received our soup, we would go down to the cellar, which was used for illegal dealings conducted by the privileged inmates. This was where an inmate from Grodno, Margolis, who was by trade a shoemaker, sat and repaired shoes on the quiet for the convenience of those big shots who preferred to wear made-to-measure shoes instead of the ones available in camp. Margolis, a man of about forty, tried to live by the rules of Jewish dietary law. He would not eat the piece of sausage that we got twice a week and exchanged it for bread. When he would find a grain-sized piece of meat in his soup, which was a rare occurrence, he would throw the soup out. As only Margolis used the cellar, our group from the Pruzhany ghetto gathered there during our hour-long break to discuss politics. Quite often, we listened to a young man named Diesatnik, who had a pleasant voice, sing sentimental Russian songs, of which he had a large repertoire.

Margolis was especially busy that spring and summer, making sandals for the big shots, and I nearly landed in trouble and lost my "distinguished" job as a shoe polisher and laundry man because of those sandals. One July day, I was carrying a pair of these sandals under my jacket for the kapo or his assistant. As we approached the gate to camp, we were stopped. A rumour spread in our ranks that a strict search was taking place. The sandals would surely be found in a thorough search, and I did not dare keep them on me, but I did not want to throw them away. We were still a distance from the gate and in between the rows of the pigsties, where pigs were raised for the SS. There were plenty of heaps of garbage, building materials and tools there. I stuck the sandals into a pile of garbage. The inmates working there were on the way to camp or inside already, and on the next day, we would pass by there before they arrived.

As soon as I entered the *Stube*, I told Zygmund what I had done and assured him that the sandals were safe and that I would retrieve them the next day. I could see the resentment on his face. We had bread soup that evening, but I did not get any. The next morning, as we marched out to work, I ran out of the column, grabbed the sandals and stuck them under my belt. I brought them to Zygmund in the office. Within a couple of days, thanks to the intervention of Leon Kulowski, we made up and things returned to the way they had been.

Sometime in July, the camp administration decided to rid the camp of the plague of fleas. After the evening *Appell*, we were led to the bathhouse, leaving our clothes and underwear in the *Stube*s. While we were being disinfected and showered in the bathhouse, special disinfecting *Kommandos* sealed the blocks hermetically and fumigated them. Returning from the bathhouse, we had to stay outside in the nude for hours while the building was being aired. After a couple treatments, we finally got rid of the fleas.

In places where kapos could not stand with sticks over the inmates in their charge, like in our factory, the camp administration thought of another incentive to make the tradesmen produce more. A certain number of marks were given to each kapo to distribute among his men as he saw fit. It was entirely up to the kapo's discretion. For those camp marks, one could buy from the canteen a few cigarettes, half a litre of sauerkraut or half a litre of snails marinated in mustard. Those two food items had no value, for what good is half a litre of mustard with a few snails in it when your stomach is crying out for bread or potatoes. The only good item was the cigarettes, which could be exchanged for a piece of bread or a few potatoes. As soon as it became known in camp that cigarettes were available in the canteen, those who had marks went to buy them.

As with other good camp positions, such as in the *Paketstelle* or the slaughterhouse, the canteen was staffed by Polish inmates. Even German inmates could not get jobs there. One evening, I arrived there to find the place mobbed. I finally made my way through, got to the counter and handed my five marks to the young man there. He glanced at me and saw a Jew.

"You are here for the second time tonight!" he yelled at me. He ran out from behind the counter, grabbed me by my lapels, and started shaking me and yelling, "You are here for the second time this evening! Admit it!"

Scared and confused, not knowing what crime I had committed, I answered, "No, I have not been here before."

In the blink of an eye, there were half a dozen Polish workers around me, and my accuser held on to me with one hand and stuck his index finger into my chest, yelling, "I caught him! He is here for the second time this evening!"

One of the men surrounding me asked, "Is it true?"

I answered desperately that it was not. He punched me in the face, and the ceiling began to move in circles while the floor came toward me. Lying on the floor, I was surrounded by the group of Poles, who seemed to be deciding what to do with me. Then, another Pole appeared, a man of medium height and age, slender in build, with a distinguished and aristocratic face and dressed in a nice inmate's uniform.

"What is happening here?" he asked. Before anyone had a chance to speak, he continued, "You do not do those things."

One of them protested, "But he is here for the second time this evening."

The man answered in the same calm voice, "You do not act like this. Let him go."

He turned around and walked away. The others dispersed too. But that young Pole who originally accused me of having been there before took his revenge. He still had my five marks in his hand. He walked over to the counter and stamped them. The stamp read, "Not valid for cigarettes." I left the canteen, hurt for being falsely accused, and what's more, deprived of the few cigarettes that could have fetched me a piece of bread. But I thanked God for sending that nice Pole in time.

I had never really spoken to an SS man except the usual "Jawohl"—*Yes, sir*, to an order, which usually sounded more like a bark than a human voice and most of the time was accompanied by a blow from a stick or a kick with a boot. That summer of 1943, I heard an SS man speaking with a human voice. It happened when the kapo had to send carpenters to the house of an SS officer to do repairs. The house was in a suburb of the town of Oświęcim, after which Auschwitz was named in German, two kilometres from camp. As usual, a couple of assistants went along with the carpenters. I was one of them. Three SS men were assigned to accompany the eight of us from the moment we left the enclosure until we returned.

The entire Auschwitz-Birkenau complex was surrounded by a chain of watchtowers manned by SS men with machine guns. Several roads led from the enclosure, and those coming or going, like the few civilians who supervised work in the camp, had to have a permit to pass. Even the SS guards who accompanied prisoners had to have permission to pass. That morning, we collected our tools from the factory and set out on our own to the end of the guarded perimeter where three SS men were waiting for us, and they accompanied us to the SS officer's house in a neighbourhood of Oświęcim. There were several groups of prisoners there. One group was cleaning the yard and landscaping it. Another group was repairing the fence, and another was putting down hardwood floors in the house. Each group came with their own SS guards, making over a dozen of them. Why so many to guard us?

Apparently, the guards had that thought too, so they came to some understanding, and soon half of them disappeared.

Because we could not be back at the factory by noon for our lunch, we would have to work the entire day until five o'clock on the portion of bread that we had received in the morning. A few of us risked approaching one of our SS guards to ask if he would escort us to the watchtower from where we would walk to the factory, receive our soup and then return to the town. What we did not tell him was that we planned to get an extra litre of soup, one at noon and one that had been set aside for us for when we returned to the factory at five. After a short conversation with the other two guards, the SS man agreed. At 11:30, we told him that it was time to go, and to our surprise, he told us to start going, and he followed, the other two guards staying behind in the officer's house.

We couldn't believe what was happening. He was breaking all the rules. We were eight men, and the regulations called for three guards to be with us at all times. But who were we to argue? We started walking, not like in a drill but as a group, and the SS man followed behind us. When we were some distance from Oświęcim and there was nobody around, we heard him say to nobody in particular, "One dog is dead. Now it is time for the other."

We knew what he meant but didn't dare say anything. We didn't even dare turn our heads to look at him. A day earlier, a rumour had spread that Benito Mussolini had been arrested by the freshly formed provisional Italian government. I thought to myself, *Does he want to provoke us, or is it possible that he knows that the war is lost and he wants to repent?* We were glad to hear such words coming out of an SS man's mouth, even not knowing if they were treacherous or sincere. Now, in retrospect, I believe that they were sincere. He brought us to the guard line and repeated a couple of times that we should be back at one o'clock, dead or alive.

We worked at and around the SS officer's house for several weeks, yet we never saw the officer at home. His wife, however, a young, good-looking blond with a one-year-old baby was always at home. They had a maid, a middle-aged woman who was an inmate with a purple triangle that classified her as *Internationale Bibelforscher-Vereinigung*, a Jehovah's Witness. The Jehovah's Witnesses in the camps were Germans who refused to serve in the army, work in munitions factories or in any way contribute to the war effort. Hitler demanded that they renounce their conviction, which meant renouncing their faith, which they categorically refused, and so they spent their time in a concentration camp instead. They were treated better than any of the other groups and were given good positions in camp. The woman with the purple triangle conducted herself in the SS man's house as if she were a member of the family, looking after the baby and eating with them. She once gave me an apple. It was the only fruit I tasted in the four years since the Germans had entered Shershev.

Sometimes other wives of SS officers came to visit. They were all about the same age, well dressed, some with small children. Because of the work going on and the banging in the adjoining rooms, they were compelled to speak louder from time to time. The bit of German that I knew came from my knowledge of Yiddish, which has Germanic origins. The German that I learned in the ghetto and the camps consisted mainly of name-calling, cuss words, curses, and words of abuse and degradation. Although I did not pay particular attention to their conversation, I concluded that there was also a nicer type of German language than the one I was exposed to every day from before sunrise to night.

Sometime in August, our kapo arranged to send a group of carpenters from our factory to the women's *Krankenbau* in Birkenau. We did not understand the reason for it. True, the barracks needed repairs, but it was not so urgent to have to send carpenters from DAW. There were other carpenter *Kommandos* in Auschwitz that were smaller and less specialized, or there were carpenters in Birkenau that could do the job. It must have been in our kapo's interest to send men from our factory. A few times, I was sent there as an assistant carpenter.

On one of my outings there, I saw how a female kapo was treating a group of women prisoners. The group of some thirty women was harnessed to a huge roller, two metres high and four metres long, that they were pulling over a piece of road covered with crushed stones. They kept pulling it back and forth. The female kapo with the green triangle, which identified her as a criminal, kept beating them while heaping on them all kinds of abusive names and curses, so that even the SS men could have taken lessons from her. When they stopped at noon, they got their soup, and I moved closer. To my surprise, I recognized among them a girl from Shershev, Feigl K. She told me that this was a penal group, and she had been sent for some camp transgression. Surprisingly, this girl survived Auschwitz, one of the half a dozen Shershev girls who survived.

On a sunny day in early fall, I was again in the hospital section of the women's camp in Birkenau. We worked independently, without supervision, so whenever there were no SS men or kapos around, we would wander around in the hope of finding something to eat.

Once, as I passed a row of barracks, I noticed that in front of three of them and their wide-open doors, stood a well-fed woman, each with a stick in her hand wearing the unmistakable green triangle of the German criminal. I walked by slowly and looked in, but because of the bright sun, I saw nothing. It seemed to me as if someone had deliberately darkened the windows running along the skylights on both sides of the rooftop. That there was something prohibited inside, I was sure. Perhaps it was food?

One of the women at the doors saw that I was curious and said, "You can go in."

I stopped, perplexed. If one was permitted to go in, why was she guarding the door? What did she have in mind? She could hit me anytime. She needed no excuse. Yet she did not look threatening and said again, "Go in. I will not hit you."

I walked in. It took me several seconds to get used to the darkness, but slowly a picture appeared before my eyes. That picture took away my breath. I could make out the familiar three-tier Birkenau bunks, naked bodies spread out on them. *What were they?* I thought to myself. They must be human, but they were not of this world. Some bodies were sitting or half sitting, leaning, some leaning against each other. Some were squatting. Some sat on the edges of the bunks, immobile, as if frozen, while others gesticulated strangely. The narrow space between the bunks was crowded with the same creatures who barely seemed to move. Even the long flue running the length of the barracks was covered with bodies. They sat and toppled over. Others tried to sit them up again but had no strength to lift them, and they remained on the barracks' muddy earthen floor. At first glance, I took those creatures to be men, for their upper bodies gave no indication of anything else, but I soon realized that they had once been women. I often saw male *Muselmänner* but could not imagine what women *Muselmänner* might look like. How could I have imagined this? In such a barracks in Birkenau we had been three hundred men. Here I was looking at the same size barracks holding at least twice as many women who were condemned to death. It seemed they were being kept without food or water, and most of them were delirious, waiting for the SS to take them to the gas chamber.

The scene felt unreal, as if I were looking at an old, faded, slow-moving film. One small creature, a skeleton, muttered to me incoherently and tried to drag herself closer. As soon as she freed herself from the mass of wretched souls around her, she shuffled toward me. Now I could see her fully and jumped back as I saw that some of her innards were hanging and reaching to the ground from between what should have been her legs, now finger-thin bones covered with grey skin. The sight was so frightening that I ran out of the barracks.

By that time, I had been in Auschwitz-Birkenau long enough to have seen many unbelievable things, but that scene surpassed the most horrible sights I had ever seen in my life. It was everything—frightening, terrible, revolting, heart-rending and incomprehensible. It was something from another world that comes only in a nightmare.

In the late afternoon, when we gathered to return to the DAW factory, we were told by a couple of our men who had dared to venture deeper into the camp that an intense and concentrated selection had taken place in both the men's and women's camps in Birkenau. What I had seen an hour earlier was a result of the women's selection. The return trip to the factory passed without anybody uttering a word. We were all thinking about the selection and about the thousands of young lives that were picked out to be taken to the gas chambers after months of slave labour, torture and pain, of trying to survive in inhumane conditions with the misleading hope that maybe, maybe....

After returning to camp and as soon as the *Appell* was over, we Jews were lined up for a selection, which seemed to me to be the most severe one in the camp since I had arrived and, from what I heard, in the entire history of the camp.

26
Waiting

ALTHOUGH NEWSPAPERS AND radios were not permitted in the camp, a trickle of news filtered through from time to time. I do not know how but a piece of a page from a German newspaper appeared in our *Stube* and started to circulate. Everyone was eager to read it. I was too. On that small piece of paper that contained no more than a dozen lines, I read, "In the last few days, the Soviet command has awarded 10,000 Jewish generals and officers of the Red Army medals for bravery. Let the German people and army take note of it and keep it well in mind to make sure that no Soviet soldier ever sets foot on German soil." For us Jews in our *Stube*, there could not have been any better news, but the Poles in our *Stube* were not at all happy. In fact, they tried to belittle it by saying that there were not as many Jewish officers in the Red Army, or that the Germans deliberately wrote the article to motivate their soldiers to fight harder.

A couple of weeks later, on a Sunday afternoon, a rumour spread in camp that in an hour or two all Jews in Auschwitz I would be taken to Birkenau, meaning to the gas chambers. If Jewish inmates in Auschwitz-Birkenau talked about the possibility of surviving the war, it was no more than wishful thinking. We knew only too well that the Nazis could not and would not leave alive any witnesses to the horrible crimes and mass murders they committed there. We knew that the Germans were retreating on the Eastern Front, and so the rumour that the Jews would soon be taken to the gas chambers sounded logical and believable. My kapo, Janek, sitting on his bunk almost opposite me, said, "Już najwyższy czas"—*It's high time*. This grieved me deeply, for I did not expect to hear this sentiment from him. After all, 80 per cent of his workers were Jews, and their craftsmanship and effort made him the most influential kapo in DAW. Secondly, I had risked my life so many times to bring things into the camp for him, receiving no more than a bit of soup in return.

I felt such confusion, and also grief for having spent eight or nine months in this hell of Auschwitz only to die now that my situation was beginning to stabilize. I was in anguish as I felt time ticking by terribly fast, and I cried to God that he should stop time forever. I remembered that I had hidden in my straw sack a ration of bread as a reserve. I quickly got it out and ate it up, not having a reason to save it any longer.

We sat on our bunks waiting for the announcement to line up in front of the block to be led to Birkenau. Afternoon became evening, and it was quiet in the *Stube* as well as in the entire camp. We figured that the Nazis were waiting for night to commit their grisly work. Then, it was nine o'clock, and the gong sounded, signalling "lights out." We got onto our bunks and waited for the lights to go on and the *Blockältester*'s announcement for us to get out. I tried to imagine how they would lead us—would they let us get dressed, or would we be forced to march the three-and-a-half kilometres from Auschwitz to Birkenau naked in the autumn night?

Eventually the exhaustion of the week's work and the tension of that day took over, and before we knew it, the gong was ringing, and it was 4:30 a.m., our wake time in the summer. Everyone was rushing to straighten their bunks, get washed and stay in line for their piece of bread.

About a month later, as the denizens of our *Stube* were getting ready to settle in for the night, one of the foremen, a prominent inmate who slept alongside the other big shots, announced, "I feel terrible; I don't know what is happening to me." The next morning, he remained in the *Stube* when we went out to the *Appell* and to work. When we came back after work, his bunk was empty. The following evening, we were ordered to go to our *Stube*. The *Blockältester* announced that there was typhus in our *Stube* and we were being quarantined. We were to remain in the *Stube* until further notice and could use the toilets only while the others in the block were at work. For emergency use, a large barrel was put in the less honourable part of the *Stube*, in the Jewish section. Food would be left outside our door.

At the start, it felt like a holiday for us, especially for the Jews, who worked hard twelve hours a day on a nagging, hungry stomach. Imagine, in Auschwitz, sitting all day long, undisturbed, lying stretched out on a bunk and sleeping to your heart's content, getting up just to receive a piece of bread in the morning and soup at noon! I was extra hungry for the first couple of days, as we did not get the extra half piece of bread or the bread soup. But after four or five days, we all lost our appetites. I was able to satisfy my hunger with half the amount of bread in the morning, and I hid the other half in my straw sack.

There were several reasons for the lack of appetite. We were confined to a small space and had to lie on the bunks almost motionless. The lack of movement, the confinement with a hundred others in close quarters with doors and windows closed, and the large wooden barrel that was being used as a toilet filled the room with an unbearable smell was enough to make anybody sick. Additionally, a rumour began circulating in the *Stube* that the Germans were planning to transfer us to Birkenau. We Jews took the rumour about Birkenau very seriously while the Poles shrugged it off, refusing to believe that Poles would be taken to the gas chambers.

When locked up twenty-four hours a day with a hundred people, one can't help but overhear all sorts of conversations. My bunk was close to the big shots, so I was in a good spot to listen to their conversations.

I found out that the sick inmate had contracted his typhus from a girl in Birkenau women's camp. The Birkenau camp was terribly filthy, full of lice and other vermin. It was never fully eradicated of typhus. Listening to the big shots tell of their escapades, I thought that their stories sounded somewhat exaggerated and boastful. One would think that these men were not in the hell of Auschwitz but in a country house where all their thoughts were directed toward women. It became clear to me that the reason our overseers were eager to find us work in the Birkenau women's camp was the women, and we carpenters gave them access. It was sad to listen to them bragging about how they could buy the favour of any Jewish girl for a portion of bread. Poor, unfortunate Jewish girls, innocent and untouched by men, had been brought to that place and violated. They were degraded to a situation that forced them to sell their innocence and dignity for a piece of bread, which, in the end, did not save them from losing their young and tormented lives in the gas chambers.

We remained quarantined for two weeks. At the end of the two weeks, we were taken to the bathhouse, disinfected and showered, and we returned to the *Stube* to receive clean underwear. The next morning, we went to work.

And so, we went on with anguish, hunger, despair and helplessness, and the middle of December 1943 arrived. The Poles in our *Stube* were becoming a little sentimental. They talked among themselves about prewar Christmases, wondering what was going on in their homes, what preparations were taking place. To us Jews, their homesickness seemed so trivial, so insignificant in comparison to our calamity. They were sorry for being unable to be with family to celebrate Christmas, for the loss of a couple years of freedom. We all knew that Germany was losing the war and that the Poles would be free and would return home, where their families were waiting for them. We Jews had come here with our extended families and saw them going up in smoke and flame.

On Christmas Eve, the Poles had a feast in the *Stube*. The big shots took up their places around the table, which was extended to make room for more men. The others sat on the surrounding bunks. Each of them contributed some goodies from their parcels that they had received from home. We Jews sat on our bunks, watching as they ate to their fill while our mouths watered. We did not go to work on Christmas Day, but the next day we did. As we marched out to work that morning, the ground as far as we could see was covered with a pure white blanket of snow that hid for a moment the purgatory beneath it. An hour later, the whole terrain had been trampled by human caricatures who turned it back to its original hell. In those conditions, I lost count of the days, weeks and even months. I didn't even know when the month of January 1944 came and went. February 1944 marked a year since my arrival in Auschwitz.

In mid-February, a sizable group of workers from our hall started to work near Birkenau, installing windows and doors in barracks for the Luftwaffe, the German Air Force. The barracks were less than a kilometre from the nearest buildings, which were the barracks of Birkenau. The work progressed slowly in the cold. The ten hours of work on empty stomachs, plus the hour's march to and from the factory in the freezing cold, dressed only in our camp garb, was unbearable. When we returned to the factory at the end of the day and received our soup, we could hardly hold our spoons.

During my time in Auschwitz, there were a few attempts by prisoners to escape. The attempts were made by Polish prisoners.[7] Jewish inmates believed that for Jews to escape was senseless, for if even they succeeded in getting out, which was doubtful, where would they run? The very first Pole would betray them, and if not the first, there were many others. However, Poles could run to families, friends and acquaintances with whom they could hide. Still, the few who managed to get out were

7 Few Jews managed to escape Auschwitz, but there were some, most famously Rudolf Vrba and Alfréd Wetzler, who escaped in April 1944 and wrote a report about the mass killings at Auschwitz. At least two hundred prisoners altogether escaped over the course of the camp's existence (Dr. Piotr Setkiewicz, Auschwitz-Birkenau Memorial and Museum).

caught and were on display, dead, at the gate of the camp. Others were hanged in public on the *Appell* grounds for all of us to see.

And yet, I felt that I must at least think about escape, for when I would be led into the gas chambers, which I had no doubt would happen, I wanted to have no regrets about not having tried to save myself. To be honest, I approached the whole idea half-heartedly, remembering my attempts to get out of the ghetto. I reasoned that if I could not get out of the ghetto, my chances of getting out of Auschwitz were nonexistent. Nevertheless, I thought of a plan. My plan was to hide in one of the outhouses we were building, which were being taken from our factory to where we were working, near Birkenau. Once there, I would hide in one of the many empty barracks until nightfall and then try to make my escape. When it would be discovered that I was missing, the search would take place in the Auschwitz perimeter because they wouldn't know that I had sneaked out. After two or three days of hiding, I would make my escape.

The plan seemed theoretically achievable to me, but my co-workers had to know about it, as they were the ones who loaded and unloaded the outhouses. As soon as I told them my plan, they turned on me with accusations and charges of wanting to kill them. You know, they claimed, that once it becomes known that we helped you escape, or even knew about it, we are doomed; they'll hang us all. With that, my plan of escaping from Auschwitz ended.

Although the SS tried to keep us isolated from the world, some news continued to filter through, and we knew that the Germans were falling back from the Eastern Front. Exactly where the front was at a given time, we didn't know. It was up to anyone's imagination and prayer. However, good news from the front did not spell good news for us Jewish inmates, and we knew that as the Red Army approached, so did our end. Yet our desire to even know that Germany was losing the war was greater than our sadness that we would not see it happen.

In the middle of a spring night in 1944, we were awakened to the wail of the camp siren. Usually, the wail of the siren was a signal to alert the SS that an escape had been made or attempted. But this always happened during the daytime, while the inmates were outside the camp and within the guards' perimeter. It never happened at night, for there was no escape from within the camp. The entire camp was surrounded by two rows of electrified barbed wires, around which was a tall solid cement wall. All this was brightly lit and surrounded by many guard towers manned by SS men with machine guns.

The next morning we found out that there had been an air raid. There was no visible damage, and we didn't hear a single explosion. One thought was on the minds of the Jewish inmates: how lucky we would be to die from an Allied bomb instead of being driven into the gas chambers by the accursed SS.

The snow was gone and the sun soon dried the large, partly paved square between the main factory building and the subsidiaries of the DAW. One day, during the midday break, I noticed inmates gathering around some large wooden crates in the square. I walked over, and one of the inmates pointed out to me a certain spot on the board of a crate. I saw writing in Hebrew letters and began to read. It was partly a letter, partly a will and testament, but, above all, it was a prayer to anyone who would read it. It read:

> Let it be known that the Jews from this camp worked with these crated machines, that their last assignment was to crate these machines, which would be their last task in their lives, for right after the crating would be done, they would be taken to the open pits that were already waiting for them outside the camp.

Their plea was to a Jew who would read it and by some miracle survive, that he should let it be known that this camp was liquidated on such-and-such a date, and its inmates were put to death. We looked for more messages and found many names as well as short and long messages—all of them containing a farewell word to the reader and to life itself. I thought, *How long will it be before we will be writing such messages and wondering if there is still a Jew in the Nazi domain left to read it?* Judging by the countless trainloads of Jews coming daily to Auschwitz and being sent straight to the gas chambers, I doubted if the legacy of European Jews would ever be shared. Now, over half a century later, I realize that it was a mistake not to try to remember the names of that camp and its history. But then, I didn't think that I would live to write about it.

27
Sosnowitz

ON MAY 4, 1944, before we were even driven out of the *Stube* to the *Appell* in the morning, the block clerk, or *Blockschreiber,* came in and read out two numbers, mine and another man's. He told us that we would not be going to work that day and that right after the *Appell* we should return to the *Stube*. Every inmate dreaded hearing his name being called out; it always meant bad news. As soon as all *Kommandos* left the camp, the *Blockschreiber* led the two of us to the bathhouse, a preliminary to a transport. We joined a larger group and were completely shaved, disinfected, given clean underwear, and a clean jacket and pants. There were close to two hundred of us. I heard Yiddish, Polish, Russian, German and Greek being spoken. It was way past midday, and there was no sign of soup; the stomach growled. Finally, two trucks arrived. We climbed in and were in total darkness as they drove off.

Eventually, we stopped and got out. We were standing on a small elevation, and before us we saw a small camp consisting of a few low barracks and small buildings, all painted green with black tarred roofs. The most unusual thing was the fence surrounding the camp. It was an ordinary wooden fence that one puts around a garden, a fence that could not stop anyone from getting in or out. At that moment, my mind was not on escaping, yet the whole thing seemed bizarre.

We were divided into two groups, and each group was led to a barracks. Inside, there were two-tier wooden bunks. On each single bunk was a straw sack and two dark brown blankets. That evening, we were not permitted to leave the barracks. But looking out of the windows, we saw that the Nazis had left nothing to chance. There were electric lights lighting up the entire enclosure, and beyond the fence stood SS men surrounding it.

The next morning, right after the *Appell*, we were divided in work groups. Among the two hundred inmates were half a dozen Germans who came as supervisors, kapos and block elders. There were also a dozen Poles who were the cooks, registrar and kapos. The minority were sixteen Russians who were supposed to receive the same treatment as we Jews, but they had the additional job of carrying the soup container into the camp, for which they received an extra litre of soup plus the privilege of emptying the remains from the barrels.

Only we, the remaining 150 Jews, were left to do the heavy labour. Among us Jews were many newly arrived Italian Jews, who were given the numbers from 180,000 and up. Except for a couple of them who spoke German, we could not converse with each other. They were uninformed about Jewish persecution and were bewildered and lost. The yelling and cursing in German and the beatings confused them totally. They looked like a sorry lot. The other Jews were me and two others from the Pruzhany ghetto, one from Grodno, a couple from Silesia, and two to three each from central Poland, Germany and France.

We were told that we had been brought there to fence in the camp with an electrified double-barbed-wire fence. After we fenced ourselves in, a large group of *Zugänge*, new arrivals, would come from Auschwitz, and we would start working in the nearby ammunition factory.

Like in Auschwitz in the summer, we got up at 4:30 a.m. Right after the *Appell*, we got a loaf of bread to share among three men. At midday, we had the customary litre of soup, and at night, a cup of camp tea. Leibel Bliskowsky, Shmuel Rosenbaum—also from the Pruzhany ghetto—and I became partners in sharing the daily loaf of bread. Cutting it up in three even pieces wasn't an easy task. How do you divide a loaf of bread and be satisfied that neither you nor your friend has been wronged, not by a bite of bread but even by a crumb? Bread was as important as life. So we cut the loaf into thirds as equally as possible. After each portion passed our scrutiny and we all were satisfied that they were equal, one of us would turn around and another would point at a piece and ask, "Who is this portion for?" and the one who had turned around had to decide. Of course, we took turns being the one to turn around and being the one to point. In this way, we made sure that nobody was wronged.

Here again, we Jews returned to the strict camp ration. The big shots, like the *Blockälteste* and kapos who dished out the soup, took for themselves all they wanted, not to mention the cooks who cooked all kinds of delicacies for themselves. Even the Russian prisoners who were working with us got the extra litre soup for bringing it out from the kitchen. For us Jews there was no opportunity for an extra spoonful of food.

On one narrow side of the camp was the gate, outside of which was a long barracks that served as the living quarters of the SS and the camp commandant, as well as the commandant's office and the kitchens. The ammunition factory in which we were going to work was a kilometre from the camp. Past the road that led to the factory was the outskirts of the city of Sosnowiec. On Sundays, we could see its inhabitants walking leisurely at the edge of the city. We imagined we could see their smiling faces, warmly acknowledging our young lives, soon to be cut short.

Our first task was to walk to the factory, pick up fifty-kilogram bags of cement and carry them back to the camp. Exhausted and hungry, I felt that at any minute I would collapse under the weight of the cement. But that would spell my end, so I summoned my last bit of strength. The only respite from this labour was the walk back to the factory for another bag of cement.

Within a few days, one of the empty barracks was filled with sacks of cement, and we went out to the factory to get iron rods, which would be used as skeletons for the cement posts of the camp fence. Those rods were tied in bundles and carried by two or three men. Carrying those bundles on our shoulders reminded me of the *Holzplatz* in DAW, but it was more bearable without the murderous Pilarek around.

We were divided into groups, and each group was assigned a task: making the wooden frames for the posts, making the skeletons, working at the cement mixer, bringing bags of cement from the barracks or carrying the sand. The kapos did not spare the stick, but worse than them were the countless SS men who watched us day and night. Many of them were young men, straight out of SS training school, with lots of ambition and vigour. They did not leave us alone for a moment. But even worse was the *Arbeitsdienst*, the work supervisor. He was a German inmate in his mid-twenties, handsome and well built with a red triangle. This was unusual, as German inmates with red triangles were usually middle-aged men. Young German inmates had green triangles, which meant they were criminals. When he came to see how the work was progressing, his behaviour toward us made the SS men look like angels. We could not understand why a political prisoner, and therefore Hitler's opponent, would be such a murderer.

Several days later, this young German had a disagreement with the *Lagerältester*, the camp elder, and he was demoted to an ordinary foreman over the sand haulers, among whom I worked. There couldn't have been worse news for us. We wondered how long we could last under his supervision. To our surprise, he told us to put down the baskets and delivered a short speech, telling us that our group would be the best group to work in. Most of the men in our group were Italian Jews. He asked one of them how to say "stop" and the answer was "fermati." "Forward?" "Avanti." He repeated the words a couple of times. We picked up the heavy baskets and walked. As we advanced, he yelled, "Fermati!" We put the baskets down for a couple of minutes and then heard, "Avanti!" We picked them up only to be stopped again twenty metres farther along. We were confused, as were the SS guards around us who walked away in disgust. As if in spite, he would always make us stop when the *Lagerältester* passed by, or the camp commandant, the large SS man who instilled fear and trembling in us.

As the days went by, our foreman talked to us. We found out that he had been in the Schutzpolizei assigned to the Krakow district and had worked with the department of supervision over the Krakow ghetto. He told his stories with visible longing for the days when he would go to the ghetto and come out with a briefcase full of money. When he was caught betraying his leader and his party, he was sent to Auschwitz for punishment, where he turned into a murderer but acted like an angel when it served his purpose.

We suggested that he not antagonize his superiors. He replied, "Have no fear, I know the law better than them, and I'm acting accordingly." What did we Jews know about the law? All we knew was that for us Jews the exit from there was via the crematorium chimney. Eventually, this foreman was sent back to Auschwitz. We never found out why.

The barracks we occupied were neglected, and the rain came in through the roof. A few of us were given the task of tarring the roof. We had to melt hard lumps of tar and spread it thickly over the roof. Although it was May, standing all day on the roof, exposed to the wind, was far from comfortable. Another problem was getting the tar off our hands, which was impossible until we received a mixture containing sulphuric acid. After pouring a few drops in the palms of our hands and quickly rubbing it in, the tar began melting. We had to stick our hands under running water immediately. They became clean but were red and raw. We finished that job in a week.

It seemed that the Germans planned to enlarge the camp, for they started to fence in a much larger area than the few barracks needed. A system was created where some inmates made the cement posts, others brought them over and lay them down near the holes and others dug the posts into the holes. The digging progressed nicely until the commandant noticed that the posts were not in a very straight line, and he ordered the holes to be dug again. More men were sent to do that job, including me. I had experience digging postholes from the ghetto, and I lined up the posts. This time they remained in the ground.

Slowly, the innocent little camp began to look like a concentration camp. The posts stood five metres apart, and we strung barbed wire on them and attached powerful electric lights. Two doctors arrived from Auschwitz, both Hungarian Jews, and an empty barracks was converted into an infirmary. In another barracks, a small space was partitioned off to be the *Bekleidungskammer* (clothing room). The SS sent in a truckload of underwear, and from then on, we changed our underwear weekly. We were allowed to shower any time, even daily.

By the end of June 1944, the camp was ready. The fence was in place with bright lights on the posts that were lit up all night, and the watchtowers were equipped with powerful spotlights and guards with machine guns. We were told to expect the *Zugänge*. The next day they arrived, some 650 Jewish men who had been in another camp and were taken to Auschwitz, where they received their tattooed numbers and went through all the formalities, like shaving, disinfecting showers and receiving clean clothing, and then they were sent on to us.

They were acquainted with life in camp, though not with Auschwitz. They hadn't even gone through a selection, maybe because they were not emaciated. In fact, they looked like a healthy group of men between the ages of twenty and forty. They arrived in Sosnowitz dressed in civilian clothes with the addition of long, wide red strips on the legs of their pants and red crosses painted on their jackets. Their shirts, which were supposed to serve as undershirts, were new or almost new, which did not escape the notice of our overseers. The first thing they did was order the new arrivals to take them off, and they were given real camp undershirts. Those new shirts became currency in the hands of our overseers who exchanged them for meat, sausage, butter and liquor with the civilian Poles who worked in the factory.

We started working in the factory the day after the new inmates arrived. We were divided into two twelve-hour shifts, and the day shift, which I was in, set out on a well-worn road that went past a small lake. The building we were to work in had been a wire factory, and the Nazis had converted it into an ammunition factory. In one part, they produced heavy artillery shells and in the other anti-aircraft guns. Upon entering the plant, we were divided into two groups and taken to the different sections of the factory. The factory employed French civilians, Poles from the city and vicinity, and now Auschwitz inmates. My group was to produce cannon barrels, and the thirty of us Jews were assigned as assistants to the civilian workers. Our job was to sweep the cement floors around the huge machines, pick up the metal shavings, and hand the tradesmen wrenches and other tools. In a word, we were errand boys.

Here, for the first time, my experience in the technical trade school in Brest-Litovsk came in handy. Although our kapo accompanied us to work, he had nothing to do there, not having any concept of what was going on. The work was specialized, and there were enough engineers and artisans who knew how to work and how to supervise. I was assigned to a Frenchman who operated a large lathe. In the first few hours, he saw that I knew something about operating a lathe, and he encouraged me to try it. When his eight-hour shift ended and a Pole came to replace him, he told the Pole that I was a tradesman and he could let me work a bit on the lathe. The Pole was delighted and let me work on the crude parts of the barrel. Convincing himself that he could count on me, he walked away to socialize with other workers.

Because we worked twelve-hour shifts and the Polish and French civilians worked eight, I got to know all three men who worked at that lathe. The kapo was seldom seen, and the civilian workers had no authority over us except when it concerned work. So I would walk around, interested in what it took to produce a cannon barrel.

It didn't take long for the supervisor of our part of the factory to notice that my civilian boss was loafing around and I was doing the work. He soon made me independent, and I had no boss over me. From then on, I spent twelve hours a day, six days or nights a week at the lathe. Each group worked the day shift one week and the night shift the next.

Next to me was another lathe, which was operated by three men over the course of a twenty-four-hour day, two Poles and a Frenchman. They had very little to do with each other. To my regret, I never got to know the Frenchman, partly because of the language barrier, but also because he spent every free moment with his fellow Frenchman who was working nearby. When so far away from home in times of war, when longing for dear ones, even the sound of one's mother tongue can give some comfort.

I became friendly with one of the Poles, Tadek Indelak. He hailed from Katowice, some ten kilometres away, and he commuted to the factory daily. He was a friend in the full sense of the word. Polite and trusting, he confided in me as if I were his childhood best friend. He shared with me all his innermost secrets, even details about his relations and experiences with his girlfriend. Quite often, he expressed his sympathy with the Jews. He never used the word "Żydzi" (Jews) which many Poles used in a derogatory, disrespectful connotation. Instead, he used the words "ci ludzie" (those people). He was careful not to apply to me the words "arrested" or "interned." When he spoke about my past, he didn't say "before you were brought here" or "before you were arrested," but instead "w cywilu" (in civilian life). His language showed his decency and modesty.

The second Pole was a man of about thirty. He was not so polite when speaking of Jews, although he showed a fair amount of tolerance toward me. He justified it by the fact that I was the only craftsman among all the other Jews who worked in the plant. It did not do any good telling him that I came from a shtetl where all tradesmen, craftsmen and artisans were Jews and that in all the shtetls around mine it was the same. His girlfriend, a girl of about my age, worked in the same factory. When they worked at night on the same shift, she would visit him during the half-hour midnight break, when all the civilian workers ate a meal. They would come from the factory kitchen and sit down to eat while we inmates watched, our mouths watering. I once watched as his girlfriend took two mouthfuls of food, turned up her nose and threw the food in the garbage can. I thought to myself, *She knows that we are hungry, why doesn't she offer it to me or another inmate instead of throwing it out?* A few nights later, the Pole and his girlfriend returned from the kitchen, he with his container of food, she empty-handed. I understood that she did not approve of the factory's food and did not even bother taking it. Another week or so passed, and again we were working the night shift. At the midnight break, the civilians went to get their meal. I saw the Pole coming from the direction of the kitchen alone and holding a container of food in each hand. He walked over to me, stretched out one hand and said, "This is from my girlfriend. She wants you to eat it."

I took the container and looked inside. I saw that the food was untouched. It consisted of a heaping ladleful of mashed potatoes covered with gravy and, on top, a piece of warm sausage. I hadn't seen such food in years. After I finished eating, I got up to wash it. The Pole would not hear of it, saying that his girlfriend would wash both containers. When I asked him where she was so that I could thank her for such a treat, he replied that she was embarrassed to come over and I should not feel obligated to her. This happened several times. Her boyfriend told me that she did not like Jews but that I was the exception. It was too good to last. A short time later, she got a permanent day job in the factory, and the day shift did not get lunch.

As I became close to Tadek, I discovered that he came from a poor family. He did not help me with food simply because he had nothing to give. He ate the midnight meal with much gusto. One day he asked me if I could procure a pair of camp drawers for him. This question intrigued me given that camp underwear had a special design for prisoners. They were a medium blue colour with narrow dark blue stripes running through them. Tadek told me that an acquaintance of his got a pair from an inmate for a loaf of bread and succeeded in dyeing them a darker shade, which made them unrecognizable as camp underwear.

A few days later, when we were changing underwear, I tore my pair into two pieces and instead of turning in a pair of underwear, I threw half a pair into the dirty pile. The *Stubendienst* saw me throwing two items, a shirt and underpants. A week later, I tossed the other half. I now had an extra pair, which I took to work and gave to Tadek. The following morning, he brought me a loaf of bread. And so we began to barter. Every two weeks, I brought him a pair of underwear, and he would bring me a loaf of bread. The loaf of bread did not go far to quiet my hunger, but it helped.

The big shots in camp now had one of their own in the clothing factory and started bartering with the civilian Poles in the factory for sausages, meat and liquor. Each of those big shots found a Jewish inmate to act as middleman between them and the Poles. They would decide on the price, and the hungry Jews had to haggle with the Poles. One of the kapos, a German inmate of about sixty who wore a green triangle and looked and acted as if he had spent his life behind bars, approached me and proposed that I be his middleman, and I gladly accepted. One of this kapo's jobs was to be at the gate and help the SS men count us as we marched out in the morning and returned in the evening. When it became known that we were stealing things from camp and selling them to the Poles, the SS started to search us on our way in and out. This kapo helped them search us. He would pretend to search me and place a flat package inside my jacket, then let me through. At work, I would open the package and offer it to Tadek, quoting the price the kapo had given me, adding half a loaf of bread for my trouble.

Those transactions took place two to three times a week. Having tested me and finding me trustworthy, he started bringing me the nice shirts that the Jews from the labour camp had come with. Those shirts were unobtainable in war-torn Poland, and one was worth a kilogram of sausage or meat, or even a bottle of liquor. For my trouble, I never received more than half a loaf of bread, and I shared it with my friend Leibel Bliskowsky, one of my two partners in the bread ration. By that time, our third partner had moved to the other shift and to another block. Leibel and I remained friends and shared every bit of food. I can say in all sincerity that in those days I was the bigger earner, although Leibel tried to reciprocate.

A couple of times, we received a few cigarettes. I didn't smoke, so I gave them to Leibel, who did. The next morning, as we received our bread, Leibel cut off a piece of his bread and slid it over to my side of the bench. I am so glad that I did not accept it, otherwise I would not forgive myself, even today.

As in Auschwitz proper, in Sosnowitz the privileged or prominent inmates had it relatively good. For them it was a matter of time until the war came to an end and their sentence would be revoked. Their aim was to stay alive and make their being there as bearable as possible. To this end, they organized different amusements. Of course, the object of their ridicule and mockery had to be the Jews. Our first *Lagerälteste*, a German inmate in his mid-thirties who wore a green triangle, was a giant of a man who took delight in watching Jews being beaten. He introduced boxing matches at which two starving Jews would fight it out with bare fists over bruised faces and bleeding noses for a piece of bread.

One such match got him so excited that he wanted to participate himself, even though it made no sense to have a match between a man who was 6'4" and 250 pounds and one who was 5'8" and 90 pounds. The *Lagerälteste* called for a volunteer. As most of the inmates at that time were Italian Jews, his call had to be translated into Italian. To everybody's surprise, a young man stepped forward. We all thought that he did it as a joke or that maybe he didn't understand the challenge. A German-speaking Italian Jew explained to him twice more what it was all about, but that young man insisted on challenging the *Lagerälteste*. The two of them got into the makeshift arena. The *Lagerälteste* was a head taller than his opponent and weighed three times as much. The scene was laughable. The *Lagerälteste* sent for two pairs of boxing gloves, and the two men faced each other. The *Lagerälteste* turned to the interpreter and said, pointing at his opponent, "Tell him not to be afraid to hit me back; make him understand it."

When the Italian heard what the interpreter said, he replied, "I am not afraid of him. He should be afraid of me." His reply brought a smile on everyone's face—such empty bravado.

When the round started, we all realized that the Italian Jew was an excellent boxer and was not joking when he said that the *Lagerälteste* should be afraid of him. When the fight was over, the Jewish young man was the undisputed winner and, notwithstanding the *Lagerälteste*'s embarrassment, he took the defeat well. Some of the big shots gave the winner some extra bread for his hard work.

A couple of weeks later, that *Lagerälteste* left the camp for Auschwitz due to a sore that developed on his leg and refused to heal. In his place came a German with a red triangle, a man of about fifty whose face expressed both intelligence and authority. During the *Appell,* he would speak to us for a few minutes, issuing new orders or decrees. One couldn't help but admire his bearing, as well as his voice and his diction. He evoked so much respect that even the always-yelling SS men fell silent to listen to him.

On our way to and from work, we were required to sing. We Jews did not feel like singing, but the Russian inmates, who were fed better and hoped to get out alive, sang patriotic Soviet songs. Eventually, my friend Leibel and I joined them in singing. To us, it was a secret protest against Nazism and all it stood for. When the SS found out the meaning of the words, they forbade singing Russian songs, so we sang vulgar Polish songs instead. The more obscene the words, the more the Polish Jews sang, especially when we lined up in the factory before marching back to camp, when all the Poles watched and listened. This too was a sort of protest, and act of contempt for the guards, for the people around and for humanity at large.

One summer morning, as we were marching back to camp after a night's work, we passed by the small lake halfway between the factory and the camp and saw a man floating face down in the water. The next day we found out from some civilian Polish workers in the factory that the man was a Jew who had apparently killed himself. Every Jew in the camp talked about it, and I am sure that everyone was bothered by the question—what drove him to it? How did a Jew manage to stay alive until the middle of 1944? Was he hidden by a Pole whom he paid and was driven away when his money ran out? Or maybe the Pole feared for his life and told him to go? How hopeless was his situation that it forced him to suicide? What tragic stories did that man take with him? I felt more sorry for that Jew than for myself. As far as I was concerned, my fate was already sealed. It was only a matter of time. But I imagined that for that poor Jew, every minute, every hour, was a struggle. How many times a day did his mood change from hope to despair? How many times a day did the sky fall on him, and how many times did he manage to lift it only for it to come crashing down on him again? There was no end to Jewish suffering, to Jewish misery.

That event stayed in my mind for a long time, maybe because it was an exception. The drowned man was no ordinary *Muselmann*, the skin and bones who were dying daily by the hundreds in Auschwitz. This Jew had dared to fool and outsmart the Germans and tried to survive them. To me he was like a falcon shot down in mid-flight.

On Sundays, when we did not work, many of us would sit on the ground leaning against the barracks wall, watching the civilian population walking leisurely on the city sidewalks a stone's throw away from us. We felt a terrible melancholy enveloping us, as we couldn't help but imagine our final moments. Yet during the hypocritical two-hour compulsory bedrest on Sunday afternoons, we would lie on our bunks and dream aloud about the miracle that we fervently prayed should happen—that we should somehow come out alive—and about what we would do then. Many of us wished to be guards around gas chambers into which the victorious army would herd the Nazis, just like they were herding us now. How naive we were to even think about surviving, and even more so to think that the world, the leaders of the powers whose armies were now squeezing the Germans from every side, would give a damn about the Jews.

Among the Jews who came to our camp from the labour camp, one could find a diversity of characters and intellects, from total ignoramuses to PhDs. One person I got to know had a PhD in chemistry. Some were ordinary Jews—humble, meek, non-pretentious—and others were self-respecting, to a degree vain and proud, maybe more than was good for them. There were many who had some kind of talent. A few of them showed virtuoso qualities as singers, and they entertained us—if that is the right word—with old-time sentimental and moving Yiddish songs while we got ready at night. I know of two from that group who survived and are now cantors in Toronto. Others were artful storytellers with an inexhaustible supply of stories from their own lives. Most of the men were in their late teens and early twenties, but there were also men in their late twenties and thirties who had studied in Austria, Italy and even in Germany up to the mid-1930s.

Our camp eventually numbered close to nine hundred men, 95 per cent of them Jews. Now and then a group of new inmates would arrive from Auschwitz to replace those who had died, and of course, only Jews died. The non-Jews were a privileged group, holding the best positions, like the *Blockälteste*, kapos and cooks. Even the Russian prisoners had it better than us Jews. They mostly kept to themselves, though my friend Leibel and I were treated more warmly by them because we spoke Russian and came from the part of Poland that had been annexed to the Soviet Union in 1939, so we were considered countrymen. We found out that among these inmates were four Red Army lieutenants, one of them a Jew by the name of Naftaly. The Germans did not know that he was a Jew, but a couple of weeks after arriving he himself made it official. There were also two former Ukrainian policemen, Nazi collaborators who must have committed some transgression. And then there were a few former Soviet soldiers from different detachments. While they were telling each other stories from the front, I overheard one say how during a retreat on the Ukrainian front, a truckload of Soviet Jews escaping the German advance had caught up with them, and how the Soviet soldiers had forced the Jews off the truck and abandoned their position so that they could flee deeper into the Soviet Union, leaving the Jews at the mercy of the approaching Germans.

The eldest former Soviet soldier, who was between forty-five and fifty and nicknamed "Uncle Grisha" by the other Soviet prisoners, questioned me about Auschwitz, and especially about Birkenau. He wanted me to describe every detail, from the moment the trainloads of Jews arrived to the moment the doors of the gas chambers closed behind them, even the process of burning the bodies and disposing of the ashes. Uncle Grisha was close to one of the lieutenants, a tall, handsome man who listened in on our conversations. I wondered why Uncle Grisha asked these questions. Less than two months later, I understood.

It was about ten at night, and I was working the night shift when we suddenly heard a piercing whistle. Many of the machines fell silent, and the kapo yelled, "Fall in! Everybody fall in!" By the time we were lined up properly, SS men were swarming around us. We were counted several times, and we were two inmates short. Uncle Grisha and the lieutenant were missing. The SS immediately started a search, and we were ordered to return to work. The search continued all night with no success. The missing inmates were not found. In the morning, the Russian prisoners were ordered to take off their civilian clothes that were marked with large red crosses, and they were given the standard Auschwitz striped uniforms instead. Their leather footwear was taken away, and they were given shoes with cloth tops and wooden soles. Two weeks later, four prisoners went missing. The SS conducted a search and again came up with nothing.

The first two escapees must have simply turned their clothes inside out so that the red crosses were not seen and put on civilian caps acquired from Poles to cover their shaven heads. They could have simply walked by the guard, who did not bother to check their IDs. The second group overwhelmed the guard. The next day a truck arrived and took the remaining Soviet prisoners back to Auschwitz.

Two days later, the camp commandant ordered us to dig in two wooden posts a metre and a half apart and to fasten a piece of pipe to connect the two posts at the top. The contraption was in the middle of the *Appell* square. We were speculating about its purpose. The next morning, after the night's work, the door of our barracks opened, and two of the four escapees walked in. Suddenly the purpose of the two posts with the metal bar across became clear—it was a gallows. We all wanted to know what had transpired since their escape and what happened to the other two who escaped with them, but we did not dare to ask them questions at such a moment.

The two escapees sat on a bunk facing the window. Looking out, they could see the *Appellplatz* and the newly erected gallows. The younger of the two turned to me and asked, "When did they put up this *turnik* [horizontal bar used in gymnastics]?"

"The day after you escaped," I answered. I reasoned that they had not yet been caught on the first day after their escape, so it would not seem as though the gallows had been made for them. It seemed for a moment that I had succeeded in setting their minds at ease. But after the distribution of the midday soup, the camp kapo came in holding a razor and started to shave their necks, and they lost their composure. After the kapo left, there was dead silence in the barracks. Many long minutes passed before some of us began whispering to each other. But those close to the two Russian men didn't dare utter the slightest sound.

The two condemned prisoners continued to sit next to each other, looking out the window. The younger was murmuring to himself, and tears were rolling slowly down his cheeks. Nobody said anything. What was there to say? Still, I went over and sat near the younger one, joining him in looking out the window. Now, being close to him, I could identify his murmur as an old Russian parting song, sung by a son to his mother. I had heard the song for the first time from my parents when we were in Khomsk, when we sat in the dark on those long evenings in 1941. In those despair-filled nights, my parents would quietly hum this song, a depressing song befitting a hopeless situation. I am not sure if I said anything to those two escapees, but even if I did, I doubt they heard it.

The barracks door opened, and a couple of SS men and some kapos marched in. They took the two escapees into the washroom, from where they soon emerged with their hands tied behind their backs. We were ordered to leave the barracks and form a large quadrangle around the gallows. Every SS man and guard in the camp, except those in the watchtowers, was there, and they stood around us. For the first time, there were machine guns in the camp proper. To me, to all of us, this display of force looked ludicrous. What were they afraid of? That we would oppose the hanging? The camp kapo tied two nooses onto the metal bar and placed a short bench underneath it. The two Russian escapees were helped up onto the bench and stood with the nooses dangling in their faces while the SS registrar read out their death sentence in German—not that they understood, not that it mattered to them. The camp commandant nodded, and the camp kapo kicked the bench out from under them. Their bodies were taken to Auschwitz that same afternoon.

My close friend Leibel worked at assembling the cannon barrels. The cannon barrel consisted of tubes that fitted into each other, and the inner tube consisted of two parts. The lower part took the impact of the explosion during the firing and got damaged much sooner than the upper part, so it had to be replaced often. The joining of those two parts required delicate work with special tools. One excessive motion with a file or slam with a rubber hammer could cause many hours of extra work. Still, Leibel, with his Polish civilian co-worker, managed to sabotage those locking mechanisms in such a way that it could not be detected during the final inspection.

Leibel became very friendly with that Pole, who was a true socialist and carried no animosity toward Jews. Once he offered to sell Leibel a handgun for ninety German marks. The idea of possessing a weapon appealed to me very much, for after the successful escape of the first two Russians and two out of the second group, the idea of escaping had awakened again in me. Unfortunately, it was impossible to procure the ninety marks.

During the midnight break, we Jews would gather in quiet corners of the plant and conduct political debates. The civilian Polish workers often joined in. Not fearing betrayal from either side, we exchanged ideas and opinions freely. During one such midnight break, I walked over to my friend Leibel for a chat and found him deep in conversation with several inmates and Polish civilians. One of the Jewish inmates was saying, "If we should survive...," but before he had the chance to finish what he had in mind, he was interrupted by a Pole who said loudly, "If you will survive, we Poles will finish you off." I noticed that a couple of the Poles felt uncomfortable with his pronouncement, but nobody objected out loud.

The *Lagerkommandant* was a typical SS man of the old guard, a person without education or moral depth who rose from being a store window washer to his SS rank because of his unquestionable devotion and cruelty. His rudeness manifested not only toward us inmates but even toward his equals.

When the Allies liberated France in the summer of 1944, many Nazi bigwigs found themselves back in Germany without the high positions they had held in France, and so they were appointed to all sorts of jobs in factories. Such a man was appointed to a position in our factory. What his assignment was, we did not know, and I doubt if he knew. He would wander around aimlessly among the workers and the noisy machines. One day, this middle-aged German started beating up one of the inmates. He only stopped when he ran out of steam. Within a few minutes, I saw the *Lagerkommandant* striding in. His threatening appearance made us uneasy. We had never seen the huge SS man in such an uncontrollable rage, his long black leather coat unbuttoned and flapping open on each side of him like the foreboding wings of the angel of death. The sight terrified us, and we wondered who his victim would be this time.

To our astonishment, he strode over to that newly arrived Nazi Party big shot and barked at him, "What right do you have to order my men around?" using the words "meine Leute" (my men). It was the first time in the camps or in the ghetto that I had heard a German referring to us Jews as men. It seemed that the camp commandant didn't receive a satisfactory answer, for he raised his voice even higher. From then on, that civilian German had nothing to do with us inmates. We knew only too well that the camp commandant hadn't acted out of love for Jews. He simply resented that a civilian had interfered in matters that were under his jurisdiction.

We knew much about the military situation from the friendlier civilian Poles. We knew that the Red Army was already at the Vistula River—so near, yet, for us Jews, so far. Perhaps, with the next offensive, the Red Army would reach us. But would the Nazis wait until that offensive to annihilate us, or would they start sooner? And so, the autumn of 1944 passed, accompanied by the unachievable dream of liberation.

On Christmas Eve, we went to work. The civilians were allowed to go home two hours early. The Poles I knew came over to wish me a happy holiday. Suddenly, all the engines stopped for the first time since we started working there. The silence was eerie. We sat or stood in groups, not knowing what to do with ourselves. In that strange stillness, while all the civilians, the free people, left for their homes or families, the rest of us felt the deep hurt and pain for everyone and everything we had lost. There was no reason for us to stay in the factory, so we were lined up and marched to the camp. To our surprise, we received potatoes with a spoonful of jam for dinner. When we finished, we received another portion of potatoes but without jam. It was the first time in years that I went to sleep without hunger pangs.

28
Death March

ON JANUARY 17, 1945, we arrived at the factory at 6:00 p.m. to work the night shift. A certain tension could be felt among the workers, as a day or two earlier a rumour had spread that the Red Army was starting an offensive along the Vistula River. Common sense dictated that the Germans would do something with us Jews. The question was: Would they take us to Birkenau to be gassed or would they shoot us here? If there was ever a time to try to save ourselves, it had to be then. We continued our work, but at a slow pace, and the overseers did not pay attention. The inmates went from one person to another, asking for ideas or advice. The closest friend I had there was Leibel Bliskowsky, and I wanted to be alone with him for a few minutes. But as soon as I went over to him or he came to me, other inmates surrounded us. Because of our longer stay in Auschwitz, the others thought that we might have some sort of solution to our desperate situation. As we were in this state of confusion, time was running out.

At about ten o'clock that evening, we heard a whistle, and a large number of guards appeared at the entrances. We were ordered to line up to go back to the camp. *Here*, I thought, *the game is over. Now they will take us to Birkenau or shoot us in the camp*. As we stood in the factory yard, lined up five in a row and surrounded by guards, all the lights suddenly went out throughout the entire plant, and everything was in total darkness. This was the time to run and hide in the factory, but I needed a few seconds to get used to the darkness so that I wouldn't run into SS men. The SS men were everywhere. Those precious few seconds were wasted, for as I was preparing for my dash, the lights came on. I looked around and saw that all the rows were even; nobody was missing. I knew then that for the second time in my life I had missed the chance to save myself.

We were led into the camp and told to prepare for a march. We received a whole loaf of bread each, which I cut into quarters and put in my pockets. We were told to take a blanket and stand outside the barracks. At 5:00 a.m. on January 18, 1945, we were led out of the camp, five abreast, into the unknown. We were led through Sosnowiec as the city was awakening. It had been a long time since I walked down a street between houses. Now and then a person walked by, looking at us with curiosity but without stopping. Then we were out of the city and in an open field. The wind cut into my face and neck and penetrated my so-called coat, chilling me to the bone. I saw that some others had wrapped their blankets around their bodies, and I did the same. The blanket did break the wind. I observed our guards and was surprised they were mostly older men between forty and fifty, and they were dressed in air force uniforms. They walked stooped alongside us, the collars of their coats turned up against the wind. They didn't look at us and seemed to be preoccupied with their own thoughts. They straightened up and became aggressive only when SS men got closer. The SS men walked up and down our column, making sure there were no stragglers. If someone fell behind, he got beaten, and if this did not help, he was ordered to get off the road and was shot. At the very end of the column, there were a few dozen prisoners pulling and pushing a fully loaded large farmer's wagon.

With nightfall, we entered a town called Bytom. We were locked inside a school. At least we were protected from the wind and there was enough room to stretch out. I ate a quarter of my bread and made sure the other three quarters were deep in my pockets. Apparently, I slept too well, for when I woke up before daybreak, I found only two quarters of my bread. I felt the loss, but I did not begrudge the thief. I knew only too well the feeling of hunger.

At daybreak we continued the march. We did not receive anything to eat or drink, and I ate one of my remaining two quarters of bread. We continued marching all day long. It was already dark when we passed through Gleiwitz. On the other side of town, we were herded into a public building in which there was hardly enough room to lie down. In the middle of the night, I got up to use the bathroom and had to step on people to get there. When I finally made it back to my spot, there was no place to lie down, and I had to spend the rest of the night on my feet. That morning, I finished my last quarter of bread, not knowing that that was the last piece of bread, or any food for that matter, I would have for almost two weeks.

After marching the whole day, we were locked up again in a building where we were just as tightly crowded as the previous night. That night I had to use the bathroom again. I wasn't about to spend another half a night standing, so I urinated on the floor where I was lying. My blanket sucked up some of it, and by morning it was dry.

In the wagon that some of us were forced to pull and push were the guards' knapsacks and loaves of bread, tins of meat and other cans of food, which the guards ate while escorting us. Those pushing the wagon tried again and again to stick their hands in the wagon to pinch off a piece of bread. However, if a guard noticed, he gave the guilty one such a beating that he would remember it for the rest of his just-shortened life. It was worse still if the SS men noticed. They simply took the transgressor to the side of the road and shot him. It was even worse for those who were harnessed to the wagon. They had to pull with their last bit of strength without even having a chance to try to get a piece of bread. If they fell, they were replaced by others. If the one who fell could still get up, he was sent to march, and if not, he was dragged off the road and shot.

That night, we were herded into a school building. It was a large two-storey building, well lit and roomy enough to walk from room to room and from floor to floor. A few of my acquaintances approached me to suggest that we attempt to escape. Their plan was to jump from the window down onto a guard below, throw a blanket over him and make a run for it. It was a bold idea but seemed impractical. Where would we run—hungry, exhausted, in prison garb and on German soil? To me the plan meant suicide. I refused to join them, and they would not go without me.

At daybreak, we continued our march. Later that morning, we entered another town, onto a main street. It was cold but sunny, and without a breeze it was bearable. Our camp commandant walked in the middle of the street as usual. On one side of him marched the reporting officer, or *Rapportführer*, and on the other, a non-commissioned SS officer whom we referred to as "the Executioner," as he seemed to take delight in shooting. Behind them, we marched five in a row, a long line of *Häftlinge*, or inmates, surrounded by guards, and at the very end was the large wagon pulled by prisoners.

We arrived in another town. There were people in the street, and they looked at us with some curiosity and yet with an expression that indicated that they would rather not see us. Their faces betrayed tension and anxiety. From the sidewalk they called out to our camp commandant, "What shall we do? Shall we run or stay?"

He yelled back to them, "No, no, stay. You have lots of time."

Above me, I heard a voice. I looked up and saw a hefty young blond German woman leaning out from an upper-floor window, saying, "We are not moving. We are not running away. We have no fear."

The camp commandant was beaming. Along the street people kept asking him what to do. He was now a big man, the former window cleaner, and people were asking him advice and showing him respect. In his wisdom, he told them all to stay.

I couldn't believe my ears. Was it possible that the Red Army was already so close that Germans would become refugees, leaving behind their homes and possessions? Were they indeed losing the war? I realized that my situation was hopeless and that I would not see the final victory. Nevertheless, to see Germans on German soil contemplating running from the approaching Red Army was exhilarating.

That evening, we reached Ratibor. We were led up a large ramp and into an unheated slaughterhouse, a building made entirely from stone and cement. The huge sloping slaughter ramp was still wet and slippery from the day's slaughter, and the smell of blood and intestines hung heavy in the air. It was so cold that we spent the night hugging each other in order not to freeze. In the morning, a few men lay on the wet platform, dead, their bodies swollen.

It was already daylight, yet we were not moving. An hour went by and then another. We heard a rumour that they were going to cook soup for us. We got livelier. It was almost a week since we'd had any cooked food, four days since I'd had anything to eat or drink. How long could we go on like this? If somebody had told me in Sosnowitz that I could go for a week without food or drink, I would have laughed in his face. And yet here I was, still alive and on my feet.

In the afternoon, we were lined up for soup. Bowls appeared from somewhere, and the first few dozen men received their soup, but then they ran out of bowls. The rest of the men would have to wait until the first group finished and turned in the bowls. The first group had not yet finished their soup when our *Rapportführer* walked in with a group of SS guards and ordered us to fall in line. Suddenly, we were being driven outside and ordered to march quickly. We were proceeding much faster than before, and I could sense the guards' urgency. Still, the main thing on my mind was the bowl of soup that I had been deprived of. I also wondered how the few who did get the soup but didn't have the chance to finish it felt.

We were now marching on a side road between snow-covered fields, passing a farmstead every few hundred metres. A column of German soldiers caught up to us. They were dressed in ordinary German armed forces, or Wehrmacht, uniforms, and they sat on or ran alongside small sleds pulled by undernourished horses. As they passed us in a single line, they gesticulated in such a way as if to say, "It is all over." Some of them said in Ukrainian, "In a few hours you'll be free."

I realized that they were Ukrainian volunteers who had joined the German army. The mind did not want to or was unable to accept such good news. However, as if to confirm their words, we suddenly heard the staccato of machine-gun fire coming from behind us. Could it have been gunfire from the Red Army?

We entered a small forest that was crawling with German soldiers working feverishly at mining the trees. They were tying three to four sticks of explosives around each tree trunk so that the fallen trees would form a barricade against the Soviet tanks. The soldiers were so absorbed in their work that they didn't even glance at us, as if the close to a thousand men passing right by them were ghosts.

As darkness fell, we were still marching—the first time we marched at night. The Soviets couldn't be far behind, I thought, and there might be a chance to sneak away, but what then? Going back into the forest was not feasible because it was filled with soldiers, and wandering around behind the front line, I would either get caught or shot. If I hid in some bushes, I would freeze or die of hunger. So I kept on marching. Anyone who fell behind was shot.

I don't know how to describe that night. We were on an endless march, liberation was only a few kilometres behind us, judging by the thunder of cannons and yet, we were still in the hands of beasts and our chances of survival were very low. Still, the march continued. Before dawn, as I dragged my feet, my eyes started closing, and I was falling asleep. Drained of strength, beyond exhaustion, walking in a daze, one prayer kept repeating itself in my mind: *Let me have just one more warm drink. May it even be the camp tea, and then you can put an end to my anguish.* My eyes just didn't want to stay open. Each person tried to hold on to the next one, who shook him off, for he had trouble walking himself.

With daylight, the sleepiness eased off a bit. The march continued. The road we were on looked abandoned, and so did the scattered farms alongside it. There was total silence, except for the occasional explosion, and there was not a living soul in sight. We hoped that the Soviets were getting closer. We passed a cluster of houses. Did I see it or just imagine a person's head in a window?

We arrived at a crossroads where we saw a vehicle packed with civilians. In the afternoon, we approached a town. Our march had changed into feet dragging. Ahead of us was a bridge over a river, and the outskirts of town was visible along the opposite bank. While on the bridge, I noticed a long row of shallow holes on the far shore, and in each of them stood or sat a single soldier. Even to me, inexperienced in military matters, the whole thing looked very unprofessional. The soldiers seemed too exposed. As we got closer, I saw that they were boys, no older than sixteen. I thought to myself, *They will not save Germany*.

However, once we entered the town, my opinion changed dramatically. There was a constant stream of military trucks, coming and going in all directions. There were soldiers at every street corner. Officers were walking around purposefully and were stopped every so often by the countless military police, or gendarmes, who were patrolling and checking their papers. Our camp commandant, in all his largeness and glory, walked down the middle of the street, flanked by the *Rapportführer* and the Executioner, and we walked behind him, surrounded by the guards. However, this did not prevent a couple of gendarmes from stopping him to ask for papers. He obliged with great fanfare, saying in a loud voice and with a dramatic wave of his hand in our direction, "And there are all my people," taking in with one sweep the guards and the guarded.

We passed a van with a few gendarmes hanging around it. One of them opened the rear door, and a pile of cartridge belts fell to the ground. One of the gendarmes yelled out to our guard, "Here, take some bullets! You will need them."

One of our guards yelled back, "We have enough!"

Soon we left that town behind and arrived at a barn, where we collapsed, exhausted. Where were they taking us? How much longer could we keep going without food? After forty-eight hours of marching, we could finally sit or lie down and speak freely. Everyone had their own thoughts about what was happening. Some came up with worthless plans. Somebody proposed hiding in the hay in that huge barn. But the Germans had counted us as we were driven inside the barn, and they would be sure to count us in the morning. They would look for those hiding, find and shoot them. Our chances of surviving were slim, yet the Soviets were so close and getting closer by the hour.

In the morning, we were counted and some were missing. A few SS men remained behind, and when they caught up with us, the barn was already out of sight and earshot, so we could only imagine what had happened. We were now on a side road that ran through open fields. The wind blew through my blanket and penetrated every bone in my emaciated body. In some spots, the blowing wind deposited a lot of snow on the road, which made walking harder. The only part of my body that had not felt the bitter cold during the march so far was my feet. Suddenly, I felt as if I had stepped with a bare foot into a pile of snow. I pulled my foot out of the snow and saw that the entire bottom of my shoe was gone. *This is all I need now*, I thought. I would not last long walking barefoot. In desperation, I ripped off a piece of blanket and wrapped it around my foot. Then I tore off two longer strips and used them to fasten the first piece tighter. And so I proceeded, one foot in a shoe, the other wrapped in a rag.

We got to a wider and better road with a fair amount of foot traffic, people walking in the same direction as we were marching. There were people of all ages, men and women, many with knapsacks on their shoulders, others with suitcases. Some were pulling small sleds loaded with as much as they could hold, others were pushing baby carriages piled high. Slowly my frozen mind started to realize that they were Germans who were trying to escape the Soviets. I tried to imagine how they must have felt, from being the rulers of Europe, now reduced to homeless wanderers. Yet they did not awaken in me any pity or sympathy. They caught up to us but were not in a hurry to overtake us, as if they felt safer near us. We were pleased with their presence. Our guards, and even the SS men, behaved properly in front of the German civilians. They not only stopped using foul language and beating us, but, more importantly, they stopped shooting those who could not continue the march. Instead, they ordered some of us to help the weaker ones. We knew that it was only a matter of a few hours until we would be herded into some barn along the road while the civilians continued on. Then everything would return to the way it was. Still, even a temporary respite was welcomed.

It was getting dark, and we were still marching. Midnight must have passed, and we plowed on. The night was bright. I could clearly see the faces of the civilians who walked alongside us. How gladly I would have exchanged places with them, even in defeat. They might be homeless for a while, but they would live. Eventually, we got off the main road and entered a large barn.

In the morning, after leaving behind the many bodies of those who had died during the night, we continued our march. This time, we were on a remote road that led through forests and snow-covered fields. One would think that we were on a trip to discover new horizons, as there was not a sign of a human being around. But suddenly, we began to see dead bodies in striped camp uniforms lying along the roadside. We could not tell if they had been ahead of us by a few hours or days. We no longer needed road markers; the bodies indicated the direction for us and what lay ahead. We spent that night in a barn, and in the morning, many were missing. As we marched away, some SS men stayed behind to search the hay.

In the last few days, except for the short interval when we walked alongside German civilians, our guards had lost any pretense of civility. If a prisoner fell down, he was dragged off the road and shot whether he tried to get up or not.

That afternoon, another group of inmates caught up with us, about the same size as our group. They were guarded by SS men, but what took us aback was that their kapos and *Blockälteste* carried weapons and played with them like children with toys. Those camp big shots with green triangles were shooting the inmates at will. That group somehow got mixed in with us, and I saw with my own eyes as one of their kapos shot three inmates for no reason at all. In fact, he shot them in the back as they were marching. It seemed to us that the SS guards must have made a satanic agreement with the big shots of that group, who were all German criminals, to dispose of the several hundred Jewish inmates and then disappear in the confusion of the fast-approaching front. The inmates of that group were so agitated and in such terror that although we were marching alongside each other for thirty minutes, we did not exchange two words with any of them and did not even find out what camp they were from. As suddenly as they had appeared, they disappeared. Their guards had driven them into a little forest. Their desperate gazes haunt me still.

Again, that night we were driven into a large barn and then continued marching in the morning. Hiding in the hay became a daily event. The guards would look for hidden inmates as soon as we were outside, even before the count. We got used to the shooting of those found hidden as if that was how it was supposed to be.

Every evening, as soon as we were driven into a barn, I tightened the piece of blanket around my foot and retied the two strips of cloth, as they slackened during the day. I could not do this during the day because I would have to step out of line, and the SS men would have gladly shot me. Besides, my hands were so cold and my fingers so numb that I could not do anything with them. A couple of days earlier, when I had to urinate during the march, I was unable to button my fly, so I buttoned my camp coat over my pants and continued. The next day, I was unable to button my jacket, and I marched with it unbuttoned and flapping in the wind. The only bit of protection from the wind was my shrunken blanket, which I was using up, piece by piece, to wrap around my bare foot.

The following few days and nights were like a walking nightmare in which I could not discern between being alive or dead. Nothing was of any interest or importance. I no longer bothered to look back to see how many and who was being shot. I lost count of the dead, and I did not remember how long we had been marching. I no longer felt hunger pangs or thirst, and I lost count of the days since I had eaten my last piece of bread.

It must have been around January 28 when we were driven out of a barn and led down a side road for about two kilometres. We marched through a large farm, passing by a couple of barns and stables. At the end of the farm near some sheds there were freight cars, their wide doors open as if they were beckoning us to get in. We were told to get in. In the confusion and bustle, I saw some wooden boxes with raw potatoes near one of the sheds. I left the line, ran over to a box, grabbed a handful and put them in my pocket. Even now, I do not know if I dared to do it because I was indifferent to the consequences, or if I was in a state of delirium. In any case, I got away with it. The doors on the freight cars slid shut and were padlocked, and we remained in total darkness. There was enough room for each of us to sit on the floor. Although the cars were unheated, the wind that had accompanied us for the last days and cut into our flesh like knives was broken. We folded our blankets and sat on them, as our bony backsides hurt from sitting on the wooden floor. It didn't take long before the cold penetrated our camp uniforms and we began to shiver. We decided to pair up, sitting on one blanket and wrapping ourselves with the second.

After many hours, the train began to move. There was a narrow crack between one side of the wall and the roof, only large enough to tell if it was day or night. The train made many stops, and we lost track of time. It became almost impossible to tell the length of time between the stops or to estimate the length of the stops themselves. It made no difference anymore. When the train stopped, the banging of the wheels died, and a dead silence overwhelmed us. Slowly, some of the inmates started talking in low voices, not out of fear but because of lack of strength. In our semi-delirium, we attempted to speculate about our next torment. Would they keep us locked in here until we were all dead, or were they taking us to yet another camp? The conversation led to the subject of food. How long could we survive without food? It was already twelve days since we had been given something to eat. We had held out longer than I ever imagined possible. How much longer could it go on? The discussion turned to the topic of cannibalism. One person mentioned that the liver was the most nourishing part of an animal, and he assumed that it was applicable to human flesh too. I looked around in the almost complete darkness of the wagon and wondered whose liver I would be forced to eat, or would it be my liver that would be eaten? Someone pointed to a couple of bodies already lying motionless on the floor. A shiver went through me, and I turned my head away. I resolved that no matter what, I would not eat human flesh. If somebody wanted, let them wait and eat mine. Nobody made a move toward the two bodies. It seemed that after all that talk, the thought of cannibalism was alien to our nature. And so, the first day and night on the train passed slowly.

With the break of day, which we determined by looking at the crack above our heads, I ate one of the five raw potatoes in my pocket. It did nothing for me. At this point, I no longer felt hunger or thirst. The following four days were a confused mixture of reality, lucidity and delirium. We still did not know where we were being taken, nor did we care. Mentally, we had already resigned from life. Still, I ate one raw potato every morning. On the fifth day, I finished my fifth and last potato. That day, our train stopped. By the voices outside, we could tell that we had arrived at our destination. A few minutes later, the doors slid open and we were told to get out. I don't know how many remained in the wagons dead or dying. Those who could still stand up and walk were lined up five abreast and ordered to march. The road went uphill, and I found it difficult to march. As I began to fall back, two of my close acquaintances grabbed me under my arms and helped me walk. One of them was Leibel Waszkiewicz, who was my age and from the shtetl of Lomza. He held me with powerful hands. I asked him how he could muster so much strength to hold me up after not having eaten for over two weeks. He told me that he had been in the same car with some big shots. At several stops, the local authorities had brought food for us inmates but those big shots accepted the food on our behalf, took it into their car and ate it themselves, never sharing it with us. They had so much food that they did not mind if he helped himself to some.

After walking uphill for several hundred metres, we saw a wall built of large rectangular stone blocks, giving the appearance of a fortress. I was too weak and too exhausted to care about further surprises or even what was going to happen to me. I did not know that I was facing the gates of Mauthausen.

29
Mauthausen

THE LARGE ENTRANCE gates of the camp opened up for us, and we were led in. Our guards remained outside. We were now under a new authority, surrounded by kapos who were leading us between two large stone buildings. We remained between the two buildings for a long time, when suddenly two large wooden crates full of bread were brought to us, and each of us received a slice.

We were counted several times and were told that out of the almost 900 who had left Sosnowitz fifteen days earlier, we were now 400, including all the big shots, about 50 men, of whom none had perished, of course. That left only 350 Jews who survived the march from Sosnowitz to Mauthausen.

By then we had forgotten what day of the week or month it was. One of us asked an overseer for the date. "The second of February," came the answer. Something clicked in my mind; somehow the date was registered in my memory. Then, despite the state that I was in, barely aware of what was taking place around me, it hit me. Two years earlier, I had arrived in Auschwitz on the same day.

It turned out that we were next door to the bathhouse, and we were ordered in and got undressed. Our hair was cut, and a five-centimetre-wide stripe was shaved down the middle of our heads from front to back. Here too, like in Auschwitz, we were permitted to hold on to our belts and shoes. Those whose shoes were falling apart, or who had lost a shoe, received a pair of shoes with a wooden bottom and cloth top. Then we were led into the shower room. I felt so weak that I sat on the floor. I do not know if we got much cleaner, as we had no soap. After some minutes under the showers, we were driven into an adjoining room, where each of us received an undershirt and underwear—no pants, no jacket and no coat. As we were leaving the bathhouse, we were registered. Each of us gave our name, age, nationality and profession. Unlike in Auschwitz, where they tattooed a number on our arm, here they gave us a small rectangular piece of tin on which our numbers were embossed. I received number 125465, and with it, a short piece of wire to tie the piece of tin around my left wrist.

Dressed only in undershirt and underwear, we were led outdoors on that February day, then lined up and marched through the camp. The buildings were made of stone blocks and seemed to be built to last forever, or at least for the "thousand-year Reich" that Hitler had promised his people. We entered a separate part of the camp, where I saw a wooden barracks surrounded by a barbed-wire fence and guard towers. Next to that barracks was another one just like it, but this one was not fenced in, and I could not see any guard towers around it. We were led inside that second barracks and ordered to sit on the floor and spread out our legs so that another person could sit between them and spread his legs for the next person. And so, we were squeezed in, taking up the entire floor. The barracks was empty of bunks except for a room in one corner, which was the accommodation of the *Blockältester* and his *Stubendienste*.

It was late afternoon when we were packed in there, and we were still sitting there in the evening and through the night. The one good thing was that it was warm when we leaned against each other, but it was difficult to sit. We were not allowed to move, and the floor was hard and hurt our behinds. With daylight, we were given permission to stand. Our overseers, the *Stubendienste*, were not Germans or Poles like in Auschwitz; they were Spaniards. Those inmates were supporters of the Republic who had fought against Franco in the Spanish Civil War. When Franco took power, they escaped to France, who sympathized with them. However, when the Nazis occupied France, they were arrested and sent to concentration camps as anti-fascists and anti-Nazis. While in Mauthausen, I noticed that the Spanish kapos and *Stubendienste* did not display the same antisemitism that was so prevalent in Auschwitz among the non-Jewish inmates.

That morning, we received a quarter of a loaf of bread each and at noon a bowl of soup. It was only then that our hunger was newly awakened. We remained in that barracks all day, watching through the windows as inmates dragged bodies from the neighbouring fenced-in barracks to the crematorium. We found out that the neighbouring barracks served as a bunker, or penal barracks, in which inmates who broke the law in camp were held under inhumane conditions. The day before our arrival, the six hundred inmates in that barracks had decided to break out. All of them were shot.

On our second night in Mauthausen, we were allowed to lie down, and surprisingly we succeeded thanks to a bit of ingenuity and the sticks of the *Stubendienste*. We were ordered to lie on our sides as close to each other as possible. In the morning, we received the quarter piece of bread, and at noon we had the soup. What we could not understand was that there was no *Appell*. This, compounded by the fact that we were still in underwear, created suspicions that turned into rumours that they were going to dispose of us very soon.

On the evening of the second day, we each received a whole loaf of bread. This confused us, but the joy of holding an entire loaf of bread in our hands chased away any dark thoughts from our minds. There were all kinds of theories about the bread. The most prevalent one was that the camp expected a large arrival of inmates from camps that were being transported deeper into Germany. However, these arriving transports were much smaller than expected because thousands had died on the way. As their tortured bodies lay by the wayside, we were eating their bread, wondering who would eat our bread and when.

A couple of days later, we received pants and jackets and were transferred to another barracks, which had three-tier bunks like those in Auschwitz. In Auschwitz, we had slept singly on those bunks, but here in Mauthausen we slept two or three on a single bunk. One night, four of us shared one bunk. Not only did we lie on our sides, but we had to have our heads in opposite directions with our neighbours' feet sticking in our faces. In that barracks, we were mixed with inmates from other camps. Our commonality was that we were all Jews and shared thoughts about our expected final fate.

Mauthausen was overflowing with inmates who had been brought in from all the camps in Polish territory, including Auschwitz. Many inmates were simply dragging themselves around the camp with one thought in mind: *Find something to eat*. Some volunteered to go to work hoping to find food there. I was taken with a group to work in the kitchen. *What could be better than working in a kitchen?* I thought. At least I would get a bowl of soup. We were led into a cellar, where we saw some fifty Soviet prisoners of war peeling potatoes. All of them were amputees, missing one or both legs. The mystery was that the Germans bothered to amputate their legs while at the same time they were shooting perfectly healthy Soviet soldiers. We were assigned to peel potatoes, and I slowly worked my way closer to the Soviet soldiers. I could see from their well-worn uniforms that the lowest rank among them was a major. Was it possible that the Nazis kept them as bargaining chips? The bowl of soup I hoped to get did not materialize, but I did succeed in slipping a few raw potatoes into my pocket, and I ate them on the way to the barracks. I was not fortunate enough to be picked for kitchen duty again.

In those days, many transports of inmates arrived in Mauthausen every day. One early evening, a large transport of inmates arrived, it was rumoured from Gross-Rosen. Nobody was permitted to get close to them. They were led into the bathhouse and then forced outside, where they remained all night. They stood there, naked, hugging the stone wall, huddled together. When we went over to see them in the early morning, only a few were still on their feet, but were near collapsing.

The rest were lying on the ground, motionless. We were not permitted to watch them and were chased away.

Just like Auschwitz, Mauthausen had its affiliated camps. The largest were the two camps Gusen I and Gusen II, which held tens of thousands of inmates. In Mauthausen, we heard horrible stories about these subcamps. It was known that each day, five hundred inmates left Mauthausen for the two Gusen camps. King Solomon wrote, "All rivers flow to the sea, but the sea never overflows." So it was with those two Gusen camps. They consumed inmates by working them to death.

Mauthausen itself had horrific legacies of its own. It was mostly infamous for its stone quarry. I remember how a Roma inmate sat on the top bunk in our barracks and said to us, "You Jews think that you have it tough here. You should have been here in 1939, when father and son, holding hands, would jump down from the top of the quarry, almost two hundred steps down into the abyss. Their bodies would be torn to shreds from the sharp edges of the rocks below."

A day or two after this conversation, I happened to come across a group of the *Strafkommando*, the punishment company that worked in the quarry. I was told that their work consisted of them being led to a pile of heavy granite blocks at the bottom of the quarry, and each had to pick up a block, put it on his shoulder and carry it all the way to the top, the entire two hundred steps, dump it there and go down for more. They did this twelve hours a day without rest.

One morning in the middle of February, the *Blockschreiber* called out some numbers, mine among them. He took us to the *Appellplatz*. Many other groups joined us there until we were about five hundred men. We were led out of the camp and marched on a side road. We were in farm country, and every few hundred metres there was a farmhouse surrounded by various buildings. The snow had begun to melt, and we could see spots of fertile black soil. Nobody was looking out the windows of the farmhouses, and nobody looked at us as we passed by.

Suddenly, in front of us was a wide, high gate. We were used to the sight of such gates but wondered what was behind this one. We were led inside. Our escort of SS men remained behind, and we were surrounded by new overseers, the majority of whom were Germans with green triangles. They recognized us as a group of Jews, although on our triangles we only had the letter *P* for Polish, as we had not yet received the yellow inverted triangles identifying us as Jews. When we had received our pants and jackets in Mauthausen, we also received triangles and were ordered to write on them the initial of our country of birth. Everybody wrote the letter *P* for Poland. Thinking that our camp commandant had not brought the archives with him, I hoped to get by as a Soviet prisoner because they stood a better chance of surviving than Jews. So I marked a letter *R* for Russian on my triangle. Throughout our two weeks in Mauthausen, nobody seemed to notice or made a fuss over it, and I was hoping that this *R* might help me at some point.

We were told that we were in Gusen I. Our new overseers referred to us by the diminutives of our Jewish names, like Shloimkah, Yankelah, Moishelah and Berelah, pronouncing them with so much mockery and contempt that we immediately understood what kind of Jew haters we were among. We were in the *Appellplatz*, and a couple more big shots approached us. One read out names from a list. One name sounded familiar to me—Rosen. I looked around and saw the former kapo of DAW in Auschwitz, the Jewish engineer who had supervised the repairs of all the engines in the factory. He was probably the only kapo who never raised his voice or hand against anybody. When I suddenly saw him in that hell, I felt as if I were meeting a long-lost friend.

Those few men were led away, and the overseers broke us up into smaller groups and assigned us to different barracks. I was assigned to block 15. Half of the fifty men in my group were from the Sosnowitz camp, all my acquaintances and some even friends. There was one more barracks behind us, number 16, which housed German inmates and criminals who had recently volunteered to join the army. The German army was so short of men that they were willing to overlook their crimes. Those criminals were dressed in the Afrika Korps uniforms for which the German army had no use anymore as the force ceased to exist with the German defeat in Africa in 1943. Those half-inmates, half-free people were hardened criminals who became foremen, kapos and even *Blockälteste*. Because they cooperated with the SS by doing their dirty work, they were allowed to leave the camp for training.

Our barracks, although wooden, was a bit better than the Birkenau ones, the *Pferdestallbaracken* (horse-stable barracks). This barracks consisted of two *Stubes*. In between the two rooms were the entrances to the barracks and a separate room for the *Blockältester*. The *Blockältester*, a tall slim German with a green triangle, had been the *Lagerältester*, but was demoted to *Blockältester* for some transgression. His legacy as a murderer was no secret and followed him everywhere. Our *Stubendienst* was a twenty-five-year-old Ukrainian, a raving antisemite.

Our room was filled with three-tier Auschwitz-style bunks. However, here, we were paired two per bunk. My partner was a boy my age who had been with me in Sosnowitz, Henry Czesielski. We did not receive any food that day. When I lay down on the bunk, I was surprised to find so much room and thought, *Here we are, two grown men on a sixty-centimetre-wide bunk, and we could find room for one more.*

The gong woke us before dawn. As I arrived at the lavatories, which were in a small adjoining building, I noticed a group of inmates surrounding a large wooden barrel the height of a man in a corner of the room. I became curious and went over to look in. For a moment, all I could see was water almost to the rim. Looking closer, I saw a pair of shoes swimming upside down in the water. Then I noticed a pair of legs leading downwards. The first thought that came to my mind was that the man had taken his own life. Turning to the person closest to me, a Russian inmate, I said, "He must have had enough."

The Russian looked at me strangely, as if to say, "Don't be such a fool," but quietly said, "They drowned him."

There was no time for questions. I ran back to the *Stube* to get my quarter loaf of bread and ran outside for the roll call. Right after the roll call, we were all lined up and marched out of the camp. We had not gone far when we came to a row of wooden barracks, where most of the column dispersed while we newcomers remained standing outside. A few SS men appeared with some overseers, called out our numbers and assigned us to the different barracks. I was led into a barracks in which there were two lines of lathes. Every ten or twelve lathes formed a unit that performed a specific task and had a supervisor, or *Einsteller* (adjuster), whose job was to make sure that the cutting blades on the lathes were placed properly. The lathes were automated, and the operator did not have to be an expert. He needed to secure the piece of metal properly in its place, check the cutting knives to make sure they were not dull, and push a button. The machine did the rest. When finished, he took out that part, checked for the correct measurement and put it on a specially designed wagon. When the wagon was half full, it was taken to the next section.

My *Einsteller* was a young Russian, my age. He noticed the letter *R* on my triangle and took me for a Russian, and in no time, we became friends. Our kapo was a Lithuanian, the first and only Lithuanian I ever met in the concentration camps. He was friendly with the Russians but hated Jews. He also took me for a Russian and was polite to me. I had no problem with the work. I did not even need the *Einsteller* to adjust the blades. Just the same, he came over for a chat. I was eager to speak with him, as he had been there for some time and knew the camp; I could learn something from him, and he wanted to find out about other camps. Of course, I had to fill my quota of work, but I knew I could do that and so did he. I found out from him that all twelve thousand inmates in this camp were working in this factory and produced six hundred light machine guns every twenty-four hours. In each barracks a different part of the machine gun was made. In our barracks, we were making the gun barrels. He told me that if a worker did not fill his quota, he was hanged right on the spot in the factory. The executions were conducted under the supervision of the *Oberkapo*, the head kapo, who was nicknamed "the General," a German inmate with a green triangle. The inmates feared him even more than they feared the SS.

That evening, we got nothing to eat, not even the camp tea. I had nothing to do, so I went to explore the camp. The entire camp consisted of wooden barracks, except for a large storehouse and the kitchen, which were built of bricks and stone. There was a bathhouse, a *Krankenbau* and the inevitable crematorium. I also came across a couple of firemen who were guards in the camp, swaggering in their fancy uniforms with more arrogance on their well-fed faces than the SS.

I noticed immediately, based on over two years of camp experience, that the hunger in Gusen I was worse than it was in the other camps I'd been in. Returning to the barracks that first evening, I took a good look around at the room and my roommates. Half of my roommates were Jews who came with me. The others, the non-Jewish inmates, had received parcels from home until recently. Now they were waiting impatiently for the defeat of Germany. They were just starting to feel hungry as their parcels dried up. The Soviet prisoners had not been receiving parcels and had been in Gusen for some time by this point. Some of them succeeded in finding a niche in the camp system by which they managed to procure some extra food and even help a friend. One had to admire their desire, their ardour for living, their talent to improvise and make do. Their reckless behaviour, which brought on inhumane and terrible punishment, I witnessed a short time later.

A young Soviet prisoner, a teenager, stole a piece of bread from another boy of the same age, and the wronged boy denounced the thief to the *Blockältester*. The *Blockältester* woke us up in the middle of the day (as at that time we worked the night shift), lined us up and announced, "You will now witness the punishment for stealing bread." Turning to the young thief, he said, "Do you have any friends you would like to say goodbye to, for you are going to die."

None of us took his words seriously, and I doubt if the young man did. Still, he shook hands with a few of his friends in our *Stube*. The *Blockältester* tied the young man's hands behind his back and led him to the lavatory to the large barrel filled with water. The *Blockältester*, with the help of the *Stubendienst*, lifted the boy and threw him into the barrel, headfirst. I was not too close to the barrel, but when I saw his body going over the rim, I turned away. I did not know when his body was taken away.

I was still wearing the letter *R* and being taken for a Soviet prisoner by those who did not know me. About two weeks after my arrival, I noticed some Soviet inmates carrying bowls with soup during the midday break, and I followed them to a small stall where there was a barrel with thick noodle soup in the middle of the floor. A man held a ladle and was dishing out the soup to a few Soviet prisoners standing in a short line, while another man wrote down the recipients' numbers. Desperate for food, I got in line. When my turn came, the one who was writing down the numbers asked me where I worked. I nodded toward the barracks. He wrote down my number and said to me, "Remember to bring the two cigarettes tomorrow." I assured him that I would. As I ate the soup, I was trying to figure out how these men had managed to swipe a barrel of such good soup, for it certainly was not intended for us inmates. The bowl of soup did not satisfy my hunger, but I was pleased with the unexpected treat. As far as the payment went, I never had cigarettes or saw those Soviet prisoners again.

Some days later, our *Einsteller* cut off a finger when he was adjusting the blades of the lathe and was taken to the camp hospital. Our kapo, the Lithuanian antisemite, appointed me as the blade adjuster. It was now my job to make sure that the blades on the lathes were properly adjusted and that the lathes were always in working condition. I doubt that kapo would have appointed me as blade adjuster had he known that I was a Jew.

As I was now free to move about, I could admire how well the work was organized and how good weapons could be produced so efficiently by starving prisoners. The fifteen lathes I was responsible for were producing machine-gun barrels. The first lathe would get a piece of rusty steel with a barely noticeable hole running through it. By the time the steel passed through all fifteen lathes, it looked like a brand-new shiny machine-gun barrel. Nobody stood over us to rush us, and we were not beaten. We all knew what was awaiting us if we did not fill the quota. In contrast, those who worked in the transport column, who were hauling the raw material all day long, were constantly chased and beaten. They fell by the dozen daily. When I saw them bringing in the heavy rusty metal, I thought of my work in the *Holzplatz* in Auschwitz.

At noon we got the litre of thin soup, which I gulped down right away. After everyone had received his soup, the kapo called the blade adjusters for seconds. I stood last in line, unsure if I qualified or not. The kapo made no fuss and poured me another litre. I could not believe it. It was too good to be true, and I wondered how long my luck could last. The hunger was taking its toll, even among those who worked at the lathes, and the mortality rate due to starvation was high. In my group, most of the workers on the lathes were Jews from my *Stube*. I could not see it so much on myself, but I could see it on them, how they were burning out. With long workdays on only a quarter loaf of bread and a litre of watery soup a day, how long could an exhausted human being go on?

When we returned to the barracks after a twelve-hour day, our Ukrainian *Stubendienst* would punish us for not making our bunk straight enough. He used a thick piece of cable to beat us mercilessly all over our bodies. I, too, was privileged to be beaten by him a couple of times, and I had marks on my body for weeks.

The fear of not filling the quota was great, and many panicked if they were falling behind with their work. When I worked on the lathe, I had no such problem. My training at school in Brest-Litovsk and my experience in Sosnowitz came in handy. Others, however, found it difficult. Quite often, I would leave my place and go over to the next guy to help him catch up. I can now say with a little pride that at times I did help my friends and suffering brothers with their work, as that was the only thing I was able to do for them. After the war, one of them would say to me, "Moniek [the name the Polish Jews gave me], you saved my life many times in Gusen." I did not feel that I was doing such a great deed back then, or even when he reminded me after the war. But now, over half a century later, it feels good to know what I did.

An order was issued in the camp that all Jews had to put on a yellow stripe above their red triangle. The next day at work, nothing seemed to have changed. At noon, we lined up for our soup. I got my soup and drank it quickly, ready for when they would call the *Einsteller* for seconds. They called, and my turn came. The kapo took a look at me, saw the yellow stripe and said, "You do not get extra soup. You are only a temporary *Einsteller*."

I left the line heartbroken. The extra litre of soup had kept me going. Now it was a question of weeks before I would collapse like so many before me. Every few days, new workers from other camps arrived to replace the departed, and soon, a new *Einsteller* came to replace the one I had taken over from. He was a Pole, a former kapo and a well-fed young man. He had no inkling what was going on, but he got the extra bowl of soup while I did the work, his work.

It was April. The snow was gone, and it was warm in the sun. One sunny afternoon, sirens suddenly wailed. All motors stopped, and the kapos yelled, "Run to the air -raid shelters!" I ran with everybody else, through fences and over grassy ground to the nearby hills and into holes in the sides of the hills, like caves. Inside, there were long corridors in which prisoners were working. Some were using pneumatic drills, and others worked with pneumatic chisels to slice away chunks from the stone walls and ceilings, making the tunnels wider and longer. The part that I could see was roomy enough to take in our entire factory. The tunnels were filled with different machines, some already connected with electric wires, seemingly ready to be operated. While still in Mauthausen, I knew that inmates were taken daily to the nearby towns to clean up after the frequent allied bombardments. We all knew that the German industry was being destroyed from the air. As I was looking at the maze of tunnels under the mountain, I was overwhelmed by what the Nazis had accomplished to protect their war industry. But I was mostly concerned with the inability of the Allies to destroy it.

The alarm did not last more than half an hour, and we started to return to the factory. We had run to the tunnel, but on the way back we walked. I had no strength to run, and apparently neither did others. As we were walking back, I noticed a sprig of clover amid the young grass, and I pinched it off and put it in my mouth.

That was my first air raid in Gusen, but certainly not the last. They started going off several times a week. Each time, running became more difficult. Despite all those alarms, I did not hear a single explosion in or around the camp. It was a great mystery to me why the Allied planes did not bombard the wooden barracks that stood no more than ten metres apart from each other and produced six hundred machine guns every twenty-four hours. One bomb could have incinerated all the barracks at once.

We could tell that the situation was getting worse for the Germans by the shortage of raw material. The twelve-hour shifts were shortened to eight-hour ones—from 6:00 a.m. to 2:00 p.m. and from 2:00 p.m. until 10:00 p.m. For the first time, the factory stayed idle at night. The thin soup became even thinner. The distribution of the soup that had taken place at work was now taking place in the barracks at 3:00 p.m. for the morning shift and at noon for the evening shift. As the soup became thinner, we would push for a better position in line to reach the barrel. If you were among the first in line, something might float on top, and if you were lucky, the *Blockältester* might fish it out. Or if you were one of the last in line, perhaps there was something at the bottom of the barrel. While the inmates were literally dying of hunger, our *Blockältester* was walking around in the barracks, drunk and well fed.

Sometime in April, a rumour spread like wildfire all over the camp that the over six hundred sick inmates in the *Krankenbau* had been gassed. As there was no gas chamber in Gusen, the windows and doors had been boarded up with a small opening left for a can of gas. What was surprising was that the majority of those killed were non-Jews; they were mostly Russians, Poles, Frenchmen, Dutchmen, Spaniards and even, it was said, a few Germans. When this rumour was confirmed, we Jews completely lost our last shred of hope. If they could do this to non-Jews, what chance did we Jews have of getting out alive?

In such a mood, we lay down, got up and went to work. A couple of days after we heard about the gassing, we returned from work dejected and depressed, but still with our intense and constant hunger. We lined up for the soup, and as soon as the *Blockältester* opened the barrel and dipped the ladle, we started jockeying for a better position in the line. The *Blockältester* lifted his eyes from the barrel and said, "You stupid Jews. What are you pushing each other for? I received orders that as soon as the other shift returns from work tonight, I am to take you all to the *Krankenbau*, where all the Jews in camp will be gassed."

So, this is the end, I thought. It should not have come as a surprise. I knew all along that this was how it would end, but the knowing didn't prepare me for the moment when it arrived. We did not push each other in the line anymore. We took our bowls of soup with dejected indifference, knowing that this would be the last meal that any of us would ever have. As if to confirm what we had just heard, two kapos walked by, and one opened the door and yelled, "Lagersperre!"—*Blocks closure!* This meant that nobody was allowed outside. We could not go out to confirm with Jews from other blocks what we had just heard. The Ukrainian *Stubendienst* hammered down a couple of loose boards in the floor. I thought to myself, *How foolish of him. What Jew would be stupid enough to try to hide under the floor in front of a hundred people, and what good would it do him?*

I got up on my bunk. My bunkmate worked the other shift, and I envied him, for he did not yet know the terrible news and would be spared the last agonizing hours. I sank into my thoughts and mentally went through all the suffering, all the agony of the last years, especially the two years in Auschwitz. To have suffered so much, so much—who could recount all the suffering that I went through, every minute of every agonizing day? I felt so much regret for all the torment, the torture, the drudgery that I had gone through. What for? So that I would die a couple of days before liberation? I felt a terrible heart-wrenching remorse for not having gone with my family on that memorable

Saturday morning of January 30, 1943, when all of them—my parents, sisters and brother—were taken by sled to the railway station. Deep down I had known there was no real chance of getting out of the ghetto. I could have spent two more days with my parents in the cattle cars and could have helped them with the children in their final agonizing moments. It is not possible to recall and reconstruct all the dark thoughts that went through my mind as I lay there on my bunk.

It was a long wait till 10:00 p.m., when the other shift would return from work, and I fell asleep. In all the dreams I'd had in the camps, I never dreamt about the future, always about the past or the present. Now, a few hours before I was going to leave this world, I had an extraordinary dream. I was standing near railway tracks, and I saw a train passing by very slowly. The train was full of passengers and was so crowded that some were sitting on top of the train, others sticking out of the windows and doors. The passengers were dressed in civilian clothes and were waving to me. I recognized many of them—Jews from France who had been with me in the same *Stube* in Auschwitz, others who had been with me in Sosnowitz, and still others whom I'd met right here in Gusen. I called out to them, "Where are you going?" And they replied, "To Switzerland." I woke up. What a sweet dream and what a bitter reality! Again, the question surfaced; in fact, it had never left me: *Why?*

Every Jew in the room was sitting or lying on his bunk, absorbed in his thoughts. Hardly anyone said a word, and if they did, it was a whisper. I did not feel like talking. What could anybody tell me except how he imagined his last moments? The time dragged on, and yet it passed too quickly. The minutes were long but the hours short. I wished that it had been in my power to stop all the clocks in the world, so that ten o'clock would never come.

It was nine o'clock. In another hour, the second shift would be back. I knew that we were not the only ones and that the Nazis intended to get rid of every Jew under their jurisdiction. Was it possible that no Jews would be left in Europe? I lay and listened to sounds from outside, wondering if miracles still happened. Then I heard the shuffle of feet, the treading of shoes. They were here. Holding my breath, I waited for the *Blockältester*'s command to fall in. He most likely wanted to have his fun and was letting us stew. Slowly, I raised my head and looked around. I did not see him, and the tired workers who had just arrived went straight to their bunks and lay down. I asked my bunk partner, Czesielski, if he had heard the news. He hadn't. He was too tired for conversation, and I was not even sure he heard me. In a minute, he was asleep. I lay on the bunk. An hour or two later, I fell asleep. The gong awakened me in the morning. I did not believe I was still alive. We came to the conclusion that the *Blockältester*, the drunkard, had played a callous joke on us.

One could feel and smell the end of the war in the air. Inmates who went to work daily on the main road told of heavy military traffic and frequent air attacks. Our soup got even worse, and we received only an eighth of a loaf of bread instead of a quarter. In mid-April, the French, Belgian, Dutch and Danish inmates were collected and taken away, but not the Jews. Rumour had it that the Western European inmates were being sent to Switzerland. In the camp there were now German criminals, the majority of whom were being trained as soldiers, as well as Poles, Russians and Jews.

A few days after the departure of the Western European inmates, as we were getting ready to go to work right after the morning *Appell*, the Jewish inmates were told to go back into the barracks as we would not be working that day. Immediately, our suspicions arose. It was only days earlier that the *Blockältester* had mentioned that we'd be taken to the bathhouse to be gassed. When all other work columns left the camp for the factory, our *Blockältester* announced that the Jews would soon be going to the camp canteen for parcels from the International Red Cross. He told us to pair up, and that one in each pair should take a soup bowl with him.

We listened in astonishment. What new trick was this? He already told us that we would be gassed. We were ready then, and we were ready now. Why did he use this kind of deceit? Would the red camp bowl calm us on our way to our deaths? Through the window, we could see the overseers gathering, each with a heavy club in his hand. Now we knew for sure that they would lead us to the bathhouse, but why all this tumult, this agitation? We Jews knew how to go to the gas chambers.

At eight o'clock, the *Blockältester* walked in. We stayed in pairs as ordered and followed him out of the barracks. We expected the clubs to start falling on us, but no — the *Blockältester* walked calmly, and we followed with the overseers all around us. They did not act in their usual hostile style. Two overseers stood at the entrance to the canteen. They told one man of the first pair to take off his jacket, and they led the two men in. A minute later the pair appeared at the door with beaming faces. One was holding the red camp bowl, which was now almost filled with some kind of meat. The other had his arms around his bulging jacket, which he was carrying carefully. We went in two at a time, coming out with loaded arms. I walked into the large room with my partner, Leibel Waszkiewicz. Halfway across the room was a counter, behind which stood a few overseers and some SS men. One inmate brought out a tin from behind a wall. He opened it with a can opener and dumped its content into the red bowl. There were solid chunks of meat! The other opened a sealed carton with a knife, and dumped its contents onto my jacket, which was spread out on the counter. I did not believe my eyes. In front of me was a heap of biscuits, marmalade in plastic bags, cubes of sugar, packets of cigarettes, tins of sardines and even chocolate bars. The SS men grabbed the chocolate, sardines and some of the cigarettes from the top of the heap and then told us to get going. I grabbed the jacket and ran out to join the others. All the overseers who had accompanied us from the barracks were still standing around us with their clubs in hand, alert, as if ready for action. We couldn't make sense of it all. Were they going to lead us to be gassed, and the parcels were only planned to mislead us?

Soon we were all back together and were following our *Blockältester*, escorts all around us. We were passing by the first barracks after the canteen when a dozen or so Soviet inmates ran out from behind it, throwing themselves on several men and scattering the goodies all over the ground. Our escorts clobbered the Soviet inmates indiscriminately. The few wronged Jewish inmates picked up whatever had not been grabbed, and we continued marching. The same thing happened as we passed the next block, and the next, all the way to our barracks. Now I understood why the camp administration had sent with us such a feared escort. If not for them, we would have returned to the barracks empty-handed.

The whole situation was very strange. Our escort consisted of *Blockälteste* and kapos, the very same men who until now had beaten us, tortured us and killed us. Now they were walking alongside us to protect us. We were still inside the camp, Jews condemned to die, escorted by the hardened German criminals with their heavy clubs. What was happening here? We reached our barracks, not the hospital for gassing. Our escorts remained outside and dispersed. We got onto our bunks to divide our newly acquired treasures.

Leibel and I sat on my bunk, and we opened my jacket and found items I had forgotten existed. Besides the biscuits, there were sugar cubes, marmalade, a can of condensed sweet milk, sugar and four packages of twenty cigarettes. We each took two packages of cigarettes, which I put in my pocket.

At 3:00 p.m., the other shift would return from work. If they didn't try to snatch whatever we had left right away, they would try it at night. After drinking the thick sweet milk, we turned to the bully beef. Next, we ate the biscuits and marmalade, and then the rest. We did not leave anything. The safest place was in your stomach. I was surprised at how much my stomach could hold. All I had left were a few cubes of sugar.

In the morning, we paid the price for those parcels. Many of us were so ill that we were unable to get out of our bunks. The younger and healthier inmates watched as those whose stomachs and intestines had been ruined by years of hunger, starvation and lack of proper nutrition, succumbed to normal food. Those affected expired within three days. I do not want to minimize the importance of those parcels. Without question they sustained the lives of many of us, maybe even mine. They gave us the impetus to hold on to life at the most difficult time in camp. It was the first time since we had been confronted with Nazism that we saw a sign that someone, somewhere, cared about us or even thought about us.

The work in the factory went on despite the shortages of material and the critical situation on the front. The shortage of food in Germany continued to be reflected in the camp, and they now divided one loaf of bread between twenty inmates. We continued to run to the shelter when Allied planes flew by. In those weeks, the Allied flyers became daring and flew so low that we could see their faces. One day, the Allied planes shot some horses on a road near the camp. The butchers from nearby villages cut off the bony parts that no one wanted, like the lower legs, and gave it to the camp. There was no meat on the bones, but they chopped them up and used them in the soup. As the *Blockältester* was dishing out the soup, it was my good fortune to get an entire horse's knee. I got hardly any soup, and of course no meat, but there was a yellow jelly-like substance between the joints, and that tasted delicious to me, the starving skeleton. Right there and then I made myself a promise that, should I get out alive, I would cook myself a horse's leg.

The next day, the soup was again the usual boiled water with a few tiny pieces of dried turnip floating in it. However, I succeeded in finding some Soviet inmates who managed to steal a barrel of soup every day and sold the soup for cigarettes. The going price was two cigarettes for a litre. There was not much to the soup, but I had some cigarettes available, and even that soup was important.

Despite the obvious signs that the war was drawing to an end, the camp discipline did not slacken. It was as strict as if the Germans were winning the war. This enraged the inmates, who felt that in those final days of the war and the certain defeat of Germany, those criminals should have tried to atone for their conduct up to that time.

At the beginning of May, at about three in the afternoon, we had just received the bowl of boiled water that they tried to pass for soup when a couple of SS men walked into the barracks. Without even looking at us, they went over to the wall on which there was a board that was covered with all kinds of warnings concerning the behaviour of the inmates. All those warnings ended with the words "will be shot." The two SS men tore off all those warnings, stuffed them in a bag, and left. Their action evoked much conversation and many assumptions. It also struck in us a spark of hope that we might, just might, live to see the liberation.

30
Liberation

ON FRIDAY, MAY 4, we went to work as usual at 6:00 a.m., but it became clear at the outset that it was not an ordinary day. The motors and lathes were running, but we walked among them, talking to one another. The kapos pretended not to see. Sometime before noon, I left my lathe and went to have a look outside. I leaned on the barracks wall next to the door so that if an SS man appeared, I would be able to sneak back in. It was a beautiful sunny day, and the sun warmed my emaciated body. I relaxed for a moment and let my guard down. By the time I noticed two SS men passing by. It was too late for me to get back into the factory barracks. They were so close that I could touch them. They wore no caps, and their dark blond hair was tousled by the wind. Their jackets had no epaulets, and their collars were missing the SS insignias; the colour of the cloth where they had been was darker. They looked at me and smiled as they went by. It was the first time that I had seen an SS man smiling to a Jew without a mocking expression. Even to me, the pessimist, the German defeat was obvious. Would they let us see it?

At two o'clock, we lined up and went to the camp. The other shift, which was supposed to be at work already, was still in the barracks. The barracks was buzzing with rumours. After the *Appell*, we went to other barracks to find out if they had more information. We saw soldiers digging a hole for a cannon on the hill behind the camp, and they soon started shooting over the hill to the far side. That night, sleep did not come easy. The cannons boomed continuously, and our mood was tense.

At some point in the night, the door suddenly opened and in came several well-dressed, well-fed inmates, Poles and Germans with red triangles, political internees. They told us to wake each other up. They said that the war was coming to an end, but that we were still under German jurisdiction. We were to pick a few strong men to stay on guard all night. Should any SS men come into the barracks, we should throw him out. Should he try to shoot, we should kill him. In any case, we should resist.

I had never dreamt that I would hear such words in camp. I could not even visualize that we would be able to hit an SS man back. I could not grasp such a moment. But these words were coming from prominent inmates. They left us, making sure that the guards we appointed had something in their hands to defend themselves with, like a club, an axe, a hammer, even a stone. It was quiet in the barracks, but the shooting continued. Sometime in the night, we heard a powerful explosion. We ran to the windows and saw that a huge fire was burning in the spot where the cannon had been. The fire burned for a long time, and the shooting stopped.

The gong woke us at the usual time, and we fell in for the *Appell.* Nobody mentioned work. We received a thin slice of bread, our daily bread ration, and hung out around the barracks for a while. Slowly, we drifted farther away. The camp was full of inmates. Everyone was excited but tense. People kept asking each other if they had heard anything. Others did not know more, but there was no shortage of assumptions, conjecture and just plain guessing. I took a walk around the camp with some friends. Here was the bathhouse to which we were taken a couple of times, where we stood under the showers while our antisemitic Ukrainian *Stubendienst*, Stasiek, yelled and hit us. A short distance away was the *Krankenbau*, in which some six hundred men had recently been gassed. The windows were still boarded up, but the doors were ajar. We did not want to go in there. A few steps farther we passed the crematorium, where hundreds of bodies were burned daily. We came near the barracks that housed the prominent inmates, the big shots, where a Jew dared not enter. It was interesting that the big shots were not visible now. Before, they were everywhere, those well-fed inmates with sticks in their hands. Now the camp was full of *Muselmänner*—emaciated, exhausted, dejected caricatures of human beings. No SS men were seen in the camp.

In mid-afternoon we heard loud shouting. There was a group of prisoners on the roof of one of the barracks, and they were pointing in the direction of Gusen II and yelling. Apparently, they had seen a column of tanks and concluded that they were American. At about five in the afternoon, the *Blockältester* started getting us ready for the *Appell*. It took longer than usual. The first two lines were in place, but the lines behind were restless and did not stand properly. The *Blockältester* and his *Stubendienst* yelled commands, and they had almost gotten us all in line when suddenly those closest to the exit broke away, and all the lines fell apart. Some inmates started running, others followed them, and then we were all running.

I ran with the crowd, excited, not knowing exactly where I was going or why. People ran from every barracks in the direction of the main *Appellplatz*, which was right in front of the wide gate, the entry into the camp. The square was filling up quickly with inmates. The gate was wide open. Outside it was a small open jeep. Two soldiers were standing in it and another two were nearby. Their uniforms were unfamiliar to me. One of them was a Black man, the first I had ever seen in my life, and I realized that they were Americans.

With unbelieving eyes, I saw the guards on the watchtowers behind the electrified fence climbing down, bringing their machine guns with them. They did not carry them like soldiers but dragged them by the straps. An SS man dragged his machine gun with the barrel pointed backwards. We saw him, and he looked back at us. It seemed to me that there was fear hiding behind his eyes. Nazis were coming out of the nearby barracks just outside the gate. They emerged with knapsacks on their backs and with a suitcase in each hand. They came over to the jeep and threw their rifles to the ground. They unbuckled their military belts, on which their bayonets, revolvers and leather cartridges holding bullets were hanging, and threw them all down. The Nazis had been ready. Their belongings were already packed, and all they were waiting for were the representatives of the Allies. Yet they guarded us to the very last moment.

As soon as our former guards got rid of their weapons, they lined themselves up three abreast, hundreds of men, and remained standing, waiting for an order. Until this point, the inmates had been standing inside the gate, blocking the exit. Suddenly, the mob of inmates ran out of the gate and started grabbing the guards' suitcases and knapsacks. I looked on with astonishment as the SS men, who only half an hour earlier had full control over our lives and deaths, stood there motionless while they were being relieved of their possessions by the Polish and Soviet inmates. I did not see any Jews among the grabbers. We Jews stood singly or in small groups, looking like uninvited guests at a celebration. We, the permanent dwellers of the bottom, the obscure, the destitute, the lowest in the abyss, the remnants of entire families, entire towns, cities and camps, had nothing to celebrate. It reflected in our eyes, in our faces and in our conduct. I stood by myself and looked at the event that was taking place before me as if I were looking at a film that made no sense. I felt that I was not there. Only my atrophied, invisible ghost floated there.

I talked to myself: *Moishe, do you see what is taking place here? Do you know that you are free? You survived Hitler and lived to see the defeat of Germany. You went through so much suffering, all in order to see this moment, and you lived to see it. Rejoice. Be happy.* In a flash, the events of the last four years ran through my mind. The expulsion from Shershev, Khomsk and Pruzhany, then Auschwitz, Sosnowitz, Mauthausen and Gusen. Yes, I was alive, but who did I have left? No father or mother, no sisters or brother, no grandparents, no uncles or aunts. Not even one cousin left of my family in Europe. What did I have to celebrate?

Our former guards recovered from the sudden loss of their belongings, and they received an order to march. They set out, followed by an American jeep. I heard loud noises and turned my head to see a large group of people running from one corner of the camp. It was the German inmates, the hardened criminals, the former big shots, the *Blockälteste*, kapos and foremen who had recently volunteered to join the German army. They were still wearing the Afrika Korps uniforms and were noticeable in the crowd, and a mass of inmates was throwing itself at them in a rage. The accumulated months and years of suffering spilled over, and the crowd did not let up until these big shots were dead. And although the majority of the overseers' victims had been Jews, I did not see Jews participating in that grisly slaughter.

Having satisfied their thirst for revenge, the former inmates dispersed. As I walked into our barracks, I saw several men drinking soup. I was directed to the next barracks, but by the time I got there, the barrel of soup was empty. Among many others, I looked around, hoping to find something to eat. Unfortunately, I was too late. What I did find was a pair of men's socks, which I immediately put on—my first pair of socks since I arrived in Auschwitz!

The hunger did not let up. Since we were now free to move about after dark, we wandered to other barracks, hoping to find something to eat. I remember walking into a barracks where a small cast-iron stove stood close to the door. Next to the stove stood a young Soviet inmate, holding in his hand a freshly skinned rabbit hide. He stuck the end of the hide into the fire, waited a moment for it to singe, and as soon as the fur was gone, he bit into the raw skin. He held the end of the skin tightly with his teeth and pulled with all his might to tear off a piece. He succeeded and chewed that piece for a long time. I realized that I would not find any food, and I returned to my barracks to sleep, exhausted and hungry.

There was no gong to wake us, but we got up at the same time anyway. We formed groups of friends and acquaintances from former camps. Nobody wanted to be alone. I formed a group with my bunk partner,

Czesielski, and a few others, and we walked around the camp looking for something to eat. Many were leaving the camp, and my comrades suggested that we do the same. I insisted that I would not leave the camp on an empty stomach. As we got to the centre of the camp, we saw a mob besieging the camp warehouse. They had succeeded in breaking the metal bars of a window that was a ways off the ground. We joined those pushing to get in but then realized that we had to let those inside get out before we could get in. An inmate appeared at the window with a large unopened case of margarine. The moment he jumped down from the window with the case in his arms, the crowd threw itself on him. In less than a minute, the heavy cardboard case was torn apart, and the packages of margarine were snatched away. The same thing happened to everyone who came out through the window. My group decided that when we got to the window, one of us would go in, and as soon as he came out, we would throw ourselves at him.

Sure enough, one of my group got in and soon appeared with a case of margarine. In the ensuing struggle, we managed to hold on to six packages of margarine. We didn't know what we would do with margarine, so we decided to continue looking for food. After a while, we came across some acquaintances who had managed to get some potatoes, which they were cooking in a pail over an open fire between the barracks. For two cubes of margarine, we bought a partnership in the potatoes and waited for the water to boil. As if in spite, it did not boil. After a long wait, we saw bubbles around the rim of the pail, and we thought the potatoes were cooked. We poured out the water and grabbed the potatoes. They were still raw.

For another two packages of margarine, we bought two packages of dried onions, then we joined the exodus from the camp. My desire not to leave the camp hungry was not fulfilled. All I had on me was the camp uniform, and I carried my blanket. The march from Sosnowitz to Mauthausen had taught me not to part with it.

BOOK FIVE
The Wandering Refugee
(1945–1948)

31
A Strange World

MY FRIENDS AND I passed through the wide-open camp gate, not registering the importance of that moment in our lives. Hungry, exhausted and dejected, we were making our first steps into a new and strange world, leaving behind a world capable of unimaginable cruelty, a world that had deprived us of everybody and everything we'd had. We did not know what this new world was like and what the future held for us. The camp was still in every fibre of our beings, in every part of our bodies. We wanted to distance ourselves from it, the farther the better. But our first instinct was for food. Everyone around us was looking for it, and we joined that searching flood of humanity. As far as my eyes could see in front of me and behind me, there were people like me.

We reached a main road that was just as crowded as ours with freed inmates. They were coming from Mauthausen. "And where are you going now?" we asked. Some shrugged their shoulders; they were just following the crowd. Others said, "Linz." I had heard of Linz. When I was in Mauthausen, the Nazis would take people to clear the streets of Linz daily after air raids.

It occurred to us to try one of the farmhouses we passed for food, but no matter where we tried, others had beaten us to it. We decided to leave the main road and stopped at a farmhouse on a side road. A middle-aged woman answered the door. We gave her the packages of margarine and the dried onions and ask her if she could give us something to eat. She told us to sit at the table, and she disappeared behind a door. We looked around, not daring to say anything. It was a small house, and the furniture was well used. We got the impression that this was not a rich home. A good quarter of an hour passed, and the woman was not back yet. Had she gone for the Germans? Our fear of Germans had not disappeared overnight. Another few minutes passed, and she walked in holding a large frying pan containing potatoes and onions that had been fried in margarine. The room filled with the most pleasant aroma. It was the tastiest meal we'd had in years, though we could have eaten more of it. We thanked her nicely and left to join the others on the road.

We soon encountered groups of German soldiers. They carried no weapons, at least as far as we could see. Whenever they found themselves in the midst of liberated inmates and someone would frown at them, they would say, "We are not German; we are Austrian," as if that made a difference from our point of view!

A couple of hours later, our hunger awakened again, and we knocked on another door. An elderly woman answered, and not having anything to barter with, we simply asked her for something to eat. She complained that she was a poor woman and that her son's pay was small. One of us asked her what her son's line of work was, and she replied, "He is only a guard in Mauthausen." We shuddered. We felt that we had the right to take whatever we liked, but she was an elderly woman, and we just turned away in disdain.

On the way back to the main road, we criticized each other for letting her off so easily. Joining the crowd on the road, we pointed out the house to a group of Soviets, and from a distance, we saw them leading a goat from its yard. Their conscience did not bother them. At that moment I was thinking about us Jews, with our scruples and ethics. Was it a wonder that anyone and everyone had taken advantage of us throughout the generations?

With night approaching, we started looking for shelter. We didn't dare go into a German house, so we found a barn to sneak into when it was dark. There was a huge bin full of dry corn kernels, and we spread our blankets over it and went to sleep. In the middle of the night, a couple of farmhands came in, and they laughed when they saw us lying on the corn. We could not fall back asleep, expecting the German owner to evict us at any minute.

During the night, one of my acquaintances mentioned that corn kernels were edible, so before daybreak, we filled a small bag with kernels and quietly sneaked out of the barn. After half an hour's walk down the main road, we found a tin can and filled it with kernels and water. We cooked the kernels for hours, and still they did not become soft. We spent the entire morning cooking the corn, and, too hungry to wait any longer, we ate them. It was almost midday when we set out on the road to Linz. A couple of hours later, we could almost make out the city in the distance. I started feeling sick and had a terrible stomach ache. I could not continue and stretched out on the grass, knowing that something was wrong with me. I told the others to go on, not wanting them to watch me expire. The boys would not hear of it. I mustered all my strength, and we slowly continued walking. None of us felt good, and we concluded that the uncooked corn kernels had started to expand in our stomachs.

At about five in the afternoon, we made it to Linz. To us small-town folks, everything in Linz seemed large. The streets were almost deserted. Here and there we would see a figure that would quickly disappear. Soon we met an American soldier, and we followed him into a large yard. The first thing I noticed was that there were children playing. Children! I had not seen children for so long. These children were playing games, running and laughing, unconcerned and ignorant of the world we were coming from. How beautiful their world seemed. Visions of my little brother Liova and my two little sisters, Sonia and Leiba, appeared in my mind, and I thought about how they had been so cruelly, so mercilessly, taken from this world. I was quickly brought back to reality by the laughter and chatter of these children. There was a pain in my chest, and the question arose again—*Why?*

Around the courtyard, there were groups of women sitting comfortably on chairs and benches, conducting *gemütlich* conversations. Many of them were knitting while talking. Those not so deeply engrossed in conversation noticed us intruders and glanced at us with annoyance and suspicion. The American soldier led us to one of the doors. It was locked. The soldier moved back a few steps and then kicked the door in. The slam of the door startled the women in the yard, who now looked at us with obvious fear. The soldier waved his hands, signalling us to go in, but he stayed outside. I thought, *Why don't you lead us in? We do not dare to go into a German house by ourselves.* But the soldier did not move, and after several minutes of waving his hands, he walked away with a disgusted expression on his face. The completely closed-in yard reminded us too much of the camp, and we got out of there.

We wandered aimlessly in the empty streets and alleys and then started looking for a place to spend the night. We came to a large lumberyard in which there was a wooden shed, the watchman's quarters. In the shed was a bed made of boards, almost two metres wide, and on it, a straw sack, a sheet and a blanket. There was also a cast-iron stove and a few utensils. It all looked like it had been left in a hurry. We piled onto the bed, which to our surprise, was wide enough for the six of us.

The only thing we were capable of thinking about the next morning was food, and we went out to the streets to look for it. Now and then a truck or jeep with a white star painted on its side passed by. A few soldiers threw us their K-rations, and we gulped them down quickly, but this only made us hungrier. Some civilians were in the streets, mostly women of middle age or older, some older men, but there were no young men in sight. After wandering for a few hours, we returned to our new home. There was an American truck parked nearby, and a few soldiers were loading boards onto it. We went over to them cautiously and began to help them. When we finished, they threw us some K-rations and drove away.

The next morning, they were back again, and we earned our breakfast. Again, we walked the streets, looking for our next meal. We saw some survivors like us, but mostly Soviets, former forced labourers. In those early days after liberation, their hatred of Germans manifested in an unbridled lawlessness. They would break into German homes and help themselves to whatever they wanted. Many German homes and apartments had been abandoned, and after a group of Soviets was through with one such home, they told us to go in and help ourselves. We ran in, and I saw a basket with onions. I grabbed it. On top of the basket lay a pair of men's shoes, which I threw away, not having the presence of mind to exchange them for the wooden-soled pair I had on from camp. I noticed a brown envelope on the floor, and I picked it up. It contained cancelled postal stamps, which triggered memories of my childhood hobby, so I took it with me.

Onions do not make a meal, so we continued wandering the streets. We passed a large gate that seemed to lead into a subterranean passage. Two American soldiers guarded the gate. We asked some local passersby what the place was and were told that it was an entrance to a huge underground German supply depot and that the guards came at six in the morning. We were there at five the next morning. The warehouse took up the entire block, and it was filled to overflowing with all kinds of food in boxes, crates, drums, sacks and huge glass jars. We could not believe our eyes. We likely faced the same conflict as those who got in before us—not being able to decide what to take first. We finally made up our minds, grabbed some things and headed toward the gate. Suddenly, American soldiers appeared at the entrance. We were trapped. Behind us we heard a voice: "This way!" We dropped everything and ran after another one of the raiders to an exit on the other side of the warehouse. The soldiers were chasing us, and I found myself running side by side with Leibel Waszkiewicz, the friend who had helped me up the hill from the railway station to Mauthausen at the end of our march. He was hanging on to a paper bag full of sugar cubes. The bag broke, and the cubes were pouring out, and we ran leaving a trail of sugar cubes behind us. Soon the Americans gave up the chase, and we ended up with some sugar.

More and more American trucks came to the lumberyard for wood, and we got to know them and helped them load their trucks. In return, they showered us with food, particularly K-rations and canned food. No more did we have to go looking for food in the streets. We could not resist eating and, not being accustomed to such rich food, we soon developed diarrhea. I recall making nightly promises to myself to stop eating so much during the day, yet when day came and I saw so much food around, I could not resist it. The others and I paid for it by spending most of the night running to the toilet, which, for us, was the entire lumberyard. I could not put an extra pound on my eighty-pound frame after liberation.

In our free hours, we walked around the neighbourhood to look at the destruction brought about by the Allied bombardment. Once we came upon what looked like a giant factory and rail yard that had been levelled to the ground. The extent of the destruction was such that it was impossible to tell where the buildings had stood. One could see railcar after railcar destroyed on the tracks, with some of the rails twisted like wires around them. Two locomotives were sitting upright, as if on their bottoms, their wheels entangled like they were in a final embrace. The contents of the freight cars—sand, cement, gravel and stones—had spilled around them. There was not a living soul around to ask what had been standing there before. Later, we found a local person to ask about it. The answer was "Göring Reichswerke"—the largest and most well-known steel factory in Germany, carrying Hermann Göring's name. We walked away feeling grateful to the Allied airmen for having done such a thorough job.

A few days later, we had a visit from three Germans. One of them said that he was a butcher and that he would like to butcher a horse in the empty part of our shed. In return, we would be rewarded with a choice cut of the horse's meat. I recalled that day, not even a month earlier, when I had received a horse knee in my soup in Gusen, and the promise I had made to myself. We agreed. The next day, the three Germans appeared with a horse in tow. I did not want to be around when they killed it, so I walked away. When I returned to our quarters, there was no sign of the three Germans or the horse. As payment, they had left a chunk of meat from the neck.

From occasional meetings with survivors, we learned that a small displaced persons (DP) camp was being opened nearby for Polish Jews. We went to see it for ourselves. It was a former labour camp, consisting of three or four huts, each further partitioned into several rooms. In each room were about seven cots with straw sacks. It had running water, and more importantly, it was already set up with a little office run by an elected committee of survivors. They were registered with the local authorities and were receiving a daily allotment of food. We liked what we saw and joined them. The American K-rations and the cans of bully beef on which I had been gorging myself, the cause of my being sick at night, were gone. Here I was back on a diet quite close to what we had in the camps—coffee and bread for breakfast, a bowl of thick soup at noon, and again coffee and bread at night, none of these to excess. Within a week, I was cured and slowly began to put on weight.

Near our new camp was a former German military barracks where American soldiers were now quartered in modern brick buildings. The buildings were connected by one central heating and water system that was in the basement of one of the buildings. I do not remember how, but the six of us got the job of attending to and stocking the furnace. We had to be at work at 5:00 a.m. to make sure there would be enough hot water by 6:00 a.m., when the soldiers would be getting up. We worked two shifts until 9:00 p.m. We had permits that allowed us to come and go as we pleased. In return for our labour, we lined up with the soldiers at breakfast and lunch, never failing to impress them with our insatiable appetites, and, indeed, we ate a lot. There was a private shower for our use in the basement, and soldiers who did not want to wait in line upstairs came down to use ours. Many left us presents, like cigarettes and chocolate, and sometimes even their discarded clothes.

A kilometre away from our camp was another camp for survivors, housing former inmates and forced labourers from different countries. I heard that my friend Leibel Bliskowsky, with whom I had shared extra food in Sosnowitz, was in that camp. We had been in Mauthausen together too, but not Gusen. I decided to go and look for him. I got to that refugee camp at sunset, and in the dim light of the setting sun, somebody pointed out to me a small figure squatting by a fire in an empty field. As I approached, I saw Leibel heating something in a small tin can. He recognized me and extended his hand but still kept an eye on the tin can, which contained chicken feet. Without saying a word, I kicked the can and it went flying, scattering the chicken feet all over the place.

Leibel looked at me and asked angrily, "Why did you do that? It was my supper."

I said, "Come with me, Leibel; I have something better than this." That evening, he came to our room, where he had his first proper meal six weeks after liberation.

A few weeks later, we began to hear rumours that our part of Linz would be handed over to the Soviets, and the dividing line would be the Danube River. To get to the other side, we had to cross a bridge that was guarded by American soldiers, and foreigners would need a special permit from the American authorities to cross. Everybody in our small camp wanted to get over to the American side, and we began to make preparations for it.

One day, a jeep pulled into our refugee camp, and four military men got out. We saw the word "Palestine" sewn on their upper sleeves. They greeted us with a "Shalom" and continued conversing with us in Hebrew. Those of us who did not speak Hebrew conversed in Yiddish. They were soldiers from the Jewish Brigade of the British Army, and they were looking to establish contact with Jewish survivors. They told us that the British government was blockading the shores of Palestine, and that the Yishuv, the Jewish community in Palestine, was trying to break that blockade by illegally smuggling in survivors. As Allied soldiers, they could move freely in formerly German-occupied Europe, searching for the surviving European Jews. Their mission was to get as many Jews as possible out of the territories overtaken by the Soviet Union.

A week or so later, the soldiers of the Jewish Brigade began to transport small groups of Jewish survivors across the bridge. Some of us were told to try to make it on our own, as the soldiers found it difficult to get everybody across. The American base where the six of us were working began to pack up, but we were asked to stay on till the last moment so that they would have hot water. Close to the end of July, the Americans drove us across the bridge to a large city, where they dropped us off in a crowded yard.

We were in a refugee camp in Salzburg. It was filled with people from all over previously German-occupied Europe. We soon found some of the guys from our camp in Linz who had left a week or two earlier, and we were given a place to sleep in a corner of a room. The food consisted of a piece of bread and tea in the morning, a bowl of soup at noon and tea and bread at night. There were not sufficient facilities to wash in, and there were no toilets. The crowd could be divided into two main groups: former inmates of concentration camps and former forced labourers. The majority of the concentration camp survivors were Jews, with some Soviets and Poles. But all the forced labourers were non-Jews, among whom were former Nazi sympathizers and collaborators, as well as kapos from the camps who were parading as refugees. Some were recognized by survivors and were dealt with harshly.

In general, the camp in Salzburg was one big mess, with hundreds of people arriving and leaving daily. I was reunited again with Leibel Bliskowsky, and a few days later we were sent to Innsbruck, to a camp for Jewish survivors only. Several days after our arrival there, a small group from the Jewish Brigade arrived, and one of the officers addressed us, telling us that we would be going to Italy as it was as close to Palestine as they could get us. The only way to Palestine was by sea. "You might have to wait in Italy a long time," he said, "and we are not promising you anything in Italy except for a beautiful blue sky. So if anyone wants to back out, now is the chance."

A few days later, we boarded a long freight train that was carrying Italian nationals back to Italy. It was early August, and we kept the sliding doors and windows of the freight car open and had a good view of the countryside as we moved south. We travelled very slowly, stopping at every station. Some of the stations had Red Cross stands where they handed out bread and bottled water. At times we stopped in the middle of nowhere and were surrounded by beautiful nature. The fast-flowing little rivers looked inviting and we bathed in them. Before long, we were moving through the Brenner Pass with its beautiful views of the Alps and then into Italy.

32
Italy

AFTER THREE DAYS of slow travel, we arrived in Bologna, where the Jewish survivors were put up in tents provided by the Jewish Brigade. Two days later, trucks took us to Modena, in northern Italy. Somewhere in the middle of the city was a huge and impressive building, built in the style of late-nineteenth-century Italian architecture, with spacious rooms and hallways. It had served as a military academy until the end of the war, and it now housed Jewish survivors and, in one distant corner, a few dozen SS women who were guarded by American military police. Into this aesthetic building, the Allied forces had squeezed in some five thousand of us. We were told to find a place to sleep, which meant anywhere on the stone floor. We lay along every wall and in rows in the middle of the rooms, sleeping in the same spot each night and sitting in it during the day. In the mornings, we lined up for our piece of bread and black coffee, and at noon for macaroni, and at night again for a piece of bread and coffee. With this diet, we were constantly hungry, although it was not the same hunger we had experienced in the camps.

To supplement our diet, some of us began to sell our belongings. I sold the few pairs of discarded US military pants and shirts I had brought. With my earnings, I went to the nearby bakery to buy rolls, but as the baker had no bag to put them in, I stuffed them in my pockets and carried the rest in my arms. Some rolls fell to the ground, and while bending to pick them up, I lost two or three more. I do not remember how many rolls I came back with, but I remember telling Leibel Bliskowsky that it was no good going for rolls alone, as I kept losing them. Beryl Bluestein, a man some twenty years older than me who had his sleeping spot not far from us, overheard this remark and offered to go with me. I gratefully accepted. On the way back, without asking or saying anything, he started eating the rolls, never stopping until we got back. After that, he would always go with me to the bakery. In no time, I managed to dispose of my possessions, and we ate up the value of the few pairs of pants and shirts and were back to the bare minimum. There were rumours that in some refugee camps one could get a new pair of shoes or pants, or both, upon arrival. In other camps, one got a few hundred liras. That was worth a dollar or two, but to one who had nothing, that was money.

Not having anything else to barter and unable to fill our stomachs, Leibel and I decided to travel to Milan. And so, we joined a mob of hitchhikers at the outskirts of Modena. All we had with us was the address of the Jewish community centre in Milan: Via Unione 5. After a long wait, we succeeded in getting on a truck, which took us as far as Parma. From there, we hitchhiked to the Po River, where we joined a long line of vehicles waiting to cross the pontoon bridge erected by the Allied forces. We could see the original bridge, which had been destroyed, its massive supporting pillars toppled over, lying on their sides as if they had been pushed over by a giant hand.

We found the conditions in the refugee camp in Milan no better than in Modena, so after a few days, Leibel and I decided to head back. This time, we went to the railway station and found out that there would be a train to Modena in the morning. We settled down for the night on the stone floor among a mass of people in the huge train station. Back in Modena, I noticed how many Jewish survivors there were, though the American soldiers were more noticeable. They were, of course, more respected and better treated because they were the liberators for many Italians too, particularly for the northern half of Italy, which had been under Nazi rule longer than the south. The Americans were rich, and even the poorest had his pockets full of cigarettes, chocolate, gum and women's pantyhose. They used to take girls out to the amusement park at the outskirts of town and to restaurants and dances. But soon we noticed that there were fewer American servicemen, as they were going home. Leibel was a smoker, and he would follow the Americans and pick up their cigarette butts. With fewer Americans, he was forced to smoke less. Eventually he gave up smoking.

My only source of enjoyment in Modena was going to the movies. The movie houses were open all night, and once inside, one could spend the night there. Some of us would do that not so much to watch the movies as to have the experience of being under a roof in a strange city.

Leibel and I decided to undertake the long trip to Turin, where there was also a refugee camp because we thought we might be better off there. We hitchhiked as far as Piacenza, where we got off at the police checkpoint on the outskirts of town and waited. After a long wait in the midday Italian sun, an army truck pulled up and stopped almost in front of us. We didn't run to the truck, knowing that Allied vehicles did not pick up hitchhikers. But these soldiers were dressed in British uniforms, and we saw "Palestine" on their shoulder badges. A little hesitantly, we approached and tried to listen to their conversation. They noticed us and looked at us with a sense of recognition—we somehow saw brothers in each other. We found out that they were a group of entertainers who travelled to the bases of the Jewish Brigade to entertain the soldiers. There were two women in that group. They all surrounded us, showering us with questions. One of the soldiers was from Białystok, and as Leibel was originally from a village near Białystok, the soldier asked him about his family. The entertainers saw that we had nothing and brought us tins of meat and fish, loaves of bread, chocolate and even a suitcase of military clothes from the truck. After a long and amiable conversation, they apologized that they could not take us closer to our destination, and they left. What an impression they left on us—a fantastic feeling of having seen, spoken to and physically touched Jewish soldiers in a strange land, among strangers, after years of Nazi tyranny. The encounter injected in me a new hope, a kind of happiness that I had not felt in a long, long time.

Leibel and I looked at our unexpected riches and realized that we could not continue to Turin carrying it all. Besides, who needed Turin anymore with all that food? So we crossed the road to get a ride back to Modena.

In the next two weeks, I took in all the movies I could, two after lunch and two at night. In the mornings, all of us would line up along the balcony that ran around the large cobblestoned yard of the academy to watch the American military police taking the SS women for a walk around it. We were not permitted to remain on the ground floor at those times, so we hurled abuse at them from above. And we were good at it. After all, we had learned from them, though many of us did not understand the meaning of the words we used, including me.

After a while, British soldiers replaced the American military police, and their escort of the SS women became comradely. One could get the impression that they were British gentlemen competing to win the favour of fair maidens, rather than guards upholding justice for hundreds of thousands of defenceless and innocent victims. Now the murderers were being paraded in front of thousands of witnesses whose families had been slaughtered by those very beasts, and who themselves had been victims of their brutality.

No more than two weeks after my encounter with the soldiers of the Jewish Brigade, I was back in the poor house. A few guys decided to go to Turin, and I joined them. The trip was difficult and took a long time. Upon arriving, we were directed to a Jewish centre. In the evenings, a few young people, the remnants of the once large and prosperous

Jewish community of Turin, would gather and reminisce about their families, who had been taken away, never to be heard from again. We decided to stay there that evening. About a dozen young people showed up, mostly girls, for women had found it a little easier to hide among the Italians than men. However, there was the problem of communication. They spoke Italian or French, since Turin is close to the French border, and we spoke neither language. Then one of the girls said something in Hebrew. None of my group spoke Hebrew except me. I was in my element, and the entire conversation was conducted through the two of us.

Later in the evening, a couple of Jewish soldiers from a South African detachment stationed nearby came in. We were told that they were frequent visitors. One of them played the piano, and we started dancing. That was my first dance after those nightmarish years, and my first as a mature man. That evening that I spent in Turin holding a girl in my arms awakened in me feelings that I had forgotten existed. But Turin had no more to offer than Modena, and we travelled back.

That summer, I bumped into a Shershevian I never expected to see alive—Eli Schneider, the older brother of my friend Hershel Schneider, with whom I had walked on Sundays in the birch alley in Auschwitz in the spring of 1943. Eli was a tall, polite and good-looking young man who had been active in Hashomer Hatzair, the left-wing Zionist organization, from his youth. He had been drafted into the Polish army in 1938 and was one of many who didn't return home after the collapse of Poland. It was accepted that he had been killed, and his family mourned him. Now I learned that he had survived by passing as a non-Jewish prisoner of war with the help of his friends in his battalion and was sent to work on a German farm for the remainder of the war. Seeing him in Modena was like witnessing a return from the grave. He had come to Italy with the intention of going to Palestine. Because of his leadership experience in Hashomer Hatzair in Shershev, he was put in charge of a group of minors in a small camp outside of Modena. After we met, he would visit me every time he was in Modena.

He asked me many questions about the months before and after the expulsion from Shershev, the life of his family in the Pruzhany ghetto, and about my few conversations with his brother on those Sunday mornings in Auschwitz.

One morning, he came to me and asked if I wanted to go to Palestine. "Sure I do!" I answered.

"Then get ready," he said. "In a few days, my entire group of minors will be taken at night to a secret place where they will board a ship to Palestine."

At that time, some quarter of a million Jews, survivors of the Holocaust and returnees from the Soviet Union, languished in refugee camps after the war, waiting for a country to open its doors to them. It was a not-too-well-kept secret that ships were departing from Italy to Palestine with illegal immigrants—survivors and refugees of the Holocaust. The British tried to stop this activity by all possible means. They kept an eye on the Jewish Brigade, knowing that they were the main force behind this movement. They checked all suspected vehicles on the roads of Italy, looking not only for potential travellers, but also for anything that might be required for longer journeys over land or sea. They tried to find the spots of embarkation, so they could seize the boats. And finally, they blockaded the shores of Palestine with their navy.

I was thrilled, but then I remembered my friend Leibel Bliskowsky, who was eighteen years my senior. I said, "You will have to take the two of us with you."

Eli, having met Bliskowsky through me on an earlier occasion, told me that it could not be done. I could pass as a minor, but he couldn't. They would not let him aboard. I was caught between my life's desire to go to the Land of Israel, and my loyalty to a friend with whom I had shared so much suffering and trust, whom I had known to be an honest and unselfish person and a true friend. I said that I would not go without him, and Eli left.

In the late summer or fall, refugees in Milan began to receive some 1,500 lira monthly. Refugees did not have to pay passage, but the railway system was in general confusion, and most of the Italian passengers did not pay either. Not only was there usually standing room only, but some people sat on the roofs and had to duck down or drop flat when the train entered a tunnel. On that first trip to Milan to collect my money, we were so tightly squeezed together in the car that upon arriving in Milan, the backs of my hands were swollen, a result of having kept my arms pressed tightly to my body for over twelve hours. On the way back, I was not lucky enough to get inside a car, and I had to sit on the buffer between two cars all night, hanging on to a protruding bolt to keep myself from falling onto the tracks.

Sometime in October, we were informed that our entire refugee camp was going to be transferred to camps farther south, to the very heel of Italy. Shortly afterwards, every few days some of us were taken by truck to the railway station. By then, my partnership with Leibel had expanded to include Beryl Bluestein, and when our turn came, we travelled south together. We travelled in ordinary freight cars with the doors wide open on either side. We sat on our knapsacks, which held our meagre possessions, and when possible, stretched out on the floor for a nap. For food, we were each given a few packages of biscuits and a couple of tins of canned meat. Here again, we were thrown together with survivors from all over Central and Eastern Europe. The great majority were men between the ages of twenty and thirty. About 10 per cent were women in the same age range. We all felt a kinship that held us together and expressed itself in the way we approached one another and spoke to each other, as if we had known each other since birth. This was made easier by our common language, Yiddish, even though we came from at least half a dozen countries.

As we travelled south, I could see mountaintops in the distance to the right. To the left, no more than a few hundred metres away, was a dark levelled plain. I asked what it was, and someone told me that it was the sea, the Adriatic. *So this is what the sea looks like*, I thought.

After three days, we came to the small railway station of Otranto. From there, we travelled in trucks downhill on a winding road through rocky terrain alternating with small plots of red soil and spotted with olive trees. Some trees seemed to grow out of the rock.

We drove into a village and stopped in front of a building, where we were registered and given an identity card and an address. Then we wandered through the village with its beautiful villas, palm trees and gardens. The villas looked terribly neglected, as if nobody had touched them in years. In the streets we met some non-Jewish refugees. They were from our part of the world, and they too did not go home after liberation, even though they had parents, siblings and members of their close families there waiting for them. We felt like we knew these refugees. We knew them too well! They were the ones who had welcomed the Nazis as soon as they came into our shtetls, the ones who had pointed to us and pointed out our homes to the Nazis and helped themselves to whatever they wanted. They were the ones who joined the local police, who helped the Germans round up the Jews, drive them out of town and shoot them at the edge of the ditches that the Jews were forced to dig for themselves. They were the ones who volunteered to fight with the Germans against their own country and their own people. And now they could not return home, fearing that they would be tried and executed as traitors.

The house we were assigned had two storeys and was built on a slope so that it had entrances on two different streets. A family from Yugoslavia occupied the bottom floor. They were not Jewish, and we wondered why they were not going home. The upper floor had several rooms, and the three of us got a room with a window looking out on a neglected palm tree and on a stone wall surrounding the front of the house. We could see that this must have been a nice villa once.

We were in a town called Santa Maria di Leuca, one of half a dozen summer resorts along the very tip of the Italian heel. The place had many beautiful villas, the summer homes of wealthy Italians. This refugee camp was better organized than the previous ones we had been in. It had been here for a while because the war had ended in southern Italy more than a year previously. The camp was run by American and British semi-military personnel, with the paid help of qualified Italians, though the British seemed to be running the show. The villas these people lived in had been repaired and furnished. They had housekeepers, cooks and gardeners who were paid Allied wages, as were the administrative personnel. There were also some American volunteers from religious organizations.

Apparently, somebody in the UNRRA (United Nations Relief and Rehabilitation Administration) realized that putting Jewish Holocaust survivors with refugees among whom there were Nazi collaborators was not a good idea. Within two weeks of our arrival, the non-Jews were transferred to other refugee camps.

Those two weeks gave us a chance to get organized and to take over positions that had been held by the departing refugees. We elected a committee to run the internal affairs of the camp and a cultural committee. We organized workshops and training courses for all kinds of trades. And we even put together a group whose job it was to keep law and order in the camp. Not that it was really needed. We had been murdered, but we were not murderers; everything had been stolen from us, but we were not thieves. Besides, we had nothing of value for anybody to steal. In fact, this camp seemed to be the safest place I had known since the beginning of the war, maybe even before that.

In those early days, we each received a bed of sorts. It was a wooden frame made of two-by-fours. Chicken netting was stretched across the frame and covered with a straw sack for a mattress. It was better than the stone floors in Modena. We used a discarded crate as a table, and thus our room was furnished.

Some larger groups who knew each other from camps or who came from the same vicinity or shared the same Zionist affiliation organized what they called a kibbutz. They occupied one building as a group, pooled their rations and cooked food for their entire group together. Approximately a dozen groups, or kibbutzim, existed in Santa Maria di Leuca. The rest of the camp members would go to the central kitchen to receive their daily ration of bread with coffee in the morning, soup with some pieces of meat for lunch and coffee at night. Once a week, there was no meat cooked with the soup, and we received a small tin of salmon. Every morning, one from our group lined up in front of the kitchen with all kinds of containers for the coffee and our three ration cards. Each card was made out for the month ahead, indicating each meal of each day. When the person presented the card, a hole was punched out for that meal. In those early months in Santa Maria di Leuca, I went to bed hungry.

True to the promise of the soldiers from the Jewish Brigade, I had not seen a cloud in the beautiful Italian sky. We were so close to the blue sea, we could almost jump into it from the window of the villa. The shoreline was sharp volcanic rock except for a short stretch of sand. The waves were strong, and one had to be careful not to be thrown on the rocks when getting out of the water. For most of us, this was our first time in the sea, but we became pretty good swimmers. We spent most of our days at the seashore that autumn, and the sea and sun worked wonders for us.

I, along with many other refugees, was now receiving 3,000 lira a month from Milan, provided by a refugee aid organization. Those who qualified had to travel by train to collect it, a trip of three days in each direction. It wasn't a lot of money, but it was of some help. However, we stopped receiving money by November 1945.

In early December, the camp committee announced that a marine school for survivors was being formed someplace in Italy, and I applied and was accepted. I was sent to Bari, where I joined three other Jewish men who were to be teachers in the school. They were two Hungarian engineers who had succeeded in avoiding being shipped to Auschwitz and a Soviet engineer who claimed to have been the captain or first officer on the Soviet submarines known as Stalinets. I was attached to the three engineers because of my knowledge of Hebrew and Yiddish, for they did not speak a word of Hebrew and very little Yiddish. All the arrangements for the school were conducted in Hebrew, as it was being organized by people from British Mandate Palestine.

To get an idea of what the school should be like, we were sent via Rome to the sea town of Ostia, thirty kilometres west of Rome, on the Tyrrhenian Sea, where such a school was already operating. After spending a few days there, we went to the small fishing town of Fano, on the Adriatic Sea. We joined the already settled body of students and staff, all together about 150 people. The conditions were primitive, and there was nothing much by way of furniture or even kitchen utensils. Food was not more plentiful than it had been in the previous refugee camps, except that we could get a slice of bread with thinly spread lard every couple of hours from a member of the kitchen staff.

As some of the teachers were local Italians and the books we were using were written in Italian, it was decided that the lectures would be conducted in Italian as well. So the first item on the agenda was to teach us Italian right away. In the meantime, the three Jewish teachers who came with me from Bari began to teach their subjects. Their lessons were conducted in an unspecified language, that is, any language the teacher could make the students understand. This was where my knowledge of Russian and Polish came in handy. The teacher from the Soviet Union could hardly speak Yiddish, so most of the lecture was conducted in Russian, and I would translate it on the spot into Yiddish or Polish, whichever was better understood by the students. The two Hungarian teachers had a harder time. Their Yiddish was poor and they did not know Polish, yet their classes were 95 per cent Jews from Poland. They had to make do with a mixture of German and Yiddish. During those first weeks, I befriended the Russian teacher, who would make sure that I understood the lectures before they started.

Out of the eight hours of daily lessons, four were taken up with Italian, and slowly we began to master the language, though, the moment the classes were over, we reverted to speaking Yiddish. The only bit of free time we had to ourselves was on the weekends, when we would go into the town for short visits. On Friday afternoons, I would go with some of my friends to the wharf in Fano and watch the fishing fleets returning from the sea with their catch. On one of these visits, we watched as one of the crew on a fishing boat divided a catch of octopus into as many parts as there were crewmembers. The crew stood, and one member turned around while another pointed at a portion and asked, "Who for?" The one who was turned around called out the name of another crewmember. In this way, the octopuses were divided among the members. It was reminiscent of how we divided bread in Sosnowitz. I wondered how they could support their families. They left home on Monday before sunrise and returned late Friday afternoon, all for a few kilos of octopus. I was hungry myself, yet I felt sorry for those Italians.

I was one of the privileged ones who had been picked for the captain course and was kept busy with studies and homework. In the second half of January, we began to talk about what was awaiting us after completing this four-year captain course. The instructor said that our diploma would entitle us to command a boat or a schooner the size of those we saw in the local harbour. The bubble had burst, and my dream of commanding an ocean liner evaporated in a second. The life we had envisioned was in stark contrast to the reality we saw on the fishermen's wharf in Fano. Shortly thereafter, students began to leave and return to the refugee camps they had come from. The Soviet instructor tried to persuade me to stay, even promising me that by the time the course would be finished, I would know everything he knew, and that I should not squander such an opportunity. I knew he was sincere and meant every word he said, but at twenty-two, the idea of spending four years with the promise of becoming a fisherman with the pay of a few kilos of octopus per week did not appeal to me.

I left Fano with about six others and went to Rome. There, we registered in a refugee camp on the premises of Cinecittà, the studios where Italian movies were produced before the war. It was a large place with some hangar-like buildings, surrounded by a high fence. A gate led inside, and unarmed police from among the refugees manned the guardhouse. They were husky men from Yugoslavia, and I couldn't help but wonder if they were afraid to return home for fear of being prosecuted for collaborating with the Nazis. We survivors could easily imagine them wearing the Ustaša uniforms of the Croatian fascist organization.

In those unheated hangar-like buildings, hundreds of refugees from all over Europe were quartered, and there were rows of cots from wall to wall. As newcomers, we received a blanket to cover ourselves with and nothing else. In the week I spent in Rome, I did not feel warm even once. And yet, despite my constant discomfort and the fact that I came from a small Eastern European shtetl and had never learned about architecture, I could not remain indifferent to what I saw. The beauty of Rome's magnificent palaces, the splendour of its villas and edifices and the grandeur of its monuments impressed me. I promised myself I would come back someday to look at it all on a full stomach.

The empty stomach was the best incentive for us to return to the camps in the Italian heel. Returning to the villa in Santa Maria di Leuca, I passed through a room occupied by a few other boys, and they jumped at me, yelling with joy, as if a long-lost brother had returned. Half following and half carrying me, they brought me into my room, where my primitive cot was waiting for me, and so were my two roommates. I was struck at once by the loud conversation and what seemed to me to be a crude, even vulgar, use of language. I had been exposed for ten weeks to a different environment, and I must have been influenced by being around people who were trying to improve themselves and learn something. I began to have regrets for having left the school.

After everyone calmed down, my roommates and I exchanged news. Leibel had good news for me. In my absence, a letter had arrived from New York, from my uncle Shloime Auerbach, my mother's oldest brother. I remembered how in the Pruzhany ghetto, on January 30, 1943, when my mother accompanied me to the porch to say goodbye, her last words to me were, "Go my son and hide. Maybe by some miracle you will succeed to avoid the Nazis and survive the war. Remember my child, you have two uncles in America, my brothers Shloime and Pesach. If, God willing, you will survive, go to them and tell them how we lived and how we perished." Then she told me the address of her brother Shloime: 2133 Daly Avenue, Bronx, New York.

When I was in Auschwitz and the other camps, Bronx was replaced in my memory by Brooklyn, and the letters I wrote after the war were lost, and one of them returned to me in Italy. There were quite a few Jews among the American troops in Europe, and Jewish soldiers would visit the refugee camps and take names and addresses to relatives in the United States. I am sure I gave my uncle's name and address too. However it happened, my uncle Shloime found out where I was and sent a letter to me care of the Milan Jewish community. They forwarded his letter to Santa Maria di Leuca. Leibel knew the importance of this letter to me and opened it immediately. It was not the first letter my uncle had written to me. He expressed joy that at least one member of the family had survived and wrote that he could not wait to see me, but that, in the meantime, I should let him know what I needed. Leibel had answered right away, writing that I needed everything.

A few weeks later, I received a notice from a bank in Taranto that money had been sent to me. In Taranto, I discovered that my Uncle Shloime had sent me 10 dollars for which I was given 2,200 lira. I was rich!

33
Possibilities

THE REFUGEE CAMPS in southern Italy were not like other camps with typical barracks or military accommodations and fences. True, we slept on primitive bunks with no furniture or outdoor plumbing and not much to eat. Yet we lived in villas and could move around freely and travel around Italy. The blue Mediterranean was at our feet, and there was an even bluer sky above. In those early months of 1946, the camp was beginning to take shape. A few dozen non-Jewish families remained, mostly Russians, but also several Yugoslavians and Spaniards. There was a communal bathhouse, with different hours for men and women. However, almost everybody spent many hours a day at the seashore, so the bathhouse was empty most of the time. Next to the bathhouse was a cultural centre, where we could sit and read old Hebrew newspapers from Palestine, as well as a Jewish newspaper printed in Rome called *Bederech* (On the Way). We sometimes had dances, where an orchestra made up of survivors played. As most of us were men, and there were not enough girls to go around, boys would dance with boys. The evenings had to pass somehow. There was a cultural circle and a theatrical circle, and each Zionistic faction had its own activities. All those groups solicited members and welcomed newcomers, so one could keep very busy if one wanted to. Yet most of us did not belong to a particular group, preferring to attend activities without obligations or commitments.

In the spring of 1946, I made contact with my father's first cousin in Netanya, in British Mandate Palestine. Chaim Shemesh had been the very first commander of Betar in Shershev and had left for the Land of Israel in 1932. His wife, Sonia, had come for a visit to Shershev with her baby during the Soviet era. I also established contact with my mother's cousin Sheine Rochel and her husband, Zev Chemelnitzky, who had moved to the Land of Israel in 1935. I received a letter from Sheine Rochel, telling me to get in touch with a soldier in the Jewish Brigade named Kirshenbaum, who was stationed in Milan. Kirshenbaum hailed from Pruzhany and had gone to the Land of Israel as a *chalutz*, a Zionist pioneer, some years earlier. So I again made the long trip to Milan and found Kirshenbaum. I was not sure what I expected from him, perhaps that by some magic, he would pull out of his pocket a permit to go to Palestine. This was not to be. He showed me a letter from the Chemelnitzky's, asking him to get in touch with me and help me financially. I still remember the wording: "Give him as much as he wants if he will only take it." I felt proud of such a recommendation. After all, they were only my second cousins and had left Pruzhany when I was twelve years old. In the ten years since they had left, I could have grown into a crook, a cheat or worse. Yet they had so much trust in the family tradition that they were giving me a blank cheque. I could have used a few liras then, but I was so overwhelmed by their trust that I refused to take anything from Kirshenbaum. He looked at me with astonishment and incomprehension and asked me, "What am I going to tell them?"

In one of the letters I received from the Shemesh family, I was told that in Santa Maria di Leuca there was a family by the name of Berger, and they had five British pounds for me, which their son from Netanya had brought for me. Since the money was already in the camp, I swallowed my pride and accepted it.

Sometime in May or June of 1946, my roommate Beryl Bluestein returned from a meeting of the camp committee, of which he was a member, and told me that the camp storehouse needed a man who knew some English. He suggested that perhaps I should apply for the job. The man in charge of this storehouse was an American sergeant who was not keen on going back home and had transferred to the service of UNRRA. He was not known as a nice person and was quite abrupt, sometimes even outright rude. As I was constantly in need of money and had picked up a few words in English, I applied and got the job. The man I was replacing stayed on for two weeks to teach me the bookkeeping skills needed in the warehouse. He was one of the two Germans in the camp, in his mid-twenties, very polite and helpful. One can imagine the questions we had regarding those two Germans, but their politeness, which we certainly lacked, and their willingness to help was so disarming, that we could not muster the courage to ask them point-blank what they did during the war.

My job was to receive the daily allotment of food that arrived on trucks and divide it up according to the number of people in every group or daycare centre. Then the trucks would deliver it to its destinations. Special rations were provided for the Allied employees of the camp, quite different from what we refugees received. The refugees who worked in the storehouse could only look at it and feel our mouths water. Our initial pay was 3,000 lira per month. At that time, one could get a pair of US Army pants for 1,000 liras, or a pair of shoes for 1,500 liras, and a kilogram of bread cost 100 liras. As survivors, our dream for years had been a full stomach in the short run, and to come out alive of the Nazi hell in the long run. And so we felt that there were many possibilities with 3,000 liras a month.

There were fringe benefits to this work, perhaps not achieved by what would be considered the most honourable behaviour in times of plenty. When a shipment of fresh fruit or vegetables arrived, the workers, including the supervisors, of whom I was one, would "taste" them, which was against the rules. At times, we received shipments of fresh meat. Everyone in the camp suspected some irregularities concerning the meat. At the beginning, we received frozen Australian sheep of good quality. But later, instead of the sheep, we began to receive half carcasses of slaughtered local oxen. Those oxen were used in southern Italy as beasts of burden and were slaughtered after they had outlived their usefulness. I had never encountered meat like it in my life. Eating it was like chewing rubber. No matter how long it was cooked in the camp kitchen, the small pieces that we received in our soup were not edible and had to be thrown out. It was our belief that somewhere along the way from the port to the distribution centres, the Australian sheep were substituted, and the ox carcasses that were unfit for consumption were sent to us instead. We were also sure that there were people high up in the UNRRA organization in Italy—British or American—who were involved in that switch. As refugees and survivors, we did not dare to make a fuss over it. Sometimes we got a truckload of supposedly freshly caught fish from the distribution point in Maglie. By the time we got it, it was not fresh at all. The best way to put it would be that we could smell the fish before we could hear the approaching trucks.

I am writing about an era when the world, particularly Europe, was trying to come to grips with the aftermath of World War II. For us Jews, it was a calamity from which the Jewish people of Europe would never recover. With the destruction of Central and Eastern European Jewry, we lost the creative source of our rich and diverse Yiddish language and literature. It was as if the womb of our people had been wrenched out. Jews all over—those who remained of our people across the sea or in the Land of Israel—had united in the attempt to ease the pain of the quarter of a million survivors who were languishing in hundreds of refugee camps across Germany, Austria and Italy. World Jewry was trying to find permanent homes for us. The liberators, the Allies, were content to let us be where we were rather than open their doors. The United States let a trickle of survivors in.

Abandoned by the world, all we could do was beg, but nobody heard or cared to listen. So we became vocal, and a period of protest marches started in every refugee camp, including ours. Not a week went by without one. There was no shortage of leaders among us, capable, intelligent, educated and dedicated survivors in their thirties and forties. We got a boost from some of the former members of the Jewish Brigade who volunteered to stay behind to prepare us for the coming struggle with the British to enter the Land of Israel, as well as to adjust to the life there. Others came from the Land of Israel as volunteers for the UNRRA but also with the secret mission to organize and work with the Bricha, the underground organization whose mission was to smuggle us refugees into the Land of Israel. I recall one of those volunteers, Aryeh, a well-built young man in his late twenties and an excellent athlete, who would take a large group of us out every morning for exercise. He visited me at work, asking what new products had arrived so that he could write out requisitions for them. Supposedly the requisitions were for the camp, but I knew that a truck would take the products to the embarkation points for use on the boats carrying illegal refugees to the shores of Palestine.

His replacement, Schwartz, was an exceptionally bright and smart man in his thirties. He was always dressed in his military uniform. Once, four Italian sailors were arrested by the British at an embarkation point and put in a jail near Maglie. Schwartz, dressed in a British officer's uniform, managed to get those Italians out with forged papers. The British investigated but never found the impersonator or the four Italians. Schwartz was replaced by Nisht, who was from a Polish shtetl and had immigrated to Palestine before the war. When he came to our camp, he was in his fifties. Up to that time I had never met a smarter, more intelligent, understanding or wiser man than Nisht. When he spoke, one would not dare to interrupt the flow of wisdom coming out of his mouth. Despite the fact that he and I were on the opposite poles of the Zionistic movement, and I had never won an argument with him, I loved to listen to the sensible articulation of his convictions.

As the camps on the heel of Italy were almost entirely Jewish, all offices and warehouses were closed on Saturdays. The top executives were former Allied officers, and the administration employees were mostly Italians and Christian, so everything was closed on Sundays as well. That gave me two full days of free time as well as the evenings.

Having received during that time a few parcels with clothing from my Uncle Shloime, I was reasonably well dressed for a refugee. In the beginning, I did my own laundry, washing one pair of underwear while wearing the other pair. But after receiving those parcels, I had clothes in reserve. I even found an Italian woman whom I paid a small fee to do my laundry. Her nineteen-year-old daughter often waited for me after dark in the bushes that grew around their house, wanting a bit of affection.

As the camp took roots, the theatrical group began to put on performances more often. We were even visited by travelling Italian theatrical groups. The Joint (American Jewish Joint Distribution Committee) sponsored a travelling group consisting of survivors, whose performances were of good quality, and they were dear to our hearts. At that time, there was no greater delight.

Sometime in the middle of 1946, the warehouse workers started receiving a civilian salary. That meant a leap from 3,000 lira per month to 13,500 liras. I converted the Italian money into American dollars and put most of it away.

Santa Maria di Leuca had a couple of restaurants where one could buy as much cheap table wine as one desired. As far as food was concerned, they only had fried fish or almonds. Because the wine was cheap, many of us could afford to go there for a glass of wine and a half kilo of almonds once a week. We would not eat the fish. There were also some small grocery stores, an outdoor movie house and a café. Admission to the movie house was cheap, and we went there every time a new film arrived, roughly every week. The café was near the movie house, and the few of us who could afford it would go there for ice cream, which was made on the premises.

Many of us survivors made contact with relatives overseas during that time and began to receive parcels and money from them. No longer was one considered rich if one had two pairs of pants or three changes of underwear. Some of the parcels contained clothing that was too small or too large, so people began to sell those items, and in time it became a full-time occupation for some, buying items from other survivors and peddling them in the surrounding villages.

Mail service had finally been established in postwar Italy, and I started to receive regular mail, mostly from my uncle Shloime in America, but also often from my parents' cousins in the Land of Israel. I also established contact with my only remaining aunt from my father's side, Sarah Kantorowitz, who had been married to my father's brother Shalom, in Argentina, and with Menachem, now Melvin, Goldfarb, a cousin from Pruzhany. Like me, Menachem was the sole survivor of his family.

We had been sitting in Italy for over a year, with no hope of getting into Palestine. The British blockade was getting tighter. The few barely seaworthy boats that were trying to get to Palestine had little chance of making it. Some of us began to lose hope, some of us courage, some both. A fair number of us who had succeeded in contacting relatives across the ocean were tempted to join them. I tried to resist the temptation, holding on to the hope that, eventually, I would somehow get to the Land of Israel.

I can still recall a letter I received from my uncle Shloime in which he wrote,

> Remember Moishele, you are all that remains of our family in Europe and all that is left. We want you to be with us. You have suffered enough. As far as defending the Yishuv, I had three sons in the US Army during the war, and they came back alive, thank God. If need be, I will send them. You have paid your dues. Come to us.

It was not the eloquence of the letter as much as his love and concern for me that moved me and triggered a thought that perhaps I should reconsider my plan.

In the fall of 1946, I received a letter from Chaim and Sonia Shemesh from Netanya. Sonia wrote with some concern for my safety:

> The situation here is getting worse and more dangerous by the day. There is no peace or tranquility here now, and it cannot be assured in the future. Should you decide to come, do not expect much.

My uncle Shloime began to look for a way to bring me over to the United States. It was necessary to provide papers with a guarantee that the potential immigrant would not become a burden to the government. The richer the guarantor, the better the prospective immigrant's chances. My uncle was a poor man, so he turned to his nephew Irving Auerbach for help. Irving was the son of my mother's youngest brother, Lippa, who had died as a young man in the United States. Among our family in New York, Irving was the "rich" man. He jumped to the occasion and began working on papers to bring me over.

Life in camp became routine. The only thing that kept changing was the weather. In November and December, the beautiful blue sky was covered with clouds, and heavy rain became a daily occurrence. The inviting sea turned rough, and high waves continuously pounded the rocky shore. On those evenings, we would sit and talk about the situation in Palestine. We talked about how unjustly we had been treated, and were still treated, by the world and by the British, who were not allowing Jews into Palestine. On such a cold, cloudy, rainy and depressing day, we said goodbye to 1946 and welcomed 1947, wondering what it would hold for us.

34
Bari

IN JANUARY 1947, rumours began to circulate that changes would be made at refugee camps in southern Italy. In February, some of the neighbouring camps were transferred farther north. Two camps with non-Jewish populations were already mostly empty. Many of the refugees had left for the United States and Canada, South America and Australia. To enter those countries, a statement that they were anti-Communists or anti-Bolshevik sufficed. It did not matter if they had been Nazi sympathizers or Nazi collaborators, or even worse, that many of them may have been murderers who served in the Nazi-organized battalions that took part in the slaughter of Jews.

The two new camps for Jews were near the port city of Bari. The one closer to Bari was called Transit Camp No. 1. The other, a little farther away, was called Palese. Yet our camp, Santa Maria di Leuca, remained intact. By the beginning of April, all the neighbouring camps were empty, and we learned that we would all be transferred to the two camps near Bari. We wanted very much to get out of the camp, but we wanted to go to a permanent place where we could start rebuilding our lives. To be dragged to another camp, which would probably not be as good as this one, did not appeal to us at all.

Transit Camp No. 1 in Bari was quite different from Santa Maria di Leuca. It consisted of a dozen cement barracks with asbestos roofs. Each barracks was partitioned into six sections by brick walls, and each section was divided into four parts by a cloth partition about two metres high. The entire upper part of the space was open, and every sound carried right across the barracks. At night, if you turned off the light in your sections, you could see what was going on in your neighbour's section through the cloth. Each group of three or four was assigned one such partition, and Bliskowsky and Bluestein had held a space for me.

A dusty unpaved road led to the one entrance of the camp, which was surrounded by a barbed-wire fence, reminding me of the Nazi camps I had been in. Besides the barracks, there was a kitchen, a bathhouse and a larger building that served as the camp's main office and post office. There was also a cultural centre, where one could find a daily local Italian newspaper or some Hebrew papers from Mandate Palestine. A small building served as a canteen, which was run by the camp community.

Refugees from all the camps in the Italian heel had been sent to Bari. I met *landslayt*, or landsmen, people from the same area as me—from Pruzhany or from surrounding shtetls and the Pruzhany ghetto. Some of them I knew personally, some by name only and some not at all. We were around twenty men, including me and my two roommates. Together, we got in touch with the Pruzhaner association in New York. And just as the ghetto authority in Pruzhany in the early 1940s had responded warmly to the plight of refugees who arrived there, so did the Pruzhaner association in New York. During my stay of over a year in Transit Camp No. 1, I received parcels from the Pruzhaner community twice.

Sometime in the middle of 1947, the Joint began to supplement our food rations once a month. We received a can of evaporated milk, half a kilogram of cheese and half a kilogram of salted beef. Bliskowsky, Bluestein and I pooled our rations and cooked the meat on a borrowed Primus stove at once, as we didn't have anywhere to store it. It took many hours for the beef to cook, and three quarters of it was fat, so our meat supplement lasted for one meal only. We had not seen or tasted milk in years, so we treated ourselves by pouring the three cans of milk into one large can, adding some cocoa and boiling up a royal drink. We were more frugal with the cheese, and it would last for a week.

Our lifestyle changed quite a bit in the new camp. Many of us were used to the privacy of our own rooms as well as having an entire village to roam in. In Bari, we were confined to the oppressive heat of the crowded barracks, or, if one preferred to be out in the sun, we could walk back and forth on the dusty road. We were free to leave the camp, but the city of Bari was a few kilometres away, a long walk on a hot day.

I had managed to save a nice sum while working at the warehouse in Santa Maria di Leuca. In fact, I came to Bari with almost three hundred US dollars in my pocket. But without the monthly paycheque and with the temptation of spending it in Bari, it became too easy to part with it. We sometimes got a ride to Bari with the trucks that brought supplies to the camp, or a few of us would take a *carrozza*, or carriage, into the city. We would go see performances and operas at the theatre, Teatro Petruzzelli. I developed a taste for the theatre and became a sort of connoisseur among my peers. For this, I am indebted to Itzik Chopper from the town of Wolkowysk. He was twenty years my senior, a friend of my two roommates and he had survived Auschwitz. He was a man of means before the war and told us of his frequent trips to Warsaw, where he attended the theatre and the opera. If I had ever been skeptical about his stories before, I was proven wrong going with him to the opera in Bari. He knew every bar of each aria and immediately noticed any wrong note, which the Italian audiences reacted to instantly. Bari was a large city and had its share of amusement parks, movie houses and parks, and I remember fondly the park near the waterfront, where we used to walk in the late afternoons and early evenings.

What we missed most in the transit camp was the sea. It was bad enough to be cooped up in the crowded barracks, but being fenced in on a dusty and rocky plain under the summer sun after almost two years on the Mediterranean was very difficult. True, Bari had its own beach, but visiting it entailed a trip to the city, and from there, a tram ride to the beach. A luxury like that was too expensive for the average refugee. Palese was more convenient and cheaper for us to visit, and we would often spend a day or more there. I even attended a bris there. The camp was right on the Adriatic Sea, the water was clear and transparent and the rocks on the beach were flat, clean and smooth. I went to Palese several times during the long summer of 1947. I would sleep over for a night or two at my friend Zygmund Suchter's. We would spend the days in the water or at the seashore. In return, I played host to Zygmund when he came to the transit camp, where his girlfriend was. As we had no spare cot in our room, I let Zygmund sleep in mine while I slept on the floor, exposing myself to the ridicule of my two roommates.

The centre of Jewish activity in Bari was on Via Garruba. I hardly went to the city without making a stop there to find friends and acquaintances, catch up on the latest news from the Land of Israel and find out the black-market price of the dollar. All official and non-official orders regarding the displaced Jews in the camps came from there. It was there that the decision was made about who would go on the next illegal boat to Palestine, and it was there that one could donate a weapon for the cause. Shortly after arriving in Bari, I got hold of a Colt, and I donated it.

Because of the crowding in our new camp, one did not have to go far to look for company. In my barracks, there were many former partisans from different groups. Their stories were full of suffering, persecution, fear, bravery and heroism. In Santa Maria di Leuca we had lived among the local Italian population, so it was impossible to meet all the refugees there. But because Bari was so crowded, we met people whom we had not met before as well as people from other camps. My friends and acquaintances until now were mostly former concentration camp inmates, and I had not had the chance to meet those who survived in hiding or with Aryan papers. There were even two people in the camp who had survived by passing as Germans in the army. There were a few people, and even whole families, who had survived in hiding, on their own or with help from gentiles. They were hidden in dugouts, cellars and attics. Some had spent years in these hiding places. No wonder they were affected—mentally, physically or both.

There were two women, a mother and a daughter, who would walk in front of our barracks every day. The girl was no more than twenty and attracted attention because of her beauty. Her mother, who could not have been more than fifty, looked like she was seventy. I was curious as to why such a beautiful girl would always walk with her mother and never with a male companion. About a month after I noticed them, the mother approached me on the main road of the camp, saying that she had heard good things about me. She took me aside and began to tell me what had happened to them during the war. She told me about being hidden in a closet for three years and how it had affected her daughter, causing her to fear and distrust people. She asked, would I mind going out with her daughter one evening? She hoped that by being in the company of a young man, her daughter might come out of her shell. I gladly agreed, looking forward to spending an evening in the company of a very pretty girl. A few days later, I went to their little partition. When I invited the girl for a walk, she got up like an obedient student and walked out with me. We walked for a couple of hours up and down the main road of the camp, from the gate to the back fence. I quickly found out that even though by my side was a beautiful twenty-year-old woman, I was actually dealing with a naive and innocent fifteen-year-old prewar girl, with whom I had no intention of getting involved.

When I was still in Santa Maria di Leuca, sometime around the end of 1946 or beginning of 1947, I received a letter from a Mrs. Leiba Zbar from Kingston, Ontario, in Canada. She was from Shershev and a friend of both of my parents from childhood. In the 1920s, she had married and immigrated with her husband and two children to Canada. She had gotten my address from my uncle Shloime and asked me if I knew anything about her family in Shershev. I knew them well. I wrote to Mrs. Zbar, telling her as delicately as I could how and when they were killed in Drohitchin. After some time, I received another letter from Mrs. Zbar, in which she asked if she could be of any help to me. By then, I had papers for America, which my cousin Irving Auerbach sent me. According to the information I received from the American consulate in Napoli, I would have to wait at least three or four years to go to the United States. At my uncle Shloime's suggestion, I asked Mrs. Zbar to try to bring me over to Canada, and from there I could decide if I wanted to go to the United States. At least I would then be out of the hopelessness of the DP camp. I would be closer to them and could try to rebuild my life. As I was writing to Mrs. Zbar to see if she could help me get to Canada, my roommate, Bluestein, requested that I ask her if she could also help him. I wrote as he requested. Soon, I received her answer that she would do whatever she could to bring the two of us over.

The DP camps in Germany, Austria and Italy were still bursting at the seams. The few countries that were letting in refugees, among them Canada, were under constant pressure to let in more and more. The Canadian government, traditionally antisemitic and smelling the prevailing mood among Canadians, did everything in its power not to let in the Jews. To come out openly a year or two after the Holocaust and state, "We do not want Jews" would have been too embarrassing for the Canadian government. So instead, they tried to prevent Jews from immigrating by using the euphemistic excuse of needing workers with particular skills, such as miners or lumberjacks. I knew some Jews who hid their Jewish identity and went to Canada as lumberjacks and actually worked in the forests upon arrival in Canada. They felt as if they were committing a crime by coming to Canada on a false pretense. It took many of us time to shake off the shackles of fear and unworthiness instilled in us by the Nazis and European nations during the German occupation. Canada was also looking for farmhands, and as Jews had not been permitted to own land in most Eastern European countries, the chance of Jewish farmers applying for immigration was very low. However, the great demand for farmhands in Canada meant that farmers could sponsor farmhands to come to Canada providing they could ensure them employment for a year.

In Kingston, Ontario, a Jewish man by the name of Abramsky owned several department stores as well as a five-hundred-acre farm near the small town of Picton. Mrs. Zbar asked Mr. Abramsky if he would sponsor two survivors on his farm, and he agreed. So, the wheels that would bring me to Canada began to turn.

The summer of 1947 was highlighted by frequent demonstrations against the British policy of restricting immigration to Palestine. Those demonstrations were held in front of the British consulate in Bari. We came from the two nearby camps, several thousand strong, with large placards in hand. We marched through the main streets of Bari, stopping traffic, but the Italian police never interfered with us until we got to the consulate. Standing across from the helmeted and armed Italian police surrounding the consulate, we would yell all the "down with" slogans that came to our minds. After an hour or so of yelling, our delegation was usually admitted into the consulate to deliver a petition, and then we would disperse.

As we got up early one morning in October 1947, we found that the camp was surrounded by Italian police. The few employees of the camp and the British camp director, who were permitted to move about, were as surprised as we were. They were going from barracks to barracks, telling us not to go outside. All we knew was that the police were conducting searches, but no one knew what they were looking for. I had in my possession a Beretta handgun and ammunition I had bought in Santa Maria di Leuca and did not want to get caught with it, so I stuck it into the toilet flush box and flushed the spare bullets down the toilet. The curfew lasted all morning. When the police finally left, we found out that all refugees from Yugoslavia had been taken away. At this time, the relations between Italy and Yugoslavia were strained, and displaced people and refugees of Yugoslavian origin became suspect. Some organizations prevailed upon the Italian authorities to let out those who had papers.

After this event, there was always a presence of Italian police at the camp gate. They did not interfere with the comings and goings of the camp, but they would stop us on the streets of Bari to check that we had a *soggiorno*, a document issued by the Italian authorities to refugees. The experience of being surrounded at night, the searches and arrests, were reminiscent of the dark days gone by and awakened in us survivors an intense, almost uncontrollable urge to leave the DP camp for our destinations, wherever they might be.

The situation in Palestine was getting worse every day. We were hearing about Arab attacks on Jewish settlements and daily casualties. The Jews were surrounded by Arab neighbours bent on slaughtering every Jew and were facing often openly hostile British forces. The Jews of Palestine began to improvise ways of smuggling weapons in. A secret call went out to all refugee camps to contribute any available arms, which would be sent to the Land of Israel. Some former partisans had sidearms, and then there were concentration camp survivors like me who saw no worthier cause than defending Jewish lives and who obtained weapons whenever possible. It was not easy to give away my most cherished possession, but it was then that I parted with my Beretta. A much more difficult task was getting the arms into Palestine. The only functioning port was Haifa, and it was under strict British control, so sending them by ship was out of the question. And so the smugglers began to seal dismantled revolvers in tins of canned meat or fish and send them by mail as parcels of food to private addresses.

When the United Nations voted for the Partition Plan for Palestine on November 29, 1947, we spent the night glued to the radio. The next morning, the camp authorities ordered a full barrel of wine to be put in the middle of the camp, free for all to drink.

Most of the refugees in my camp had papers to go to the United States, Canada, South America or Australia by that time, or they were expecting them at any moment. Yet the news of the partition moved us deeply, particularly the announcement that the British would pull out completely by the middle of May 1948. Our discussion turned to the most pressing topic of the day, the future of the Yishuv, the Jewish settlement in the Land of Israel. Following the United Nations vote, Arab attacks on Jews intensified. We spent many hours listening to the radio to get the latest news. We tuned in mostly to the BBC, because many hours of their foreign programming were done in Polish. We could have sworn that these broadcasts were deliberate attempts by the British to antagonize and upset us survivors, as many of us understood Polish, and their reporting was so clearly anti-Jewish and pro-Arab that it disgusted us. As our information came from such a venomous source, we would go to Bari for more balanced news, visiting the headquarters of the Jewish Agency on Via Garruba. The atmosphere there was very relaxed, and we would walk from room to room, trying to pick up bits and pieces of news that were more encouraging than what we heard on the radio.

Those were trying days for the Jewish people in general, for those in the Land of Israel in particular, and even for us refugees in the camps. We had so much time on our hands to think and worry, especially because of what we had witnessed first-hand so recently. Our camp was in a constant state of tension.

35
To Canada

EARLY IN 1948, the Canadian immigration authorities informed me that I would soon be called to the Canadian consulate in Rome to arrange the needed formalities. Bluestein received his notice as well, but with an immediate call to go to Rome. Within a week, he was back with a visa to Canada. Bluestein did not waste time and got in touch with his uncle in Philadelphia, asking him to pay for his passage to Canada. I was disappointed with these developments. After all, it was my parents' friend from way back who originally started the process to bring me over to Canada. Bluestein was only an onlooker who had joined in my plans. Now he had the visa to Canada, and I did not! My uncle Shloime was particularly upset with this turn of events. He too knew Mrs. Zbar from Shershev and had been in contact with her throughout all those years. However, all we could do was wait. And wait I did.

The waiting was anything but boring. For us Jews, this was one of the most tense yet hopeful moments in our history. We were witnessing the *chevlei leida*, the birth pangs of our Jewish homeland as it was coming to life. Events were taking place at a head-spinning speed. The British were pulling out of Palestine while still preventing Jewish refugees from entering. To us survivors of the Holocaust, the only people in the world willing to extend a helping hand and a warm welcoming smile were our fellow Jews in the Land of Israel, and we felt that the British were showing a contempt of justice that the whole world could see. We stayed glued to the radio day and night. We knew of every Arab attack and every British betrayal. We heard about the slaughter of dozens of Jewish doctors and medical staff when Arab forces attacked a convoy on its way to the Hadassah Hospital on Mount Scopus and of the Arab massacre at the Kfar Etzion kibbutz, and we cried. We waited, almost holding our breath, for May 14, when the last British troops would depart, wondering what would happen and hoping for a miracle.

At the end of April, a couple of days after Bluestein had left for Canada, I received a note from the Canadian consulate to come to Rome for an interview in one month.

On May 14, we in the camp shared the excitement about the declaration of the State of Israel with the rest of the Jewish people all over the world. We celebrated the occasion with another barrel of wine in the street. Yet we all remained glued to the radio. We knew that it was not only the fate of the approximately 650,000 Jews in Israel that hung in the balance, but also our two-thousand-year-old dream of returning to our promised land. It was the moment when the fate of our entire people was to be decided.

At the end of May, I left for Rome, checking into a private home that had been converted into a small hotel, where I shared a room with five other survivors. We had long before forgotten what privacy was, so sleeping six in a room meant nothing to us. We spoke the same language, Yiddish, but we also had a common past and experiences, and we understood each other instantly, as if we had known each other for years. The next day I went to the Canadian consulate, where I was given letters to different medical offices for an array of tests and a date for an appointment with a Canadian doctor several days later. In those few days, I had a chance to walk the streets of Rome, looking into the windows of the beautiful shops and at the many piazzas, statues, monuments and fountains. I had seen them before, but now, I was seeing them with a sense of nostalgia; I was already missing Rome and Italy.

On the appointed day, I went to the consulate doctor. He had my medical reports in front of him, and he gave me a checkup. Then he gave me a couple of sheets of paper and told me to present them at the consulate the next day. When I showed up at the consulate the next morning, there was quite a crowd ahead of me in the large waiting room. I sat down and looked around, expecting to see only survivors like me. To my surprise, we were the minority. Most of the potential immigrants were Italians of all ages. That puzzled me, as I was under the impression that Canada was interested in young and able-bodied people. Some of the refugees came out of the office with radiating faces and others with expressions of deep disappointment. We began asking the refugees who emerged what was going on behind the door and concluded that politics played a role in receiving a visa. That is, someone who had spent the four years of the war in the Soviet Union stood very little chance of receiving a visa. One young man I spoke to was refused a visa because a blow he had received in a concentration camp made him unable to hear in one ear. Another had the same problem with an eye. Another mentioned to the consular clerk that he had a brother in the United States, and the clerk responded, "You do not want to go to Canada. You want to go to the United States. All you want is to use Canada as a stepping stone. We cannot allow that." And so it was for us survivors in those days—a selection of another kind.

When my turn came, I was taken into a small room. A well-dressed woman in her thirties came in, sat opposite me and said in German, "Please give me a short resumé of your life." I told her my life history. The whole story took no more than a few minutes, and I received my visa. The visa was good for three months. Shortly after returning to Bari, I was notified that my passage from Genoa to Halifax on the ship MS *Sobieski* had been paid for by my cousin Irving Auerbach. The booking was for July 1, 1948.

There was only one month to my departure to Canada, but my time and attention were constantly occupied with the events in Israel. I went to sleep and woke up with feelings of guilt. I felt like a traitor, and I would chastise myself many times a day for going to Canada while my brethren in Israel were fighting for their existence. Only three and a half years earlier, I would have been happy and would have felt privileged to die for such a cause. Now that I had the chance to fulfill my childhood dream to stand in line with other Jews in defence of a Jewish homeland and Jewish lives, I was abandoning them to their fate. My uncle reminded me constantly in his letters that I was the sole survivor of our entire family and that I owed it to them to stay alive to perpetuate their memory and their name. "Besides," wrote my uncle, "after what you went through, you more than deserve it!" Nevertheless, that feeling of guilt has never left me and is as indelible as the guilt over remaining alive that haunts the survivor.

I still had most of the money that my uncle Shloime had sent me. The notion that you could find gold in the streets of America was engraved in my mind, as it was in the minds of the Eastern European masses, so I decided not to arrive looking like a beggar. I went to a tailor and ordered a double-breasted brown suit. A refugee seamstress in the camp made me six dress shirts. In a clothing store, I bought two pairs of pyjamas and six sets of underwear. After much deliberation, I bought six Borsalino hats for Mrs. Zbar's family. Not knowing what else to buy, I bought a nicely decorated musical cigarette box, a couple of cameos and a table lamp made from a large seashell, with beautiful carved designs. Having heard that accordions were expensive in North America, I bought a new Scandalli accordion, which came in its own case. I also acquired two suitcases and filled them with my new purchases. One contained the presents and my new wardrobe and the other letters from my uncle and from my relatives in Israel, as I did not like to part with any written material that was of sentimental value to me. I filled up the rest of the second suitcase with the clothes I had received in parcels from my uncle Shloime. So here I was, a refugee with two suitcases and an accordion, ready to travel to Canada.

From my travelling experience in Italy, I preferred to be early rather than late and decided to leave a week before my boat was due to depart. Leibel Bliskowsky offered to accompany me to Genoa, and I gladly accepted. That train trip is still vivid in my mind, with those small, crammed compartments. Somewhere along the trip, a group of Italian women took up a lot of space, and one of them initiated a conversation with us, but we were not inclined to chat, so we pretended to speak and understand less Italian than we did. All they found out from us was that we were going to America. I heard one saying to the others, "Look how lucky those two are. They are returning home to their families and parents, to comfort and riches." And they continued describing life in America as they imagined it. We listened to their conversation without uttering a word. I do not know what went on in Bliskowsky's mind, for he had lost not only his parents, brother and sisters, but also a wife and a child. I wanted to jump up and yell, "Stop talking! I cannot bear it! I have neither a family nor a home. I was driven out of my home seven years ago, and two years later, my family and I were brought to a place called Auschwitz, and they were mercilessly murdered, and now their ashes are fertilizing some Polish farmer's field." But I did not say anything. I sat listening to their conversation about my life, about the life of my family that could have been, that should have been but was not.

And so the train rolled on, from Bari to Barletta to Foggia to Caserta, past Rome, past Civitavecchia. I looked out at the city of Civitavecchia, which had been badly damaged in the war. I had never been there, but I knew of it because Betar under Jabotinsky had established a naval training school for Jewish boys there. It took me back a dozen years. How much had it changed since then? The train continued on to Pisa and finally reached Genoa.

There we checked into another hotel where we slept several to a room. Here we met Jews from all over, even from North Africa. All of them were waiting for the departure of their boats, a few to Canada, some to the United States, others to South America and still others to Israel. In the evenings, the men went for walks in the neighbouring streets. What impressed me most was a street along the harbour, with bars, cheap coffee houses, music and, above all, human diversity. There I saw the kinds of characters I had always imagined to be fictional, in movies only. But there they were, every bit as real as they seemed to be in the movies.

The day of my departure arrived. I paid for my and Bliskowsky's stay at the hotel, despite his objections, and we took a *carrozza* to the port. After paying the coachman my last few liras, all I had in my pocket was twelve American dollars. Saying goodbye to Bliskowsky was not easy for either of us, for we had learned to trust each other and became good friends during the last five years. In a sense, I felt guilty for leaving him behind while I was going to that "golden land." I boarded the ship and stood on the main deck to have a better look at the harbour and the city. There was a large pier below, surrounded by a marble stone balustrade, where my friend Bliskowsky was sitting. We were too far apart to hear each other, but we could see one another. I did not want to move for fear that he would lose sight of me. I stood there on the same spot for a couple of hours until the boat began to move. Everybody on shore started waving, and so did my friend, not stopping until I was completely out of sight. I felt that I had left behind one of the best friends I'd ever had, if not the best.

My cabin held eight passengers, mostly Italians. I went onto the deck to explore. We Jewish survivors found each other pretty quickly, and we soon found out more about our fellow travellers. The members of the crew, mostly Polish, were glad to talk with us. There were 1,200 passengers aboard: 50 Jews, 100 Italians, and the rest of Eastern European descent, mostly Ukrainian. At supper, I was the only Jew among mostly Italians, and the whole meal was quite pleasant.

Before midnight, we stopped in Cannes, France. There, a whole yeshiva, a Jewish institution of higher learning, came aboard—seventy-five young men with several older men, apparently their rabbis. They went down to their cabins, from which they did not emerge even once throughout the entire trip. We were told that there was a kosher kitchen set up for them in a separate dining hall.

It was an exciting day for me, and I went to bed early. Sometime during the night, I awoke with a sensation that I was being lifted up and up, and then suddenly the direction changed, and I was going down. It seemed as if my stomach was pressing upwards, and an urge to vomit overwhelmed me. Not losing a second, I jumped off my cot and ran in my underwear and bare feet to the hallway, where the washrooms were located. To my surprise and chagrin, the hallway was filled with people trying to get there ahead of me. People were vomiting on the walls, on the floor and on each other. I joined them. For a moment I felt a bit better, just enough to see what was going on around me. I saw men and women, half-naked, in such misery that they could not care less how they looked. Needless to say, I did not go to the dining room the next day.

After a few days, I began to feel better and I started to spend all of my time on the deck, going down to the cabin only to go to sleep. There I met other survivors, and we shared our experiences. I even dared to speak about the future, although carefully and with a good measure of apprehension. But my favourite occupation was to sneak up on those Eastern European non-Jews and listen to their conversations. Their faces seemed familiar to me, and I could picture them in Nazi uniforms as watchmen at Auschwitz or as volunteers in the local police or auxiliary police under the Nazi command in Shershev, Antopol, Drohitchin, Khomsk and Pruzhany. They stood in small groups or leaned on the railings close to each other. I was curious to know what they were talking about. While we were telling each other of our suffering and losses, what were they telling each other? How they had inflicted such suffering on the Jews? I tried time and time again to pass by such a group close enough to hear something, but to no avail. The moment I came within earshot, they stopped talking. This was a good topic of conversation among us survivors. We knew the moral quality of some of the immigrants who were travelling with us to Canada, and we wondered what they would pass on to their children. Whatever these people left behind in Europe, we were certain they took with them their racial hatred and intolerance.

BOOK SIX
A New Life in Canada
(1948–2000s)

36
Farming

ON JULY 10, 1948, we docked in Halifax. We were told to collect our luggage and line up to be processed. My suitcases came off the boat with the last load, so I was among the last to go through immigration. The immigration officer began to fill out a questionnaire: family name; first name; parents' names; profession; education; languages? I mentioned some half a dozen languages I spoke, but not Yiddish, which was my mother tongue, or Hebrew. I saw the satisfaction on the inspector's face. He was dealing with a literate person after the dozens and dozens of illiterates he had just seen. After a few more questions, he asked, "Do you have a train ticket to your destination?" He was holding the pen to tick off a line on the questionnaire.

I answered, "No."

He looked up and said, "Just a moment." He called over one of the men who was mingling with the Eastern European immigrants and asked him, "Why doesn't he have his ticket?"

The man asked for my name, looked at his list, and answered, "He is not on my list, you better ask Mr.____." He gave a Jewish-sounding name.

The inspector's face became serious, and he asked me cautiously, "Are you Hebrew?"

"Yes," I said.

His face immediately became stern, and he moved it closer to mine. I looked at his blond, smoothly combed hair and his light blue eyes, at a face that had seemed so friendly just a moment ago. The words that were coming out of his mouth—"You are a Jew!"—sounded like an accusation.

"Yes, I am," I said.

He straightened up and walked away, saying in a loud voice, so that the other inspectors could hear, "I got here a lulu." He was back seconds later, accompanied by another man. Pointing to me with a motion of his head, he said to him, "He is yours."

The man came over to me, stretched out his hand and said, "*Shalom aleichem*. I am from the HIAS, the Hebrew Immigrant Aid Society. Welcome to Canada. Outside this building, a train is waiting, and it will take you to your destination." He pulled out a train ticket from his pocket, handed it to me and said, "Good luck."

At the exit of the building, I was given a package of MacDonald's tobacco and a folder of Vogue cigarette papers. Both are still in my possession as of this writing. Intentionally or not, all the Jewish passengers from the boat were in the same coach. We were excited that we had finally arrived in Canada and were glad to be together for a little while longer. It took a while for the train to move, and we were getting hungry. Someone had found a store nearby and bought a loaf of white bread for twelve cents. We were impressed by the low price, and in no time, we were all buying and eating bread. We moved out of Halifax before dark. My English was the best in our coach, so I became the spokesperson for all. There were many questions for the conductor who was collecting our tickets: How much does a tailor make an hour? A shoemaker, an upholsterer, a hat maker, an electrician, a bricklayer, a carpenter? It seemed that everyone could make up to four dollars an hour. My God!! Four dollars meant thirty loaves of bread. Who could earn thirty loaves of bread a day in Poland or in Italy? No wonder this was the *goldene medine*, the golden land.

We were too excited to sleep that night. In the morning, we all sat by the windows, trying to see as much as possible of our newly adopted country. We travelled for kilometres on end before we saw a settlement. In the distance were four lonely houses. One of us pointed out that there was a car parked in front of each one of them. Did every Canadian house have a car? The day went by in expectation and excitement. Evening came, and the train continued to gobble up kilometres of track at an immense speed.

Shortly before midnight the train stopped in Montreal, and about half the passengers in my car, all of them survivors, got off. I felt a pang seeing them go. We had become close aboard the ship, and more so on the train. We felt comfortable and safe together. Now there was silence in the half-empty car. I guess we all felt the same way. When the train started moving again, we tried to resume our conversation, but to no avail. Meanwhile, the conductor passed by, announcing that the next stop would be Kingston, Ontario—my stop! I wondered what it would be like to meet Mr. and Mrs. Zbar, who were total strangers yet so nice to me, and I began to feel nervous.

At around two-thirty in the morning, we stopped at the Kingston station. I grabbed my two suitcases and the accordion and got off the train. The train pulled away, leaving me, as far as I could see, alone. As the sound of the train faded into the distance, I heard voices coming toward me from down the railway tracks. Soon, I could make out shadows of people and discern some words in Yiddish. I was standing under the lights of the station, and they were coming out of the dark. I heard a woman's excited voice saying, "He looks just like his uncle Shevach!" This really caught me by surprise. My uncle Shevach had perished as a czarist soldier somewhere on the Russian-German front, a casualty among many millions in World War I. My older sister Sheva was named after him.

As they got closer, I could make out in the dark three men and one woman. One of them I recognized immediately by his gait. It was Bluestein. The others were Mr. and Mrs. Zbar and their business partner, Mr. Berlin. After an excited and nervous introduction, we got into their car. Instead of driving to their home in town, we drove to their cottage. Everybody was tired. I was shown a couch in the living room, and we all went to bed. But despite the long and sleepless trip from Halifax, I could not sleep. As soon as I heard someone moving around in the next room, I got up too. Soon everybody was up. There were more people in the cottage than I thought. The Zbars' children were visiting from New York with their families, and there were two maids. All of them tried to make me comfortable and put me at ease, but I was tense. Even Bluestein's presence did not help. I could see that the three months in Canada had had no effect on him at all, and he was still the same refugee as he had been in Italy, which embarrassed me to a degree.

The cottage had running water, plumbing and electricity. Everything was so beautiful—the cottage, the lake, the quiet atmosphere, the children's giggles and happy shouts, their parents' laughter and the grandparents' joyous and beaming faces. It felt unreal, like a fairy tale, so out of my world! Surprisingly, I felt no envy at all. On the contrary, I felt glad for people who were so nice to me and tried to make me feel at home with them.

Our conversation was conducted in Yiddish. Mr. and Mrs. Zbar spoke Yiddish as if they had just left Shershev. So did Mr. Berlin. Their children and spouses understood almost every word and spoke some. I was sure that they spoke in Yiddish only for my benefit. After all, by then they had been in Canada twenty years. But after many decades in Canada myself, I am not so sure, for I am still more fluent in Yiddish than in English.

In the evening, Mr. and Mrs. Abramsky arrived unexpectedly. He was the farmer who was my sponsor in coming to Canada. After a short chat, Abramsky proposed that I start work on the farm the next morning. Despite Mrs. Zbar's suggestions that I stay for another day or two to recover from my trip, he was insistent. I did not want to overstay my welcome with the Zbars, and I agreed to go to the farm.

The next morning, Bluestein and I boarded the bus and got off three kilometres before Picton, where the Abramsky's farm was located next to the highway. The farm consisted of five hundred acres of land on both sides of the road, formerly belonging to several owners whose two houses still stood there. The manager of the farm lived in one house, and in the other was a Canadian family that looked after the chickens and cows. In the middle of a field overgrown by weeds stood a couple of sheds. Bluestein had been living in one of them, and I moved in with him. The shed had two rooms. One served as a kitchen and a living room, and the second was a bedroom with two squeaky single beds and just enough room for our meagre possessions. The kitchen had a wood-burning stove, a small table and a couple of wooden chairs that were held together with wires. Behind the shed was an outhouse for washing, bathing and drinking water. And down a gentle slope, some fifty metres away and forming one side of the farm's boundary, was Lake Ontario.

I changed my clothes and went right to work. I had never done this kind of work before, and I was looking forward to it. However, the work turned out to be entirely different from my expectation. The part of the farm that lay between the main road and the lake was unsuitable for farming because it was rocky. In the middle of this land stood a beautiful stone cottage, which the owner had converted into a summer home for his family. The owner's plan was to extract all the stones from the upper layer of the earth so that it could be levelled and seeded with grass, creating a manicured lawn in front of the cottage. Our job was to follow the tractor driven by the foreman, picking up stones and throwing them into a bin. It was impossible to pick up all the stones, for there were more stones than soil. Some neighbouring farmers observed us and said, "This is not farming. It is mining."

The workday started at six in the morning. We had an hour for lunch, and then we continued working until dusk, which in July, meant working until nine in the evening. We received forty-five dollars a month. Our only free day was Sunday, so we got up early on Sunday mornings to catch the bus to Kingston so that we could spend the day with the Zbars. We would return to the farm in the evening. After paying for the bus trips to Kingston, we did not have much money left for food, which we usually bought in Picton.

What helped us in those days were the weekly visits by the Zbars and Mr. Berlin. They came from Kingston to visit us almost every Wednesday afternoon because the stores were closed then. They brought baskets full of sandwiches, pies and other goodies. When they came, we would take an hour or two off work and picnic together under one of the many trees on the property. We knew that we owed all of this to Mrs. Zbar's good nature and generosity. She spent many hours preparing the food, knowing that it was not possible to finish it all in one picnic. Of course, they never took anything back with them, leaving us with enough food to last for two or three days.

And so, we got into a routine of working from dawn to dusk, with an hour's break for lunch. There was no time for anything else and barely time to think. After waking at five in the morning and a hurried breakfast of bread with jam or butter, we worked until noon. During our lunch break, we usually caught some fish in the lake and kept them alive in a pail of water until the evening. On our way back to the shed for lunch, we would pick up some eggs, which were spread all over the farm, and eat fried eggs and bread before continuing to work until dusk. After work, we would plunge into the lake to wash off the sweat of the day. Then we cleaned the fish and boiled them in a pot with potatoes. By then it was eleven or later, and it was time to call it a day.

In those days, there were Jewish families in almost every small town in Ontario. One Sunday, a man appeared and introduced himself in Yiddish. He lived with his family in Picton and had a business buying chickens from the farmers and shipping them to New York. He drove us over to his home and introduced us to his wife and young children. I found out that he had come to Canada as a young man from our part of Eastern Europe. When he learned that we were making forty-five dollars a month, he offered me forty-five a week to come work for him, plus living accommodations. He said, "You will be able to save every penny of your pay."

I asked why he was willing to pay such a good wage. He said that he wanted to hire me because his drivers were not dependable. They drank and caused accidents. He knew that Jewish boys did not drink, and that made it worth it to him.

Oh, how badly I wanted that job! But I was under the impression that the terms of my immigration meant that I had to stay on the farm for a full year. Our employer had guaranteed the government that he would keep us employed for a year so that we didn't become a burden on the government, but what we didn't know was that there was no law prohibiting us from working somewhere else. So I refused that offer.

The Zbars and Mr. Berlin could not stand to see the two of us working twelve to fourteen hours a day, six days a week, for a pittance. They also wrongly assumed that we were required to stay on a farm for at least a year, and they reasoned that we could have our own farm, so they decided to help us buy one. Bluestein and I did not have a penny to our names, so they turned to our uncles. My uncle did not have any money but managed to collect some from his children—three sons who had spent the war years on the front lines as US servicemen and two daughters who were garment workers. He collected two thousand dollars and sent it to the Zbars. Bluestein's uncle in Philadelphia, who was well off and had no children, promised to send the same amount.

The Zbars and Mr. Berlin searched the newspaper ads for a farm. After examining a few farms, they chose one in a place called Greenbush, eighteen kilometres north of Brockville, Ontario. It was a hundred acres, including arable land, pasture and woods. There was an old house, a stable for ten milking cows and two big horses, and a barn. All of them were in a rundown state. Near the house was a vegetable garden. The farmer would not let it go for less than 7,500 dollars, which was a high price at that time. The Zbars and Mr. Berlin decided to wait a while.

Since I had arrived in Canada, I was in touch regularly with my uncle Shloime in New York. My relatives in the United States were eager to see me and decided to send my cousins Helen and Harold to visit me. I still remembered them from before they left Shershev in 1930. Harold had been twelve and Helen around twenty. I was only six then, so it was no wonder I did not recognize them when I saw them. I spent a Sunday with them at the Zbars' cottage, but there were other visitors there, so it was difficult to speak with them alone and to pass on the message from my mother, which I had cherished and carried with me throughout the previous seven years, a message that echoed in my mind endlessly. All the same, it was moving to see my two cousins whom I knew from my childhood. They were part of my New York family, the family that my mother had loved so much that she never stopped telling us about them.

My cousins left the next day. On the following Sunday, the Zbars and Mr. Berlin took us to see the farm, and the decision was made to buy it. The truth is that I had very little say in this decision. It was the Zbars' and Mr. Berlin's say and money, except for the 2,000 dollars that my uncle sent, and it was mostly made because of Bluestein's claim that he had been a farmer back home and was good at it. Mr. Berlin extended us a loan for the missing 5,500 dollars.

As the lawyer was making out the agreement between us and Mr. Berlin, writing down every word and pronouncing it loudly and clearly, so that we, the two newcomers, could understand, he said, "We, the undersigned, undertake to repay the above-mentioned amount at the end of five years, with the interest rate of..." Here he stopped to hear from Mr. Berlin the interest rate he was going to charge us.

Mr. Berlin answered calmly, "None."

The lawyer, whose eyes had been glued to the paper until that moment, jerked his head up. He stared unbelievingly at Mr. Berlin, and asked, "What?"

Mr. Berlin said, "No interest."

The lawyer held his gaze on Mr. Berlin for a few long seconds. Then he turned to us and said, "You are lucky men."

When we returned to Abramsky's farm that night, we decided that one of us should go to our farm to get acquainted with the work. The next Sunday, the Zbars and Mr. Berlin took me to our farm. It was the end of September, and there was a lot of work to do. The cows had to be milked twice a day. Some of the cows, sensing a stranger who approached them awkwardly, began kicking with their hind legs. Nevertheless, I quickly learned to operate the milking machine and got used to the cows, and they got used to me. There were four acres of corn and four acres of sugar beets to take in. I was doing this by myself, as the former owner felt no responsibility for the farm anymore. A week later, he and his family left and Bluestein came.

One of the first things I learned about farming was that one could not leave the farm for a whole day. There is never a moment when a farmer can say, "Now I can relax." No matter how long the day is, it is never long enough. Our day began at five in the morning. At six, we were already milking the cows. Then the milk had to be carried in metal containers to the road, where it was collected by a truck and delivered to a dairy plant in Brockville. There, each container was tested for its milk and milk fat content. The farmers received a cheque every two weeks.

After milking the cows, we took them outside to be watered at the trough and we cleaned the stables. Then the horses and cows were taken to the pasture. By that time, it was eight o'clock, time to wash up and eat breakfast, which always consisted of leftover boiled potatoes that we fried in a hot pan with fresh onions and half a dozen eggs. As soon as we finished breakfast, we left the house, not to return until after milking the cows in the evening, which was never before eight.

In the first few weeks, we spent the days bringing the sugar beets from the field into the barn, first removing the leaves and roots. Then we had to take care of the corn. As we had no silo, we had to cut the stalks down, tie them in sheaves, and bring them into the barn. There were still potatoes in the ground, more than what we needed, so we decided to sell some. One day, I counted how many potatoes I dug up from after breakfast until milking time at six in the evening. During that full day, I filled ten sacks of potatoes. When we sold them the next day, all we got was seven dollars and fifty cents, which also covered the labour of plowing, fertilizing, seeding and weeding. I am sure that if I had gone to do the same potato digging at a neighbour's farm, he would have given me at least ten dollars for that day's work, without the plowing, seeding or weeding. That was the lot of the average farmer.

In general, farming in those parts was entirely different from what I had seen growing up. In Eastern Europe, the farmer was self-sufficient in almost every respect. He grew and raised all his own food. He grew flax to make linen, from which he made shirts, pants and underwear for the family. His sheep supplied him with enough wool to make felt for his winter outerwear and heavy felt boots, and the sheepskin made warm and durable coats. The farmer sold only the surplus so that he could supplement his most elementary needs. Here there was specialized farming. Many farms did not even keep a few hens to supply their own eggs or poultry.

The small Jewish community in Brockville consisted of fewer than a dozen families. Word swiftly spread that a couple of Holocaust survivors were living on a farm nearby. One Sunday afternoon at the beginning of October, a car pulled into our farm and four passengers got out. It was a Mr. and Mrs. Pleet and their two children: Ruth, who was eighteen, and Lenny, who was eight. They were the first Jewish family from Brockville to visit us. A Jewish family by the name of Feltcher also came to visit later on. There was another Jewish farming family a few kilometres from us by the name of Zarkover. They were fortunate to have left Poland two months before the war began in 1939. Sometimes they drove over to us on Sunday for a couple of hours, and we would share prewar memories of our lives in Poland, as well as present-day farming problems and practices.

It was also there, in rural Ontario, that I came face to face with the dislike, or rather the deep-rooted hatred, that existed between Protestants and Catholics. Yet they were neighbours who came together to help one another at harvest time or to cut wood for winter. How polite and superficial they were to one another, but when they were alone with us, they expressed their innermost feelings with no inhibition. Bluestein and I could not understand how these two Christian groups could hate each other so much, and we wondered how much more both groups must hate us Jews.

As Jews with memories of the Holocaust fresh in our minds, we made sure never to infringe in any way on our neighbours. In fact, we made sure that they owed us. When we were asked to help a neighbour bring in the corn and fill up the silo, both of us would go help when only one helper was expected to come. We never asked anyone to help us in return. While we helped our neighbours cut their firewood with a circular saw, a matter of a day's work, we spent a month pulling a saw back and forth to cut up our own wood.

The days were becoming noticeably shorter, and the weather deteriorated. We were getting up and milking the cows while it was still dark. Our summer work clothes were worn out and insufficient for the cold weather. Fortunately, we received a notice that a parcel was awaiting us in the Brockville customs office. My uncle Shloime had written to me earlier that he was sending his sons' military clothes that they had come home with from the war. They could not have come at a better time. We received pants, shirts, jackets and coats made to last, even waterproof attire. We became the envy of our neighbours, for the military clothes were perfect for our work on the farm.

During the short days of late fall, we spent the daylight hours repairing the fences around the farm. We had five kilometres of fence, all old and in bad shape. The cows apparently believed in the saying "The grass is greener on the other side," and they were always getting through the fences. We, for our part, believed in the saying "Good fences make for good neighbours," and we tried to make sure our cows stayed on our land. When the snow came, we kept the livestock indoors and spent hours chopping up corn stalks and sugar beets to feed to the cows with their ground-up oats.

We were encouraged by the Zbars and Mr. Berlin to make development plans. The barn was old and so was the stable, and we made plans to build new ones, or at least to repair them. For that we needed material. We had thirty-five acres of woods with big elm trees. We knew nothing of the characteristics of elm and decided to cut planks of wood from our trees. I will never forget our first day in the woods and the cutting down of our first tree. It was a cold wintry day. After breakfast, we hitched up two horses to the sleigh and tied another sleigh to it, and then set out across the snow-covered field to the woods at the other end of the farm. The wind was strong, and the snow was deeper than we thought, and the horses fell into drifts up to their bellies. The forest was still except for the rustle of the treetops and the flapping wings of scattered flying birds.

We left our two horses hitched up between some large trees then picked one of the largest trees and began to cut it down using an ordinary saw. We soon discovered that it was no easy task to saw through a thick elm tree. Finally, the tree began to fall. Too late, we realized our mistake of not tying the horses to a tree. The sound of breaking branches and the thud of the falling tree scared them, and they took off with the two sleighs. One behind the other, they fled through the trees as fast as they could. Fortunately, the reins snagged on some branches, and the horses stopped a few hundred metres away. Nevertheless, during their short run they succeeded in breaking both sleighs, and it took us a few days to repair them.

After a tree was brought down, the trunk had to be cut into four-metre-long pieces, not an easy task. Then the cut logs had to be brought out from the woods to the buildings, a distance of a kilometre and a half, with a creek in between. At times the snow over the creek would collapse under the weight of a log, and the leading sled would get stuck on the high bank, leaving the log and both sleighs between the two banks of the creek. It would take us half a day to get out of such a situation. Having made sure that we had enough logs, we took them by horse and sled to a sawmill, where they were cut into planks. Returning home after nightfall, the chores of milking the cows and cleaning out the stable still awaited us.

In late fall and into the winter, there was a sharp drop in the cows' milk production. The smallest cheque we received for a month's production of milk was seven dollars in February, as compared to the largest cheque, which was for three hundred dollars in September. Milk production improved in March again when the cows began calving. The whole process of calving was a new, phenomenal experience for me, though the calves required a lot of attention from us.

A couple of weeks before Pesach, Mr. and Mrs. Pleet extended an invitation to us for the two nights of Pesach, but as both of us could not leave the farm at the same time, the decision was made that I should go, providing that I would let Bluestein go to Montreal. I agreed, and he left a couple of days later. The work of milking the cows, feeding the calves and cleaning the stables fell to me. To my dismay, when I went to milk the cows the next morning, I found another newborn calf on the floor. As if in spite, during my partner's six-day absence, three new calves were born.

When Bluestein returned, his entire attitude had changed. It turned out that his purpose for going to Montreal was to try to find a wife. He had met a woman who would consider marrying him but would not live on a farm.

On Pesach eve, I hitchhiked to Brockville, arriving just before sundown. Everything in the Pleet's house was nice and clean for Pesach, and the house was filled with the aroma of good food. Mr. Pleet conducted the seder in a very traditional way. It was reminiscent of the seders I'd had in Shershev an eternity ago. For me it was the first happy seder in eight years. I did not let myself sink into gloom and acted as festive as I could. I went with Mr. Pleet to the synagogue, heard some new melodies at the seder and sang some of my own that I remembered from my childhood. I spent the afternoon walking around Brockville with Ruth. The second seder was just as festive as the first, but I felt more at ease. The next morning, I went back to the farm. I hated to take off my only suit, which I had brought from Italy, and get into my work clothes.

After he returned from Montreal, Bluestein stopped making plans for the farm. He did not say much and was preoccupied with his thoughts. Sometimes, he brought up the subject of the woman in Montreal, or he mused aloud about his future on the farm. When I showed lack of sympathy or indifference, he said, "Sure, you are smart. You are twenty-five years old and flirting with a nineteen-year-old girl. What have I got to look forward to on this farm?"

The snow melted. Green grass began to sprout, and the soil began to dry. Spring had arrived, and it was time to get to work. We had a three-disc plow that needed extensive repairs that we could not afford, so we bought a single-disc plow and began to plow our land. Our neighbours looked on in disbelief, for no farmer who had to plow that much land would attempt to do it with a single-bladed plow. Early each morning, one of us would do all the daily chores, which could take four or five hours, while the other would plow. I had never held a plow in my hands before, but soon I got the knack of it and became as good as any farmer. This kind of farm work, especially if not mechanized, is very hard. To follow a team of horses twelve hours a day, holding on to the handles of a plow tightly, is no easy task. The topsoil was fairly shallow, and beneath it was a layer of stony soil in many places. If that stony soil got hooked, it would come up in shell-like pieces, lifting with it all the topsoil, tearing the plow out of your hands, and if not stopped in time, it would tip over and fall on the hind legs of the horses, causing injury or at least spooking them. Bluestein, being an older and heavier man, could not plow for hours, so it became my task to plow from dawn to dusk, while he did the other chores. Neighbours came by to admire my resilience.

Before we started to plow, we spread the manure that had accumulated over the winter behind the stable. We did it by hand, because we did not have a manure spreader. However, we did have a grain planter, which came in handy. We also planted corn, sugar beets and potatoes, as well as some vegetables in the space allotted for a garden. My partner insisted on digging deep narrow ditches between the beds, despite the advice of the neighbours and my protest, claiming that this is how he had done it at home. It did not help arguing with him or explaining that the ground in our corner of Eastern Europe was low and swampy. He went ahead and dug those ditches, and as a result, we had a poor crop. Surprisingly enough, I managed to plow the entire fifty-five acres of land in time for sowing.

My two cousins, my uncle Shloime's daughters, Helen and Rose, came to visit us from New York and stayed with us for ten days. I took time after milking the cows to reminisce with them about the old Shershev, and of course about the families we'd had there but who were no more. Above all, we talked about my immediate family. My mother, who was their aunt, they remembered clearly. There was no end to the stories. We sat up till late at night, until it was almost time for me to get up. I was lonely when they left. Shortly afterwards, we had visitors from Toronto, two friends from the refugee camps in Italy, Zygmund Suchter and Max Moneta, along with their wives, Zena and Irka. We talked about our experiences from those three years in Italy. After a few days, they left, just in time for haymaking, which took about two weeks. We had barely finished bringing in the hay when oat-harvesting time was upon us. It took us three weeks to take in the grain, and then we had to take care of the corn.

As the barn badly needed repairs and we had prepared plenty of lumber over the winter, we got ready to fix the barn. However, we discovered that the elm planks, which had been so straight when we piled them up to dry, had twisted like corkscrews wherever they were not weighted down, and more than half of them had to be discarded. Nevertheless, we had enough straight timber left, and we began to hammer it over the weakened side of the barn. To our dismay, the nails would not penetrate the wood. Some of our neighbours suggested that we dip the tips of the nails in grease before hammering them in. That helped a bit, but the boards often split as soon as the nails were halfway through. After many trials and disappointments, we realized that elm wood was not a good building material.

It became more apparent that Bluestein's enthusiasm for the farm was diminishing, although he tried to hide it in the presence of others.

He talked more and more about getting rid of the farm, how the farm held no future for him, that no woman, certainly not a Jewish one, would leave the city for such a farm. With time, his whining had increased to a degree that he began speaking openly about leaving the farm. It seemed to me that he saw that he could not save any money on the farm. The best we could hope for was to eke out a living. And seeing that he had no investment in the farm because his uncle never sent the two thousand dollars he had promised, Bluestein had nothing to lose by abandoning it. At the age of twenty-six, I could not understand a man twenty years my senior who had lost a wife and two children. I did not understand his loneliness and despair as he watched his middle years slipping away.

Meanwhile, Ruth had given up her job in Montreal and came home so that she could come out to the farm to see me at least once a week or more. This only called attention to my friend's loneliness. During the week, Ruth called me on the telephone a couple of times. I reciprocated, but not every call, because I simply could not afford it. As all young people do, we flirted a bit on the phone until I once heard somebody trying to stifle a giggle. It dawned on me that at least one person was listening to our conversation on the party line. From then on, Ruth and I spoke in Yiddish, and some of our neighbours were deprived of their entertainment.

All that time, I was corresponding with my friend Bliskowsky, whom I had left in Italy, and with my relatives in Israel. But my closest contact was with my uncle Shloime in New York. In early fall, after long deliberations with my uncle and his children, especially his oldest son Jack, who worked for the US Department of Justice, I decided to visit them in New York. I was not yet a Canadian citizen, but I had heard of some new Canadians who had been let into the United States after proving to the US authorities at the border that they had some investment in Canada. My cousin Jack sent me his phone number at the Department of Justice and told me to ask the US border inspector to call him, and he would guarantee my return to Canada.

One of the first Jews I had met in Brockville, Mr. Feltcher, offered to accompany me across the border on the ferry from Brockville across the St. Lawrence River to the town of Morristown, New York. We docked on the opposite shore on the American side, and I was finally standing on American soil, the land that every Eastern European Jew dreamt of, the land of freedom and plenty. The welcoming committee consisted of one immigration inspector. As soon as I told him that I was born in Poland and had no visa, he ordered me into the office. I told him about my relatives in the United States and showed him the papers that proved that I owned a farm. I also gave him my cousin Jack's telephone number and asked him to call and confirm my story and identity. He said, "You can be President Truman's cousin, I will still not let you in without a visa."

I was very disappointed that I could not get to the United States, but my family in New York was even more disappointed.

The weather began to change. There were days when there was no let-up in the downpour, and it was impossible to do any work outdoors. Yet it was my biggest enjoyment to put on the rubber boots and the waterproof clothing that my uncle had sent me and walk the length of the farm to the very end, two kilometres each way. No matter how hard the rain fell, not a drop of water penetrated the suit, nor did the rain wet my face, which was protected by the hood. Walking in the rain like that took me back to my childhood, when I would sit in my friend Moishe Gelman's living room at the open window and watch the rain coming down on their flower garden, the nicest in Shershev. What beautiful memories that walk brought back. It triggered yearnings for those days and longings for those people, for the family and friends who were so dear to me and whose lives had been cut short so cruelly and mercilessly. They were taken away from this world and from me, forever. I cannot explain why, but in those empty expanses of the fields around me—for who would walk outside in that weather—in the storm, alone, I felt an unusual nearness to those departed souls. I felt sadness and warmth, as if they were near me or with me in those moments and I could communicate with them in my mind.

As for Ruth and me, our feelings toward each other changed during the year from acquaintance to friendship, and then to more sensitive emotion and sentiment. It was inevitable that the subject of marriage would come up. I recall a remark that Ruth made half-seriously during one of our more earnest conversations. She said, "A farmer will never get rich unless he strikes oil on his land. You will never strike oil on this farm."

Somehow, without much discussion or argument, the decision was made to sell the farm. I was not happy, for I realized that we stood to lose money, as we had overpaid to begin with. The loser would be me, or rather my uncle. We could not let Mr. Berlin lose any of the money he had lent us. My other reason for being unhappy about leaving the farm was different. I had never forgotten the time when I was forced to march from Shershev to Antopol, during which some hundreds of us were killed by the Nazis, how we were then reunited with our families in Antopol and then immediately expelled again and driven eastward, an entire community of two thousand souls—men, women and children. We were destitute, deprived of possessions, even a crust of bread, and we could see in the distance the non-Jewish farmers peacefully going about their daily chores while we were being driven to places and fates unknown. We were so envious of those farmers who were leading such peaceful lives. That quest for tranquility had materialized itself for me on the farm, and I loathed the idea of leaving it. However, I could not remain on the farm alone. It was based only on Bluestein's expertise and authority that the Zbars and Mr. Berlin had bought the farm in the first place. It was by the same authority that the decision to sell was made.

37
Continuity

IN THE MIDDLE of October 1949, Mr. and Mrs. Pleet held a dinner in their home for the few Jewish families in Brockville. On this occasion, Ruth and I announced our engagement. In November, we sold the farm for 5,500 dollars, just enough to cover Mr. Berlin's loan. The experience with the farm had cost us 2,000 dollars, exactly the amount my uncle Shloime had sent.

I left for Montreal, which was at that time not only the largest city in Canada, but also the centre of Canadian Jewry. I rented a room with an elderly childless Jewish couple by the name of Freedman, at 5990 Park Avenue, for twenty dollars a month. A few days after arriving, I found a job as a carpenter in a desk factory. I worked ten hours a day, five days a week, and took home twenty-seven dollars a week. From this amount I had to put away five dollars a week for rent, and the rest was mine to spend. After taking Ruth out on Saturday nights to a club and getting to and from work, there wasn't much left over. On the way home from work, I would stop at a corner store to buy a loaf of sliced rye bread, three cans of sardines and butter. At home, I buttered all the slices of bread and made sardine sandwiches. I ate a third of those sandwiches for supper, a third for the following day's breakfast and a third for lunch. When I got tired of eating bread and sardines three times a day, seven days a week, I would treat myself to a lemon for a nickel and squeeze it over the sardines. The only cooked meal I had was on Friday evenings, when I'd go to a nearby restaurant. There I'd order a hamburger, which was served with mashed potatoes and green peas, and wash it down with a cup of tea. The bill came to ninety cents, and, feeling generous on those occasions, I would give the waiter a dollar tip.

Ruth worked for Universal Pictures, and on Friday nights, we would see a movie for free. The Quebec censor board reviewed movies before approving them to be shown to the public, and employees of the company were permitted to attend and bring a guest. So we saw movies before anyone else did, uncensored too!

During the winter of 1949–1950, Ruth and I travelled to New York for my cousin Harold's wedding. This time, I knew to obtain a visa from the American consulate first, and we had no trouble crossing the border. As we were coming out of the train station in New York, I heard a voice saying, "Moishe?"

I turned my head instinctively in the direction of the voice, without thinking that there might be many Moishes in New York. There stood three of my cousins, Yankl (Jack), Avreml (Abe) and Eli. After taking Ruth to her aunt and uncle's, my cousins took me to my uncle Shloime's apartment on 2133 Daly Avenue, the same address my mother had given me on the morning before she and the rest of my family were taken to Auschwitz. My aunt Esther was there with my other cousins, Chvolkah (Helen), Rose, Lippa (Leo) and Elchonon, or Harold, the groom. After all the hugs and kisses, I went to see my uncle who was at the nearby synagogue. As we embraced, my uncle wavered on his feet and had to sit down. I took this to be a sign of his age and asked my cousin if this kind of weakness happened often. He said that it was the first time he had seen his father in that condition. After a few minutes, my uncle recovered. He had just been overcome by the excitement of seeing me.

My cousin's wedding was a beautiful affair. I had seen only a few weddings in Shershev and a few more in the displaced persons camps in Italy, and such a wedding would have been beyond imagination in either place. I met the rest of my mother's family, those who were fortunate to have left Europe before the rise of Nazi Germany, some even before World War I. Besides my uncle Shloime and my aunt Esther and their children, I met my mother's other brother Pesach (Philip), and his wife, Esther, and their children and grandchildren. I also met my uncle Lippa's son, Irving, who had paid for my passage to Canada, and his wife, Ruth, and their children. It is difficult to describe my feelings in those moments. I had newly discovered the entire family from my mother's side, and they were alive and well. Of course, I knew of them, but to see them in person, to be hugged and kissed by them, to see the tears running down their faces and to feel their affection, that is beyond my ability to describe.

On the way back to Montreal, I felt invigorated, even exhilarated, to have found them, to know that they were real and didn't just exist in my mind or through letters; they were my living, breathing, feeling, loving and affectionate family.

Ruth and I got married on June 14, 1950, at the Murray Street Synagogue in Ottawa. Mr. and Mrs. Pleet made all the arrangements and covered the expenses of the wedding, as I had no money of my own. My two uncles from New York attended, and the other guests from my side were Mr. and Mrs. Zbar and Mr. Berlin. All other guests were from Ruth's side of the family. After the wedding, Ruth and I went on a honeymoon in Old Orchard Beach, Maine, which was a destination for honeymooners at the time. This time, the border inspector gave me a hard time. He asked me questions such as "Why did you not serve in the German army?" When I responded that I was a Jew, he said, "So what?" He asked such bright questions for a good half-hour before he let us go. Old Orchard Beach had a beautiful sandy beach that stretched for kilometres, and between our hotel and the Atlantic, there was nothing but fine sand, stretching seemingly endlessly in both directions.

After our honeymoon, we returned to Brockville and spent several months there. I supposedly helped my father-in-law in his dry goods store, but he managed to run it nicely with my mother-in-law and did not need me. However, he had some credit business with several customers who at times were not prompt with their payments and had to be reminded, so I became responsible for making home calls to collect.

In Brockville, there was no active Jewish life for young people, so Ruth and I moved back to Montreal as fall was approaching. Not being able to afford rent for an apartment, we rented a room from a family by the name of Gurman on Waverly Street. Ruth got back her job with Universal Pictures, and I started looking for a job. With the help of a landsman by the name of Sam (Shepsl) Zlotnik who had come to Canada in the 1920s, I was directed to a clothing factory called Quality Pad. They were in need of a cutter, a trade about which I knew nothing, but I convinced the owner to hire me. Six months after I started working there, I was doing as much work as the head cutter, who was getting twice my pay. Our work consisted of piling up fifty layers of cloth evenly and cutting them according to the pattern that was marked on the top layer. It was big responsibility, for if you made a mistake, you ruined fifty pieces of cloth at once. The work also involved a measure of danger because the electric cutters were sharp and fast. Yet I did my work skilfully and neatly, without ever hearing a complaint.

I wanted to improve my education and become an engineer, so I registered at Sir George Williams College. Three nights a week I would go straight from work to school and didn't get home until eleven at night. I spent my Sundays doing homework. This is how the winter of 1950–1951 passed. For Pesach, we went to Ruth's parents in Brockville. I was off school in the summer, and that gave us time to do activities like going to amusement parks and taking boat rides on the St. Lawrence River with music and dancing, and the summer of 1951 passed pleasantly but uneventfully.

In the fall of 1951, my father-in-law bought an apartment building in Montreal, on Linton Avenue. As my in-laws were still living in Brockville, somebody had to look after the building. So we moved to Linton Avenue, into a two-bedroom apartment. It was a wonderful change from living in one room and having to share all facilities. The privacy, our own kitchen, the availability of a shower at any time — it was great! How easily we get used to things and take them for granted.

In early 1952, we found out that Ruth was pregnant. She continued to work because we knew that once she stopped, we could expect difficult times. My father-in-law came up with a plan for me to support our growing family. He wanted to buy a going concern, like a corner store. In those days, the owner would stay in the store from morning until almost midnight, every day of the week. By working six or seven days a week and not having the time to spend any money, the owner could be assured of a livelihood.

Ruth's parents made a list of several stores for sale, and the two of us set out to look them over. Eventually, we found one at the corner of Victoria Avenue and Linton Avenue, a block and a half from our apartment. The owner, an elderly Jewish man, was desperate to sell it. It was a large store and had a soda bar, which served cold drinks and some food, a variety of groceries, toys and sweets, as well as an assortment of handy items, like writing materials and notions. A lot of residential buildings were going up all around, and this was the only store of this kind in the neighbourhood and quite busy. The owner named his price and would not budge. Here I saw a business deal that could only be made between deeply religious Jews like my father-in-law and that elderly man.

"Fine," said my father-in-law, "it's a deal. You finish today's business and take the cash for today's sales, and leave everything in the store as is. Take nothing but your hat, and give me the keys."

They shook hands. My father-in-law gave the owner the name of his lawyer and asked him to return the next morning with his lawyer. With that, my father-in-law walked out, leaving me to learn a business in one afternoon and evening, a business of which I knew nothing. The store closed at midnight. As agreed, the owner emptied the cash. He took his hat, gave me the keys, wished me good luck and drove away. I locked the store and walked home up the street. I was in business!

The store opened at 8:00 a.m., but before opening, I had to take in the rye bread, rolls and bagels, then all the daily newspapers in English and French, which were delivered in the early morning hours. We had several people working for us to cover all the shifts. The weekends were busier than weekdays, particularly Sunday evenings, when many of our customers came home from a weekend in the Laurentian Mountains. At lunchtime, students from the school across the street came to the store to buy snacks and drinks. During that hour, the store was a madhouse, with as many children as the store could hold, yelling, screaming and shoving each other, while adult customers tried to push their way to a counter, sometimes giving up and leaving. The children were attracted to the comic books like bees to honey. They read them up to the moment the bell rang, calling them back to class. There were some who, in the dash to get back to school, ran out with comic books hidden under their jackets. We knew about it but were unable to keep an eye on everyone.

My father-in-law came in from Brockville to see how we were doing and saw how hard I was working. After a couple of visits, he decided to come in every second Sunday so that I could have the day off. I was thankful for that and used the time to catch up on needed sleep. In those days, Montreal was known for its nightclubs, rivalling New York in number and perhaps even in entertainment quality. Every second Sunday, Ruth and I would have dinner in a nice restaurant and then go to a nightclub for entertainment and dancing.

The most enjoyable times for me in the store were Sunday mornings. It was almost a tradition for Jewish men to go to their favourite bakery on Sunday morning for fresh bread, rolls or bagels and to the delicatessen for lox, cream cheese and other delicacies. In our store, they could get all they needed in one trip, plus the Jewish papers. Many Jewish newcomers lived in our neighbourhood, and on Sunday mornings the store was packed with Jewish men discussing trivial subjects like the weather or more serious subjects like world politics or antisemitism.

Everything was always said loudly, as if the power of persuasion lay in the volume of one's voice. I liked to listen to these discussions while serving the customers. Some of the arguments were silly, some bordering on ignorance, but others were brilliant. How I would have liked to join them, but I was too busy. Thinking of those conversations now, they seem irrelevant. But in the moment, they were so important, so pertinent to those individuals, to that time and that situation.

In October, Ruth stayed at home more, and I ran over to the house several times a day to see how she was doing. On Friday, October 10, Ruth began to feel contractions. In the evening, I ran home, where Ruth was alone in the apartment, much calmer than I was. When I called the taxi, I was so excited that I could not recall our building number or the apartment number. Ruth had to take the telephone and tell the dispatcher our address. I took her to the Jewish General Hospital, and then went back to the store. We were busy that night, as we were every Friday. At about 10:45 p.m., the phone rang, and I got the news that we had a baby boy. I grabbed a box of cigars from a shelf and handed them out to all the customers, yelling, "It's a boy! It's a boy!" I can still see the surprised looks of some of the customers who did not even know Ruth was pregnant, or perhaps did not know Ruth at all.

When I first saw my son in the hospital nursery, his face did not look much different from all the other babies in the room, yet I instantly felt warmth coming over me toward that infant, not yet one hour old. That feeling came to me again but with much greater intensity eight days later, when I held him at his bris. The chief rabbi of Montreal, Rabbi Herschorn, bestowed on him all the traditional blessings required at such a ceremony according to the laws of Moses and Israel and named him with the names of my father, Yitzchak, and grandfather Yaakov Kopel, who perished together in the gas chambers of Auschwitz on February 1, 1943. Holding my baby, I spoke to them all, to my parents, grandparents, sisters, brother, uncles, aunts and cousins. I spoke to them, not with my lips, but with my heart and my whole being, crying out to them: *Look, here is your continuity! You will not be forgotten, nor will your names be forgotten. Despite all attempts, you will live in him, in his soul and in the memories of you, which I intend to instill in him.* Maybe because of the passing of so many years since that day, or perhaps because of my inability to verbalize my feelings back then, I cannot describe my feelings now. All I know is that I was very excited and very agitated, and at that time I felt closer to those in heaven than to those on earth.

I was starting to feel the physical exhaustion from the sixteen-hour workdays. I was constantly on my feet and on the go. Even my meals, which consisted mostly of sandwiches, I would eat standing, one hand holding the sandwich, the other serving a customer. Even the day off every other Sunday did not restore my full energy. I decided to give Carl, our full-time worker, the keys to the store. I left him money to start paying for the early deliveries, and I came in an hour later. In the next two years, we managed to pay out the balance on the store, and we could say that we owned it. The fear of losing the store was gone.

Looking back, I would say that those were good years, especially if one does not demand too much from life. There is no question that I worked very hard, yet we managed to overcome our problems, in no small measure thanks to my perspective looking back to another era and seeing how meaningless, how trivial, those problems were in comparison to what I had witnessed and gone through.

Yes, I remember well our first two years in the store. True, I did not spend much time at home, but Ruth used to bring our son Kenneth, or Ken, to the store. To me, he always was and will be "Itzekel," after my father, Yitzchak, or Itzik. I experienced so much joy watching him grow from an infant into a toddler and then into a little boy. He was everything to me—my hope, my dream for the future, a kind of resurrection of my family and, above all, its continuity. Some of my most tender memories are of those late summer afternoons when Ruth came to the store with Itzekel. I would sit him down on one of the stools near the bar and try to feed him, taking down all the toys from the shelves to keep him amused while I sneaked a spoonful of soup into his mouth. When he became confident on his feet, he would run around the store among the groups of schoolboys who were playing cards on the floor.

In the spring of 1954, Ruth and I went to Brockville to spend Pesach with her family, as we always did. Ken was a year and a half. Once in Brockville, I decided to go by bus to Kingston to see the Zbars with Itzekel. Itzekel, who in his lifetime so far, had seen only one creature with four legs, excitedly pointed from the bus window to the distant cows, yelling, "Doggie!" The other passengers smiled. The novelty soon wore off, and Itzekel was lulled to sleep with his head on my lap as I gently stroked his head and back. Only a loving parent knows the feeling of love that pours out of your heart in such a precious moment.

It was the first time that Mrs. Zbar met Itzekel, but she knew how to put a child at ease. In no time Itzekel began to feel at home and proved it by pulling out drawers and emptying the contents on the floor. I tried to stop him, but Mrs. Zbar would not let me interfere, saying, "He is having a good time. Let him be." Dear Mrs. Leiba Zbar, that noble, kind, benevolent human being. Little did I know that this would be the last time I would ever see her. A while later I found out that she had passed away after a short illness.

38
Newfoundland

ONE DAY, A landsman came into the store and told me about his success in business in St. John's, Newfoundland. When he heard me complain about my long hours and lack of time to be with my family, he tried to persuade me to come to Newfoundland as his business partner. At first, I was cool to the idea, but after being exposed to his persistent salesmanship, I eventually succumbed to the proposition and decided to sell the store and move to Newfoundland.

When one badly wants to buy an item, one has to pay the full price for it, but when one badly wants to sell, one takes a loss, and that is what happened with the store. We sold the store for a much lower price than its full value before Pesach in 1956. After Pesach, I left for Newfoundland, leaving behind Ruth, who was pregnant, and three-and-a-half-year-old Ken. There were no direct flights from Montreal to St. John's then, so there were stops in Moncton, Halifax, Sydney, Stephenville and Gander. I got as far as Gander that evening, only to find out that the flight to St. John's was cancelled because of fog. As there was no road to St. John's, the only way of getting there was by the train colloquially called the Newfie Bullet, so named because of its slow speed. It was a narrow-gauge train with small and dingy coaches, occupied by even filthier passengers, rugged-looking men with unshaven faces, dressed in crude work clothes and heavy boots. Some had their boots off altogether. The coach was filled with thick cigarette smoke. Some men were chewing and spitting out a dark substance on the floor, and it took me a while to realize that they were chewing tobacco.

A man was lying across a double seat, and I tapped him gently on the shoulder but got no response. I tapped again, harder, expecting to hear a protest or even a curse. To my surprise, the man opened his eyes and looked at me, a stranger in city attire, and, still half asleep, he sat up and made room for me to sit down. After a while, we started a conversation. He had trouble understanding me and I found it difficult to understand his unusual English. Yet I managed to find out that the men in the coach were woodsmen returning home after a long season spent chopping wood for the large paper mill in Corner Brook. The lumberjack described life in the lumber camps—the hard work, the difficulty in making a living and the poverty at home. Despite this man's rough appearance and common language, he was a decent human being who worked hard and honestly to support his family. The train kept on winding and twisting between rocky hills and swampy valleys, curving its way around countless lakes and fir-covered hills, slowing down to a crawl at every twist and turn. Some young passengers got off the train and walked alongside it at the same speed. No wonder the trip from Gander to St. John's, a distance of 320 kilometres, took ten hours.

In St. John's, I stayed with my new partner and his family to await the arrival of Ruth and Ken. Meanwhile, I had the chance to get acquainted with the city of St. John's and the Jewish community. Our business consisted of a rented store in St. John's and two small country stores on the Burin Peninsula. Inexperienced young clerks managed both stores, and there was no supervision or proper accounting. We had half a dozen employees in the St. John's store. My partner and I would spend most of the week out of town, leaving the store in St. John's unsupervised. We drove over the rough roads of eastern Newfoundland, travelling from village to village, trying to sell a variety of clothing to the small general stores spread out among the isolated bays and inlets along the rugged shores of Newfoundland. This was the kind of work that Eastern European Jews had done when they arrived in Canada a generation earlier. The only difference was that they had carried their wares on their backs, while we travelled in a large truck full of merchandise.

At that time, there was only one hundred-kilometre stretch of paved road on the whole island. That road led from St. John's to Carbonear, and it was so full of potholes that one had to be more careful driving on it than on the unpaved roads. On the rest of the island, the roads were originally walking paths, which then became roads for horses and buggies. Some roads had been upgraded, but it was risky to travel on them with a motorized vehicle. These were the roads we travelled on, stopping at little stores and trying to sell our merchandise.

In the mid-1950s, there were still rural areas of Newfoundland that didn't have electric power. Some households had their own power generators, which could supply enough power to light up one or two homes but not a single appliance. In these areas, the population lived in the same conditions that we'd had in Shershev before 1932. It took some adjustment for me, a city dweller, especially one coming from a large city like Montreal.

There were hardly any hotels or motels in Newfoundland to speak of, just a few in St. John's and Corner Brook. In the small towns, a house with a few spare rooms was referred to as a hotel. In the smaller villages, there were boarding houses, where the owner rented out spare rooms for a night or two to a casual sojourner or travelling salesman. I would not like to guess how often the bedding was changed on the beds I slept in. We would eat our breakfast at the boarding house and buy canned meat or fish and bread for the other meals, parking on the side of the road to eat. The only fresh produce available consisted of durable items like turnips, cabbage, carrots and potatoes. The only fruit available most of the year was a kind of apple that kept in a barrel year-round.

Ruth was due to give birth to our second child at the beginning of August, and I left for Montreal to be with her at the end of July. Those were trying days for both of us. Ruth was expecting to go to the hospital at any moment, knowing that a day or two later I would have to leave for Newfoundland. As for me, I did not want to leave Ruth behind with two children. I missed them terribly. But the main reason for my tension, which I could not even share with Ruth, was my realization that my decision to go to Newfoundland had been a hasty one and was now irreversible.

On Saturday, August 4, Ruth gave birth to a baby girl. I was thankful to the Almighty for giving us a second child, our first daughter, and for the speedy, easy and safe delivery. I was glad to be given the chance to have my daughter carry on my mother's and my sister's names, Esther and Sheva, which we anglicized to Sharon. Yet I was restless and apprehensive about leaving them. Two days later, I travelled back to St. John's, where I spent the rest of the summer by myself, mostly in the small coastal communities, or outports. I came into the city on the weekends to look for an apartment to rent, but that was not easy. There was an American military base on the outskirts of St. John's. It had about five thousand personnel, and their families had taken every available apartment in town.

I finally succeeded in finding an apartment on Patrick Street. It was an old two-storey house, with the landlord living on the top floor. As the house was built on a slope, the basement led from the back of the house into the yard, which was overgrown with weeds, shrubs and some dogwoods. The basement contained the kitchen, with an old stove converted from wood to oil, a spare room and a bathroom. The landlord used the rest of the basement for storage. On the ground floor, there was one bedroom and a double parlour, a long room divided into two by an arched door.

Meanwhile, Ruth began to get ready for the transition to St. John's, not an easy job with two children on her hands. She arranged to have the furniture crated and everything else properly packed, and the entire shipment left by boat. Ruth followed with Ken and our ten-week-old daughter, Esther Sharon. With Ruth came Mrs. Chapman, the nurse who had looked after Ken for a year. Ruth brought her along to help her on the trip and until she was settled in St. John's.

After working in St. John's for a year, my partnership in the business broke up, leaving me with 10 per cent of my original investment. I suddenly found myself without money and without any means of supporting my wife and children. Those were difficult days for me. I blamed myself for giving up a good business in Montreal and getting into this mess. I had ventured into a business that was new to me in a faraway and strange place without thoroughly checking out what I was getting into beforehand. Now I was harvesting the fruits of my naive trust in others. If I'd had the money I invested in that unsuccessful partnership, I would have returned to Montreal to start something on my own. Unfortunately, I did not.

I managed to scrape together enough cash to make a down payment on a second-hand van and to buy a return ticket to Montreal. In Montreal, I went to visit the dry goods wholesalers whom I knew from my dealings in the previous year. Without exception, they were willing to extend me credit. One, a successful wholesaler and importer named Ben Mintz, said to me, "I will give you credit of a thousand dollars because I started my business over twenty-five years ago with seven dollars."

In appreciation of this man's trust in me, he got about half my business with wholesalers for the next thirty years.

After several days of acquisitions in Montreal, I returned to St. John's, and the merchandise started arriving a week later. Our living room became my warehouse. So I was in business, in an occupation I had never aspired to and in fact detested. But what else could I have done? There was nothing I could do in St. John's to support a family. So, I filled up two suitcases with samples, loaded up as much merchandise as I could in the van and set out on the rugged roads of eastern Newfoundland.

Many of the settlements in Newfoundland were strewn along its coast and were not connected to each other by land. The only access to them was by sea, and they were often isolated because of the weather or because the bays were blocked by ice. However, the provincial government, aided by the federal government, embarked on a program to connect the settlements with roads, following the footpaths made by generations of inhabitants. Those roads winded between boulders and swamps, going up hills and down low boggy grounds, where one foot to the right or left could spell disaster for a weary driver. The construction of those roads had begun with Newfoundland's Confederation in 1949 and was in progress when I started my travels.

The eastern part of Newfoundland has an incredible amount of rain, drizzle and fog, and I began working there in the beginning of October, when rain and fog were at their heaviest. The heavy clouds were so low that I could touch them when raising my hand above my head. They did not disappear until early November, when the temperatures fell below zero and the precipitation changed to snow. The cold weather brought winds, which blew away the clouds long enough to assure one that blue skies still existed above the heavy clouds. It was only when the temperature dropped below fifteen degrees that the sky cleared and exposed its heavenly blue colours.

It is difficult to imagine today the conditions of the roads in Newfoundland in 1957. They were a continuous sea of mud. My truck would sit axle-deep in mud that scraped its underside, tearing off exhaust pipes, fuel lines and brake cables. Added to that was the darkness, which started at four in the afternoon, and the fog, which was as thick as the mud below. At night it was impossible to see one metre ahead, even with the headlights on.

This was my beginning. I left Ruth and the children with a heavy heart. The pouring rain added to my misery and made me feel as if the heavens were crying with me for the hard times I was experiencing, all of my own making.

It was not easy to go into those country stores, introduce myself and try to talk a storekeeper into looking at my samples. It often happened that I would talk to a storekeeper for an hour and get him to look at my samples, but he would not buy anything. I would walk away dejected, but I knew I had to continue. I had to pay the rent and pay for the van, and above all, I had to feed a wife and two children.

In late November, the snow came down to stay, and the treacherous roads became worse. In some places, the road was blocked by drifting snow. In other places, the truck would spin its wheels going up a hill and then start sliding backwards. As soon as I left home, I wanted to go right back, but I knew I could not. I spent five days a week on the road. I would come home to pick up the merchandise, which usually took a whole day because of the poorly organized system at the wharf. Another day was taken up with checking the newly arrived merchandise, making orders in the van, and filling it with the merchandise. In between, I had to go downtown to deposit whatever money I had come back with from my last trip and then immediately send cheques to my debtors. I was still doing my best to build their trust and confidence in me. Ruth helped me with the paperwork. To save time, I would leave home in the evening and drive all night, arriving at my destination in the morning, ready to see the first customer. I soon learned not to leave in the evening if it was snowing.

Then we found out that Ruth was pregnant. That gave me the impetus to work still harder. Thinking about it today, it seems that it was as hard as it could be anyway, driving all night in the snow or the mud, spending nights in unheated homes, sleeping sometimes with my clothes on in houses lacking any sanitary facilities and eating whatever the little local store had to offer. I worked sixteen hours or more every day. Those little country stores—most of them inside homes or just next door—were open from the moment the owners opened their eyes until they went to bed. Some of the merchants preferred to see me after closing time so as not to be disturbed by their customers. Selling merchandise was difficult and often aggravating, but it paled in comparison to the hardship of the driving and the hazards of the road. In addition, my van was wearing out and needed tires, which I could not afford to buy. I once got six flat tires on a ten-kilometre stretch of road and spent all that day fixing tires.

At the beginning of 1958, business dropped off. I had five or six competitors in eastern Newfoundland, all of them working out of St. John's. It was time to go to Montreal and place orders for spring and summer goods, but I owed my suppliers in Montreal money I did not have. I was in a bind and did not know where to turn. Eventually I asked my landlord to lend me the money. I made out the cheques and left for Montreal, stopping in New York for a couple of days to spend time with my uncle Shloime. Before my fateful decision to move to St. John's, I had managed to pay my uncle the two thousand dollars he had sent me in 1948 toward my share of the farm.

In Montreal, I visited my suppliers and gave them the cheques covering the balance of the money I owed them. This time, they were not as apprehensive to extend me credit, and some seemed genuinely interested in selling me merchandise. My entire trip to Montreal and New York took a week. As soon as I got back, I went on the road.

During that first winter of driving, I had a couple of close calls. One of the traveller's worst enemies was the freezing rain that would sometimes fall all night, building up a thick layer of ice. The surface of the road would become so slippery that it was impossible to walk, even with a nail-pointed cane. It was even worse when that slippery icy road was covered with a thin layer of powdery snow. On such a road one morning, I lost control of the steering wheel, and the van slid off the road into a ditch. I made my way on foot for the next few hundred metres to a settlement and knocked on the door of the first house. A middle-aged man let me in, and I explained my situation to him. He told me to go back to the van and wait for him. In no more than fifteen minutes, he was back with a dozen men. It took them a few minutes to get me on the road and turn the van around. I was so grateful to those people that I was ready to pay them anything. I asked how much I owed them, but they just smiled. The man from the first house waved me away, saying, "Next time you come, bring a bottle of rum."

Despite all the hardships that I encountered on those Newfoundland roads, despite the rawness and inhospitable terrain, the raggedness of its shores, and the harshness of its climate, the people of Newfoundland made up for all those shortcomings.

In May, the rain ate away at the layer of heavy snow. Like in the biblical story of Noah, the land began to appear from beneath the mountains of snow, and soon the roads turned into a bottomless bog. Unlike with snow, I could not dig my way out of the mud.

The scheduled birth of our third child was getting closer. We decided that Ruth should go with the children to Montreal and stay with her parents. She left in the middle of May, and I followed two weeks later. On the evening of June 4, 1958, I took Ruth to the hospital, where she gave birth to a baby girl. She was as beautiful as the sun. We named her after Ruth's great-aunt Chaya Sarah, and we called her Aviva Simone. Ruth and the children remained in Montreal with her parents for a few weeks. I returned to St. John's two days after Aviva's birth.

By the end of June 1958, spring was in full bloom in Newfoundland, but even June had its surprises. I spent the night of June 10 in a small motel, and when I woke up on the morning of June 11, I looked out the window and could not believe my eyes. The beautiful green landscape of yesterday was covered in a thick layer of snow! In mid-morning I was at the foot of a large hill and saw a plow struggling to clear the snow, which was well over a foot deep. By the time the plow cleared the other side of the hill, the mid-June midday sun was out in its full strength, melting the snow very fast. The ditches on either side of the road became raging torrents.

As soon as the roads dried out, drivers were confronted with another nuisance—dust. A vehicle would kick up a cloud of dust that stretched for two kilometres if there was no crosswind to blow it off the road. The dust tended to penetrate every crack of the vehicle, no matter how tightly it was shut. It settled everywhere and on everything, including in sealed boxes in my van. It was most noticeable on the heads and faces of the travellers. It got to the point where you could not see a thing in front of you. In such weather, one prayed for rain. But, unfortunately, such prayers were answered more often and for longer periods than you wanted, and the rain changed the roads into a sea of mud. No wonder there were so few travellers in Newfoundland in those times.

With three little children at home, and the living room taken up with merchandise, there was no room to turn around in our apartment, and the rent was exorbitant. So I looked around for a larger and less expensive accommodation. New subdivisions were coming up at either end of Elizabeth Avenue with new streets being added, and I found out that there were houses for sale with a full basement, perfect for a warehouse, but I needed two thousand dollars for a down payment. The only person I could turn to was my good friend Philip Auerbach, or Uncle Fishel to my family. He was a Holocaust survivor from Pruzhany who had been in Auschwitz at the same time as me. I got to know him in the DP camps in Italy. He was single and an established jobber, and even though I became his competitor, we instantly became best friends and remained friends for thirty-five years, until the last day of his life. I asked Philip for help, and he gladly offered to sign for me as a guarantor for the down payment. I undertook to repay him in monthly payments, and I can proudly say that I never missed a payment, which was no small accomplishment given my financial situation. And so, at the beginning of October 1958, we moved into our new home at 21 Gambier Street. At that time, we were one of two families in the St. John's Jewish community of seventy members that kept kosher. Ruth's parents bought us a freezer as a housewarming present, and it was large enough to keep kosher meat, bread and cakes, which I bought in Montreal when I went to visit my wholesalers.

No vehicle in those days could stand the punishment of Newfoundland roads for too long, and after driving over eighty thousand kilometres a year on terrible roads, my van was finished and I traded it in as a down payment for a new one—a Ford truck, cab and chassis. I got someone to build a box with shelves and sliding doors on the back. That was a great improvement to the little old van, where all my merchandise was in cardboard boxes, and I sometimes had to empty most of them to find a certain item. Now, every item was in its place and accessible, and because the box was roomy, I could carry four or five times as much merchandise.

That winter was a hard one even for Newfoundland standards. The snow started early and didn't let up. At the end of February, after visiting my suppliers in Montreal, I decided to cover the two territories closer to home. I heard that the road to Burin Peninsula was treacherous and that the snow was high, but I could not afford to stay home an extra day or two. A fifty-kilometre stretch of the road around Terrenceville was especially dangerous. The ground was flat, with hardly a tree or a hill to detain the drifting snow. That part of the road was named Terrenceville Road, and every person who knew that stretch of road and travelled on it from time to time would pronounce that name with repugnance or aversion. In the previous three years, I had learned to respect the Newfoundland winters, but not enough I guess. That March, travelling through the snowy terrain, my desire to get home was so strong that I ignored my common sense. I knew there was no way for any vehicle to get through, yet I wanted to get home so badly. I ended up spending two nights in my truck with only a can of orange juice and two chocolate bars to eat, trapped in deep snow on Terrenceville Road before the road was cleared enough for me to get through. After that, I started carrying canned and dry food and drinks with me in the car, just in case.

On that same stretch of road, a few years later, a Terrenceville man built a small restaurant in the middle of nowhere. One winter, I was among the dozen vehicles that got stuck there, unable to continue due to the heavy snowdrifts. We had to spend the night there, but there were not enough accommodations for all the travellers. Some had to stretch out on the floor, and others spent the night on chairs. I was among the fortunate ones to be given a bed, a single bed, but I had to share with a stranger. The man, a known fish processor in St. John's, got into the bed fully dressed, and I followed suit. The bed was old, and the springs were stretched, with no elasticity left. The man, who was large, fell into the middle of the bed, and my weight could not level out the springs.

I turned on my side away from him, positioning myself on the frame of the bed. Supporting my head with one arm, I held myself in that position all night. Of course there was no thought of sleep.

In the spring of 1959, the weather had another surprise in store for Newfoundland. The forests, on which Newfoundlanders depended so much, were cinder dry and crying out for rain, but to no avail, and the fires started. The fires were not confined to the eastern part of the island, and most of the woods on the Burin Peninsula were burned too. That summer, I got stuck almost in the very same spot as in March's snowstorm, but this time it was behind a wall of fire. I was on my way home when the mounted police closed the road between Don River and Swift Current. We spent the night in our vehicles, and the following morning, a police car tried to lead us through. The smoke was thick, and cinders fell on us. I was concerned about my truck, as the box was made of wood and plywood. The police car leading the column of cars and trucks decided that it was too dangerous to continue and ordered us back to the river, where we had to spend another twenty-four hours. The next evening, we were permitted to go on, and we drove through smouldering cinders that had been a forest only two days previously.

In the early years of Confederation with Canada, from 1949 to the mid-1960s, many settlements became accessible by road, and as the ambition of every salesman was to get to settlements at the end of the newly opened roads before any of his competitors did, the news of a new road opening was kept secret for as long as possible. There were a couple of roads that I was the first salesman of dry goods to travel: between Bunyan's Cove and Port Blandford and between Trinity Bay North and Wesleyville.

In the early 1960s, the federal and provincial governments joined in constructing a cross-island highway, from the southwestern point of the island to the eastern end point, the provincial capital, St. John's.

It was no small undertaking, but it was an absolute necessity, as until that time the opposite ends of the island were connected only by a narrow-gauge railway line. In the first year, they paved fifty kilometres of road, starting from St. John's. What an improvement it was in comparison with the old road! Every Newfoundlander could not wait to see the road completed. That road was to be the last leg of the Trans-Canada Highway, connecting Vancouver on the west coast of Canada with St. John's in the east. Large signs proclaiming "We'll finish the drive in '65" appeared along the new highway being constructed, praising the glory and generosity of the federal and provincial governments.

The first premier of the province, Joseph Smallwood, tried hard to drag Newfoundland into the twentieth century, and road construction was just one aspect of the changing face of Newfoundland. The other major change was the spanning of electrical wires across the island, electricity that introduced to all settlements refrigerators, televisions, washing machines and many more electrical appliances, previously unknown to the inhabitants. The main industry, fishing, also became more advanced with the introduction of draggers, which increased the catch. Modern fish plants were built, and there was more employment. Those were memorable and good years for Newfoundland.

39
Miraculous Meeting

IN THE MID-1960S, an event of immense importance took place in my life that connected the past with the present. In those years, the fishing on the Grand Banks off the coast of Newfoundland was very rewarding, and it attracted fishing boats from across the Atlantic. The boats came from Spain, Portugal, Poland, Japan and East and West Germany, but the largest fleet was the Soviet one. The boats came into St. John's harbour for supplies, fuel and fresh water. Sometimes they came in for medical emergencies. With so many foreign boats in the port, and at times hundreds of sailors in the streets, the local population got used to seeing them and stopped paying attention.

I always paid special attention to the Soviet and Polish boats, hoping to meet a Jewish sailor. I was supported in this endeavour by my friend Lewis (Leibel) Ferman. Besides having a dry goods store on Water Street, he was also a part-time government employee, serving as a translator for the dry-dock personnel when Soviet or Polish boats came in for repairs, or when a sick Soviet or Polish sailor was brought to the hospital for medical attention. His job gave him the opportunity to get on board those boats, and he could see the crew list and look for Jewish-sounding names. But finding the names was only the beginning, for individuals from Communist countries were not supposed to be alone with foreigners. The only way to get anyone off the boat was to offer a ride to a whole group "to see the town," and take along the Jewish man. During those years, I met a couple of Jewish captains, but they were even more careful than the non-Jews. Even when they were invited to a private home, they would not go by themselves and would always bring a couple of companions with them. Still, I kept looking for a Jewish face in the crowd of foreign fishermen as I passed them on the streets or in a store.

On a late Saturday morning in early March of 1965, I was downtown with Ruth and Aviva in Woolworth's department store on Water Street. We were just about ready to leave the store as a group of foreign fishermen passed by in front of us. Out of habit, I looked at them, assessing their nationality, which I determined to be Polish. One face caught my eye. It was strangely familiar. It belonged to a man in his mid-fifties, who was wearing a beret and a long grey coat, a style that had been in fashion before the war. Where had I seen this face before? I stood there, thinking for a moment. The face triggered a memory, but it could not be! Or could it? Could it be Leon Kulowski, the man who saved my life in Auschwitz by pulling me out of the penal colony and getting me a job in the carpenter shop?

I stood there, glued to the floor, not knowing what to do. I had written to Kulowski from Italy several times after liberation but never got any response. Should I go over to this foreign man and ask him? Would I not make a fool of myself? But what if this man was Kulowski? I heard Ruth's voice asking me what I was looking at.

"That man's face looks familiar to me," I told her. "He reminds me of Leon." I knew it sounded crazy, yet I couldn't leave.

Ruth said, "Go and ask him if it will make you feel better."

I walked over to the group of fishermen and addressed the man in the grey coat in Polish.

"Are you Polish?"

"Yes," he answered.

"Have you ever been to Auschwitz?"

The man looked at me inquisitively. Slowly nodding, he said, "Yes."

I knew immediately that I had the right man, and I could feel tension growing in my stomach. I said to him, "Is your name Leon Kulowski, Auschwitz number 805?"

His mouth dropped, his eyes became wide, and he could barely blurt out, "Who are you?"

I could hardly control myself. Shivering with excitement, I was trying to tell him in one minute who I was and what he had done for me. He did not remember a thing! I took him over to where Ruth and Aviva were standing. Ruth knew all about him.

What followed was like a dream. We took him home, and the story spread in minutes all over town. Within hours, we had visits by reporters from the local television and from the newspapers. Friends called to share the excitement with me.

Only after supper did I finally stop shaking. This was Kulowski's fifth visit to St. John's. After the war, he had gone back to university and became a doctor, and he was now the ship's physician. Fishermen and fishing crews made much more money aboard the ships than doctors or university professors on land in Communist Poland. Needing to support a wife and two children, he decided to go to sea as a ship's doctor. This story spread across his ship, too, and when I took him back late at night, the entire crew was on deck, inspecting me with curiosity.

In those days, there was a chronic shortage of everything in the Communist countries, and I gave Leon whatever he dared to take in clothing and footwear. He would not take money because getting caught could mean spending the rest of his life in jail. He even had to smuggle the clothes and footwear aboard. So Ruth and I took the clothing under our coats the following day and went aboard with him, leaving everything in his small cabin. We had to make a few trips to avoid looking too suspicious with all the clothing under our coats. After two days in St. John's, Leon's boat left for home, the Polish port of Gdynia. I tried to keep in touch with Leon, but corresponding was difficult because Communist Poland censored letters from the West, so mail delivery was very slow.

40
Family and Community

SINCE THE EARLY 1900s, the Jewish community in St. John's had had an old shul, or synagogue, on Henry Street. In the 1950s, the community was growing with an influx of Holocaust survivors and with the grown children of old members. Many members became more prosperous during and after the war, so the leadership proposed building a new shul, and the members approved the proposal. We formed committees to raise money, land was bought on Elizabeth Avenue, and soon after, construction began. Members of the Jewish community were busy raising money for the construction of the new synagogue. While the men wrote cheques, the women came up with all kinds of projects—rummage sales, bake sales, card and bingo games, dinner parties, lotteries and other activities.

Before we knew it, it was spring 1960. The new shul was finished, and the community was humming with activity. The weekend when the dedication was to occur was drawing near and so was my tenth wedding anniversary. The struggling Jewish community of St. John's had seen its membership outgrow the old wooden shul on Henry Street and move into a beautiful stone edifice, worthy of a much larger congregation. At sixty-eight families, the membership of our congregation was the highest in its history, and I regret to say, higher than it ever was after that.

The Friday night service before the dedication was conducted by Rabbi Kotziner, may he rest in peace, who filled all Jewish leadership functions in our community—rabbi, Torah reader, shofar blower, teacher, procurer of kosher food and more. Rabbi Kotziner had a pleasant voice and conducted the service in a traditional Orthodox way, which had been the tradition of our congregation since its inception. The dedication was attended by many dignitaries and leaders, and at the reception on Sunday, I said to Ruth, "What a beautiful way to celebrate our tenth wedding anniversary." Of all our anniversaries, I remember that one best.

After the war, the St. John's Jewish community had problems getting rabbis or spiritual leaders. A major source of rabbis and Hebrew teachers had dried up, namely, European Jewry, two thirds of which had been destroyed in the Holocaust. As the Jewish community in North America became more affluent, the demand for rabbis grew, and almost nobody was willing to leave larger Jewish centres on the mainland to move to a faraway place like St. John's, Newfoundland, with its inhospitable climate. Moreover, the small community could not afford to pay much beyond what was required in the upkeep of the synagogue. So we had to settle for Hebrew teachers who were not as versed in the Talmud as a rabbi would be. As long as they could teach the children Hebrew and conduct religious services on Shabbat and the holidays, we had to be satisfied. In a pinch, some of our members could help conduct the services.

One of those members was Morris Wilansky, originally from near Minsk in Belarus, who had come to Newfoundland with his parents, brothers and sisters as a teenager. He had acquired a good religious education in his early years in the yeshiva in Pruzhany. His father was the first and only Jewish ritual slaughterer in Newfoundland's history. The second synagogue member to volunteer as a religious teacher was my friend Lewis Ferman, a Holocaust survivor who had been in a partisan group with his wife, Grunia, under the leadership of Tuvia Bielski, a decorated resistance fighter and a committed Jew. Mr. Ferman organized yearly remembrance services to commemorate the Holocaust, inviting distinguished Newfoundland personalities to address the gathering, which was open to the public. For those events, the synagogue hall was full. Mr. Ferman often conducted services in the synagogue. Those who knew him remember him for his magnanimous nature. Another person who helped conduct services was Ernest Mauskopf, also a Holocaust survivor. Others helped too, according to their ability, including me.

There was a short period in 1957 when the community did not have a spiritual leader for six months. I volunteered to teach the children once a week whenever I was in town. Then we got a teacher from Israel, a man named Eisenberg, who came with his wife and two boys. They stayed for close to two years and then moved to Calgary. Then we got a young couple named Fishlovitz, Hungarian Jews who came via Israel. At that time, I became a member of the shul's executive committee and was given the education portfolio. I held that function in the Newfoundland Jewish community for thirty years, until our departure. I believe I was given that position because I was the only "learned Jew," which in our part of the world meant that I knew Hebrew. For this I am thankful to my parents, who had put so much emphasis on my education. My father constantly reprimanded me for running around with my friends instead of reading, and so, I sat over books for many hours, jealous of my friends who were playing ball outside. The result was that I had a good command of Hebrew, on par even with native Israelis.

After Fishlovitz, Rabbi Kotziner came to St. John's and remained until 1962, when we managed to get Mr. Shane, a fairly new arrival from Hungary. We were fortunate to have had Rabbi Kotziner because of his qualifications as a rabbi, his voice as a cantor and his traditional Eastern European approach.

Those were the most active and productive years of the community. After the completion of the synagogue, the community set out to raise money to pay the mortgage and for the upkeep of the synagogue and the rabbi's salary. A committee was formed, appropriately named the Ways and Means Committee. In this endeavour, the women of the synagogue sisterhood excelled, organizing all kinds of events. Other committees organized dances and card games that were open to the public. One could feel the heartbeat, the pulse of an active and vibrant Jewish community in this remote and isolated place.

During those years, I did not have much time to spend with our children, being out of town most of the week. Even when I was in town, I was constantly busy. So I tried to play with the children while working. I had converted our garage into a warehouse, and on Sundays, I would load the truck, backing it up to the garage door so that I could load it out of sight of inquisitive eyes. When the kids were young, they would come down to the basement and try to help me. The loading process was quite complicated, so they were not much help, but I kept them entertained and happy by playing games with them. The game that never failed to entertain was hide-and-seek. Two of them went into the garage while I would hide the third child in a box of clothes in the basement. There was such joy on their faces and delight in their voices when they found their hidden sibling. A couple of times each winter, I would get some firewood, a tin can, kosher hot dogs, mustard, buns and matches, and we would drive out of town to an old water reservoir, where we would start a bonfire and make hot dogs.

Throughout the years, I walked around with a guilty feeling, with a sense that I had betrayed my childhood dreams and aspirations and my fervent wish during the Nazi nightmare that if I had to die, I should die for our Jewish home in Palestine, instead of perishing among millions of others without a name and without anybody knowing I even existed. The gnawing guilt was exacerbated by my awareness that I had left Italy for Canada at a time when the newly born State of Israel was fighting for its first breath. Five Arab armies attacked Israel before its people, many of whom were survivors of the Holocaust, could experience a taste of freedom and independence.

Even with independence, peace was far off. Arab terrorists attacked vehicles on isolated roads, killed people and terrorized Jewish settlements. My longing for that little corner of the world, for that realization of the two-thousand-year-old dream of my people, was beckoning to me from afar, as if to say, *Come, take a look at me. You dreamt about me so much. The least you can do is walk on my soil, so soaked with the blood of your forefathers and brethren. They gave their lives so that you can walk in the streets of my cities, in the fields and valleys, on my rocky hills, so that you can inhale the fragrant air of my mountains and feast your eyes on my beloved city, Jerusalem.*

I often spoke to Ruth about my dream of visiting Israel. But I could not afford it. The years were rolling by, and I was unable to put aside a few dollars. My other dream was to do something in memory of my parents. There was no mention of their names anywhere, never mind a gravestone. But with daily pressures and financial difficulties, I put it off.

In 1965, Ken was approaching his bar mitzvah, when a Jewish boy turns thirteen and assumes his religious responsibilities as a grown man. We came to the decision to take our son on a trip to Israel, realizing two aspirations: to instill in Ken a sense of belonging and a deep understanding of the ongoing connection between the people of Israel and the Land of Israel, and to fulfill my own lifelong dream to see that land with my own eyes. We decided to join a group trip, and Ruth found a group organized by the Jewish National Fund (JNF). The trip was to last three weeks in the summer. A couple of weeks before our departure to Israel, Ruth came up with the idea to plant a grove of a thousand trees in memory of my parents through the JNF. We arranged to pay for the trees over a period of ten years.

On the plane, our group leader told us to try to see all we could, for the first trip would be the most memorable and the most noteworthy. How right he was, for none of the trips we made later remained as vivid in my memory as the first one. Our trip was luxurious, and we stayed in nice hotels in Tel Aviv, Haifa and Jerusalem. We even flew to Eilat for a day and swam in the Red Sea, which was as warm as a bathtub. During the tour, I had the opportunity to show off my knowledge of Hebrew, the history of Zionism and the geography of Israel. For this, I was grateful to my teacher in Hebrew school in Shershev, Yoel Waldshan.

I don't have words to describe my feelings walking the streets of Tel Aviv or Jerusalem. It was so exciting to hear Hebrew spoken in the streets, to walk in the narrow alleys of the old Orthodox neighbourhood of Mea Shearim, to listen to the voices of little boys reading the Torah and translating it into Yiddish. From a rooftop, I looked with longing in the direction of the Western Wall without being able to see it. A thousand large and small attractions gladdened my heart.

It was also exciting to meet my relatives—my mother's first cousin Sheine Rochel, who had left Pruzhany in the mid-1930s with her husband and two children; my father's first cousin Chaim Shemesh, who had left Shershev in the early 1930s and was joined later by his girlfriend Sonia Pinsky. They were the only family I had besides my mother's two brothers and their families in New York. Sadly, my mother's two brothers had already passed away by the time we visited Israel.

But there was someone else I desperately wanted to see in Israel, my close friend Leibel Bliskowsky, whom I had met in my *Stube* in block 18 in Auschwitz and with whom I had spent nine months in Sosnowitz and then roomed with for three years in various DP camps in Italy. I had last seen him seventeen years earlier, sitting on the balustrade of the port in Genoa, waving goodbye to me as my ship moved out of the harbour on its way to Halifax. By this time, he was married and had a little girl. We were spending a Shabbat in Haifa, and I went to his house after our Friday night dinner. We sat into the wee hours of the morning and had a lot of catching up to do.

As Ruth and I got into the taxi on our way back to the hotel, I remarked that there was something missing. Something had been lost in my friendship with Leibel, and I did not quite know what it was. Perhaps we had lost some kind of openness and frankness with each other. Ruth, in her perceptive way, answered quite sensibly that I should not be surprised. My friendship with Leibel had been forged in a concentration camp, when we reached out to anybody who would reciprocate with a friendly gesture. It was the same in the DP camps. But now we had both built our own lives and directed our attention, commitment and love to our families.

We also visited Gottel Wiener who was from Shershev and lived in Binyamina. He was ten years older than me and had been mobilized into the Polish army in March 1939 together with my uncle Eli. Gottel had survived Auschwitz, where he had worked in the DAW on the other shift. We spent a day with Gottel, and there was no end to the stories each of us wanted to share. The same happened on all our visits with friends and relatives.

When visiting my cousin Chaim Shemesh, I told him that my lifelong dream was fulfilled.

He replied, "Do not say 'fulfilled,' for once you have been in Israel and seen it, you will not be able to stay away."

That summer evening in Netanya with Chaim and Sonia was beautiful. We sat with them on the veranda of their charming little villa, surrounded by blossoming trees, the embodiment of the Israel of my dreams. In that moment I wished that time could be frozen.

The warmth of my mother's cousin Sheine Rochel was so endemic to the Auerbachs and could not be equalled. She reminded me of my grandmother Freida Leah. When we were visiting, their older daughter, Hanna, and her husband and children, who lived in California, were there as well. We also met their younger daughter, Ita, and her husband, Yaakov, and their two children, who were living nearby. I was amazed then, and even more on our subsequent visits, by Sheine Rochel's phenomenal memory. She could recall events, names and places dating back to her childhood from the time she was two. After her husband, Velvl, passed away, we would sit for hours on end, listening to her fascinating stories about my family from half a century before my birth. She died at the age of ninety-two, a year after our last visit, and she was still in possession of that extraordinary gift, her memory. Sheine Rochel was the last surviving person of my parents' generation, and with her passing, the memories of that time became remote history. My cousin Jack wrote some of the family's history in his book *The Undying Spark*, but it doesn't compare with the wealth of information that Sheine Rochel possessed.

While in Israel, I could converse with anybody in Hebrew or Yiddish or, if necessary, in half a dozen other European languages. I felt that I was among brothers, fellow sufferers who had known persecution, and that every passerby was not only a friend but also a relative. The euphoria after the birth of the State of Israel had not yet evaporated.

During that visit we dedicated a grove of trees in the Martyrs Forest in the Judean Hills near Jerusalem in memory of my parents.

As soon as we returned home to Newfoundland, I had to go out on the road to start paying some of my recently incurred debts. Yet Ruth and I felt that we ought to do something for the community in honour of Ken's bar mitzvah, and we decided to hold a luncheon after Shabbat services. Ruth organized the event, ordering kosher food from Montreal. Ruth's parents and her brother came from Montreal for the occasion. The whole community, old and young alike, adjourned to the synagogue's social hall for a lunch fit for kings. I think that it was one of the rare occasions that the entire Jewish community, members and non-members alike, nearly seventy families, showed up in the synagogue.

After the event, it bothered me to see all the food that was left on the platters and the plates. I knew that we were in a land of plenty, and I had attended enough affairs to know that food goes to waste, but until then, I had not been involved in those events personally. Ever since my wartime experiences and the intense hunger I had suffered, I looked at food with different eyes, with much more respect and appreciation, bordering almost on reverence. Throwing out food was a sacrilege to me, the profanation of the most precious thing in the world next to life itself. I assume that many other Holocaust survivors feel the same way.

Ken's bar mitzvah was also a time for reflection. Despite my losses and hardships, there was someone to carry on the names, traditions and memory of my dear ones; there was a continuity of my family, who had been so cruelly and mercilessly slaughtered, and a continuity of my tortured and tormented people. In a small way, I was helping to manifest the prophet Ezekiel's vision of dry bones coming to life. And again, just like during Ken's bris, I spoke to my parents and grandparents without a sound and without moving my lips: *Here, look, he carries your name, your memory and your legacy into another generation. It is within him that you and your memory will go on living.*

41
Generations to Come

AND SO THE years began to roll by, with the daily problems, the difficulties of making a living and the hardships of the road. The Jewish community of St. John's was in its prime, and we were like one big family, though not everything was smooth or without friction. We had our fair share of quarrels and discord, and a good measure of gossip, rumour and even slander.

Sharon went to Israel to study at the Hebrew University of Jerusalem, quickly adapting to the local lifestyle and becoming fluent in Hebrew. Ken was studying engineering at Memorial University of Newfoundland and started going out with a St. John's girl, Lisa Nathanson, whom he knew from childhood, as they had attended Hebrew school together. In 1975, Ken and Lisa decided to get married. By then my uncles and aunts in New York had passed away, so the invitations went out to my cousins. I did not forget my friend and benefactor in Poland, Leon Kulowski. He had retired five years earlier at the age of sixty, according to the Polish law of that time. My continuous attempts to bring him on a visit to Israel were fruitless, but I was hopeful that the Polish government would let him come to a wedding in St. John's. After sending the formal invitation, I paid a travel agency for his return ticket and waited to hear from him.

The waiting days turned into weeks, and the weeks into months. I even sent a notarized letter to the Polish government, guaranteeing to cover all expenses incurred by him. Still nothing happened. All he needed was a passport to leave the country, and time was getting short. Ten days before the wedding, we received a telegram from Leon saying that he finally got the passport. Ruth and I flew to Montreal to welcome him at the airport.

After the wedding, Leon remained with us for close to six weeks. During that time, he travelled with me all over the eastern part of Newfoundland and saw more of it than most locals do. During his stay, he was interviewed on television, and our story was written up in the local newspaper. I succeeded in arranging for him a stopover in Paris for twenty-four hours on his way back, so that he could see his cousin who was living there and tour the city.

In 1976, our daughter Aviva joined her sister in Israel. Now life became much lonelier for us, especially for Ruth, who was home by herself three or four days a week. The activities in the Jewish community had decreased. Having paid up the entire mortgage on the new synagogue, there was less incentive for fundraising events, and the bingo games, bake sales and dances stopped.

And so, the long Newfoundland winter passed slowly. Ken and Lisa decided to move to Toronto. Aviva left Israel and moved to Toronto to work. Sharon continued her studies at the Hebrew University of Jerusalem and met a young Israeli by the name of Meir Gazit. They were married in Jerusalem in 1980 and their first child, a girl, was born there on March 13, 1984. They named her Orly Penny, after my father-in-law, Pinchas. I flew to Israel to welcome the new addition to the family. Again, I went through all the emotions that I had gone through when my children were born. However, I did not let on, hiding my feelings deep inside, communicating silently with my parents and grandparents, telling them that their memory and legacy would live on in generations to come. I saw in my grandchild the continuity of my family that had been so mercilessly murdered. I saw in her the permanence of my family and of our people. These thoughts and feelings would return with the birth of each grandchild.

In 1985, Sharon, Meir and Orly moved to Toronto. Now, our three children and our first grandchild were in Toronto, and our visits to Toronto became more frequent. I watched with pride and joy as our grandchild was slowly growing from a baby into a little girl, and I wanted to be able to spend time with her.

Things were changing for us in Newfoundland. The Jewish community was shrinking. Old members continued to pass away, a few retired to Florida, and the young people, unable to find work in Newfoundland, moved to larger cities on the mainland. My line of business began to disintegrate. As more paved roads were being built on the island, communication between settlements became easier, and malls were being built in major centres. Many retailers were forced to close their businesses, and I lost a good part of my income too. As my business ceased to be profitable, and with all our children in Toronto, we began to think of moving closer to them.

On May 5, 1989, the forty-fourth anniversary of my liberation from the Gusen concentration camp, Sharon gave birth to her second child, a boy. Ruth and I went to the bris, where the newborn baby was named Eitan Lavi Areyeh—Areyeh after my brother Leibel, who perished in Auschwitz at the age of thirteen. (Leibel and Areyeh mean "lion," in Yiddish and Hebrew respectively.) The birth of our second grandchild gave us even more incentive to be with the children, and in August 1989, we moved to Toronto.

Our second daughter, Aviva, got married in 1990 and had her first baby in 1995. She was named in the Lodzer synagogue after my father's two sisters, Sheindl and Pesl, who perished in the Holocaust and whose families were obliterated. My daughter called her daughter Ariella.

In 1992, Sharon gave birth to a boy. He was named Erez Shlomo Lev—Shlomo after my sister Sarah and Lev after my youngest sister, Leiba.

In 1997, Aviva gave birth to a girl. She was given the name Freida

Chinkah—Freida after my mother's mother, Freida Leah, who died in Shershev in 1935, and Chinkah after my father's mother, who perished in Auschwitz together with my entire family. My daughter Aviva calls her Genevieve, but to Ruth and me she is Freidala. Now I had children and grandchildren named after all the members of my immediate family as well as my grandparents. I felt that at least their names would not be erased. At the same time, I felt sad for my extended family, who had no one to carry on their names and their memory.

42
Holocaust Education

LESS THAN A month after Ruth and I moved to Toronto, I received an invitation from Ernest Condon, an educator in Labrador, to address schools, churches and legions in Labrador on the topic of the Holocaust. Even though I knew the eastern part of Newfoundland like the back of my hand, I had never been as far north as Labrador and was curious to see it.

I had started speaking to schools about the Holocaust in the 1960s after I was approached by a professor of religious studies at Memorial University of Newfoundland, Dr. Morley Hodder, who asked me to address one of his classes on the topic of the Holocaust. Apparently, the class was interested in what I had to say because I was invited back repeatedly. Before long, I was being invited to other schools in St. John's. Speaking at schools outside of St. John's was more difficult, as travelling there sometimes meant the loss of a workday for me. Still, I did not want to deprive the students of the chance to learn about the events of the Holocaust, the atrocities and the immensity of the crimes committed. I never accepted even a token of compensation. In fact, if I added up the time and loss of business, plus the many kilometres I spent travelling, the gas and vehicle depreciation, it would have come to a nice sum.

In November 1989, Ruth travelled with me to Labrador, and we spent four busy days there. On November 11, there was a march in front of the cenotaph, and I was invited to participate. I marched in the front row, between the chief of the local mounted police and the chief of the local police. Wreaths were laid in memory of members of the military who had fallen in war. Suddenly, two soldiers appeared beside me, carrying a wreath. On its wide ribbon was written in gold letters, "In memory of the six million Jews who perished in the Holocaust." I was moved to tears. A voice on the loudspeaker announced that Moishe Kantorowitz would lay a wreath in memory of the six million Jews who were killed in the Holocaust. With trembling legs, I helped carry the wreath with the two soldiers and laid it down at the base of the cenotaph. Even now, years later, when I remember that event, I get emotional. I feel a deep gratitude to the people of Labrador in general and in particular to Ernest Condon, who made us feel so welcome there.

In those four days in Labrador, I must have delivered over a dozen speeches to schools and churches, and I gave several radio interviews. Ruth and I were impressed with the city of Labrador and its friendly and warm-hearted people.

Shortly after our return from Labrador, I received a letter from Dr. Sam Revusky, a professor at Memorial University of Newfoundland. He asked me to help him translate a book his father had written shortly after the end of World War I called *In di shvere teg oyf Ukrayne: zikhroynes fun a Yidishn ministr* (*Wrenching Times in Ukraine: Memoir of a Jewish Minister*). It dealt with a short period of Ukrainian independence between 1918 and 1919 and described the slaughter of thousands of Jews in Ukraine during that era. Abraham Revusky, a Jew, had been a minister in the short-lived socialist cabinet and wrote from that vantage point. I gladly agreed, hoping to gain some experience for when I would write my story. I had started writing, in Yiddish, ten years earlier, but I put it aside after writing a dozen pages.

It took us two years to translate the book, and it was only after I finished this project that I sat down in earnest to write my story. I continued writing in Yiddish because, despite having lived in Canada for over fifty years, I still had a better command of Yiddish than English. The writing progressed slowly, with many interruptions.

In April 1995, I received a letter from Memorial University of Newfoundland. It read:

> 1995 marks the 50th anniversary of the end of World War II and the closure of one of the saddest chapters in human history. In recognition of the 50th anniversary of the end of the Holocaust, in celebration of the triumph of life over the forces of darkness and evil, and in contemplation of your personal involvement in those events as well as the years you spent as a citizen of this province teaching the consequences of racial and religious hatred, Memorial University of Newfoundland wishes to award to you an honorary degree. On behalf of the Senate of Memorial University, I therefore have the honour to invite you to be present at our annual fall convocation on October 28, 1995, and to accept the degree of Doctor of Law, Honoris Causa. The university community would also be delighted if you would agree to address convocation.

I learned later that our good friend and true humanitarian, Ernest Condon, had submitted my candidacy for this honour to the Senate of the University, and the Senate voted unanimously to approve it.

In October 1995, Ruth and I and our daughter Sharon and her two older children travelled to Newfoundland. We spent the Friday night Shabbat meal with our friend Judy Wilansky, where we enjoyed the evening with some prominent members of the community, including Ernest Condon and his charming mother. For Saturday lunch, we were invited to the lieutenant governor of Newfoundland, sharing the meal with the premier and some ministers of Newfoundland, as well as some university dignitaries. After the meal, we were all driven to the university, where the convocation took place in its huge hall. It all proceeded with great fanfare. Several hundred students received their degrees, and then I was introduced to the thousands of guests, graduating students and faculty. After being bestowed with the university cape and handed the degree by the chancellor of the university, John Crosbie, I took the podium with a good measure of trepidation. I had been speaking for years to small and large groups, but never to such a large and prestigious audience. I was told later that the content and delivery of my speech were good, and I hope they really were.

On that evening, the university held a dinner for the members of the provincial government, faculty, distinguished members of the city administration and us. On the next day, the Jewish community held a luncheon for us. I spent the rest of the day and part of the following day speaking to schools.

Back home, I returned to my favourite pursuit, writing my life story to commemorate Shershev and all those who perished in the Holocaust. I continued to address students whenever I was called upon by the Holocaust Education Centre in Toronto and taught them about the results of hatred, bigotry and racial discrimination.

Epilogue

NOW, AS I am concluding my story, I go back in my mind to my youth and my adolescent years, and I wonder if I could have changed anything in my life or in the lives of my dear ones. I still remember how, as a boy, I would listen to my father's stories about his escapades as a soldier during World War I. In my exuberant imagination, I envisioned that I would be a hero in such circumstances. How could I, my father, or anybody else imagine the terror and cruelty, the atrocities perpetrated by the Nazis and their sympathizers during that long night of unimaginable savagery? Who could have imagined that anybody could conceive of and execute a plan to annihilate an entire people, an entire race and an entire faith?

My memories take me back to the open ditches where whole families were lined up and mowed down by machine guns, where little babies were thrown in alive. I can visualize the gaping openings of the gas chambers of Auschwitz and the tortured deaths of the hundreds of thousands of camp inmates. And again and again, I ask myself if I could have done anything to change it or even a tiny little part of it. What could I have done for my family? I live with so much regret, tortured by remorse for not having done something. Yet I know that there was nothing I could do. The ten thousand souls in our ghetto tried to come up with something, but in vain. Every person wanted to save themself or a loved one. There were people who were smarter and braver than me, but we all ended up in Auschwitz. The handful that succeeded in getting out of the ghetto were killed fighting the Nazis or by antisemitic partisan groups. Very few remained to tell their stories.

I look back with so much pain to the period of a year and a half when my immediate family and I lived under the tyrannical rule of the accursed Nazis. I can still see the tears rolling down my mother's cheeks, my parents' desperate search for a way out, which they knew would not be found. I remember the innocent and frightened faces of my little sisters and brother, looking up to my parents, who looked back at them with so much pain, sadness and helplessness. They knew that there was nothing in the world that could reverse their fates.

I ask myself repeatedly: How could a civilized people sink to such depths? I think about the millions who died the most horrific deaths, their lives snuffed out prematurely. Some were only hours old, some were not able to crawl or walk or speak yet—a million and a half children. How much creative power, undiscovered and discovered talent and human ingenuity went to waste, never given a chance to grow and blossom? And what about the murdered adults? The amount of brainpower, talent and creativity lost is staggering and incalculable. Six million Jewish people were murdered, among them world-renowned personalities in every conceivable field. And the masses of ordinary people who were killed, did they not think? Did they not feel? Were they not human beings like everybody else? They knew joy and grief, happiness and sadness, satiety and hunger, health and sickness, bliss and sorrow, bounty and scarcity. Their dreams, their hopes, their plans were left unfinished, never to be fulfilled. Who will realize their dreams, hopes and plans? Who will sing their unsung songs, their unwritten music, poetry and prose? Who will rebuild a world of culture and spirituality that took almost two millennia to build?

I raise my eyes to the heavens and join the millions of my slaughtered brethren in a wrenching cry—*Why?*

Dear mother of mine, I have fulfilled your bequest to tell the world how we lived and how we perished. I survived to tell not only your brothers, but their children and grandchildren. And one more thing, Mama, your legacy is now being passed on to your grandchildren and great-grandchildren, may it be for a blessing always.

Acknowledgements

THIS BOOK WOULD not have been possible without the help of my wife, Ruth; my children, Ken, Sharon and Aviva; and my grandchildren, Orly and Eitan; as well as my three youngest grandchildren, Erez, Ariella and Genevieve, who were too young at the time of writing to assist.

A special thank you to Dr. Sam Revusky of St. John's, Newfoundland, to Leah Belfon of Toronto and to Leah Watson of Rochester, New York. I must also include an extra special thank you to Drs. Dina and Elisha Babad of Jerusalem, Israel, for their invaluable assistance in completing this book.

Jews of Shershev

IN WRITING THIS memoir, Moishe hoped to preserve and honour the names and memories of the Jews of his shtetl, the majority of whom were murdered by the Nazis. With the editorial decision to keep the memoir focused on Moishe and those closest to him, many of those names are no longer included. To honour Moishe's memory of the Jews of Shershev in the years leading up to the Holocaust, the editors have compiled a list of all the names that Moishe recorded in his original manuscript.

Pellet Aprik and his children, Avraham and Mali
Reuven Aronowicz
Shalom Aronowicz
Laizer Ber and Freida Leah (née Goldfarb) Auerbach
Shloime Chaim Auerbach
Baumriter, his wife, their daughters, Lola and Mira, and his sister and brother-in-law
Shalom Berenstein, his mother, brother and sisters
Moshe Bikstein
Aaron Bikstein and his younger brother
Chaya Chadricky
Gedalia Chadricky
Moishe Chadricky and his sons, Yosl (Joseph) and Eli
Tiebl Chadricky
Zev and Sheine Rochel (née Auerbach) Chemelnitzky and their children, Chana, Itti and Taibl
Nechemya and Rivka (née Potshinker) Der-Shteper and their three children
Yankl Berl Eisenstein, his wife and their son, Laizer
Lippa Elman, his son and other children

Shalom Yosef and Chaye Rantshe Farber, their son, David, and an unnamed daughter
Feiga Feinbir
Yaakov Feinbir
Nachum and Tzina Feldman and their son, Leibel
Sarah Feldman and her husband, Osher
Alter and Esther Golda Gellerstein and their son, Zalman
Meir and Yenta Gelman and their children, Moishe, Bunia and Chaim
Beryl Gichman, his wife and their children, Chaim Todl, Moshe and Malka
Feivel Gichman
Isser Gichman, his wife and their children
Moishe and Sara Gleser and their child
Benjamin Goldberg
Boris Leib Goldfarb
Nathan Shepsl Goldfarb
Sheine Rivka Granat
Noah Hochman, his two brothers and their father
Reuven Hochman
Shimon Izbicky
Chome Henie Judelewsky and her children, Yaakov, Eidl and Mushka
Nathan Kabizetzky, his brother David and their mother
Yaakov Meir and Sarah (née Winograd) Kabizetsky and their five daughters
Hershel and Yenta Kalbkauf and their children, Kalman, Nishkah and three unnamed daughters
Leibel Kalbkauf, his daughter Leah, his son David and unnamed children
Meir Kalbkauf and his father
Hertzke Kaminker and his family
Eli Kantorowitz
Hershel and Sheine Kantorowitz and their two children
Joshua and Freda (née Goldberg) Kantorowitz and their two children and Joshua's son Shalom
Reuven and Chashkah (née Pinsky) Kantorowitz and their children, Michla, Shalom and Shevach
Shalom and Sarah Kantorowitz and their child
Yaakov Kopel and Chinkah (née Granitzki) Kantorowitz
Yitzchak (Isaac) and Esther Beila (née Auerbach) Kantorowitz and their children, Sheva, Leibel, Sonia and Leiba
Yosl and Shainah (née Shterman) Kiselew
Yankl Kleinerman
Itzel and Molie Kleingerg, and their mother
Avrom Kolodytzky, his wife and their daughter
Nathan and Chashkah Krenitzer and their children
Rachel Krenitzer
Gershon Krenitzer
Chatzkel Krugman, his wife and their children, Shloime, Mulick, Chaya and Tevye
Temma Kwelman, her husband and their children, Avreml, Tzipora, Feigl and Gittel
Yaakov Yeshayou Kwelman and his family
Leibel Leberstein

Shmuel Leberstein and his son, Yosl
Feivel and Tzina (née Winograd) Leiman and their daughters, Sara and Chaya
Mordechai Leshtchinsky and his daughter Sara Esther
Chaim Levkovitz
Gershon Levkovitz
Rafael Levkovitz
Bendet Lifshitz
David Lifshitz
Rabbi Noah Liwerant, his wife, their son Meir, their daughter Nechama and three unnamed children
Avi London
Maykah London
Shalom London
Yitzchak London and his two sons
Gedalia Loshevitzy and his children, Lippa and Beila Deborah
Glade Loshevitzy and his son
Joseph Maletzky and his daughter
Sara Maletzky
Pesach and Brina Maletzky, their children, Nachum, Itzik and Moishe, and Brina's mother, Yachna
Avreml Meister, his wife and their child
Daniel and Malka Meister and their children, Yosl, Maya and Reuven
Srulkah Meister, his wife, their son Chaim and unnamed children
Eli Neibrief
Leibel Neibrief
Sarah Neibrief, her husband and their son, Yankl
Motl Notes
Mindl Osherkilers and her daughter
Asher Pasmanic
Shloime Pasmanic
Zusel Pasmanic
Yaakov Peker, his wife and their daughter
Joshua and Bluma Pinsky
Leibel and Sheindl (née Kantorowitz) Pinsky and their children, Sioma (Shalom) and Lisa
Shalom Pinsky and his son Hershel
Bentzy Pittel and his father
Symah Pomerantz
Reshl Pomerantz
Yosl and Brina Pomerantz
Shepsl Pomerantz, his brother Itzel and their parents
Kepele Potshinker and his wife
Meir Yona Reitman
Miriam Reitman
Pesl (Pola) (née Kantorowitz) and Zelig Remez, their son Max and two unnamed children
Chaikl Roselewsky
Avraham Rosuchowsky
Zalman Rosuchowsky
Yosef and Raya (née Pinsky) Rotenberg and their children, Laizer, Litek, Pola, Lisa and Minah
Itti Ruben
Shepsl Rudnitzky, his sister and their parents
Zisl Saposhnik
Zalman Schneider, his son Reuben and unnamed children
Beryl Schneider and his sons, Eli, Hershel and Shloime
Beryl and Helkah (née Roselewsky) Shames
Yosl and Chaye Zlate Shames and their daughter, Esther
Chaim and Sonia (née Pinsky) Shemesh
Avrom Shlomo and his son, Kulie

Moishe Eli Shocherman
Moishe Shocherman and his son, Motl
Chaya Leiba Shterman
Laizer Sznajder
Chaim Tenenbaum and his sons, Itche and Beryl, and Beryl's wife Drezl (née Pomerantz)
David Tenenbaum and his son, Beryl
Moishe Tilter
Joseph Tuchmacher
Moishe Tuchmacher, his wife and their children
Israel Tzemachowitch and his wife
Shmuel Tzemachowitch, his wife and their daughter
Reuben Valdman, his wife, their daughter Rivka, and five unnamed children
Yoel Waldshan, his father, his wife and their sons, Yaakov and David
Yekutial Wapenstein
Yehuda Wiener and his children, Gottel, Rafael, Pinchas and three unnamed sons
Israel and Gittel Winograd, their son, Avreml, and unnamed children
Moishe and Pesha Winograd
Yankl Winograd
Reuven Winokur
Israel Wisoker
Peshkah Zaritzky
Yudel Zatotzky, his wife, their sons Beryl and Yehudl, and unnamed children
Areyeh Zlotick
Yudel and Reizl Zubatzky and their children, Shloime and two unnamed daughters

Full Name Unknown

Avrom Ber, his wife and their son and daughter
Avromkah
Channania
David, his wife and their children
Dolman
Feigl K
Glier, his wife and their daughter
Hertzke Fishel
Reb Isaac, rabbi of a synagogue
Lipkind
Meir Chaim, his wife and their children
Mordechai, his wife and their son, Baruch
Nitzberg
Shmuel and his daughter, Feiga
Shmulevitch
Tzadik
Tzalkah fun di zamden
Tzivia, granddaughter of Nyomka (Benjamin)
Yankl der beder
Yudke

Names Unknown

Elderly lady who sold pancakes
Goose seller, his wife and their children
Shershev *soyfer stam* (ritual scribe)

Afterword

FORTUITOUSLY, I HAD the opportunity to read Moishe Kantorowitz's original manuscript several years ago. In reading this newly edited version, I remain as captivated by his richly detailed accounts of Jewish life in his beloved shtetl, Shershev, as I was during my first reading. Kantorowitz's expressive literary style depicts Jewish life in the interwar period in Poland (now Belarus) with a vitality that today lives only in the remembrances of those who survived the Holocaust. For Kantorowitz, the memories contained in the pages of *Lament* were more than a narrative account of the past—they were born out of an abiding sense of duty to remember and honour family and friends murdered in the Holocaust and to bear witness for future generations.

Lament, however, is not only a witness account of the past, but also a narrative of rebirth, resilience and a restored belief in humanity. Kantorowitz's experiences gained in the over thirty-five years that he lived in St. John's, Newfoundland, serve as an ethnography of a particular era in the province's history. As a Holocaust survivor from Poland, his depictions of life in the early post-Confederation era in Newfoundland provide a unique perspective, and that is what I want to offer a deeper reflection on here.

My focus will be on three aspects that define *Lament* as an important contribution to the social history of Newfoundland. The first is how

Kantorowitz experienced the people of Newfoundland; second is how his recollections of the economic and infrastructure development add to a deeper understanding of the sweeping changes that took place as a result of Newfoundland's union with Canada; and third is how the small number of Holocaust survivors who moved to St. John's contributed to and shaped the Newfoundland Jewish community.

When Kantorowitz settled in Newfoundland in 1956, the island was still in the throes of transition as it continued a trajectory of modernization and economic development initiated when it became Canada's tenth province in 1949. Although seemingly shocked by the milieu during his first visit to Newfoundland, Kantorowitz also discovered a familiar reference point in his surroundings. He writes, "In these areas, the population lived in the same conditions that we'd had in Shershev before 1932." Perhaps most significantly, he found the local populace to be warm and welcoming. This warmth was essential in his journey toward healing and rebuilding a new life after experiencing the horrors and devastation of the Holocaust. Indeed, it was the relationships that he formed with local Newfoundlanders that left an indelible impression on him. In 1995, when Memorial University of Newfoundland awarded Kantorowitz an honorary doctorate of laws LLD, he paid homage to the spirit in which he was welcomed by Newfoundlanders when he addressed the convocation with these words:

> And now if I may, a few words to you as Newfoundlanders. To you who dwell on this island, on this rock if I may say so. Like this rock that withstood the onslaught of the cold a cruel Atlantic with its bone-chilling winds, fog, drizzle, rain, snow and ice for millenniums, so have you, its people, who dwell on this rock for generations, withstood the onslaught of the venomous racist hate propaganda that assails these shores. In fact, you have made me, one of the remnants of European Jewry, welcome with open arms and you shared with me the roof over your head and your food, scarce at times, at your table; among you where in thirty-three years I have never heard a racial slur or remark.... To you, my

> friends, not only the deprived and persecuted, but every decent person will bow his head in respect and gratitude.[1]

Kantorowitz's impressions of Newfoundlanders and their qualities were formed during his career as an itinerant salesman who travelled the outport communities of Newfoundland. These recollections provide contemporary readers with a window into a past that is unfamiliar to most people born in post-Confederation Newfoundland.

Kantorowitz's writing is also characterized by a proclivity to include detailed descriptions of the climate and geography. Newfoundland's unpredictable weather, rugged coastline and rough roads occupy a special place in his memories. Perhaps this is not surprising since these factors were central to his livelihood and shaped his experiences in rural Newfoundland. For today's readers, these descriptions provide a vista depicting the realities of everyday life in Newfoundland. Kantorowitz was a witness to the tremendous societal and cultural upheaval that accompanied the union with Canada. Whether it is his recollections of travelling by the train known as the Newfie Bullet, witnessing the construction of the Trans-Canada Highway that replaced rudimentary roads or seeing electricity installed in homes become commonplace, Kantorowitz captures the spirit of change that accompanied this early era after Confederation.

Finally, Kantorowitz, like the other Holocaust survivors who settled in St. John's, contributed to the cultural landscape of the Jewish and broader community. In an oral history recorded in 1990, he talks about the changes in the Jewish community:

> [They were mostly] survivors like myself, Jews of European background who spoke Yiddish, who were in a sense traditional.

1 Moishe Kantorowitz's convocation speech was published in *The Gazette*, Memorial University of Newfoundland's paper, in the November 2, 1995, edition. The speech can be viewed online through Memorial University's Digital Archives Initiative: https://collections.mun.ca/digital/collection/mun_gazette/id/4281/rec/3.

> And that injection of new blood, if I can say, sort of helped the community expand, and gave this community a new lease on life. Newfoundlanders, as a whole, I must say, know of no anti-semitism. At least I have never felt it. I have felt friendship, and I must say that Newfoundlanders have always welcomed me with open arms.[2]

Kantorowitz was a bridge builder who made the Holocaust personal and relatable for the thousands of Newfoundlanders who heard him speak. He was among the first Holocaust survivors to speak publicly in Newfoundland about his experiences. Whether he was speaking to schools, religious institutions or in public educational forums, he bridged the gulf between the understanding of the historical significance of the Holocaust and making the inconceivable more tangible and personal.

In writing his memoir, Kantorowitz fulfilled one of his stated goals of ensuring that his family members are remembered in perpetuity. As he wrote, "For deep in my heart, I believe that my life was spared in order to bear witness to the tragedy that befell my people during the darkest era in Jewish history." Having read his searing testimony of the Holocaust, we too share the responsibility to safeguard the collective memory of the Holocaust and to remember the people and conditions of society that fostered the resilience and renewal of the survivors who made Newfoundland and Canada their home.

Dr. Carson Phillips
Gratz College
Holocaust Survivor Memoirs Program, Azrieli Foundation
2025

2 Interview conducted by David Magder, Archives of the Holocaust Project, Toronto, 1990, Sarah and Chaim Neuberger Holocaust Education Centre.

Photographs

1

2

3

4

1 Moishe's mother, Esther Beila, with her parents, Freida Leah and Laizer Ber Auerbach, and her brother Lippa standing on the left. Shershev, Poland (now Šarašova, Belarus), circa 1903.

2 Moishe's mother, Esther Beila. Shershev, circa 1913.

3 Moishe, sitting on the right, with his sister Sheva and their parents, Esther Beila and Yitzchak (Isaac). Domatcheva, Poland, circa 1927.

4 Moishe with three of his siblings: Moishe is standing on the left, his sister Sheva on the right, his sister Sonia between them and his brother Leibel in front. Shershev, 1933.

1

2

3

4

1 Moishe's cousin Lippa Auerbach (standing, left) and uncle Eli Kantorowitz (standing, right) with two friends. Shershev, 1929.

2 Moishe's uncle Hershel Kantorowitz. Shershev, circa 1930.

3 Moishe's aunt Pesl (Pola) Remez (née Kantorowitz). Shershev, circa 1930.

4 Moishe's uncle Reuven Kantorowitz. Shershev, 1935.

1

2

1 The Shershev synagogue built in the seventeenth century, partially destroyed before World War I and demolished by the Soviets in 1941. Shershev, 1920s.

2 Moishe's family's house built in 1932 at 29 Platz Pilsudzkiego, Shershev. Photo taken in 1970.

At the funeral of Moishe's maternal grandmother, Freida Leah Auerbach (née Goldfarb). The headstone marks the grave of Moishe's grandfather Laizer Ber Auerbach. Standing from left to right: with her arm on the headstone, Moishe's sister Sheva; behind the headstone, Moishe's uncle Reuven; to the right of the headstone, Moishe, with his hand on his brother Leibel's shoulder; in the centre, Moishe's father, Yitzchak, and to the right of him, Moishe's mother, Esther Beila; front and centre, Moishe's sister Sonia. In the foreground is the body of Moishe's grandmother Freida Leah. Shershev, 1935.

1

2

3

4

1 Top row: Laizer Rotenberg (left) and Moishe (right). Second row from the back (left to right): Tevye Krugman, Itzik Maletzky, Yankl Neibrief. Third row from the back: Hershel Schneider, Moishe Gelman, Kalman Kalbkauf. Bottom row: Litek Rotenberg, Yosl Leberstein. Shershev, 1934. Three of these boys survived the Holocaust.

2 Moishe's sister Sheva. Shershev, 1935.

3 Moishe's mother, Esther Beila. Shershev, 1935.

4 Moishe's father, Yitzchak. Shershev, 1935.

1

2

1 The Shershev division of the Betar Zionist youth group. Moishe is in the first row, reclining, third from the left. Shershev, 1933.

2 Moishe's Grade 7 class. Moishe is standing in the top row, second from the right. Shershev, 1938.

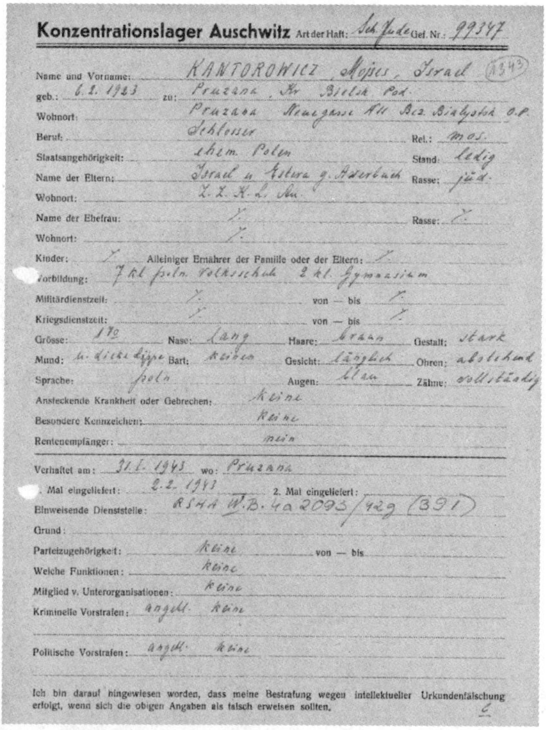

Konzentrationslager Auschwitz Art der Haft: Sch. Jude Gef. Nr.: 99347

Name und Vorname: KANTOROWICZ Mojses, Israel
geb.: 6.2.1923 zu: Pruzana, Kr. Bielsk Pod.
Wohnort: Pruzana Neuegasse Nr. Bez. Bialystok O.P.
Beruf: Schlosser Rel.: mos.
Staatsangehörigkeit: ehem. Polen Stand: ledig
Name der Eltern: Israel u. Estera g. Aderbach Rasse: jüd.
Wohnort: Z. Z. K. L. Au.
Name der Ehefrau: /. Rasse: /.
Wohnort: /.
Kinder: /. Alleiniger Ernährer der Familie oder der Eltern: /.
Vorbildung: 7 Kl. poln. Volksschule 2 Kl. Gymnasium
Militärdienstzeit: /. von — bis /.
Kriegsdienstzeit: /. von — bis /.
Grösse: 170 Nase: lang Haare: braun Gestalt: stark
Mund: m. dicke Lippe Bart: keinen Gesicht: länglich Ohren: abstehend
Sprache: poln. Augen: blau Zähne: vollständig
Ansteckende Krankheit oder Gebrechen: keine
Besondere Kennzeichen: keine
Rentenempfänger: nein

Verhaftet am: 31.1.1943 wo: Pruzana
1. Mal eingeliefert: 2.2.1943 2. Mal eingeliefert:
Einweisende Dienststelle: RSHA IV.B.4a 2093/429 (391)
Grund:
Parteizugehörigkeit: keine von — bis
Welche Funktionen: keine
Mitglied v. Unterorganisationen: keine
Kriminelle Vorstrafen: angebl. keine

Politische Vorstrafen: angebl. keine

Ich bin darauf hingewiesen worden, dass meine Bestrafung wegen intellektueller Urkundenfälschung erfolgt, wenn sich die obigen Angaben als falsch erweisen sollten.

1

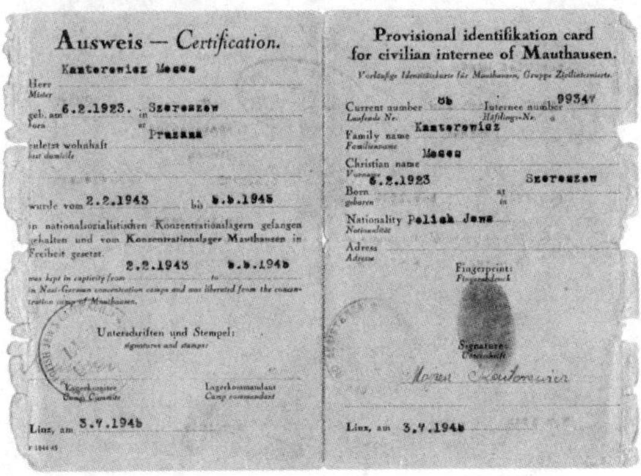

Ausweis — Certification.

Herr / Mister Kantorowicz Moses
geb. am / born 6.2.1923. in / at Szereszew
zuletzt wohnhaft / last domicile Pruzana
wurde vom 2.2.1943 bis 5.5.1945
in nationalsozialistischen Konzentrationslagern gefangen gehalten und vom Konzentrationslager Mauthausen in Freiheit gesetzt.
was kept in captivity from 2.2.1943 to 5.5.1945 in Nazi-German concentration camps and was liberated from the concentration camp of Mauthausen.
Unterschriften und Stempel: / signatures and stamps:
Lagerkomitee / Camp Committee — Lagerkommandant / Camp commandant
Linz, am 3.7.1945

Provisional identifikation card for civilian internee of Mauthausen.
Vorläufige Identitätskarte für Mauthausen, Gruppe Zivilinternierte.

Current number / Laufende Nr. 55 Internee number / Häftlings-Nr. 99347
Family name / Familienname Kantorowicz
Christian name / Vorname Moses
Born / geboren 6.2.1923 at / in Szereszew
Nationality / Nationalität Polish Jews
Adress / Adresse
Fingerprint: / Fingerabdruck
Signature: / Unterschrift Moses Kantorowicz
Linz, am 3.7.1945

2

1 A Nazi document from Auschwitz with Moishe's prisoner information on it. Courtesy of Arolsen Archives.

2 An identity document issued to Moishe in Linz, Austria, in 1945, after his liberation from Mauthausen.

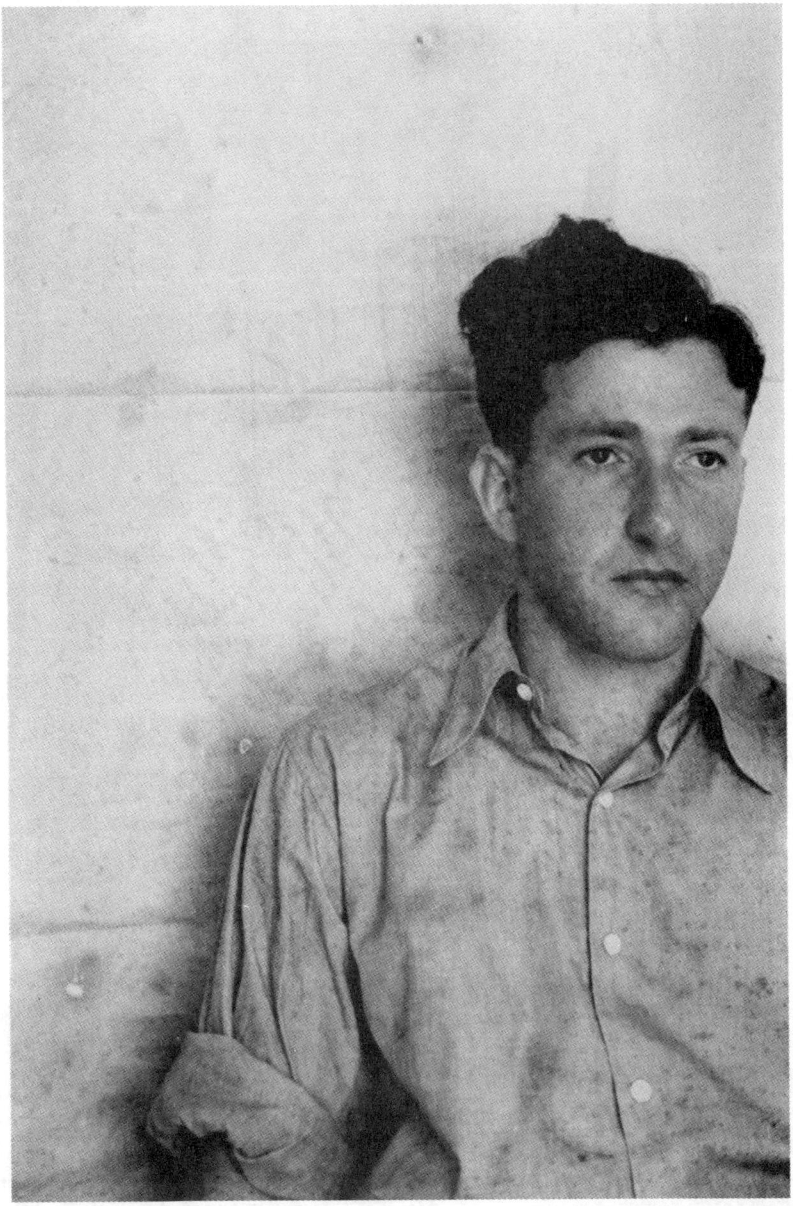

Moishe after liberation. Place unknown, 1945.

1

2

3

4

1 Moishe. Place unknown, 1945.

2 Moishe. Santa Maria di Leuca, Italy. February 25, 1946.

3 Moishe. Palese, Italy. September 26, 1947.

4 Moishe. Bari, Italy, circa 1947.

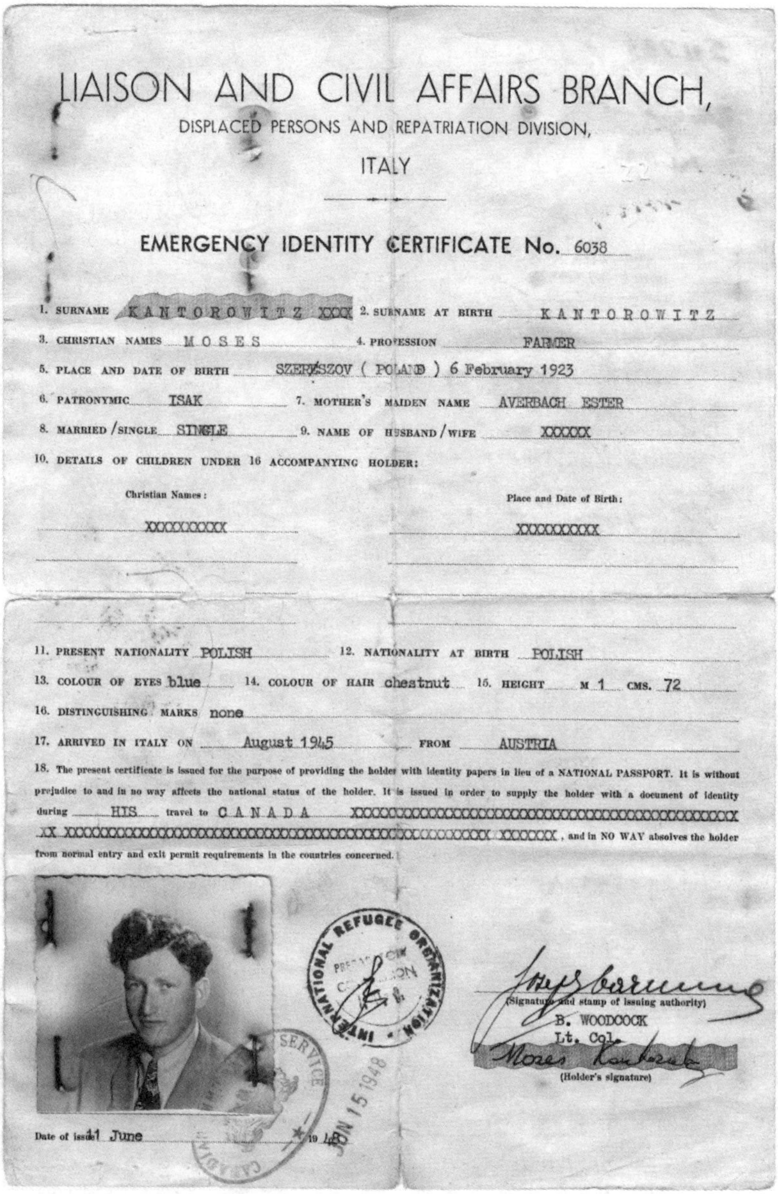

LIAISON AND CIVIL AFFAIRS BRANCH,
DISPLACED PERSONS AND REPATRIATION DIVISION,
ITALY

EMERGENCY IDENTITY CERTIFICATE No. 6038

1. SURNAME KANTOROWITZ XXXX 2. SURNAME AT BIRTH KANTOROWITZ
3. CHRISTIAN NAMES MOSES 4. PROFESSION FARMER
5. PLACE AND DATE OF BIRTH SZERÉSZOV (POLAND) 6 February 1923
6. PATRONYMIC ISAK 7. MOTHER'S MAIDEN NAME AVERBACH ESTER
8. MARRIED / SINGLE SINGLE 9. NAME OF HUSBAND / WIFE XXXXXX
10. DETAILS OF CHILDREN UNDER 16 ACCOMPANYING HOLDER:

Christian Names:	Place and Date of Birth:
XXXXXXXXXX	XXXXXXXXXX

11. PRESENT NATIONALITY POLISH 12. NATIONALITY AT BIRTH POLISH
13. COLOUR OF EYES blue 14. COLOUR OF HAIR chestnut 15. HEIGHT M 1 CMS. 72
16. DISTINGUISHING MARKS none
17. ARRIVED IN ITALY ON August 1945 FROM AUSTRIA
18. The present certificate is issued for the purpose of providing the holder with identity papers in lieu of a NATIONAL PASSPORT. It is without prejudice to and in no way affects the national status of the holder. It is issued in order to supply the holder with a document of identity during HIS travel to CANADA XXXXXXXXXXXXXXXXXXXXXXXXXXXXXXXXXXXXXXXXXXXXXXXX XX XXXXXXXXXXXXXXXXXXXXXXXXXXXXXXXXXXXXXXXXXXXXXXXX XXXXXXX, and in NO WAY absolves the holder from normal entry and exit permit requirements in the countries concerned.

INTERNATIONAL REFUGEE ORGANIZATION

(Signature and stamp of issuing authority)
B. WOODCOCK
Lt. Col.
Moses Kantorowitz
(Holder's signature)

Date of issue 11 June 1948

JUN 15 1948

An identity certificate issued to Moishe in Italy in 1948.

1

2

3

1 Moishe and Beryl Bluestein on the farm they worked on near Picton, Ontario. 1948.

2 Moishe and his wife-to-be, Ruth Pleet. 1949.

3 Moishe (centre) walking down the aisle on his wedding day. On the right is Mrs. Zbar, who sponsored Moishe to come to Canada, and on the left is Moishe's uncle Shloime. Ottawa, Ontario. June 14, 1950.

Moishe and Ruth on their wedding day. Ottawa, June 14, 1950.

1

2

3

4

1 Moishe and Ruth. Sainte-Agathe-des-Monts, Quebec, 1955.

2 Moishe and his son, Ken. St. John's, Newfoundland, 1958.

3 Moishe with his daughters, Sharon on the right and Aviva on the left. St. John's, 1959.

4 Moishe and his children (left to right): Ken, Aviva and Sharon. St. John's, 1962.

EPILOGUE TO AN ORDEAL

Two Inmates of Auchwitz Meet In Water St. Store

"Do you speak Polish?"

"Yes".

"Were you in Auchwitz during the war?"

"Yes".

"Is your name Kulowsky?"

"Yes".

"Shake! Put it there!"

That was the conversation carried on between Maurice Kantorowitz, of 21 Gambier St. and Dr. Leon Kulowsky of Poland in the store of Lewis Ferman and Company, 338 Water Street, around two o'clock Saturday afternoon.

SHOCKED

It took place after Maurice recovered from shock — the shock of recognizing a man who had saved his life in a Nazi extermination camp 21 years before. He thought he had seen a ghost.

PRISONERS

The two men had been inmates together at Auchwitz in Poland, the most dreaded of all German concentration camps. Dr. Kulowsky had been sent there in 1940 and Maurice Kantorowitz in 1943. In 1944, Dr. Kulowsky was transferred to Sachenhousen and neither knew if the other was dead or alive until they met in the Ferman store.

COMPARE NOTES

After comparing notes, each found out what had happened to the other during the intervening years: Maurice had been freed by the U.S. 5th army on May 5, 1945 and had afterwards come to Newfoundland.

BECAME M.D.

Dr. Kulowsky had been liberated by the Russians, also in 1945. After that he studied medicine and became an M.D. Finally he joined the Polish trawler "Uran" which, last weekend sailed into St. John's.

INTERPRETER

Here he met Mr. Ferman who acts as interpreter for both Polish and Russian crews. So the rest can be guessed. Both decided to pay Mr. Ferman a visit at exactly the same time.

Mr. Kantorowitz, who is fluent in English, spoke both for himself and Dr. Kulowsky who speaks no English at all. He had this story to tell.

HIS STORY

When the Germans moved into Poland they surrounded the Jewish quarter, in which he lived, with barbed wire, penning him in the ghetto from August, 1941 to January, 1943.

IN AUCHWITZ

Then he was sent off to Auchwitz to find Leon Kulowsky already there. Maurice was assigned to a group destined for slow extermination through hard work and little or no food.

MARKED FOR DEATH

There were 50 in this group at the start but they were being killed off at the rate of five or six every day. They didn't just drop down and die they were actually killed. When the "foreman" saw a man who was too weak to work, he just hit him with a stick. And when the man fell he simply put the stick across his throat and pushed like a savage until he choked him to death.

SAVED

Maurice said he could not have stood it more than another few days, when along came Leon Kulowsky and gave him a break. Leon was in the carpentry group and, being the oldest, was in charge. This gave him the power to pick other men for his group. And by taking compassion on Maurice he saved his life.

Dr. Kulowsky and Mr. Kantorowitz.

This did not mean that the new job was a big bed of roses, he said. But carpentry work was skilled

(Continued on Page 8)

Epilogue To An Ordeal

(Continued from Page 3)

labour. The job had to be done right and it just didn't pay to push the men.

FAMILY MURDERED

While Maurice survived the ordeal of Auchwitz, his family did not. His parents, three sisters and a brother all went to the gas chamber, he said.

NUMBERS

Both men had their Auchwitz prison numbers tattooed on their arms. Maurice rolled up his sleeve and revealed No. 99347 still plain to be seen.

IN UNDERGROUND

Lewis Ferman, the man who brought them together, had marks of his own — bullet wounds in both his face and his head. He fought the Nazi menace in the underground, serving mostly in Lithuania, he said.

Although neither Dr. Kulowsky or Mr. Kantorowitz expressed any particular bitterness towards the Germans, that there was no love lost between them and Mr. Ferman he left no doubt.

An article from *The Newfoundland Herald* about Moishe and Leon Kulowski's meeting. 1965.

1

2

3

1 Moishe (right) and Leon Kulowski after reuniting in St. John's. March 6, 1965.

2 Moishe, left, with Leon. St. John's, 1966.

3 Moishe and his family (left to right): Moishe, Aviva, Ruth, Sharon, Ken. St. John's, 1968.

Moishe at the Western Wall. Jerusalem, Israel, 1969.

At Moishe's son Ken's wedding. Back row (left to right): Moishe's cousin Harold (Elchonon) Auerbach and his wife, Eva; Moishe's cousin Leo (Lippa) Auerbach; Moishe's wife Ruth's brother and sister-in-law, Sheila and Leonard Pleet. Second row from the back: Moishe's father- and mother-in-law, Pinchas and Devorah Pleet; a friend of the family Rose Rockstein; Moishe's wife, Ruth; Moishe; Leon Kulowski; Moishe's cousin Leo's son Steven. Third row from the back: Moishe's cousin David Auerbach; Moishe's daughter Aviva; the bride and groom, Lisa and Ken; Moishe's daughter Sharon; Moishe's cousin Eli Auerbach's daughter Jane; Moishe's cousin Eli. Front row: Moishe's cousin David's wife, Ida; his cousin Abe's wife, Rebecca; Abe Auerbach; name unknown; Moishe's cousin Eli's wife, Shirley. St. John's, 1975.

1

2

1 Moishe and Ruth. Brazil, 1983.

2 Left to right, standing: Sharon, Ken, Moishe, Aviva. Sitting: Ruth. 1984.

1

2

1 Moishe in the Chamber of the Holocaust Museum on Mount Zion. The headstone above him and to the left is for Shershev. Jerusalem, 1986.

2 Moishe standing front and centre at the head of a procession in memory of fallen World War II soldiers and Holocaust victims. Labrador City, November 11, 1989.

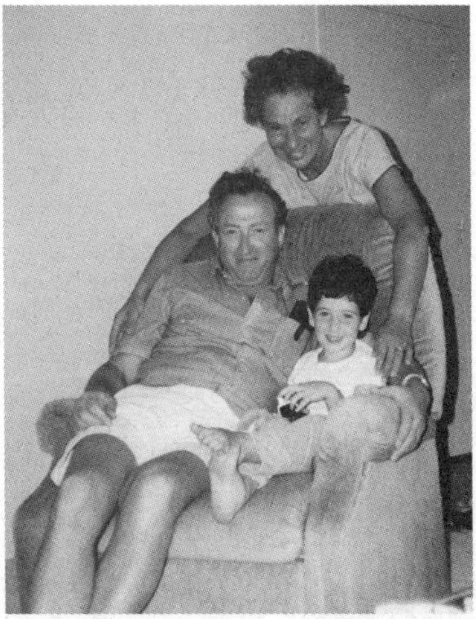

1

2

3

1 Moishe and Ruth with their first grandchild, Orly. Toronto, Ontario, 1987.

2 Moishe and Ruth with their granddaughter Orly at her bat mitzvah. Toronto, 1996.

3 Moishe and Ruth with their grandchildren (left to right): Ruth, Erez (in front), Eitan, Ariella, Moishe holding Genevieve, Orly. Toronto, 1998.

Moishe on the day he received his honorary degree and addressed the convocation at Memorial University of Newfoundland. St. John's, 1995.

1

2

1 Moishe and Ruth in the Martyrs Forest, standing next to a plaque honouring their donation to plant trees in Moishe's parents' memory. Jerusalem, 2000.

2 Moishe and Ruth celebrating their fiftieth wedding anniversary. Toronto, 2000.

1

2

1 Moishe and Ruth with their grandchildren (left to right): Erez, Ruth, Genevieve, Eitan, Orly, Ariella, Moishe. Toronto, 2001.

2 Moishe with his grandchildren Erez (left) and Eitan at Erez's bar mitzvah at the Western Wall. Jerusalem, 2006.

1

2

1 Moishe and Ruth with their grandchildren at his eighty-fourth birthday party. From left to right: Eitan, Ruth, Genevieve, Moishe, Ariella, Orly, Erez. Toronto, 2007.

2 Moishe and Ruth with their family. Standing in the back, from left to right: Ariella; Aviva; Orly; Sharon's husband, Meir Gazit; Erez; Ken. Front row, left to right: Ken's wife, Lisa; Genevieve; Ruth; Sharon; Moishe; Eitan. Toronto, 2007.

Moishe. Toronto, circa 1995. Photo courtesy of the Toronto Holocaust Museum.

Glossary

Aktion (German; pl. *Aktionen*) A brutal roundup of Jews for mass murder by shooting or for deportation to forced labour, concentration and death camps.

Aliyah Bet (Hebrew) A clandestine movement established to bring Jewish immigrants without immigration permits to British Mandate Palestine before, during and after World War II. The name, which means "ascent B," differentiates the movement from the immigrants to whom the British granted permits. Aliyah Bet organized ships to pick up Jewish immigrants from different points on the European coast in order to make the perilous journey to Palestine. Many were turned back. *See also* British Mandate Palestine.

American Jewish Joint Distribution Committee (JDC) Colloquially known as the Joint, the JDC was a charitable organization founded in 1914 to provide humanitarian assistance and relief to Jews all over the world in times of crisis. It provided material support for persecuted Jews in Germany and other German-occupied territories and facilitated their immigration to neutral countries such as Portugal and Turkey. Between 1939 and 1944, Joint officials helped close to 81,000 European Jews find asylum in various parts of the world. Between 1944 and 1947, the JDC assisted more than 100,000 refugees living in DP camps by offering retraining programs, cultural activities and financial assistance for emigration.

Anschluss (German; union) The annexation of Austria into Germany in March 1938, as part of the Nazi plan to unite all German peoples into a Greater Germany. A plebiscite held under strict Nazi supervision on April 10, 1938, was 99.7 per cent in favour of the Anschluss. Austria was renamed Ostmark and ceased to exist as a separate nation until 1945.

Auschwitz (German; in Polish, Oświęcim) A Nazi concentration camp complex in German-occupied Poland about 50 kilometres from Krakow, on the outskirts of the town of Oświęcim, built between 1940 and 1942. The largest camp complex established by the Nazis, Auschwitz contained three main camps: Auschwitz I, a concentration camp; Auschwitz II (Birkenau), a death camp that used gas chambers to commit mass murder; and Auschwitz III (also called Monowitz or Buna), which provided slave labour for an industrial complex. In 1942, the Nazis began to deport Jews from almost every country in Europe to Auschwitz-Birkenau, where they were selected for slave labour or for death in the gas chambers. In mid-January 1945, close to 60,000 inmates were sent on a death march, leaving behind only a few thousand inmates who were liberated by the Soviet army on January 27, 1945. It is estimated that 1.1 million people were murdered in Auschwitz, approximately 90 per cent of whom were Jewish; other victims included Polish prisoners, Roma and Soviet prisoners of war. *See also* Birkenau.

Betar (Hebrew acronym for Brit Yosef Trumpeldor, Josef Trumpeldor Alliance) A Zionist youth movement founded in Riga, Latvia, in 1923 that became part of Vladimir Ze'ev Jabotinsky's Revisionist Zionist political party. The movement, which existed mainly in Eastern Europe, encouraged the development of a new generation of Zionist activists, promoting vocational training, learning Hebrew, military training and defence, immigration to Palestine and the establishment of a Jewish state on both sides of the Jordan River. By 1938, Betar had 90,000 members from 26 countries but was most active in Poland. During the 1930s, Betar organized the illegal immigration of thousands of European Jews to Palestine, and during the Holocaust, its members played an active role in the underground and in ghetto uprisings. After World War II, the movement was centred in Israel, and it still has chapters around the world. *See also* Jabotinsky, Vladimir Ze'ev; Revisionist Zionism; Zionism.

Birkenau Also known as Auschwitz II. One of the camps in the Auschwitz complex in German-occupied Poland and the largest death camp established by the Nazis. Birkenau was built in 1941, and in 1942 the Nazis designated it as a killing centre, using Zyklon B gas to carry out the systematic murder of Jews and other people considered "undesirable" by the Nazis. In 1943, the Nazis began to use four crematoria with gas chambers that could hold up to 2,000 people each to murder the large numbers of Jews who were being brought to the camp from across Europe. Upon arrival, prisoners were selected for slave labour or sent to the gas chambers. The camp was liberated in January 1945 by the Soviet army. An estimated 1.1 million people were killed in the Auschwitz camp complex, most of them in Birkenau and the vast majority of them Jews. *See also* Auschwitz.

Bricha (Hebrew; escape) The name given to the massive clandestine movement that organized the illegal migration of Jewish refugees from Eastern Europe to pre-state Israel after World War II. Estimates of the number of Jews who reached Palestine with Bricha range from 80,000 to 250,000. Although the goal of the organization was to smuggle Jews to pre-state Israel, some used the group and its connections to escape from Communist countries to displaced persons camps in Austria and Germany.

British Mandate Palestine (also Mandatory Palestine) The area of the Middle East under British rule from 1923 to 1948 comprising present-day Israel, Jordan, the West Bank and the Gaza Strip. The Mandate was established by the League of Nations after World War I and the collapse of the Ottoman Empire; the area was given to the British to administer until a Jewish national home could be established. During this time, Jewish immigration was severely restricted, and Jews and Arabs clashed with the British and each other as they struggled to realize their national interests. The Mandate ended on May 15, 1948, after the United Nations Partition Plan for Palestine was adopted and on the same day that the State of Israel was declared.

concentration camp A location in which people are held without recourse to rule of law, usually under difficult conditions. Under the Nazis, a large network of concentration camps was developed where prisoners—including Jews, Roma, homosexuals, political prisoners, prisoners of war and others considered "undesirable"—were used as slave labour and exploited for economic gain. They were provided with little food or other necessities, often resulting in death due to starvation, illness, exposure, beatings and execution. The camps were run by the SS, the elite police force of the Nazi regime that was responsible for security and for the enforcement of Nazi racial policies.

Deutsche Ausrüstungswerke (DAW; German; German Equipment Works) A company established by the SS in 1939 that used concentration camp inmates and Nazi ghetto inmates as forced labour to produce military equipment and supplies for Germany's war effort. *See also* SS.

displaced persons (DP) camps Facilities set up by the Allied authorities and the United Nations Relief and Rehabilitation Administration (UNRRA) in October 1945 to resolve the refugee crisis that arose at the end of World War II. The camps provided temporary shelter and assistance to the millions of people who had been displaced from their home countries as a result of the war and helped them prepare for resettlement. *See also* United Nations Relief and Rehabilitation Administration.

Einsatzgruppen (German; task force) Units of Nazi SS and police that were charged with securing the territories occupied by Nazi Germany after the invasion of the Soviet Union in 1941. With the support of local collaborators, these mobile death squads rounded up and murdered over a million Jews and many others in mass shooting operations. They were a key component in the implementation of the Nazis' so-called Final Solution in Eastern Europe.

Endek Another name for Endecja, the acronym and common name used for the National Democratic Party in Poland, a right-wing, nationalist and antisemitic political party founded in 1893 by Polish politician Roman Dmowski. The party advocated for boycotts of Jewish businesses, a redistribution of wealth from Jews to Poles and Jewish emigration from Poland.

Free City of Danzig The name of the city that is now Gdańsk, Poland, when it was under the protection of the League of Nations after World War I. Under the terms of the Treaty of Versailles, Germany was forced to cede West Prussia to Poland. However, Danzig, a port city in West Prussia, was mostly ethnically German, and it was determined that it would a "free city," belonging to neither nation but with special rights given to Poland. In spring 1939, Hitler demanded the annexation of the Free City of Danzig to Germany as part of his mission to reclaim German territories that were lost in the Treaty of Versailles and create an empire that included all ethnic Germans.

Gestapo (German; abbreviation of Geheime Staatspolizei, the Secret State Police) The Nazi regime's brutal political police that operated without legal constraints to deal with its perceived enemies. During the Holocaust, the Gestapo set up offices in German-occupied countries and was responsible for rounding up Jews and sending them to concentration and death camps. They also arrested, tortured and deported those who resisted Nazi policies.

Gusen The first subcamp in the Mauthausen-Gusen complex, built five kilometres from Mauthausen in the winter of 1939–1940. Prisoners did physical labour at nearby sites, and in 1944, two subcamps were added as more prisoners were brought to the region to work in armaments production. In May 1945, there were 20,487 prisoners in Gusen, vastly exceeding its original capacity of 4,000 to 5,000 prisoners. An estimated 35,000 people were killed in the camp over the course of its existence. Gusen was liberated by American troops on May 5, 1945. *See also* Mauthausen.

Hashomer Hatzair (Hebrew; The Youth Guard) A left-wing Zionist youth movement founded in Central Europe in the early twentieth century to prepare young Jews to become workers and farmers, and to establish kibbutzim—collective settlements—in the Land of Israel. Before World War II, there were 70,000 Hashomer Hatzair members worldwide, and many of those in German-occupied territories led resistance activities in the ghettos and concentration camps or joined partisan groups in the forests. It is the oldest Zionist youth movement still in existence. *See also* Land of Israel; Zionism.

Jabotinsky, Vladimir Ze'ev (1880–1940) A Zionist activist, writer and leader who split from the official Zionist movement in Europe to found the Revisionist Zionist party in 1925. He also founded a new branch of nationalist Zionism, the New Zionist Organization (NZO). Jabotinsky advocated for the mass immigration of European Jews to British Mandate Palestine, promoting the ideals of Jewish self-defence and self-determination, and for Jewish sovereignty over the entire territory of the British Mandate. In 1937, he became the commander of the Irgun Zva'i Leumi (Irgun), which carried out armed struggles against the British and the Arabs in Palestine between 1937 and 1948. *See also* British Mandate Palestine; Revisionist Zionism; Zionism.

Jewish Brigade A battalion of approximately 5,000 volunteers from Palestine, formed in September 1944, that was under the command of the British Eighth Army and fought against the German army in Italy. After the war, the Brigade played an important role in helping Jewish refugees in Europe and organizing their entry into Palestine. The Jewish Brigade was disbanded by the British in 1946.

Jewish National Fund (JNF; in Hebrew, Keren Kayemeth LeIsrael) A non-profit organization founded in 1901 to buy, lease and develop the land of Palestine and later Israel for Jewish settlement. JNF's ongoing projects include water conservation, land development for Jewish immigrant communities and tree planting. JNF has planted hundreds of millions of trees in Israel and currently owns 13 per cent of the country's land.

Kanada The warehouses in Auschwitz-Birkenau that stored the belongings and clothing confiscated from newly arrived prisoners. The name, adopted by the prisoners working there, came from the widely held belief that Canada was a land of wealth. *See also* Auschwitz; Birkenau.

kibbutz (Hebrew; pl. kibbutzim) A collectively owned farm or settlement in Israel, democratically governed by its members. Also, a collectivist group committed to the idea of the Jewish homeland in Palestine. *See also* Zionism.

Land of Israel (in Hebrew, Eretz Yisrael; also Holy Land, Promised Land) The traditional and biblical name for the land that, according to religious Jewish belief, was given to the Jewish people by God. The borders of the current State of Israel overlap with but are not the same as the borders of the Land of Israel as outlined in the Bible.

Mauthausen A notoriously brutal Nazi concentration camp located about twenty kilometres east of the Austrian city of Linz. First established in 1938 shortly after the annexation of Austria to imprison "asocial" political opponents of the Nazis, the camp grew to encompass 50 nearby subcamps. By the end of the war, close to 200,000 prisoners had passed through the Mauthausen forced labour camp system and almost 120,000 of them died there—including 38,120 Jews—from starvation, disease and hard labour. Mauthausen was classified as a Category 3 camp, which indicated the harshest conditions, and inmates were often worked to death in the brutal Wiener Graben stone quarry. The US army liberated the camp on May 5, 1945.

Muselmann (pl. *Muselmänner*; derived from German; Muslim) A slang term used by camp prisoners to describe prisoners who were near death and seemed to have lost the will to live. Some scholars attribute the use of the word Muslim to the fact that the prostrate and dying prisoners were reminiscent of devout Muslims at prayer.

Nuremberg Laws The race laws passed by the Nazi government in September 1935 that legalized antisemitism and the separation of Jews from broader German society. Under the Reich Citizenship Law, German Jews were stripped of their citizenship and classified based on how much Jewish ancestry they had. Under the Law for the Protection of German Blood and Honour, marriages or sexual relations between Jews and Germans/"Aryans" were forbidden. *See also* Reich.

partisans Members of organized groups of fighters or resistance movements that were formed to oppose armies of occupation. During World War II, clandestine partisan groups were widespread across Europe and ranged from those fighting Nazis and fascism to nationalist groups that opposed all foreigners, including Jews. There were approximately 20,000–30,000 Jewish partisans who fought against the Nazis in Jewish partisan units or as members of non-Jewish groups in the forests of Eastern Europe.

Piłsudski, Józef (1867–1935) Polish socialist leader and revolutionary who was the first head of state of the newly independent Poland, from 1918 to 1922, after more than a century of Poland's partition between Russia, Austria and Prussia. Piłsudski organized a coup d'etat in 1926, after which he served as minister of defence and remained politically powerful and popular among Polish citizens, including many Jews because of his opposition to antisemitism. Piłsudski attempted to form alliances with western powers and other European countries and signed non-aggression pacts with the Soviet Union and Germany in 1932 and 1934 respectively.

Przytyk pogrom An anti-Jewish riot that took place in the largely Jewish town of Przytyk, Poland, on March 9, 1936, during which a mob destroyed dozens of Jewish stores and homes, attacking their inhabitants. Two Jews and one non-Jew were killed, and more than twenty people were wounded.

Reich A German word meaning empire or realm. The term "Third Reich" is often used to refer to Germany under Nazi control from 1933 to 1945. The Nazis believed that they would rule a "Thousand-Year Reich" in Germany.

Revisionist Zionism The right-wing Zionist movement founded in the early twentieth century in Eastern Europe by Vladimir Ze'ev Jabotinsky. The movement opposed Labour Zionism's socialist ideals and emphasized Zionism as a political ideal with a goal to establish a Jewish state in all British Mandate Palestine and Transjordan. The movement supported military action against Arabs who carried out attacks on Jews in Palestine. *See also* British Mandate Palestine; Jabotinsky, Vladimir Ze'ev; Zionism.

shtetl (Yiddish) A mostly Jewish market town in Eastern Europe before World War II. Life in the shtetl revolved around Judaism and Jewish culture and was defined by the closely intertwined economic and social lives of its residents. Shtetls existed in Eastern Europe from the sixteenth century until they were wiped out in the Holocaust.

Sosnowitz (also Sosnowitz II) A Nazi concentration camp in Sosnowiec, Poland, that was a subcamp of Auschwitz, established in May 1944 at the request of the Ost-Maschinenbau GmbH (OSMAG) arms company. The camp provided slave labourers who produced anti-aircraft cannons and shells. The population of the camp was 95 per cent Jews who had been deported to Auschwitz in late 1943 and early 1944. Sosnowitz was evacuated in January 1945, and the approximately 860 remaining prisoners were forced to march for twelve days to Opava (in current Czech Republic), where the survivors of the march were put on trains to Mauthausen. *See also* Auschwitz; Mauthausen.

Spanish Civil War (1936–1939) The war in Spain between the Nationalists—who were led by General Francisco Franco and supported by conservative elements and Nazi Germany and Fascist Italy—and the democratically elected Republican government, which was supported by socialists, Communists, the Soviet Union and an international contingent of volunteers. After an initial coup that failed to win a decisive victory, the country was plunged into a bloody civil war until Franco's victory in 1939, when he established a Fascist government that lasted until 1975.

SS (abbreviation of Schutzstaffel; Defence Corps) The elite police force of the Nazi regime that was responsible for security and for the enforcement of Nazi racial policies, including the implementation of the "Final Solution"—a euphemistic term referring to the Nazis' plan to systematically murder Europe's Jewish population. The SS ran the concentration and death camps and also established the

Waffen-SS, its own military division that was independent of the German army.

Star of David (in Hebrew, Magen David) The six-pointed star that is the most recognizable symbol of Judaism. During World War II, Jews in German-occupied areas were frequently forced to wear a badge or armband with the Star of David on it as an identifying mark of their lesser status and to single them out as targets for persecution.

Treblinka A Nazi death camp in German-occupied Poland about eighty kilometres northeast of Warsaw, established in 1942. Treblinka was the third death camp built specifically to implement the planned mass murder of the Jews in occupied Poland. Approximately 900,000 Jews and unknown numbers of Poles, Roma and Soviet prisoners of war were killed in Treblinka.

United Nations Relief and Rehabilitation Administration (UNRRA) An international relief agency created at a 44-nation conference in Washington, DC, on November 9, 1943, to provide economic assistance and basic necessities to war refugees. It was especially active in repatriating and assisting refugees in the formerly German-occupied European nations immediately after World War II.

Zionism A movement promoted by the Viennese Jewish journalist Theodor Herzl, who argued in his 1896 book *Der Judenstaat* (*The Jewish State*) that the best way to resolve the problem of antisemitism and persecution of Jews in Europe was to create an independent Jewish state in the historical Jewish homeland of biblical Israel. Early Zionists also promoted the revival of Hebrew as a Jewish national language.

Index

The Azrieli Foundation was established in 1989 to realize and extend the philanthropic vision of David J. Azrieli, C.M., C.Q., M.Arch. The Foundation's mission is to support a wide spectrum of initiatives in education and research. The Azrieli Foundation is an active supporter of programs in the fields of education, the education of architects, scientific and medical research, and the arts.

The staff members dedicated to the Holocaust Survivor Memoirs Program are: Jody Spiegel, Arielle Berger, Catherine Person, Marc-Olivier Cloutier, Carson Phillips, Catherine Aubé, Matt Carrington, Devora Levin, Michelle Sadowski, Elizabeth Banks, Monika Kolanka, Candace Alper, Susanne Bachert, Mark Weissfelner and Emily Standfield.